The Development of British Amphibious Operations 1882-1914

The Development of British Amphibious Operations 1882-1914

Joseph Moretz

Pen & Sword
MARITIME

First published in Great Britain in 2025 by
Pen & Sword Maritime
An imprint of
Pen & Sword Books Ltd
Yorkshire - Philadelphia

Copyright © Joseph Moretz, 2025

ISBN 978 1 03612 134 1

The right of Joseph Moretz to be identified as the Author of this work has been asserted by him in accordance with the Copyright, Designs and Patents Act 1988.

A CIP catalogue record for this book is available from the British Library.

All rights reserved. No part of this book may be reproduced, transmitted, downloaded, decompiled or reverse engineered in any form or by any means, electronic or mechanical including photocopying, recording or by any information storage and retrieval system, without permission from the Publisher in writing. NO AI TRAINING: Without in any way limiting the Author's and Publisher's exclusive rights under copyright, any use of this publication to "train" generative artificial intelligence (AI) technologies to generate text is expressly prohibited. The Author and Publisher reserve all rights to license uses of this work for generative AI training and development of machine learning language models.

Typeset in INDIA by IMPEC eSolutions
Printed and bound in England by CPI Group (UK) Ltd, Croydon, CR0 4YY

The Publisher's authorised representative in the EU for product safety is Authorised Rep Compliance Ltd., Ground Floor, 71 Lower Baggot Street, Dublin D02 P593, Ireland.
www.arccompliance.com

For a complete list of Pen & Sword titles please contact

PEN & SWORD BOOKS LIMITED
47 Church Street, Barnsley, South Yorkshire, S70 2AS, England
E-mail: enquiries@pen-and-sword.co.uk
Website: www.pen-and-sword.co.uk

or

PEN AND SWORD BOOKS
1950 Lawrence Rd, Havertown, PA 19083, USA
E-mail: uspen-and-sword@casematepublishers.com
Website: www.penandswordbooks.com

To say that he committed errors is to say that he made war.
                                        Sir William Napier

To Ecaterina

Contents

Acknowledgments		ix
Note on Style		xi
Abbreviations		xii
List of Illustrations		xiii
Introduction		xiv
One	Into Egypt, 1882	1
Two	Out of Egypt…into the Sudan	13
Three	Suakin-Berber Operations Redux	30
Four	On the Road to Mandalay: Upper Burma, 1885–86	35
Five	Gordon Avenged: Sudan, 1896–98	40
Six	Suffering No End of a Lesson: South Africa, 1899–1902	46
Seven	China and the Boxer Rebellion, 1900	55
Eight	Somaliland, 1901–1904: Chasing the "Mad Mullah"	71
Nine	The Russo-Japanese War, 1904–1905	82
Ten	Assessment	95
Eleven	Joint Operations and the Educational Response, 1882–1914	108
Twelve	Toward a *Manual of Combined Naval and Military Operations*	133
Thirteen	*Deus Ex Machina*: Reform from Above	154
Fourteen	Came a New War: Executing Expeditionary Warfare	187
Bibliography		**205**
Endnotes		**222**
Index		**275**

Acknowledgments

In the research and writing of this history, I have incurred countless debts while receiving unstinting kindness and assistance. Alan Jeffreys has been a font of knowledge on the history of the Indian Army. His help in unlocking the mysteries of that service and his willingness to provide an early venue for airing my thoughts on one aspect of a larger topic is deeply appreciated. Likewise, David Kohnen allowed me to offer some early thoughts on the experience and lessons derived from British amphibious warfare at a conference hosted by the U.S. Naval War College in 2019.

Jim Beach, Gary Greco, and Peter Robinson have all offered recurring support and advice along a path that never quite seemed to come to closure where, for the researcher, another file awaits to be drawn. Mark Stanovich of the U.S. Naval War College was kind enough to review and offer critical comments on a portion of the work, and his assistance is kindly acknowledged. Likewise, I benefited from sharing a portion of his findings at a session of the Military History Seminar of the Institute for Historical Research. To Professors Andrew Lambert and William Philpott, my sincere thanks are extended for the hospitality and comments.

The research pursued would not have progressed but with the aid and assistance of the archives consulted. Undertaken amidst a global pandemic, the challenge proved greater still. Crown copyright material held within the National Archives appears by permission of His Majesty's Stationery Office. The use of the many private papers consulted has invariably enhanced the accounting presented. Accordingly, my deep appreciation is extended to the Churchill Archive Centre, Churchill College, Cambridge; the Imperial War Museum, London; the Liddell Hart Centre for Military Archives, King's College, London; the National Army Museum, Chelsea; the National Archives, Kew; and the Middle East Centre Archive, St Antony's College, Oxford. Though I never visited the National Archives of Australia or the Australian War Memorial, the resources accessed online were no less essential in supporting the conclusions reached. My warmest thanks are extended to each of these institutions, especially Gemma Hamilton, Penny Hutchins, and Katherine Thomson.

The editors, Tara Moran, Kerri Landis and Harriet Fielding of Pen and Sword, have been helpful and accessible in the editorial and production of this work. My thanks and appreciation are warmly extended to them and those unseen who make an idea a reality. The kind assistance of Lee Curran at Alamy in negotiating the rights to the illustrations and photographs adopted is warmly noted, and while I have attempted to identify and secure permission from all holders of copyright, any omission is entirely accidental. As always, the errors present belong to the author, while the good existing represents the hands of many. May there be precious few of the previous and those present merely incidental to the larger story.

Note on Style

In a work anchored in primary sources, the author has elected to follow the patterns of contemporary usage and note through parentheses any modern equivalent. Titles, ranks, and names of individuals are rarely static, and the convention employed has been to refer to individuals by their rank, title, and full name upon first reference, with subsequent mentions adopting the appropriate diminutive thereafter. A Christian or first name is employed where common surnames might lead to confusion.

Abbreviations

adc	aide de camp
BGGS	Brigadier General, General Staff
CIGS	Chief of the Imperial General Staff
CDC	Colonial Defence Committee
DMO	Director of Military Operations
DNI	Director of Naval Intelligence
EMS	Eastern Mediterranean Squadron
FSR	Field Service Regulations
GHQ	General Headquarters
GOC	General Officer Commanding
KAR	King's African Rifles
KOSB	King's Own Scottish Borderers
MLO	Military Landing Officer
NID	Naval Intelligence Department
OC	Officer Commanding
ODC	Overseas Defence Committee
PNTO	Principal Naval Transport Officer
RFR	Royal Fleet Reserve
RIM	Royal Indian Marine
RIMS	Royal Indian Marine Ship
RMA	Royal Marine Artillery
RMLI	Royal Marine Light Infantry
RND	Royal Naval Division
RNR	Royal Naval Reserve
RNVR	Royal Naval Volunteer Reserve
RUSI	Royal United Services Institution
USN	United States Navy
WAFF	West African Frontier Force

List of Illustrations

1. The Bombardment of Alexandria, Egypt 1882
2. The Effects of Naval Bombardment
3. Landing Sailors and Marines at Alexandria 1882
4. Sir Garnet J. Wolseley
5. Advancing Up the Nile 1884
6. The Black Watch Salute General Wolseley 1884
7. Captain Lord Charles Beresford on the Nile
8. The Battle of Abu Klea 1885
9. The Naval Flotilla in Burma 1885
10. The Victor of Khartoum: Major General Lord Kitchener
11. Gunboats at Omdurman 1898
12. A Naval Gun Crosses the Tugela River
13. Admiral Seymour's Retreat on Tientsin 1900
14. The Japanese Army Landing Hores at Chemulpo, Korea 1904

Introduction

...that the techniques and attitudes of joint-service co-operations which had largely accounted for the flawless planning of all the large-scale combined operations of the Second World War should be deliberately inculcated from the very start of an officer's career.[1]

Fitting for an island nation possessing a storied military past, projecting military force to a distant shore has come to be seen as a uniquely British way of waging war. To be sure, many of these operations would now be classed as administrative landings with battle, if occurring at all, only following sometimes afterward. Others, of course, merit the label of opposed landings. To contemporaries of the period covered by this multi-volume study, the evolutions went by the appellation of "conjoint or combined operations." Less important than how they were styled remains the thought and the purpose giving rise to these ventures. In the decades before the First World War, professionals appreciated the myriad difficulties and dangers associated with amphibious operations. The laity, including statesmen, thought relatively less of these matters, but could recount numerous examples of their occurrence before 1914. Indeed, whatever operational failings Britain demonstrated during the First World War, a corpus of relevant experience was the least of these.

What is now styled as "joint amphibious operations" were difficult because they were never of a single type. Naval support to a military force standing on the defensive, raids, feints, blocking operations, riverine operations, and, yes, an opposed landing, spoke to a series of joint operations of ever-increasing complexity. Meanwhile, as every operation must at some point end, even the manner of evacuation came to be viewed as a particular type of combined operation to be understood and learned. Finally, in a campaign of the grandest scale, examples of each might feature at differing moments along the way.

Of opposed landings, the campaign in Gallipoli testifies to what may await a force so bold as to meet an enemy forewarned and forearmed. Of course, administrative landings before 1914 were challenging enough, never mind the record of meeting an enemy head-on. What military and naval authorities thought feasible before the onset of the First World War in the realm of joint operations is a neglected field of study—a surprising omission given the ink that has been spilled retelling the debacles experienced at Gallipoli, Mesopotamia, and East Africa. Every campaign has its context—operational and strategic, to be sure—but also political, doctrinal, and bureaucratic. How Britain elected to wage war in 1914 proved a product of these variables just as surely as the military and naval capabilities it could muster. The literature discussing the state of British pre-war thinking regarding power projection is relatively sparse. Tying the strands of pre-war military experience and thought in the realm of joint operations is this study's chief purpose, which takes as its starting point 1882 and the British assault against Egypt. The choice is far from arbitrary, as the moment saw several earning their spurs and later playing a central role in the amphibious operations executed during the First World War. If the operations in Egypt did not lead to these subsequent campaigns, it did influence much of the training and planning that followed. It certainly changed Britain's relationship with the Ottoman Empire, which never fully recovered in the intervening years.[2]

To the extent learning is more than the product of self-experience, this work pays special attention to the Russo-Japanese War. Thinking officers appreciated that fundamental changes were occurring in the nature and style of war. A learned public also appreciated this courtesy of works such as Ivan Bloch's *Is War Now Possible?*[3] Notwithstanding what British officers understood on the eve of the First World War, the problem of time and scale remained. Many of the operations executed were, at best, division-level affairs and of amphibious landings, not even rising to that level. During the 1882 Egyptian campaign, the military deployed 35,000 troops, of which only 16,000 were part of the field force. In the South African War, the largest British campaign of the period, the total military force approached 450,000.[4] These were campaigns of sizable proportions for Britain, though paling in scope to the demands of what awaited. Operational experience, while important, is never sufficient for solving future problems as circumstances are never congruent. This alone should give one pause before chiding others over past mistakes. This study looks at what was thought, what was taught, what was expected, and what was done in the thirty years before Britain found herself facing a scale of conflict not witnessed in a century.

Of course, this history is but a part of a greater story. The breadth of the British Empire gave rise to a breadth of corresponding experience. This study cannot attempt to recount every action, but it does try to account for the lessons drawn. What follows is not a history of pre-1914 joint operations so much as an evaluation of the doctrine and preparation registered beforehand married to relevant experience that informed the development of British thought. This forms the substance of this volume, and from that telling, the context of British joint operations in the 1914–1916 period is examined through the evaluation of three case studies—Mesopotamia, Gallipoli, and Tanga—to be analyzed in a subsequent volume. Together, both volumes provide a portrait of the doctrine and operational capabilities of British forces in the realm of joint amphibious warfare on the eve of and during the first days of the First World War. Any discussion on a "British way in warfare" necessarily needs to be mindful of this story.

One

Into Egypt, 1882

Mr. Gladstone wrote to me the other day that we had only been able to struggle through the Egyptian difficulty, as a Cabinet, by the exercise of the greatest conciliation and marked forbearance. This is very amiable of us, but I don't think it has produced very good results in Egypt.[1]

Hartington, 1884

In our cynical age, prestige as a vital quality of governance is easily derided. Yet, for an empire always maintained on the cheap, it assumed an import to contemporaries not to be dismissed. Always lurking was the fear that a setback in one locale might spell danger elsewhere, particularly if both locales were possessed of like co-religionists. Here, the worry was always India, which in the period of this study remained neither a unified country nor a polity anchored so heavily in the Hinduism of today. The legacy of the mutiny made such worries acute, and the future of the Ottoman Empire, the proverbial "Sick Man of Europe," only exacerbated matters. The lines of this political and strategic context need not concern us unduly. Still, they establish why British naval and military forces became active in the eastern Mediterranean in 1882.

The cover provided by British maritime superiority anchored on the Mediterranean and the East Indies Squadrons made intervention in Egypt feasible in the first instance. Further, British forces need not worry about their lines of communication running from England and India absent the intervention of a hostile naval power.[2] Though France came to object to British actions, Paris had been at the fore in setting things in motion. Others acquiesced in what followed. This included the Sublime Porte, the nominal sovereign who reigned but did not truly rule Egypt.[3]

A nationalist revolt within the Egyptian Army led by Colonel Ahmed Urabi, which had its roots in the replacement of native officers by Turks and Circassians, had been simmering for months. Under the cry "Egypt for the

Egyptians," Urabi demanded the dismissal of War Minister Osman Pasha Rifki. When this was allowed in February 1881, more demands ensued. By September, the Khedive was facing a *coup d'état* but, more than that, his third revolt in as many years. His response was to banish Urabi and his regiment to the interior.[4]

If professing the subordination of Egypt to Turkey in theory, it was not a point Britain and France desired to see in practice. The present Khedive was very much their man, having gained power at the expense of his profligate father through an earlier joint effort. Thus, a continuance of khedival authority and the financial control presently enjoyed could not be but a vital interest now for London and Paris. Such was the situation in late 1881 when France proposed joint military control of the country to Britain.[5] London was not ready to go so far, but it did contemplate sending a warship to Alexandria to reassure its nationals; France soon equaled the response.[6]

Matters only became more worrying with the new year, as Urabi desired to increase the size of the Egyptian Army, which had been shorn following a war with Abyssinia. Regrettably, owing to its international debt, Egypt could not afford a larger army, and any policy that attempted as much was to be resisted by those most exposed financially: Britain and France. Thus, the issuance of a dual note by both on 8 January affirmed the status quo.[7] Reginald Brett, the young private secretary to Spencer Compton, the marquess of Hartington and British war minister,[8] questioned its propriety, believing the cabinet had not considered the implications.[9] Brett was correct on three levels. Firstly, the implications for Britain and France were not congruent. Problematically, Léon Gambetta's Ministry fell on 31 January 1882. Secondly, given the recent French occupation of Tunis, the note meant something different in Cairo. Now, Britain stood no better than France in the eyes of many Egyptians.[10] Thirdly, the note threatened the interests of others, notably Russia, Italy, Greece, Germany, and most assuredly, Turkey.[11]

At the War Office, preparations for eventualities had already begun with Colonel Richard Harrison journeying to Egypt in November to survey the Suez and Sweetwater canals.[12] This effort was mirrored by the Intelligence Department's Major Alexander Tulloch, who reconnoitred Cairo, Alexandria, Port Said, Tel-el-Kebir, and Ismailia in January 1882. His intelligence allowed an 1875 plan covering the occupation of Egypt to be updated. At this point, the idea was to deploy a two-division force from Britain and India.[13] Interestingly,

Tulloch came across an unnamed naval officer performing much the same work, though beginning from the canal's southern end. The War Office printed Tulloch's report in May 1882 and then provided copies to India and France the following month. Encompassing all aspects of the Egyptian Army, the report's preparation had been facilitated by the Egyptian Army's Chief of Staff, General Charles Stone, an American.[14]

Another War Office–sponsored survey led by Professor Edward Palmer and Captain William Gill, RE, also operated in the area. Palmer's association with the Sinai was longstanding, but his present task was to judge the tenor of Bedouin feeling in the Egyptian hinterland. To what end can only be surmised as his party came to grief that August, but ensuring the non-intervention of Arab tribes should Britain intervene that summer appears the likely reason.[15]

Meanwhile, the Khedive temporized. In meeting the demands of some 50,000 rebels, he adopted steps operating at both the Sultan and European Powers' expense. Insisting their stance was to safeguard the interests of the Sultan, elements of the French Mediterranean Squadron under Rear Admiral Alfred Conrad and Britain's Mediterranean Squadron under Admiral Sir Beauchamp Seymour rendezvoused at Souda Bay, Crete. Departing on 18 May, the fleet carried out exercises en route to Alexandria.[16] In Constantinople, Dervish Pasha and 4,000 troops were readied for service in Egypt. Designated as the force's chief of staff was a cashiered British officer, Valentine Baker.[17] The ostensible mission of the Anglo-French fleet was to protect European life and property.[18] Its ultimate purpose was to backstop the negotiations for an Egyptian ministry that was friendly to Allied interests.[19] The fleet's presence offered muscle where before mere entreaties sufficed. The Khedive, understanding the dictates of *force majeure*, yielded readily enough. Still, where a position is secured at the expense of others, a response from those adversely affected must be expected, and ever more so when their hands retain the levers of control. Thus, the military stood firm for Urabi.[20]

The situation led many Europeans residing in the interior to seek refuge elsewhere. Their departure posed an immediate problem to Cairo's coffers as the grain harvested could not reach market, with a portion of the proceeds following to the taxman.[21] While negotiations with the disaffected officers were underway, rioting broke out in Alexandria, leading to the death of fifty Europeans, the wounding of many more, and much destruction.[22] Among the injured was Charles Cookson, the British consul. This was not the moment for intervention, though it would not be long delayed. Tellingly, the British fleet of fourteen ships and the French naval squadron of six acting in concert and steaming within eyeshot of the disturbances did not intervene. However, many Europeans took refuge in the nearby ships. Indeed, with so many seeking the ships' comparative safety, the fleet's effectiveness was in danger of being compromised.[23]

At home, the fleet's inaction sparked a storm of criticism. Having been returned to office in 1880 on a pledge of peace, William Gladstone faced a split within the cabinet and the wrath of the Tories beyond.[24] Responding to the worsening situation, elements of the Channel Fleet sailed to reinforce Britain's naval presence. That measure, along with the decision of 5 July to send troops, suggested a more assertive policy was unfolding. The reality was something less. With John Bright voicing resignation while Joseph Chamberlain advocated for yet still more robust measures, Gladstone struggled to maintain unity among his party's Radical and Whig factions.[25] Tipping the scales toward action was the strengthening of Alexandria's defenses, as these posed a risk to the fleet underwriting the safety of foreigners. With the Tories threatening to raise the whole in parliament, Gladstone upped the ante ever so slightly again. Orders were issued to Admiral Seymour to forestall the strengthening of Alexandria by force, if necessary.[26]

Those defenses consisted of smoothbore, rifled guns, and heavy mortars of a dated provenance ensconced in forts. Perhaps more worrisome was the fear that an attempt would be made to block the port by sinking stone-laden barges.[27] Tulloch, having returned, met with Admiralty and War Office representatives to review the details of his reconnaissance, which had documented Egyptian positions at length. Sensing that at least one service was on the cusp of war, he willingly offered his help to the Navy. With the Admiralty accepting the offer with alacrity, Tulloch found himself at Admiral Seymour's side within the week.[28]

Early July saw the chartering of ships to support the evacuation of the 55,000 Europeans residing in the city, of whom only some 3,000 were British. Seymour now received the authority to act unilaterally if the situation demanded.[29] The change in instructions reflected the difficulties of fashioning a timely, collective European response, but from that change stemmed a commitment few could have foreseen.[30] When a close reconnaissance of Alexandria by Lieutenant Henry Smith-Dorrien confirmed the improvements underway at Fort Silsili, Seymour warned off the Khedive's Navy.[31]

With the eight major warships of the British fleet divided into inner and outer squadrons, the shelling of Alexandria's forts commenced at 7 a.m. on 11 July 1882.[32] At the fore was the battleship *Inflexible*, which mounted four 16-inch guns and fired 1,700-lb shells from two twin turrets. New for a warship, the 10,000-ton vessel incorporated electricity and stood as the last word in naval technology. The balance of the bombarding squadron remained a mixed force with inferior armaments spread across several different calibers. With individual targets allocated to the attacking ships, initial shooting conditions were ideal, with the sea calm, visibility fine, and ranges varying from 1,300–4,000 yards. Surprisingly, given the justification for the assault, the fleet did not engage Fort Silsili. Instead, the *Temeraire*, *Inflexible*, and *Monarch* steaming slowly engaged the forts ranged across Alexandria while others did as much though firing at anchor.[33] As the action progressed, ships closed the distance to combat the poor visibility created by the residue of so much shooting with rocket and 1-inch guns joining the equation.

Though an ammunition ship was scheduled to arrive the next day, Seymour cautioned captains to be judicious in firing as each ship only carried approximately eighty rounds per main gun. In the event, the expenditure in heavy ordnance proved severe. Meanwhile, the fires registered were not all in one direction. Several ships suffered punishment, including the *Alexandra*, being hit no less than sixty times and fortunate to escape. Meanwhile, the *Inflexible*, if less knocked about topside, received damage beneath the waterline, necessitating her docking in Malta for repairs.[34]

If the shooting claimed some magazines and silenced a few guns, the results, when set against the effort expended, appeared paltry. Lieutenant Percy Scott held that only ten Egyptian guns had been hit for the expenditure of 3,000 British rounds.[35] Many shells failed to explode or exploded prematurely, with 80% of fuses failing. Meanwhile, in the *Alexandra*, two of its muzzle-loading guns suffered damage from firing that might have resulted in critical failures if the action had continued.[36] Lieutenant Commander Caspar Goodrich of the U.S. Navy reported that measures were in hand to correct matters. Still, the performance of British shells would remain a vexatious issue in the years ahead. With few guns destroyed outright, real success required laying gun-cotton charges to destroy the artillery's powder, thereby rendering their further use problematic.[37]

At the end of the day's action, British casualties stood at five dead and twenty-eight wounded; Egyptian casualties numbered in the hundreds if not thousands.[38] Crews now transferred ammunition from the *Humber* to their respective vessels. This effort proved only partially successful as that ship failed to bring any fuses for the shells being passed. As elements of the Channel Squadron were to arrive momentarily, the critical period proved to be the days following.[39] Notwithstanding the misstep, shooting resumed on the morning of 12 July but soon desisted, as it appeared the garrisons would at last yield. That was fortunate, for sea conditions had deteriorated, rendering effective fire impossible.[40]

Ashore confusion reigned as authority collapsed. Indeed, a greater calamity began to unfold as fires raged in the city, leading to carnage and wanton mayhem. Before running its course, over 2,000 Europeans had died, and order ashore only followed when the operation assumed the proportions of a direct military intervention. Such mayhem and confusion served its purpose, allowing Urabi and his cohorts to quit the city.[41] Quitting too was Bright, who avowed, "I cannot accept any share of the responsibility for the acts of war which have taken place at Alexandria. I cannot see to what they may lead, and I know not to what greater wrong and mischief they may force the Government."[42]

With the defenses swept aside, the landings made by the British fleet were of an administrative nature and initially tackled the guns commanding the harbor. A follow-on force occupied the palace at Ras-el-Tin on 13 July, with the operation coming under the *Inflexible*'s pugnacious commanding officer, Captain John Fisher. So terrible had conditions ashore become that German, Greek, and American forces landed to secure their consulates and the Western quarter. Not until 17 July, however, did the first regular British soldiers appear when a brigade previously staged in Cyprus from units already found in the Mediterranean area disembarked.[43] Their arrival immediately doubled the size of the intervention and would have come sooner, except that they had had work to do at Port Said first. They did not arrive, however, in the troopship *Orontes*, which reached the scene without embarking any troops. The *Orontes* captain, Hilary Andoe, had served as the resident transport officer in Natal in 1880 and would act as the principal transport officer during the Tokar Expedition in 1884. In short, Andoe was the navy's point man for any trooping duty under active service conditions.[44]

Admiral Seymour welcomed the one-armed Major General Sir Archibald Alison and his infantry, the latter of whom was now assuming responsibility for the city's occupation. The military, however, remained subject to Seymour's overall authority, who had been appointed local supremo in the absence of Sir Edward Malet, Britain's consul general to Egypt.[45] The turnover suited the War Office if not quite Gladstone, who would have been happy to have seen Seymour retain direct responsibility for the entire operation. The stumbling block was deemed the Army Act, which specified that the legal chain of command for deployed forces ran solely through *military* channels.[46] The point might be thought academic, save in the previous year, doubt existed whether Marines once landed operated under any vehicle of formal discipline, be it naval *or* military.[47] That and a desire to see the fleet's personnel commanded through their own chain of command moved Seymour to insist that the naval forces landed be kept intact. This Lieutenant General Sir Garnet Wolseley did, though keeping the Royal Marine Light Infantry apart from the Royal Marine Artillery, believing they "get on very badly together."[48] Administrative niceties aside, Seymour's stance reflected that the landings of July 1882 had denuded the fleet as a warfighting entity. With several senior officers ashore, command of some ships had devolved for a time to junior executive officers.[49] That expedient owed everything to the absence of the British Army immediately following the bombardment.

Considering the earlier outrages occurring and the standing orders to protect life, Seymour's failure to anticipate events would appear to stand as a mark against his judgment. Allowing that his initial force was too small to do much else, such a verdict would be too strong. Though military reinforcements were on the way from Gibraltar and Malta, even these were insufficient to meet the scale of rebellion unfolding.[50] Seymour acted when he did because London feared the risks accruing against the fleet. In electing to force the issue unilaterally, London was not wrong, merely precipitous. It would not be the last time a Mediterranean naval squadron initiated an action against a landward objective with too few ships on hand and absent an immediately available military force. Yet, acting when it did, minus military support guaranteed the wanton death and destruction that followed.[51]

Though preliminary measures had been taken, the decision to mount a greater expedition and to what ends remained open as late as 20 July. Earlier, the queen had sought to learn from the secretary of state for war the name of the intended commander. Hugh Childers could not answer that question because the cabinet had yet to weigh the lines of any intervention. The War Office was thinking, however, of a corps-size force. However, the bombardment and the deployment of infantry under Alison now forced the issue. The British desired the porte to send a force to Egypt; the sultan continued to temporize. Childers now pressed the cabinet to grasp the nettle. Responding, on 21 July, they accepted the War Office's plan for occupying Egypt, and Wolseley was appointed to command an expedition soon following.[52] In turn, Wolseley tapped others occupying key positions in the home establishment to join him.[53]

Though the naval bombardment had been a unilateral British act, the hope remained that the French would join future efforts. Already sharing intelligence, Lieutenant General Sir John Adye, the designated chief of staff to the expedition, intended to travel to Paris to discuss a French contribution when the Chamber of Deputies voted against further involvement.[54] Unknowingly, the vote ceded French influence in Egypt to the British for the next 70 years. Elsewhere, with sanction given to call out the reserves, maneuvers were conducted at Aldershot for those bound for Egypt. These serials were limited to battalion-level drills and did not include the higher staff and transport arrangements, which only joined the expeditionary force following its arrival in Egypt.[55] Still, the movement of 26,000 troops and 5,000 horses from Britain and the Mediterranean environs, along with another 8,000 troops and followers from India, represented a feat few could match; it also required numerous lateral movements as units sent to the scene of action had to be backfilled by others.[56] Fortunately, Admiral Sir William Mends, the admiralty's long-serving director of transports, proved equal to the task possessing as he did an unsurpassed knowledge of the trooping problem.[57]

Though a city had been subdued, a country remained afire. Urabi retreated to Kafr-el-Dawwar (Kafr ad Dawwâr) while a growing number of sympathetic uprisings began. Alison's policing efforts are not germane to this study save that the dearth of crew-served weapons meant ratings from the fleet continued to man the machine guns landed. Securing Alexandria now allowed the Europeans to return. It also allowed the logistics for subsequent operations to be anchored on the city for the canal and Cairo stood as the ultimate levers to be controlled if the rebellion were to be smashed.[58] Accordingly, Rear Admiral Sir William Hewett's East Indies Squadron tackled the southern end of the former when a party from the corvette *Euryalus* under Commander Ernest Rolfe occupied

Suez on 2 August. Rolfe, no stranger to Africa, Hewett, or the soon-arriving Wolseley, would play an outsized role henceforward in Egypt, the Sudan, and Abyssinia. His connections to both officers extended to the previous decade's Ashanti War, where he served in Hewett's ship, the *Active*, before acting as Wolseley's naval *aide de camp*.[59]

As for Wolseley, owing to illness, he only arrived on 16 August.[60] Separately, two divisions of infantry and another of cavalry made a parallel passage to that city. On August 18/19, a portion of that force re-embarked in seventeen transports. Escorted by eight warships, they made for Aboukir (Abu Qir), seemingly with the intent of taking the Egyptian Army stronghold at Kafr el Dawar.[61] Anchoring in the afternoon, this was but a ruse fostered, as the forts protecting Aboukir meant any landing there faced immediate opposition.[62] Wolseley's real objective remained Port Said. Seizing the northern end of the canal, Wolseley intended to march on Ismailia and, thence, Cairo in a move that promised to outflank the Egyptian Army and negate the geographic disadvantages presented by the Nile River Delta. Thus, small boats headed shoreward at dusk under a covering fire while the main force spread across 113 vessels raised anchor and sailed.[63] Not without some difficulty, however, as engine breakdowns plagued the *Nerissa* and the *Rhosina*, two of the transports.[64] Nevertheless, all reached Port Said on the morning of 20 August.

Already, that town was being screened by the *Monarch* and *Iris*, and under cover of darkness, parties came ashore and surrounded the barracks of the local garrison. Though armed, the weapons of the naval landing party were not loaded because the aim was to overtake the rebels with a minimal amount of force. Directing the coup was Tulloch and suggests something of the nature of his earlier reconnaissance of Egypt. Meanwhile, another party under Commander Herbert Edwards from the *Northumberland* and the *Penelope* assumed control of Kantara's telegraph offices, while a larger body from the *Orion* seized Ismailia. Throughout the day, these forces fought several minor actions until reinforced by Major General Gerald Graham's 2 Brigade, which formed a part of Lieutenant General George Willis' 1st Division.[65]

Of note, the orders drafted by Rear Admiral Anthony Hoskins specified the forces to be employed and the primary objectives to be secured. Emphasizing the need to minimize civilian casualties and property damage, it was left to the discretion of Captain Henry Fairfax, the senior naval officer present, to retreat if faced with a superior force. Conversely, those issued to Captains Edward

Seymour of the *Iris* and Robert Fitz Roy of the *Orion* and operating in support of Fairfax remained more abbreviated.[66]

Admittedly, the absence of the army owed nothing to idleness. Instead, it merely reflected the poor landing facilities available, which hindered the building up of men and stores.[67] In the first instance, an advance body from the York and Lancaster and West Kent Regiments reached Ismailia in the gun vessels *Falcon* and *Beacon*.[68] Concurrently, Hewett's East Indies Squadron patrolling near Suez closed the Maritime Canal. Blocking further access was the gunboat *Mosquito*, which later that evening, in company with her consort the *Seagull*, landed two companies of the Seaforth Highlanders to seize Chalouf-el-Terraba.[69]

With the above, the British controlled the entire waterway, and it remained for Wolseley to reduce Egyptian resistance in the country's interior. These operations culminated at Tel-el-Kebir, an Egyptian military camp located on the Sweetwater Canal, where following a 5-mile silent night march guided by Wolseley's naval *adc*, Lieutenant Wyatt Rawson, the British routed the Egyptians on 13 September. Claiming 2,000 nationalists, Urabi himself escaped to Cairo, 60 miles distant. Fearing another calamity, two squadrons of cavalry offered quick pursuit. Cairo, however, would not share Alexandria's fate. With Colonel the Hon. Reginald Talbot capturing Urabi the following day, Wolseley entered the city on 15 September.[70] Four days later, the Khedive dissolved his Egyptian Army.

This success, achieved at little cost in British and Indian lives, owed much to Egyptian disorganization, for the expedition's logistics remained a "hand-to-mouth" affair, in the words of Royle. With the road network poor to non-existent and the rail line severed, a flotilla of minor craft supplied the front and evacuated the wounded via the Sweetwater Canal, a waterway connecting the Nile to the Suez Canal. Even then, getting ammunition, food, feed, and water to the front posed endless difficulties, reducing some to live off pigeons while others rustled cattle; not a few were reduced to drinking foul water. Forced to retain a brigade at Alexandria to maintain order against a first-class enemy offering real opposition, British fortunes would have been bleak.[71]

Paradoxically, the supply and transport arrangements of Major General Sir Herbert Macpherson's Indians offered a notable contrast.[72] They arrived complete with 2,500 mules and did not expect to hire camels locally to meet their needs as the force deploying from Britain did. Further, the horses of the Indian Cavalry withstood the rigors of the campaign better than their British counterparts. Moreover, the ships bringing the force had been specially modified for their trooping duties. To that end, thirty-five ships had been hired to service a force expected to reach two brigades augmented by 3,000 followers. This included the transport *Hydaspes* converted into a hospital ship under Captain John Hext.[73] Leasing ships was more financially sound than maintaining a permanent fleet of transports and freed naval personnel from manning those ships when being held in a caretaker status.[74] More remains to be said on the matter, but having a cadre of active troopships *and* the ability to contract for others retained an advantage not to be dismissed lightly.

Victorious, Wolseley wasted little time quitting the scene. Residual actions remained, including the occupation of Aboukir on 2 November.[75] In the wake of the intervention, the Khedive returned to a disarmed Cairo, though there could be no mistaking where the levers of power now resided.[76] That power was being exercised within decided limits, for Britain had little desire to retrieve all of Egypt's misfortunes. Most especially, this included those arising in Sudan.[77] Thus, Britain announced on 7 November her intention not to intervene in Sudanese affairs. Further, Britain barred any retired officers from offering their services to the Khedive. That was a belated climbdown, for the Foreign Office had sanctioned their use only a month earlier. Though the change might be interpreted as a means of limiting involvement, the more likely reason remained the objection of seeing Baker Pasha—Valentine Baker, a cashiered cavalryman—commanding British officers.[78]

Two further measures ensued. Firstly, the East Indies Squadron continued to protect Egyptian interests in the Red Sea, including the Sudan littoral.[79] This confirmed Egyptian control of Khartoum and Suakin while hindering the slave trade, ensuring the broader safety of Aden and India, and forestalling the influence of France. Suakin was especially prized as it served as an important relay point for the Eastern Telegraph Company through its cables to Suez and Aden.[80] Secondly, at the prodding of Colonel Sir Charles Wilson, Lieutenant Colonel Donald Stewart proceeded to Sudan to "report upon the state of affairs" found there. A superb staff officer, Stewart's six-week sojourn took him from Khartoum to Massawa via Senaar and Kassala. When received at the Foreign Office, Stewart's report read as a litany of woe.[81]

Meanwhile, Dufferin,[82] Britain's minister to Constantinople, came to Egypt to identify what reforms might forestall further turmoil.[83] True to his remit, a bevy of recommendations followed, including placing the Egyptian Army and gendarmerie on sounder lines. Indeed, Baker was already pursuing as much. Two problems remained, however. Firstly, his leadership would be problematic if British officers were to be employed in a reformed Egyptian Army. Secondly, his plans regarding Sudan were more fulsome than Dufferin allowed.[84] The political cost of employing Baker became a factor Gladstone could not ignore. That the prime minister hosted Major General Sir Evelyn Wood to dinner the very day the Foreign Office was requesting the War Office to find a suitable alternative to Baker suggests the costs already incurred.[85] Thus, the appointment of Wood as sirdar of the Egyptian Army ensued leaving Baker to reform the gendarmerie. Wood's efforts would produce only limited results for other claims would be made upon his office, foremost, managing the lines of communication during a future Sudan campaign. Yet, even if such distractions had not been present the largesse to achieve more in the way of reform simply did not exist.[86] Dufferin and Wood, however, did accept a key aspect of Baker's reorganization plan: the secondment of British officers in the service of Egypt. Still, two further measures remained very much on the back burner: Dufferin's endorsement of a Suakin and Berber rail line to facilitate Egyptian control of Sudan and the suggestion that General Gordon be induced to return to Khartoum. Both stood idle for the moment, but their hour would yet come.[87]

Ironically, Britain wasted little time reducing its military presence just as its political influence assumed greater dimensions with a steadily diminishing force of 12,000 troops remaining. With Urabi banished to Ceylon (Sri Lanka), Britain appeared triumphant. Appearances, however, can be deceiving, and so they proved now. Egypt's fate was inextricably linked to Sudan, where 40,000 troops in virtual penal servitude extended the Khedive's remit. The occupation worked against Egypt's already straightened finances, and thus, one did not require the skills of a Baring to appreciate the undesirability of retaining control of Sudan on that score.[88] In the words of Milner, Britain now adopted a policy of "limited liability." Unfortunately, others not in the service of the queen-empress thought in more expansive terms. Fighting and Britain's part in it had barely begun.[89]

Two

Out of Egypt...into the Sudan

The man is not worth the camels.[1]

Redvers Buller, 1884

The occupation of Egypt, if meeting initial success, gave vent to further problems. Cholera and typhus, to be sure, but also nationalist and religious fervor. By June 1883, the former had claimed one per cent of the British Army of Occupation.[2] By August, 1,000 Egyptians a day were dying. Ironically, this medical crisis only cemented British administrative and political control as civil and military authorities responded to the worsening situation.[3] Though with decidedly clipped wings, on the credit side, the Khedive had been restored to power. Yet, occupation by Christians proved loathsome to Nationalists and Islamists alike, bringing discredit anew to his rule. As the font of opposition was anchored in the Egyptian Army, it was natural for the British to disband and reform that body. That measure, however, created an opening for those despising the yoke of Egyptian rule in Sudan.[4] Guided by Muḥammad Aḥmad ibn al-Saiyid "Abd Allāh, a religious warrior *cum* Sunni prophet but known forever as the Mahdī, the nationalist revolt in Egypt created the space for Mahdism which the British attempts at reform only fueled."[5] Troublesome for some time already and confirming nature abhors a vacuum when Egypt redeployed troops from Sudan to deal with the crisis in Egypt when the incipient rebellion became general.[6]

Subsequently, the Khedive turned his sights on reclaiming Sudan and sought British help. If London demurred, they insisted any expedition be British-led and suggested any of several officers. Valentine Baker thereupon selected Lieutenant Colonel William Hicks, late Bombay Staff Corps.[7] With a party of seconded British officers, all left Cairo via train for Suez and then by ship for Suakin in February 1883.[8] The task facing Hicks Pasha was in every regard prodigious, for his command required reorganization and training before it could embark on operations. That it included many who had followed

Urabi did not bode well. Hicks aimed to meet the rebels in the Kordofan, a lonely, scorching environment southwest of Khartoum. Possessing limited freshwater, more worryingly, this was the Mahdī's very center of gravity. If beginning well, Hicks proved unequal to the task, with his command of 11,000 being handled roughly over several days culminating with its annihilation at Shaikán on 5 November 1883. Not since Moses had faced down the legions of Pharaoh, it was said, had an Egyptian force been so ill-treated.[9]

Almost as bad followed when 500 Egyptians, accompanied by Lynedoch Moncrieff, a retired naval officer and British consul, came to grief at Tokar. Attacked by a smaller force, that Tahir, the officer commanding, survived merely added insult to injury.[10] The debacle set bells ringing in London, where *The Times* likened the affair to Major General Sir William Elphinstone's 1842 retreat from Kabul.[11] With her prestige at a nadir, Britain abandoned its self-proclaimed goal of withdrawing all remaining troops in Egypt lest the tide of Mahdism subsumed the entire Nile region. Still, Sir Evelyn Baring, Britain's consul general to Egypt, argued against direct involvement in Sudan. In a prescient signal to home authorities, he warned that once embroiled, Britain would find it impossible to leave.[12]

All this moved Hartington and Wolseley to propose backstopping Egyptian efforts with British officers.[13] Northbrook, the First Lord, advocated withdrawal from Sudan's interior while retaining its Red Sea ports. Dufferin, meanwhile, believed Egypt should keep the region east of the White Nile.[14] Meeting that December, the cabinet temporized: Britain would not provide troops, but it would not object to the assistance of Turkey, the nominal suzerainty. That palliative proved too much for Egyptian coffers—a point London appreciated. What the Khedive could do was send another force to Sudan. London now had to come clean and advise that evacuation from the interior was the proper response. That demand proved too much for Mohamed Sherif Pasha, the Egyptian prime minister, who resigned. Unable to display such flexibility, the Khedive remained. Implicitly, the British were jettisoning their policy of limited liability.[15]

With British Red Sea naval operations resting on Suakin and Aden, threats to either were always strongly deprecated. London now reinforced its naval presence.[16] Authorities in Cairo and London also concluded that accommodation with Abyssinia by Egypt over outstanding frontier issues was a must, for it offered one means of forestalling the Mahdī's influence in Senaar and Kassala while allowing Egypt to focus on the Red Sea littoral. To that end, Hewett of the East Indies Squadron met with King John to fashion a rapprochement.[17] The initiative sprang from the Sudan explorer Sir Samuel Baker.[18] That it would suffice was doubted, for the War Office pursued the additional measure of recalling Gordon on 15 January 1884. Gordon likely learned of Hewett's mission at this time.[19] He certainly was not in doubt what his role in the unfolding drama was to be: Wolseley tasked Gordon with reporting on the manner of withdrawing the remaining 24,000 Egyptian troops from Sudan and, more importantly, given the outrages previously occurring in Alexandria, how best to evacuate its remaining European population. In short, Gordon's task was to outline the means of conducting a noncombatant evacuation operation in a far from permissive environment.[20]

That public mission was misleading. Firstly, one did not need to send a general or a former governor general to survey and report. After all, Donald Stewart had already done much the same. Gordon was being sent to command the Egyptian garrison at Khartoum.[21] Evacuation might follow, though given Gordon's antecedents of independent duty and Britain's interest in maintaining a foothold in the Sudan littoral, perhaps not. All would depend on events. Secondly, though Gordon's appointment appeared to be answering an ongoing press campaign, the truth remained that the government had been touting his services to the Khedive since December.[22] The inspiration belonged to Major General Sir Andrew Clarke, the inspector general of fortifications.[23] More directly, Clarke held the concurrent appointment of commander of the Corps of Royal Engineers. Finding Gordon, a fellow sapper, a position commensurate to his status must be reckoned as a key motivation and one that animated Wolseley, too. Indeed, the public call for Gordon's return has all the hallmarks of a campaign orchestrated to provide a level of cover for the *volte-face* being adopted.

Gordon received his instructions on 18 January in a final planning session chaired by Granville, with Hartington, Northbrook, and Sir Charles Dilke of the Local Government Board also in attendance.[24] If explicit on what was to be reported upon reaching Khartoum, Gordon's guidance on evacuation remained opaque.[25] At no point during these preliminaries did Gordon meet with Gladstone, suggesting the prime minister was not genuinely vested in the scheme even if the cabinet endorsed matters on 22 January.[26]

Meanwhile, the Khedive attempted to retrieve Sudanese fortunes by his own means. The 1,300 troops garrisoning Fashoda retreated north to Khartoum, joining the 4,000 bayonets already there, while a body of gendarmes was sent to secure the communications connecting Khartoum, Berber, and Suakin.[27] This step followed as the British would not sanction the use of the army.[28] Unfortunately, Baker Pasha's command proved as ill-composed as that under Hicks Pasha. Indeed, its antecedents were distinctly bad, with many deemed responsible for the worst of the Alexandria rioting of the previous year.[29] The younger brother of Samuel Baker, his pedigree for a policeman was uncommon except by the standards of nineteenth-century Egypt. A former colonel of Hussars, Valentine Baker, had been sentenced to penal servitude in 1875 for sexual assault. The indiscretion ended one career but begat another: Within a year, Baker found employment on the staff of the Turkish Army. Following Cairo's occupation, Pasha Baker assumed command of the Egyptian Army. The appointment soon ended when some at Westminster heard of it to the benefit of Evelyn Wood.[30]

Departing Cairo on 19 December 1883, Baker's task was to protect the route to Berber. Wood modified these orders in mid-January to secure the evacuations of Sinkat and Tokar. Knowing of Baker's sordid reputation, Baring anticipated a battle would occur if only to redeem that cashiered officer's standing. Baring was soon proved correct when an inferior Mahdist force overwhelmed his command of 3,500 at El Teb on 4 February 1884. Said to include "the sweepings of Egyptian gaols," if so, then many of the warders were British officers.[31] The rebels' success operated at the peril of Sinkat and its garrison, located 50 miles away from Suakin. Despairing of any support, Tafiq Bey and his garrison attempted to retreat to Suakin. Disaster and another defeat ensued. Meanwhile, Baker and 2,000 survivors reached Suakin on 5 February, where the *Ranger* and *Decoy* stood offshore.[32]

Immediately, a naval landing party landed to forestall a general uprising. In turn, the *Euryalus* sailed from Suez, bringing Hewett to assume responsibility for civil and military affairs from Baker.[33] Hewett quickly organized the surviving forces while all available marine officers were directed to Suakin from the Mediterranean Squadron. More would yet come from the home depots. A further measure saw the removal of Egyptian officers from the command of Sudanese troops.[34] Nominally, Hewett and the East Indies Squadron were acting in support of and under Khedivial authority, but Baring remained the real power behind the throne.[35]

The expanding military crisis gave vent to a parallel political crisis. British Near East policy appeared in tatters leading Salisbury and the Tories to charge British actions toward Egypt were feckless, if not dishonest and illegal.[36] The harsh measures Hewett adopted appeared to add shame to scuttle as rebels and natives were flogged while a reward was promised for the capture or death of the leading Mahdist lieutenant Osman Digna.[37] Both went beyond the norms of British law and policy, yet fashioning a defense to protect British subjects absent an effective force left Hewett few options. His methods were no worse than those employed by Seymour in Alexandria in 1882.[38] A veteran of the Ashanti War, Hewett deprecated using bluejackets ashore. Circumstances seemingly demanded otherwise, with the lives of Europeans at risk the spur.[39] All true, and all required a counterstroke to restore matters and, more importantly, to restore British prestige.

The knock to British prestige weighed heavy on Wolseley, but so too did the implications presented to a Gordon who had yet to reach Khartoum. By announcing that it would not fight for Sudan, Britain was forfeiting the support of tribes not yet aligned to the Mahdī. Thus, Wolseley proposed the establishment of a British protectorate in eastern Sudan lest Gordon, the presumed rescuer, require rescuing himself. Admittedly, Wolseley was not guaranteeing even this would be successful, merely that it offered a chance of forestalling a greater failure.[40] To a government that eschewed the jingoistic ventures of Disraeli, Wolseley's demarche proved hard reading. Meeting twice on 10 February, the cabinet ordered an infantry brigade from Egypt to Suakin.[41] From Malta came a battalion of infantry, and a second was sent from Gibraltar to backfill those departing Valetta. In turn, the admiralty organized a Marine contingent in Britain to augment its limited force in Egypt.[42]

Gordon reached Cairo on 24 January and now intimated to Baring that he intended to make Khartoum via Suakin. Appreciating the ongoing troubles in Kassala, the latter suggested a Nile journey instead. Over the next 48 hours, Gordon participated in at least five separate conferences where the lines of his mission were thrashed out with Egyptian authorities. Appointed governor general of Sudan at a final conclave with the Khedive, Gordon and his military secretary, Colonel Donald Stewart, departed.[43] At a minimum, the appointment clarified his relationship with Colonel Henry de Coëtlogon, the acting governor general.[44]

Gordon aimed to evacuate all via Berber and Suakin, believing the Mahdī did not present an immediate problem to those in Khartoum.[45] He also offered to make the Mahdī the sultan of the Kordofan. That gesture was wasted, but more substantially, Gordon repudiated the laws prohibiting slavery, reduced the inhabitants' taxes, opened the city's prisons, and announced the abolishment of torture.[46] These steps aimed not to eliminate the grievances standing between Khedival authority and the populace but were precursors for transitioning power to local chiefs outside the orbit of the Mahdī.[47] He also ordered the immediate return to Cairo of de Coëtlogon while seeking the appointment of al-Zubayr Rahma Mansūr as deputy governor general. Even coming from Gordon, the last should not have surprised London, for the Khedive had attempted as much in December.[48] A notorious slaver, London vetoed it then and vetoed it now.[49]

The Khedive accepted all this much as he accepted Hewett's actions elsewhere. Still, Gordon contemplated a further trick: Incorporating Sudan with the Congo and placing it under Belgium's rule. The ploy promised to limit Britain's future exposure and was consistent with his original instructions, which emphasized forestalling a return to slavery in the wake of an evacuation.[50] Of course, employing al-Zubayr undermined that strategy, as did renouncing the laws prohibiting slavery. Both, however, were means to a desired end (evacuation) not otherwise seemingly attainable.

On 12 February, Baring instructed Gordon to cease moves southward from Khartoum. If nixing a greater plan, then it also forestalled one avenue of retreat. To some, though, it appeared Gordon was drifting from settled policy. This prompted the War Office to weigh whether a force might be required to secure Gordon's arrest.[51] That did not materialize, but another expedition in the wake of Baker's defeat departed Egypt for Suakin. Spearheading the Tokar Expedition were not only British officers but also British troops. Reaching Suez via train, the force boarded the *Orontes* and arrived at its destination on 19 February. Major General Gerald Graham joined in four days a force that included 380 Marines under Colonel Henry Tuson and a contingent of 164 officers and ratings with their crew-served guns under Commander Rolfe.[52] Tokar succumbed, however, before Graham's force of 4,000 troops could effectively intervene. Whether Hewett's warning to Digna that Tokar garrison stood to be relieved precipitated the debacle is impossible to adjudicate. Still, at a minimum, it emphasized the element of time to those besieging the town.[53]

Proving too late for Tokar, Graham sought at least to redeem El Teb. He achieved that and more on 29 February at the Second Battle of El Teb when meeting a force of 6,000 rebels.[54] They suffered 1,500 dead, while British casualties amounted to some 200. Graham next marched to Tokar and recovered a cache of arms gained from Baker Pasha's earlier defeat. With the enemy proving elusive, orders to retreat followed.[55] The cabinet, however, was not yet through and authorized a further intervention. Re-landing on 11 March, the expedition, including Rolfe's brigade, advanced to Tamai, where a rebel body of 12,000 suffered a further 2,000 dead two days later. British losses totaled some 200, equally divided between wounded and dead.[56] In all this, the support of Admiral Hewett proved exemplary. First denuding the defenses of Suakin, Hewett then drew further officers and ratings from the offshore squadron, including Arthur Wilson of the *Hecla*. In turn, both Hewett and Wilson accompanied Graham.[57] Appreciating the support rendered, Graham reported, "Had Admiral Hewett himself been in command of the Expedition for the relief of Tokar he could not have done more to further its success."[58]

Nevertheless, final victory proved elusive as the British force was too small to control the vast countryside into which Digna and his followers retreated. Operations, no matter how successfully conducted, must be tied to a greater strategic purpose if their import is not to be wasted, and here, Graham's victories brought no essential change to Egypt's fortunes in Sudan. Indeed, they may have exasperated matters, for when the British retreated to the coast after torching several villages, the rebels' spirits soared. Regrettably, another season of campaigning beckoned.[59] Graham lacked the authority to advance as far as Berber owing to the absence of water along the route and the fear that his force would be overwhelmed by the Mahdists. As many troops suffered from sunstroke, the first was prudence itself. That Calcutta desired the return of its troops was probably the truer reason.[60] Regrettably, the failure to secure Berber ordained much of what followed.

If Gordon had been inclined to direct a withdrawal, the space provided by Graham's victories might have allowed for the removal of the remaining Egyptians and Europeans. That, however, did not occur. Exactly why cannot be adjudicated, though the likelihood Gordon believed the European citizenry faced greater dangers leaving the city under Egyptian and friendly Sudanese guard suggests itself. To that end, Britain entered negotiations with Abyssinia to stabilize eastern Sudan. If successful, Gordon would be presented with a clear path of exit. Alternatively, it might be Gordon understood his early departure minus a successor such as al-Zubayr, merely presented the entire Sudan to the Mahdī. Thus, he may have resolved not to quit Khartoum soon after arriving. Certainly, Donald Stewart concluded as much.[61]

While it is impossible to know how Gordon would have responded if Baring or the Foreign Office had ordered his immediate retreat from Khartoum, this never occurred. Holland argues that Gordon's appointment as governor general meant he was no longer under direct British control and that Gladstone was unwilling to adopt a course (removal) that would be unpalatable to the cabinet and the public. Hartington was probably closer to the truth when suggesting Gordon would never have obeyed the order. Increasingly, however, the war minister questioned the general's sanity.[62]

Implicit in the decision to send an officer of Gordon's stature was that Britain would send others if necessary. That was the view of Hartington; it was also the view of Wolseley. The evidence suggests Baring held as much, too, as he returned to London in late April to back the case for a military response.[63] That case argued for an autumn advance up the Nile by a force of 6,500 British troops. Pointedly, Wolseley eschewed the employment of an Indian contingent, believing its native followers would be a hindrance. That was one argument, but perhaps the more honest reason remained the emoluments of Indian officers were greater than their British counterparts. The adjutant general, however, proved more receptive to employing a naval brigade.[64] The cabinet, however, remained deeply divided, with some arguing for a more limited response. Lieutenant General Sir Frederick Stephenson, commanding in Egypt, disabused the possibility of a limited operation given the risks now accumulated.[65]

In May, the War Office directed Stephenson to prepare for a campaign in anticipation of final approval. Concomitantly, the Foreign Office pressed Turkey to reassert its authority over Zeila and Tadjoura on the Red Sea coast by sending troops. That did not happen, as Cairo could not meet the costs of a Turkish occupation.[66] Meanwhile, Commander Walter Graham traveled to Abyssinia to prepare for the arrival of Hewett.[67] If London stood firm against rescuing Gordon, a change was discernible, with Granville seeking to learn from Cairo and Gordon the scale of a relief force. To the chagrin of the Foreign Office, no reply was forthcoming, probably because Gordon thought in terms of reinforcement and not rescue.[68] Reluctantly and ever so slowly, Gladstone and the Liberals accepted a commitment in the summer of 1884 that they had abhorred the previous winter. Sudan may not yet be an imperial interest, but Egypt and British standing in the East could not be so dismissed leading Hartington to threaten resignation unless preparations to save Gordon were advanced.[69]

How long Khartoum could prevail depended partly on the supplies of the besieged but more emphatically on the scale of opposition faced. In July, Gordon estimated the city was secure for another four months.[70] Meanwhile, four primary routes existed to reach Khartoum. The most direct route consisted of a desert crossing from Suakin to Berber where the Nile could be gained with passage to Khartoum following. This, indeed, was the route Hicks had taken in 1883 under better circumstances.[71] Potentially, the route allowed a force to arrive sooner and, just as importantly, allowed for a more rapid withdrawal of those trapped.

Alternatively, a force could land at Massawa and cross the 500 miles to Kassala before advancing to Abu Haras. Here, water and transport were ever a factor, but the option remained viable if the tribes along the route remained generally peaceful.[72] A third option was an advance anchored on the Nile from Egypt. If seasonal rains abetted navigability, cataracts made the route unpassable at several points and would require the portage of boats. Finally, a hybrid advance might be attempted using the Nile where feasible, but then bypassing the river and crossing the desert at Korsoko or Korti before gaining the Nile anew.[73] No matter what the course adopted, difficulties remained. Still, a Nile advance, though longer, retained advantages.[74] Deemed a healthier approach, it would not present as many problems in freshwater supply. The passage, however, might be interrupted if the rebels gained the Sabalūka Gorge, a defile found between Khartoum and Metemmeh. This had been de Coëtlogon's fear voiced the previous November, leading him to prefer an evacuation directed toward Suakin on the Red Sea.[75]

While Wolseley conceded success was possible no matter the line of march taken, a Suakin-Berber approach demanded over 4,000 camels. Paradoxically, Wolseley discounted the number of camels a Nile advance required.[76] Events would demonstrate that while the Nile afforded access, it did so only reluctantly. Found 1,600 miles from Cairo, time would become the governing factor in reaching Khartoum.[77] Considered but seemingly discounted was an expedition anchored on more than one approach. This was vouchsafed by Admiral Lord

John Hay, the commander-in-chief, Mediterranean. Indeed, Hay believed such an approach underlined Hewett's mission to King John.[78]

Resting on the Blue Nile just before its merger with the White Nile, Khartoum seemingly offered a ready-made bolt-hole for the 34,000 trapped there. Still, no matter the approach adopted, the support of the Navy would be vital in negotiating the Third and Fourth Cataracts, which obstructed the passage of the Nile throughout the year. To this end, Commander Tynte Hammill and Lieutenant Reginald Marriott, RMA, surveyed the Nile in May–June 1884.[79] Concurrently, Colonel Horatio Kitchener and Major Leslie Rundle wooed the tribes along the Nile who had yet to declare for the Mahdī. At the same time, Major Herbert Chermside performed a similar task for those near Suakin to keep the way clear to Berber.[80]

Based on his findings, Hammill recommended advancing from Suakin, for a Nile approach necessarily meant working against current and gradient all while the depth of the river receded.[81] Hay endorsed his conclusions, and so did Stephenson.[82] Wolseley, though, had other thoughts, and, increasingly, his voice crowded out the plans of others. This included King Leopold of Belgium, who offered to deploy a force via Suakin to reach Gordon, and General Clarke, who proposed laying a railway from Suakin.[83]

Though the government had yet to commit to an expedition, measures were now taken in hand. In Egypt, British troops were directed to Aswan. In London, Hartington proposed establishing a working group composed of Admiralty and War Office representatives on 16 May. Gladstone deflated the last initiative, insisting the War Office settle its affairs first.[84] Thus, absent formal concurrence and minus an approved plan, the War Office began preparing the groundwork for both Nile and Suakin-Berber operations.

However, the cabinet's failure to address Sudan matters in a timely fashion doomed the prospect of Suakin-Berber operations. In late July, word that Berber had fallen to the rebels on 26 May reached London. This invalidated the assumption that a sizable portion of any Suakin force could be held back until the constructed rail line was finished. Now, that force must be expected to advance in step with the engineers to guarantee their safety. Unfortunately, the window for constructing a rail line evaporated with the onset of the African summer. Hartington thus wired Stephenson in August that an Egyptian-anchored approach was likely. Stephenson, though, persisted in touting the advantages of a Suakin-Berber route. The advocacy did little good, and, for his pains, the adjutant general assumed the role Stephenson held to be his.[85] Ostensibly, these reduced matters to either a Nile-anchored advance or one centered on a Massawa axis. The latter proved problematic as it required the cooperation of Abyssinia and thus presented greater risks than one residing entirely in British hands. This left only a Nile advance, leading Samuel Baker to predict that the venture would fail owing to the lateness of the hour.[86] If his warning failed to make an impression, then it was because even a bad option must be exercised when all others have lapsed.

Against his own advice to employ the least encumbrance, Wolseley traveled to Egypt with Evelyn Baring and Britain's new commissioner to Egypt—Northbrook. Along with Gladstone, Granville, and Hartington, the erstwhile First Lord stood as the cabinet's fourth member of the close-knit group controlling Britain's Egyptian policy.[87] Clearly, the to-ing and fro-ing of Stephenson over his continued advocacy of a Suakin-Berber advance had exasperated Hartington, to be sure, and behind him, Wolseley. One still believing a Suakin-Berber approach made in conjunction with a Nile advance was worth pursuing remained Cambridge, the commander-in-chief. His October 1884 proposal fell flat. That it required a commitment in trained troops Britain did not have is one explanation. That Wolseley and Northbrook believed a full-scale expedition to reach Gordon could yet be avoided remains another.[88] On balance, perhaps the strongest argument for a Suakin-anchored approach remained the advocacy of those familiar with all local tactical conditions.[89]

From Egypt, Wolseley provided a revised assessment to relieve Khartoum before the end of the year. The War Office agreed to provide the troops, though limiting their use beyond Dongola for the moment. In truth, bluff and self-deception were on full display. Wolseley argued that the deployment "of a fairly imposing British force" might prove sufficient to win the day, though, of course, that could not be guaranteed. Hartington parroting Wolseley trusted it was so.[90]

In September, nine infantry battalions were detailed for service. They were joined by a body of mounted troops under Brigadier General Sir Herbert Stewart. The men, minus their animals, sailed from Portsmouth by the end of the month and reached Wādī Halfā by late October. A two-week training period commenced for the hastily raised Camel Corps, aiming not to create a new style of *arme blanche* so much as a unit of mobility suitable for the theater of operations.[91] Necessarily, a Nile advance required shallow-draft boats. General

Stephenson proposed employing those found locally, but this was discounted.[92] Thus, Colonel William Butler and Lieutenant Colonel James Alleyne, with James Dunn of the Royal Corps of Naval Constructors, worked rapidly to design and contract for 800 35-foot shallow-draft whalers. Tellingly, Butler had never seen the Nile above Cairo, but that did not stop him from criticizing the report on its navigability when that paper reached the War Office. What Butler and Alleyne had seen was Canada's Red River when campaigning with Wolseley in 1870. Doubtlessly, Wolseley trusted Butler's judgment, but the claim "Water is water, rock is rock, whether they lie in America or in Africa; the conditions which they can assume toward each other are much the same all the world over" would prove false.[93] It would be for Butler and company to force events to conform to that premise.

The whalers began arriving within four months. Manned by *voyageurs*, Egyptian conscripts, and ratings from the fleet, the boatmen were nothing if not eclectic. They became the responsibility of Butler and Captain Frederick Boardman, the late inspector of patrol craft in Egypt. In turn, they were assisted by Alleyne, Hammill, and Commander Julian Baker. Though a regular naval officer, Buller thought Hammill out of his depth and thus sought the assistance of Captain Lord Charles Beresford.[94] In fairness, more than the quality of officership stood in the way of success. Never mind the problem of discipline; some boatmen were *very* old, while others lacked basic boat skills. Even if those drawbacks had not existed, the rapids remained to be overcome.

Thomas Cook steamers bore Wood's Egyptians, who were tasked with maintaining the enterprise's lines of communication. In hindsight, Butler lamented the congestion created, which hindered the progress of the infantry. However, the more significant problem remained the lack of an overall plan specifying the relative priority of men and materials, matched by a failure to mark the contents of boxed supplies. Yet, even if all had been correct, the men, according to Butler, worked at a sluggish pace.[95] Meanwhile, a naval brigade was created in late November. Wolseley proposed creating the force from the officers and ratings already supporting the expedition. While it did not approximate what a military officer thought of when speaking about a brigade, Beresford's force brought unique capabilities to an expedition operating on and serviced by the Nile.[96] Foremost, personnel familiar with boats, launches, and skiffs, not unlike the steamers and *nuggars* (i.e., large sailing boats) plying Egyptian and Sudanese waters.

Unfortunately, creating a naval brigade at the eleventh hour came with a steep price, as the personnel to form its ranks were scattered along the lines of communication.[97] Thus, time, a commodity in little abundance, elapsed as efforts to create the brigade proceeded. Worse was to follow as insufficient coal was on hand for the steamers. Buller, Wolseley's chief of staff, cited Major General the Hon. James Dormer, the chief of staff to British forces in Egypt, as the chief culprit for the failure. Wolseley believed the error was Buller's and his own in assuming all was correct with the establishment's logistics.[98] Allowing errors occurred, a key consideration must be afforded the lack of political direction. Failing to define ultimate aims beforehand, when the size of the expedition was doubled in September and narrowed to retrieving Gordon and Colonel Donald Stewart, the assumptions of April proved insufficient.[99] Privately, Buller calculated that there was no time to get the supplies required for the body of 10,000 now posited before Gordon's wherewithal had been expended. To that end, he pressed Wolseley to scale back the proportions of the expedition. Wolseley acceded to a point. He canceled the sailing orders of two regiments still in Britain.[100]

That September, Colonel Stewart and 2,000 Egyptian troops attempted to reach Dongola to meet the advancing force. Blocked by rebels, Stewart ordered the troops to return to Khartoum while continuing with a party of forty in the *Abbas*. Coming to grief at the Fifth Cataract, the Mahdists completed what nature had not.[101]

Writing to Gordon from Dongola in early November, Wolseley now appreciated the limitations of a Nile advance. It might reach Khartoum. It was not apt to reach Khartoum in a timely fashion. Consequently, he informed Gordon of his intention to send 1,500 camel troops across the desert to Shendy. This bypassed the reverse course the river assumed between Korti and Abu Hamed. Dividing his force, Wolseley would continue to send a column under Major General William Earle up the Nile while Herbert Stewart's mounted troops avoided the cataracts. Here, a survey made thirteen years earlier suggested Stewart's line of march and the oases available.[102] Reaching Korti mid-December, regrettably, the balance of Wolseley's command remained miles behind.

Stewart departed on 8 January for the 180-mile trek to Metemmeh. The delay owed everything to the preparations still required and the lack of coordination between Wolseley and Buller, separated by many miles. However, the hiatus allowed a portion of the naval brigade to reach Korti before the movement commenced.[103] With its skilled artificers, the brigade's presence was crucial for what followed, as only they could operate the steamers, hopefully waiting at Metemmeh.

At best, Stewart's column represented a reconnaissance in force with the dual aim of securing Metemmeh as an advance base before restoring contact with Gordon. To this end, Colonel Charles Wilson, the expedition's primary intelligence officer but, more correctly, its political officer, accompanied the column to give Gordon a letter. Its contents remain unknown, but its chief message must be that it told Gordon not to expect relief until April.[104]

Stewart's and Wilson's progress became measured in days and then in weeks. This owed everything to logistics as intermediate waypoints needed to be established along the line of march.[105] Though the days began warm with a mild breeze present, heat ruled the afternoons with nights cold. The column marched, rested, and then marched anew under the moonlight. Steadily, man and beast suffered as the provision of water became acute. Much that was carried evaporated owing to water bottles having defective skins, while the wells dotting the line of advance proved inadequate. Stewart pressed ever forward in the hope the next well would suffice. Wilson was highly critical of the manner of the march, believing more would have been achieved had they marched by day and slept by night.[106]

Meanwhile, Gordon faced his own dilemma of supply. Unable to feed everyone, he resolved to reduce at least demand; thus, he allowed some 5,000 inhabitants to quit the city.[107] Of course, Stewart's difficulties were compounded by the Berber tribesmen and Mahdists who held the wells of Abu Klea. A sharp action followed there on 17 January when a force of at least 8,000 under Abu Safia breached the British lines before the square could be formed. Costing ninety-two wounded and seventy-five dead, among the latter was Colonel Frederick Burnaby, the would-be Tory parliamentarian, pioneer of aeronautics, a friend of Gordon, and veteran of the Russo-Turkish War and El Teb.[108] Of Abu Klea, Wilson "felt when it was over that we had a narrow escape."[109] A mixed force of bluejackets, infantry, and cavalry—British and Egyptian—that had not trained together and suffering numerous breakdowns in their weapons were held as the proximate reasons for the near disaster. Of the élan of the attacking Sudanese, none could fault. Over 800 fell, defending the wells that now belonged to Stewart.[110]

With the Nile remaining miles and days away, Stewart had wanted to rest after such a desperate struggle but thought otherwise, knowing that Gordon, too, faced desperate times. Thus, a very tired column resumed its trek to Metemmeh.[111] Tragically, the column now suffered a severe setback at Abu Kru (Gubat) when forced to engage the enemy anew on 19 January. Suffering nearly twenty-five killed and over 100 wounded, included among the latter was a gravely wounded Stewart.[112] Command now devolved upon Sir Charles Wilson, a sapper of singular scientific talents though barren in the art of command.[113] Wilson understood his limitations and looked to Colonel the Hon. Edward Boscawen for guidance.[114] That officer, too, was bereft of experience such that the triumvirate of Lieutenant Colonel Percy Barrow, Captain the Earl of Airlie, and Major Frederick Wardrop came to the fore.[115]

Nevertheless, the column advanced slowly, as many wounded were present. Indeed, so weakened had the column become, Wilson deprecated attacking Metemmeh, holding that even a successful action would produce only more casualties that could be ill-afforded. Thus, he elected to establish his force above Metemmeh proper. By 22 January, the prospects of reaching Gordon in time were quickly slipping away. Omdurman, a bastion covering the approach to Khartoum, was known to have fallen. With Herbert Stewart badly wounded,[116] Burnaby dead, and all officers of the naval brigade casualties save Beresford ill and infirmed, the only thing seemingly remaining of the original plan was the object. Still, Wilson did not despair. When a patrol reported the way clear, a cautious Wilson accompanied by Beresford and a body of infantry boarded steamers to conduct their own reconnaissance as far as Shendy.[117]

That delay was met by another such that General Wilson only set out on January 24, minus Beresford, now admitted to hospital. Never mind, Wilson, three officers, 240 Sudanese troops, a handful of ratings, and twenty British decked in scarlet sailed forth.[118] The gesture was wasted as Khartoum succumbed on 26 January 1885 following a siege of 317 days.[119] Two days later, Wilson sighted the befallen city but was stopped short when met by a hot fire. Capturing the drama, he recalled:

> The sight at this moment was very grand: the masses of the enemy with their fluttering banners near Khartum; the long rows of riflemen in the shelter-trenches of Omdurman; the numerous groups of men on Tuti [Island]; the bursting shells, and the water torn up by hundreds of bullets

and occasional heavier shot,—made an impression never to be forgotten. Looking out over the stormy scene, it seemed almost impossible that we should escape.[120]

More dejected than the British were Wilson's Sudanese, who understood Gordon's loss meant their own loss as loved ones, if not dead, faced a life of slavery at the hands of the Mahdī. Hastily, Wilson beat a retreat. In truth, the return passage proved even more trying than the ascent, with both steamers lost through grounding, leaving it to Beresford and the remnant of the naval brigade to rescue a stranded Wilson.[121]

Elsewhere, Earle's Nile column advanced methodically. Absent determined resistance, getting beyond the Fourth Cataract proved difficult enough. News of Khartoum's fall reached the party on 3 February; it reached London two days later.[122] With parliament in recess, the cabinet did not meet until 6 February. Even then, concrete facts were lacking. Thus, Earle continued his advance. Meeting 1,500 rebels on the rocky knolls and high ridges of Kirbekan, he attacked immediately. Gaining the position, Earle would not live to celebrate. Brigadier General Henry Brackenbury now assumed command and pressed on for initial reporting only told of Khartoum's fall with news of Gordon unknown. Assuming the proportions of a punitive expedition, payment was exacted upon the rebellious tribes until Wolseley ordered Brackenbury to desist and retire.[123]

Culturally, Gordon's death proved a seminal moment. Boding ill for Gladstone's future fortunes, if a silver lining existed, it must be that while Gordon held Khartoum, the Mahdī dared not move on Egypt proper. With that hindrance gone, British forces were singularly exposed with retreat now a necessity where before it had been merely a virtue: if tactically successful during the advance, Wolseley's army had been severely bloodied during the process and then thereafter. To wit, William Earle and Herbert Stewart had fallen and many a lesser, too. More problematic, insufficient troops were present to meet a Mahdī no longer tethered to Gordon and Khartoum, all while the hottest period of the year approached. Accordingly, Abu Kru, so recently won, was evacuated on 13 February by Wolseley's Chief of Staff, Major General Sir Redvers Buller.[124]

Throughout the campaign, Wolseley privately castigated the abilities of his immediate staff and senior officers, except for Herbert Stewart. Wilson received an extra dose of venom with Wolseley holding him, and Gladstone for the failure realized. Gladstone's sin was one of omission, or more precisely, failing to act promptly. Wilson's sin was that of an officer unequal to the challenge of command, with the delay displayed on his part costing Gordon his life. That view was entirely self-serving, for more significant had been the failures of Wolseley, who bore the ultimate operational responsibility.[125] Sadly for Wolseley, his disappointments were not yet finished.

Three

Suakin-Berber Operations Redux

> [T]he true history of the 1885 campaign has never yet been written. If it were written I don't think any one would be tempted to repeat the experiment.[1]
>
> Cromer, 1897

News of Khartoum's fall reached London on 4 February, and with parliament in recess, the initial political backlash remained subdued. The climate did not last with the reckoning occurring within the fortnight when Gladstone addressed the House of Commons. Reminding members that Egypt's Sudan policy and, consequently, that of Britain's had been one of evacuation, he now signaled a change. With the Mahdī having gained Khartoum and its arsenal of arms, evacuation no longer remained tenable.[2] With Mahdism running rampant, maintaining a British toehold in Sudan no longer sufficed. Thus, orders followed for Wolseley to begin a fresh offensive from Suakin to break Osman Digna's power. To that end, the Commander-in-Chief summoned General Graham in February, with command of the force being raised for eastern Sudan proffered. If suiting Cambridge, the appointment of Graham did not suit Wolseley, who preferred Major General Sir George Greaves. Cambridge remained altogether unmoved, leaving Greaves to become Graham's chief of staff, with overall operations subordinated to Wolseley.

In the aftermath of the Gordon debacle, Wolseley had remained on the Nile and thus removed from the composite force, being organized around three brigades of infantry and a further one of cavalry bound for eastern Sudan.[3] Of course, the question of logistics still dominated, and here, the need for a rail line was finally affirmed. To that end, the engineering firm Lucas and Aird received a contract on 17 February 1885 for its construction.[4] The next day, the assent was secured for mobilizing the reserves, with Graham's departure from London following 2 days later.[5] With the previous seeing to the threat posed by Digna, Gladstone avowed that a further expedition would eliminate the Mahdī.

However, the time required to collect further forces precluded an immediate advance to Khartoum. Accordingly, the most that Wolseley might achieve in the near term was the gaining of Berber. Thus, a multi-year campaign, if not explicitly voiced, stood to be fought.[6]

With the Tories controlling the Lords, securing the funds to allow Gladstone's strategy to proceed was highly problematic. Thus, Gladstone stressed how a British presence in Sudan "afforded an effectual check, and a very powerful check, to the Slave Trade carried on in that region, and the question of the Slave Trade was one which we could not wholly exclude from our view." That last may have been eyewash, but it was a piece many accepted as Salisbury himself had argued along similar lines previously. More directly, Gladstone, employing a variant of another century's "Domino Theory," announced, "'Our concern in the Soudan was a concern dependent upon our concern and obligations for the safety and defence of Egypt."[7] That, too, was a dart aimed at Tory hearts, for it had been Disraeli who had acquired Britain's interest in the Suez Canal Company in 1875.

Throughout, authorities underestimated the Mahdī. Important decisions were deferred and, when finally taken, represented the minimum possible. Such was exemplified by the £300,000 credit voted by parliament. Only a portion of that required, Gladstone sought the money to forestall the resignation of Hartington and others from the cabinet.[8] Of course, Salisbury, the leading Tory, sat in the Lords, and it was from that chamber that the most strident criticisms of Liberal policy emanated. He reminded all that that deemed impossible in 1883—an advance from Suakin to Berber—now formed the central feature of the present *volte-face*.[9] The invective did not stop there and deserves to be quoted at length as it anticipates criticisms rendered in another century over another failure:

> General Gordon has been sacrificed to the squabbles of a Cabinet and the necessities of Parliamentary tactics. For these things, undoubtedly, unless the machinery of our Constitution is an absolute failure, unless the people of this country have lost all control over the policy pursued on the nominal responsibility of their Rulers—for all these things an account will assuredly be exacted. What, however, concerns us now mostly is the future. We are told that Expeditions are going out to Suakin. We want some security that they will not return with such a record

of useless slaughter and fruitless effort as the last Expedition did. We hear that great efforts are to be made to defeat the Mahdi at Khartoum. We wish to know that these exertions, which, without doubt, will cost us so much in precious treasure and far more in precious blood, will not be absolutely thrown away, and that we shall not retire from Egypt leaving behind no record of our presence, except the mischief and the confusion we have wrought and the bones of the unhappy soldiers who have been slain. My Lords, I will not now pursue this subject further. We are meeting not only in a great crisis, but under pressure of great sorrow. We have lost men belonging to this House, whose presence was highly valued, whose memory will be held dear, whose honour is an honour to the class to which they belonged. We lament their loss and the loss of many other valuable soldiers whose lives are not too valuable if they have been sacrificed really to the interests of their country, but whose fate bears with it a terrible demand of reckoning and indignation if they have been sacrificed to the imbecility of a Ministry, or to the necessity of keeping a Party in power.[10]

These strong words were entirely self-serving but not altogether wrong, given the lamentable record of the previous two years. Yet, operations occur within a context greater than the corridors of power, as Salisbury himself would come to appreciate.

With Sudan's hot season approaching, Graham could not initiate sustained operations in the time available from Suakin. Accordingly, the War Office specified the twin tasks of defeating Digna while constructing a rail link to Tambuk Wells. Unlike previous operations where the East Indies Squadron saw to the needs of the military, the limits of the Mediterranean Station were expanded to support Graham. To this end, Commodore Robert Molyneux flew his broad pendant in the composite vessel *Sphinx*, where he directed the many minor naval vessels—primarily gunboats—supporting the military while overseeing the landing of stores and men in the narrow and challenging anchorage.[11] There, an Indian brigade of 3,200 effectives with accompanying followers embarked in seventeen transports began arriving in early March.[12] In all regards, it was a force ready for business. Unlike the transports arriving from Britain, those sailing from Bombay had been tactically loaded and immediately available for service upon anchoring.[13]

An innovation of the 1885 campaign saw the laying of land mines to protect the exposed flanks of the expedition's logistics.[14] Otherwise, the *Dolphin*, acting as a guardship, directed its searchlight over the British encampment and fired at the probing enemy. Necessarily, the sleep of the British and Indians suffered, which, beyond securing intelligence of the force, was probably the point of it all.[15] With 12,000 effectives and as many animals landed supported by over 7,000 followers, Graham initiated operations on 19 March. Aiming to clear the Hadendowa territory so that construction of the railway might begin, the force advanced in typical fashion for operations in Sudan: A cavalry reconnaissance led a main body marching in tactical squares with baggage following to a preselected point where a *zeriba* was constructed fort the advance's protection. The point now acted as a depot for the column while serving as the jumping-off point for the next march. Successively repeated, the process extended control along the axis of advance while offering multiple strong points for meeting the enemy with effect by crew-served weapons. The approach, while effective, consumed British troops in the process and made for slow progress.[16]

Such caution was merited, for it was while constructing their *zeribas* that a brigade-sized force under Major General Sir John McNeill fought a twenty-minute pitched battle at Tofrek against Digna on 22 March. Fought but 6 miles from Suakin, the engagement saw over 900 rebels killed, with the British and Indian contingent suffering over 500 casualties along with 900 precious camels.[17] With further troops arriving daily, the losses were manageable. Less manageable was the public response to yet an additional display of poor generalship.[18] That political problem was now joined by a further one as the influence of outside events on high strategy laid low present operations. To wit, a joint commission chartered to demarcate the common frontier between Afghanistan and Russia threatened to collapse when an Afghan force operating under British advice was defeated at Pul-i-Khishti on 20 March.[19] At one level, the Penjdeh (Panjdah) crisis witnessed the all too familiar setback of securing British aims when working through local proxies. However, the crisis underscored India's vulnerability, so its import stood far graver. Certainly, far graver than the control of Sudan, for as Brett reminded Hartington, "A check, even a disaster, in the Soudan may be forgiven; but on the Afghan frontier, never."[20] Lord Randolph Churchill, the secretary of state, remained more sanguine. Believing the possibility of war remote, the navy could easily strike at Russia through the Turkish Straits if the eventuality should arise.[21]

Given the worsening situation, the admiralty imposed a news blackout on the movements of the Mediterranean Squadron, while the War Office warned Wolseley on 13 April that operations directed toward Khartoum would likely be terminated. A week later, that order was confirmed.[22] Ironically, given the risk India faced, an order to withdraw from Sudan did not yet apply to Graham's force nor Brigadier General John Hudson's Indian brigade. Thus, Graham pressed forward with laying a rail line. Not until 11 May 1885 were definitive orders to retire received. The decision precipitated the resignations of Northbrook and Selborne.[23]

With the rail line now abandoned, Digna wasted little time destroying the nearly 20 miles of track laid.[24] Conceding the quality of the work accomplished, Emilius de Cosson nevertheless faulted the employment of civilian contractors. If their presence owed everything to the commitment of Indian engineers elsewhere, then better to correct matters now lest future crises find only regret.[25] Britain's greater strategic interests forced Salisbury, the new premier, to temporize in a manner not unknown to Gladstone.[26] This owed much to the weakness of the Tories, who accepted office as a minority party. Consequently, British and Egyptian forces withdrew from the Upper Nile region, with the railway hub at Wādī Halfā becoming the *de facto* frontier. Unlike the missteps and setbacks that had characterized the advance, the withdrawal met with few operational difficulties. Strategically, the reverse was true, for it gave the Dongola district a gift to the rebels.[27]

In a strange twist of fate, the Mahdī died of typhus that June, even if Mahdism as a force remained. 'Abdallāhi b. Muhammad at-Ta'īshī, the Khalīfa, now sought to extend the remit of Mahdism beyond Omdurman and Khartoum. This would lead British and Egyptian forces to fight a series of defensive actions that year and in the years ahead, though that story resides outside the bounds of this accounting. Pity though Sudan, as abject misery awaited: Its population of 8,000,000 reduced to 2,000,000 by 1898 owing to war, disease, famine, and misrule.[28] Irony of ironies, the new Egyptian Army would be built around the martial tribes of the Sudan.[29]

Four

On the Road to Mandalay: Upper Burma, 1885–86

To-day Lieutenant Protheroe embarked 200 men of the Prince's Albert's (Somersetshire Light Infantry) and 250 men of the Madras Infantry on the flotilla steamer Burma—*one of those prepared to carry the troops—to ascertain whether the men, more especially the Europeans, could comfortably settle on the decks of the steamers in the space allotted. The space was found ample. The men rapidly embarked and disembarked.*[1]

After the chastisement in Sudan and narrowly avoided war with Russia, it might be thought a period of consolidation would ensue. That, however, did not occur, as India now issued an ultimatum to Thibaw Min, the Burmese king. Palace intrigues and poor governance were a feature of Burmese governance. Still, those maladies alone would not have prompted the making of a British protectorate if political and economic factors had not been at the fore. Thus, when Britain learned Thibaw had concluded a secret treaty with France the previous January, matters rapidly came to a head. The treaty promised to tie Burma closer to France to the detriment of British commercial interests.[2] When Thibaw issued a decree against the Bombay-Burmah Trading Corporation over the illegal harvesting of forests, Calcutta responded with alacrity.[3] In truth, Upper Burma had vexed Indian officials, if not their superiors in Whitehall, for several years. Unsurprisingly, plans for its subjugation dated from at least 1883, with commitments in Afghanistan, Egypt, and Sudan arguing against a more robust policy until now. If annexation was not the avowed end-state, the step became inescapable once a pliant Burmese prince failed to appear.[4]

Already controlling Lower Burma, Britain naturally took a keen interest in events affecting the balance of the country. Disturbances in Mandalay might be weathered, but the prospect of a rival enjoying an economic advantage represented a threat of another order. Being that the area was thick with jungle and swamps, what trade existed passed along the Irrawaddy in British steamers. The construction of a railroad would upset present arrangements, and more so if the patron was France, with goods flowing to Indochina.[5] In short, the situation anticipated the Berlin to Baghdad project of twenty years, save Britain now enjoyed a local supremacy unmatched by events in Mesopotamia.

In late October 1885, India prepared an expeditionary force, some 9,000 strong, drawing upon those British forces stationed in India in association with units from the Madras, Bombay, and Bengal presidencies. The following month, Dufferin, the Viceroy, appointed Major General Harry Prendergast commander. On 5 November, that officer and a battalion of the Hampshire Regiment sailed from Calcutta in the troopship *Clive* for Rangoon (Yangon) via Madras (Chennai). By the middle of the month, a division-sized force had been collected at Thayetmyo, an outpost on the British-Burmese frontier. They aimed to depose the king and occupy a region roughly the size of France. Behind them stood a brigade from the Bombay Army and a division already serving in Lower Burma. Two dozen river steamers towing at least twenty-nine barges took the force into Upper Burma.[6]

Prendergast's command included a naval brigade formed from the personnel of the East Indies Squadron under Captain Robert Woodward of the corvette *Turquoise*. That officer and vessel had been operating off Suakin in company with the gunboat *Woodlark* under Commander Robert Clutterbuck.[7] Thus, Rear Admiral Sir Frederick Richards, commanding the East Indies Squadron, did not have to look far to find officers with recent experience in joint operations. Both were joined by another veteran of recent Sudan operations, the Navigating Officer Commander Alfred Carpenter, who surveyed the way forward for the inshore flotilla.[8] Delivering tactical fires from steamers and barges, the flotilla provided the expedition's main punch from twelve 25-pounders and offered medical support via a barge under the direction of Fleet Surgeon Brownlow.[9] Admittedly, the Burma Field Force possessed its own 40-pounder heavy siege guns, 6.3-inch howitzers, and 25-pounders, but they retained limited ammunition.

Anticipating that operations would eventually transpire, stockades akin to those likely to be met had been constructed in India to test the manner of fires for their defeat.[10] All were now ferried to Minhla on commercial steamers and towed barges being augmented by the river craft of the Indian Marine. Still, unlike recent operations conducted on the Nile, contemporaries saw the advance of the military force as primarily a naval operation, though army engineers supported it. In the words of the Intelligence Branch:

> On them fell all the work of reconnoitering and guarding the fleet by surprise by water. The heavy guns were mounted on barges for river service and accompanied the Naval Brigade as escort to the fleet. The remaining steamers and flats were transports for troops and stores, and were not fighting units of the fleet. The escort headed the column of ships to clear the river in front, to prevent any attack by water from reaching the transports and to silence the guns of any positions on the banks before the transport ships had to pass them. When the guns of the escort were not sufficient for this, troops were to be landed and land operations were to be undertaken.[11]

Geography and force composition dictated the tactics adopted. Doubtless, if the campaign had been one of retribution, more forceful methods would have prevailed. Prendergast's instructions were to occupy an intact and viable Burma with minimal force. Though the siege batteries would reduce the forts guarding the Irrawaddy, they also served to awe the Burmese. Following a brief bombardment against the covering forts, the landing faced only token resistance.[12] In the process, the village proper burned to the ground, notwithstanding Dufferin's earlier instructions about limiting destruction. A repeat occurred ten days later at Ava, though now the defenders numbered some 8,000. Again, the British quickly overcame any resistance allowing Prendergast, now joined by "King Dick" Richards, to reach Mandalay soon afterward. Capturing Thibaw and deporting him to Madras, Britain claimed Upper Burma. More importantly, the remaining French and Italian traders soon departed.[13]

In the words of one protagonist, "Such opposition as there had been was childish in its feebleness and want of skill and purpose." Assuredly so, with British losses amounting to eight dead and twenty-six wounded.[14] Yet, while the expedition stymied the desires of outsiders, it did not satisfy all Burmese, with many retreating into the area's vast interior. Thus, an insurgency soon followed, testing the mettle of the British. Abetted in part by the region's lack of infrastructure, coming to grips with the recalcitrant Burmese would tax the invaders sorely.[15]

With Prendergast and Brigadier General Francis Norman's 3rd Brigade following the Irrawaddy a further 200 miles to Bhamo that December, it was left to Brigadier General George White's 2nd Brigade to pacify Mandalay.[16] Though the numbers resisting were not great, they possessed the advantage of space. Climate and disease hampered British operations, with men and horses equally succumbing. Continuing resistance necessitated the deployment of further troops so that by December 1886, the equivalent of an army corps was engaged in pacification operations. Even still, the numbers deployed were inadequate, and something approaching peace did not materialize for several years.

By this point, Prendergast had been relieved ostensibly because of the continuing resistance faced. That rings hollow, for he had been given command of all forces in Burma only on 14 February 1886. The summary execution of Burmese prisoners by the Provost Marshal Lieutenant Colonel Willoughby Hooper and the public outcry arising is probably closer to the truth with the return of the Liberals to power that same month in place of Salisbury offering scope for the change.[17] General MacPherson, the erstwhile commander of the Indian contingent in the 1882 Egyptian intervention, now assumed command, only for a moment as he quickly succumbed to malaria. This necessitated the appointment of Lieutenant General Sir Frederick Roberts, the commander-in-chief. Eventually, Lieutenant General Sir Charles Arbuthnot replaced "Bobs," leaving White to oversee day-to-day operations.[18]

The minor military and constabulary operations occurring in the interior need not concern us save that they exhibited the familiar traits of movement across rugged terrain supported by tenuous river transport with campaigning limited to benign months. Cholera, malaria, and dysentery plagued those serving, including Gerald Holland of the Indian Marine, who had performed feats of wonder in keeping the troops supplied.[19] With movement primarily dictated by the Irrawaddy and Chindwin rivers, close coordination among the services during the initial phase of operations was a must. This was no more reflected than in the prominence of the naval contribution appearing in Prendergast's final dispatch and the appointment of Lieutenant George Ballard as his aide-de-camp.[20] Meanwhile, political factors were a constant in colonial wars, and this war proved no different. Colonel Edward Sladen, Britain's former agent at Mandalay, now acted as the chief civil officer to the Burma Field Force—in effect, its political guiding hand.[21]

The pacification operations that followed required the construction of a specialized fleet of shallow-draft paddle-wheelers. Designed to a specification developed by John Hext, now director of the Indian Marine, thirteen craft were provided. Events demonstrated these to be insufficient and that more were not forthcoming must be accounted their expense. The flotilla became the workhorse of Burmese operations, with double-decked flat barges capable of bearing over 700 troops and their supplies.[22] Overall, the campaigns waged in Burma came under the tutelage of India. At this hour and until 1903, a unified Indian army did not exist. Instead, the three presidencies provided the forces required. Though a commander-in-chief existed, the separate armies' ethos, traditions, and procedures seemingly offered ample scope for operational problems. Surprisingly, this rarely occurred. Yet other issues were evidenced with climatic factors limiting the time available for conducting operations at the fore. Understandably, sustaining the force's health in the face of such conditions followed as a byproduct. Beyond establishing the objectives to be accomplished and defining prohibited practices, Dufferin did not attempt to micromanage operations, and this worked so long as the military delivered the results desired and unit actions stayed within the limits imposed. Ideally, the presence of Indian political agents guaranteed the upholding of Dufferin's dictates. Burma, however, demonstrated that theory did not always equal practice and that not even a commander-in-chief in the field could translate quick victory into something approaching peace.[23]

Five

Gordon Avenged: Sudan, 1896–98

Owing to the lateness of the Nile, the passage of the steamers over the cataracts could only be commenced on 2nd August, and was successfully accomplished under the direction of Colonel Hunter, D.S.O., who was ably assisted by Commander Robertson, C.M.G., R.N., and other officers, who all worked indefatigably on this arduous task. The flotilla of four armed and three unarmed stern-wheelers arrived at Kosheh on 23rd August, and the forward movement of the troops of the Suarda garrison to Abearat took place on the same day.[1]

From the previous, it is clear that the British operational experience was based on an altar of improvisation. Lack of clear political direction, a strategic problem, gave vent to operational challenges as inadequate and poorly trained local forces could not secure the limited goals posited. By 1884, Britain faced an asymmetric conflict requiring the deployment of regular troops to pursue limited ends against an opponent employing limited means in pursuit of unlimited ends. Granted, this was only a portion of the problem, for even a more explicit policy and better and more numerous forces were insufficient by themselves. Wolseley's praise of his soldiers' efforts and *élan* notwithstanding, the burdens of distance, time, and logistics could not be wished away.[2] These lessons did not go unlearned, and when an Anglo-Egyptian force returned to Sudan, it did so on more favorable terms. Infrastructure in place, to be sure, to support the demands of the sequential operations launched to recover the province, but also intelligence on the topography and the enemy to be faced. Seeing to the last would be an officer of singular talent and persistence: Reginald Wingate, the Egyptian Army's Director of Military Intelligence.[3]

Wingate's persistence began after the crushing of Urabi when the recently commissioned gunner arrived in Egypt from Aden. Attachment to the Egyptian Army followed, leading soon to his appointment as *adc* to the sirdar. After a full campaign in the failed effort to save Gordon, Wingate returned to Egypt, where he became its Director of Military Intelligence in 1889, where his attention turned toward Sudan and to the recovery of the Austrian officer Slatin Pasha from Mahdist captivity. That success provided a wealth of information to support future military plans.[4]

Having ceded Sudan to the Mahdists in the 1880s, an Anglo-Egyptian return in the 1890s may appear inexplicable. Reform and regeneration during the interim, though, had been pursued with relish, leading to a revitalized Egypt and a revitalized Egyptian Army. Perhaps because it was not formally part of the Empire, overseers such as Dufferin could afford to think large, knowing that the bill for their dreams would not fall on the imperial exchequer. One such dream was the construction of canals and irrigation works in the southern expanse to reduce the area's poverty. An idea mooted by Villiers Stuart in late 1882 when he surveyed Egypt's infrastructure and endorsed by Colonel Colin Scott-Moncrieff two years later.[5] Their vision would be realized and then expanded, but not without resistance from Egypt's *Assemblée Generale*. Democracy worked fine in London, but its practice in Cairo possessed decided limits under British tutelage. Thus, the Khedive was forced to dissolve the assembly before the construction of a dam to further the production of cotton and sugar could proceed. Of benefit to the economy, it was perhaps even more beneficial to Egypt's governmental finances.[6]

While Sudan remained in turmoil—three-quarters of its more than eight million inhabitants had died since 1885—embarking on large-scale works entailed risk.[7] Risks to Egypt's creditors, to be sure, but also the risk that if an unfriendly power ever occupied Sudan, any dam constructed might prove for nought as the power occupying Sudan might control the flow and level of the Nile before its waters ever reached Aswan.[8] Britain declared a protectorate in Uganda to reduce what remained latent and then secured understandings with Belgium and Italy. These arguably buttressed the defense of Egypt and worked against French aspirations. They also inevitably drew Britain deeper into the affairs of Sudan.[9]

The Italians, attempting to reap where others had sown, occupied Kassala following an engagement against the Mahdists. Two years later, it was their turn to feel the wrath of the African when they suffered a sharp rebuke at Adwa in March 1896. The misfortune removed a friendly buffer, but it did not set in motion British efforts to reclaim Sudan for Egypt.[10] It did, though, prompt Wolseley and the War Office to advance efforts. Salisbury and the cabinet now sanctioned an expedition to secure Dongola in Sudan, but the larger prize awaited. That object escaped Captain Henry Wilson of the War Office's Intelligence Department, whose efforts were directed toward assisting Italian forces.[11] If Wilson had not been briefed on ultimate aims, then it may be assumed Major General Sir Herbert Kitchener had.

Where Wolseley had advanced by the Nile and failed, Kitchener opted to extend the rail line from Wādī Halfā to Kerma before tackling 'Abdallāhi. After a false start and a year of work, Lieutenant Percy Girouard's efforts bore fruit. Concurrently, a second line running from Wādī Halfā to Abu Hamed was completed. Though advancing by rail possessed advantages, the lack of water towers along the route required locomotives to be self-sufficient, with capacity correspondingly reduced.[12] Granted, the Nile was too near not to abet Kitchener's efforts with gunboats providing tactical fires where possible. Nevertheless, its rapids and varying state made it an unreliable consort. Still, Kitchener was able to plan his advance to coincide with the Nile running at a high level in a manner unknown to Wolseley, as gaining a country and not a recalcitrant general remained the aim. Thus, the factor of time did not loom nearly so large.

Where Wolseley had employed British forces with a smattering of Egyptians, Kitchener benefited from a British-trained and British-led Egyptian force with ample experience of the theater and the enemy.[13] Moreover, Kitchener possessed the support of a government that knew what it wanted. Under Gladstone, the Liberals were always conflicted imperialists, and keeping his party onside proved to be a severe task when it came to Egypt. Not so for the Tories with Salisbury, who now acted with alacrity. Letting Kitchener be Kitchener, the Egyptian Army secured Dongola by the end of September 1896. Salisbury, being Salisbury, now presented a bill of nearly £800,000 to parliament. In truth, the Chancellor, Sir Michael Hicks Beach, upped the ante by announcing that operations would continue until Khartoum was occupied. The House cheered, and the funds duly came.[14] This was not Christmas in February, for the British Treasury was not a bank to be raided, but the Caisse de la Dette judged the use of Egyptian funds illegal.[15] This contretemps took its toll on Kitchener's mental state, and so did the fervent wish not to be superseded by a superior officer—in this case, Major General Sir Francis Grenfell. With the introduction of major British forces pending, such appeared a distinct possibility, and that the present

Adjutant General had also been a Sirdar of the Egyptian Army recalled the plight of General Stephenson thirteen years previously.[16]

The Navy was a full partner in the operations, clearing 400 miles of territory from the Mahdists. Commander Stanley Colville commanded the river flotilla, which included a contingent of the Royal Marine Artillery. With prior service in Natal in 1879 and during the expedition for Gordon's relief, Colville did not lack experience.[17] The boats now employed were shipped in sections and constructed on-site at Kosheh in August.[18] Likewise, an Indian contingent deployed, and the 2,500 troops under Charles Egerton allowed the Egyptian garrison holding Suakin to join Kitchener's advancing army. Given the frequency Indian troops featured in Africa, this step might have been thought routine. That did not mean it was welcomed, and India argued that all charges, including the pay of its soldiers, should be met by the British Exchequer.[19] London countered that India could not remain indifferent to Sudanese affairs. Of concern to this accounting were the seams of responsibility exposed.[20]

With memories of the last campaign still alive, General Adye, arguing safely from the pages of *The Times*, avowed that capturing Dongola should proceed *in the autumn* via a Suakin-Berber route.[21] March proved a time more to Kitchener's liking, and with the rail line extending nearly to Akasha, the Egyptians marched the remaining sixteen miles to Firket and won their prize on 7 June. Extension of the railway to Abu Hamed followed, and after defeating the enemy in a brisk action, Major General Archibald Hunter captured that locale on 7 August 1897. The occupation of Berber quickly ensued, and on Christmas Day, Colonel Charles Parsons secured Kassala upon the heels of an Italian withdrawal.[22]

Once more, the pace of operations owed everything to logistics and the time of the year; the sirdar would not make the mistake of attempting more than could be supported. Additionally, appreciating the limitations of his troops, Kitchener sought British reinforcements. In September 1897, four gunboats negotiated the treacherous Fifth Cataract to support the forces concentrating at Atbara. On 8 April 1898, at the price of 600 casualties, a combined Anglo-Egyptian army defeated the Sudanese, killing over 2,000 in the exchange.

A second British brigade under Brigadier General Neville Lyttelton (1st Grenadier Guards, 1st Northumberland Fusiliers, 2nd Lancashire Fusiliers, and the 2nd Battalion Rifle Brigade) arrived in July to form a British division under Major General William Gatacre. The latter's reputation as a hard taskmaster did not go unearned, with no day too hot for work. Kitchener doubtless appreciated his efforts as it allowed a force of 20,000 troops to concentrate 40 miles above Khartoum that August supported by ten gunboats, assorted steamers, boats, and barges.[23] At Omdurman on 2 September 1898, Kitchener routed the Khalīfa's horde of 60,000 to the tune of 10,000 dead and then sealed the victory by dumping the late Mahdi's body into the Nile. However, the Khalīfa and several senior followers escaped being subdued later at Om Debraket. As for Digna, he eventually yielded in January 1900.[24]

The minor flotilla had been a full partner in these operations. No stranger to the Nile, Commander Colin Keppel had served with Boardman, Beresford, and Wilson in the desperate attempt to reach Gordon.[25] The three stern-wheel gunboats supporting Kitchener were shipped in sections and assembled locally. Mounting six guns and firing a new explosive shell—lyddite—they were capable of 12 knots while drawing only 3-1/2 feet when fully loaded. Commanded by Keppel (*Sultan*) and Lieutenants David Beatty (*Fateh*) and Horace Hood (*Naser*), the gunboats scouted ahead of the advancing army and then provided tactical fires with their machine guns and 12-pounders.[26]

As a joint operation, the reconquest offered few talismans; as an example of a 'British Way in Warfare,' it remains instructive. The Foreign Office controlled operations and the War Office's responsibility was limited to supplying the wherewithal to proceed. Others would repeat the template, if not always to a successful end.[27] Effectively acting as a Commander-in-Chief, Baring allowed that no great tactical skill had been demonstrated. That the Consul General absented himself for two months during the campaign's most critical phase testifies that Kitchener enjoyed a high degree of latitude and trust. Indeed, Cromer was fulsome in crediting the sirdar with the success achieved with logistics proving the critical essential.[28] Kitchener, however, was not the army—at least not yet.

The defeat of the Mahdists broke the back of resistance, but control of the greater Sudan had yet to be secured. To that end, Salisbury outlined the campaign's next phase that summer. This specified a continued advance along the White and Blue Nile Rivers, with Kitchener expressly directed to command the force operating on the White Nile as far as Fashoda (Kodok).[29] Thus, Kitchener, accompanied by elements of two Sudanese battalions of the Egyptian Army and four gunboats, departed Omdurman for southern Sudan on 10 September. These efforts culminated at Fashoda, where a French detachment under Major Jean-Baptiste Marchand raised the tricolor the previous July.[30] The incident resides outside the limits of this account save that the power conferred by Keppel's flotilla provided the necessary muscle to enforce British demands.[31]

As the nominal purpose of these operations had been to reestablish Egyptian control over Sudan, Cairo mostly met the costs. While the Khedive's pockets were more handsomely lined than in the 1880s, much remained payable to others. Consequently, Kitchener and Baring economized on the scale of operations, a practice others would later follow, though not always to the same successful ends. The sequential operations conducted proved a model of execution or so held Helmuth von Moltke, the Chief of the German General Staff, who held no finer exploit had been accomplished in recent years.[32] Certainly, that was correct as far as casualties were concerned, with Anglo-Egyptian casualties proving slight while those of the enemy had been grievous. The financial reckoning, however, was of another order for Sudan would drain hundreds of thousands each year from Egyptian coffers.[33] More positively, the army and the Navy had demonstrated that they were indeed sister services when time was not a critical factor.

Six

Suffering No End of a Lesson: South Africa, 1899–1902

If 12,000 English troops with some thousands of Volunteers, cannot successfully resist an offensive movement in the Colonies by the Boers, it seems to me the British army must be in a very bad way.[1]

Joseph Chamberlain, 1899

The war in South Africa could not have been waged without the support of the Royal Navy. Still, allowing for that, amphibious operations never featured as a significant enabler to the broader campaign. Britain gained access to the theater through the Cape Colony and Natal and controlled the surrounding waters, meaning the Boer republics were largely isolated from outside support. By any assessment, this must tell in the end and would, but that resistance lasted as long as it did and that first honors went to the Boers testifies that what appeared latent was by no means guaranteed. Tellingly, the Boers possessed three immediate advantages. Firstly, they operated on interior lines from the Transvaal and Orange River State while the contested area exceeded the combined areas of France and Germany. Secondly, their forces enjoyed better mobility and were closer to the field of battle. Indeed, Britain stood more than 6,000 miles distant.[2] Thirdly, they seized the initiative by placing British outlying posts at risk. The last dictated initial British military moves as local political authorities were reluctant to surrender remote and exposed areas for fear of what might follow. Loss of territory, to be sure, but more worryingly, a revolt by the Boer or native inhabitants in Cape Colony or Natal. Those risks were undoubtedly real, but so too defeat in detail if the army could not defend all that was held.[3] Finally, if the affair tells us little about Britain's ability to conduct amphibious operations at the beginning of the new century, it sheds light on her higher direction of war and the strengths and shortcomings in military capabilities. Again, a deficiency in crew-served weapons by the army was manifest. If ultimately crowned with success, the operations conducted in South Africa proved as trying as any campaign Britain fought between the Russian War of 1854 and the war arising in 1914.

If long anticipated, the commitment required was not. Initial stores were inadequate, to say nothing of overall strategy and tactical prowess.[4] From an expeditionary force formed around a single corps, an army of 250,000 British and Imperial troops eventually deployed to the theater.[5] Nearly 450,000 soldiers served during the 31 months of hostilities in a level of effort substantial only by recent British standards.[6] Others, including the American Civil War, the Russo-Japanese War, and the Balkan Wars of 1912–1913, witnessed more significant efforts in mobilization and dearer costs in casualties.[7] Indeed, those wars were troubling for their very intensity, with the South African conflict remaining an outlier as British casualties reached only 5 percent per annum.

How far the South African War approximated a future conflict posed important implications operationally, tactically, and, even more so, strategically. Embroiled in a distant conflict that saw Britain suffer several early reverses, others, such as Russia, appeared ready to make trouble in Afghanistan.[8] This echoed the events of 1885, and if the threat failed to be realized, it harkened to the empire's accumulated risks. This much was appreciated while hostilities remained ongoing and moved Lord Kimberley, the late Liberal foreign secretary, to argue for a formal inquiry. Salisbury would not yet accede to this, though accepting Britain's machinery for waging war remained far from perfect.[9] His reply would not be the last word if sufficient for the day.

If the Transvaal and the Orange Free State lacked navies, they did not lack pluck. Appreciating that Britain had been increasing its forces in the Cape Colony that summer,[10] speculation became rife in early September that a large-scale augmentation of troops under General Sir Redvers Buller would occur. Already participating in a series of field exercises, Buller's preparations confirm a degree of readiness beyond the standard scheme of seasonal exercises. To what end soon became apparent when the cabinet ordered four battalions to South Africa on 8 September.[11] Meanwhile, Portugal, Britain's ally of longest standing and beholden to London's financial largesse, impeded the transfer of arms from Delagoa (Maputo) Bay to the Transvaal.[12] Elsewhere, matters were not so ordered, with munitions, sympathizers, and information continuing to flow to the Boers. Belatedly, Britain would only impose martial law on the ports servicing the Cape Colony in October 1901.[13]

Speculation became fact when Buller's appointment as general commander-in-chief was gazetted on 9 October.[14] In truth, Buller did not seek the appointment, believing Wolseley to be the better candidate; this sound advice failed to move Lansdowne, the secretary of state for war.[15] Proceeding with Buller was Colonel Herbert Miles, commandant of the staff college, to serve as chief of staff. The appointment did little good to that institution, which perforce closed its doors. The wisdom of that act may be questioned, but lacking a standing expeditionary force, the measure retained a certain logic.[16]

Ian Beckett notes that from April 1899, meetings between the admiralty's Transport Department and the Transport Division of the quartermaster-general's Department of the War Office began to coordinate the movement and sustainment of a force to support future operations.[17] This advanced matters, but real progress required the expenditure of money to secure the transport and supplies necessary to support corps-level operations.[18] Meanwhile, Lieutenant General Sir George White, erstwhile commander-in-chief, India, and presently the quartermaster-general, landed at Durban on 7 October 1899 to assume command of the Natal garrison. Two days later, the Transvaal issued an ultimatum demanding British forces vacate the shared border. With the demand unanswered, the Transvaal declared war 2 days later.[19]

If the crisis had been anticipated, the onset of war saw Britain flat-footed. Partly, this reflected the primacy of those ministers who believed the Transvaal would ultimately meet British demands. Partly, this reflected the dictates of financial stringency as deploying the 9,000 troops proposed by Wood, the adjutant-general, was a cost not to be entertained lightly. Partly, it stemmed from Wolseley's prejudice against employing troops from India "sodden with fevers, drink and venereal."[20] Five-thousand British troops, sodden or otherwise, would yet arrive from India to be rushed to Natal's border with the Transvaal in a forlorn attempt to hold the ring.[21] In this climate, the commander-in-chief raised Wood's proposal by 4,000. Unfortunately, the belated alacrity in decision-making was not followed in execution as slow rather than fast ships were hired to move the reinforcements owing to the latter's expense. Nevertheless, the War Office mobilized the reserves to meet the expanding war and benefited from the superb port facilities of London and Southampton. For those already in South Africa, the superiority of Boer artillery remained the vital concern. It was a concern that would only continue.[22]

Presently, the *Doris*, wearing the flag of Rear Admiral Robert Harris, patrolled the waters encompassing the Cape Station. Upon receipt of the Transvaal's ultimatum, the admiralty ordered Harris to guard the ports of Natal and the Cape Colony and to refrain from landing men or guns. When the governors of the two colonies requested immediate support, Harris attempted to balance the tenor of his orders with the dire circumstances facing Sir Alfred Milner and Sir Walter Hely-Hutchinson.[23] In truth, the situation exposed a latent seam in British command and control: While local military forces fell under the authority of the Colonial Office and regional governors, the navy remained firmly under admiralty remit. Thus, the force fashioned at the War Office soon found itself broken into penny packets to meet the several threats faced. That confronting Kimberley was acute, but circumstances were no less dire at Ladysmith and Mafeking.[24]

Reluctantly, the admiralty ordered a naval brigade to be formed. Thus, the cruiser *Powerful*, sailing toward Suez from China, received new orders to head for the Cape. Captain the Hon. Hedworth Lambton and the crew of the *Powerful* had been expecting to exchange ships with Percy Scott and the *Terrible* at Suez.[25] Captain Scott would yet assume command of the *Powerful*, but the *Terrible* now steamed for the Cape. So, too, the *Powerful*, though Lambton would never become Admiral Fisher's chief of staff in the Mediterranean Fleet as intended. Making for Mauritius, the *Powerful* embarked the 2nd Battalion of the South Yorkshire Regiment and continued to the Cape.[26] Upon arrival, Lambton formed a naval landing party around two 4.7-inch and four 12-pounder guns supported by Lieutenants Lionel Halsey and Algernon Walker-Heneage.[27] All proceeded to Ladysmith, a town of 4,500 inhabitants anchored on the Klip River, where the guns immediately went into action.[28] When the rail to Colenso was severed on 2 November 1899, Ladysmith effectively became a besieged town and remained so for 118 days. Most of the civil population and Major General John French, commanding the cavalry division, were among the last to leave. Four cavalry regiments were not so fortunate, and thus, the arrival of the naval brigade proved something of a near-run thing.[29]

The presence of Scott, deemed the service's foremost gunnery expert, was fortuitous. Possessing an inventive mind, where others saw difficulties, Scott saw possibilities. In Egypt, Scott had modified heavy naval guns for use ashore in 1882. Now, employing the works and talent of the local dockyard, he modified 4.7-inch and 12-pounder guns to allow White to meet the 155-mm guns of Ladysmith's besiegers on more equal terms. Of course, denuding the *Terrible* of secondary armament meant to deal with attacks by torpedo boats was only possible because of the benign maritime environment. Yet, it also spoke to the technical training officers such as Scott had received.[30]

Though a brigade had been formed, Harris husbanded further support. Unsuccessfully, Scott had attempted to secure more ammunition than the 250 rounds per gun landed. Harris refused, with the crux of the matter being Harris' Admiralty orders.[31] Meanwhile, in the absence of other troops, Scott assumed responsibility for defending Durban.[32] The creation of the naval brigade from the crews of the local squadron was an expedient and a recognition that present military forces were deficient in artillery. The contribution, however, was not limited to augmenting the firepower of those surrounded as several ratings were further co-opted to serve in Ladysmith's balloon section.

By March 1900, and after 118 days, the siege of Ladysmith was broken, though many officers and ratings were ill in hospital suffering from dysentery or enteric fever.[33] The *Powerful* and the *Terrible* returned to usual duties, leaving their makeshift guns behind. In the case of the *Powerful*, she departed for England, and in the case of the *Terrible*, making course for China.[34] This changed the makeup of the brigade but not its usefulness, as landing parties continued to support operations until the end of September 1900.[35] This included that from the *Doris*, which had landed on 22 November 1899. Commanded by Captain Reginald Prothero, their heavy guns supported Lieutenant General Lord Methuen's march to relieve Kimberley. Seeing action at Belmont and once more at Graspan (Enslin) on 25 November, Methuen prevailed, but the cost was heavy for the naval brigade. With Prothero wounded and Commander Alfred Ethleston and Major John Plumbe, the ranking marine, both dead, a contributing factor had been the want of tactical finesse. Though the gallantry of the naval brigade was all that could be asked, the officers had advanced with swords drawn while the men failed to disperse in the face of a hot fire.[36]

As true at Alexandria, the fusing of the shells often proved defective. However, this time, the problem was attributed to using delayed action rather than direct action fusing when firing lyddite. Heavy use, moreover, had told against the guns' rifling, rendering effective fire increasingly difficult. If the naval guns had performed creditable service, they were working against type.

The narrow carriages were ill-suited to the veldt's rough trails, while the long-barreled guns' high muzzle velocity remained better suited for use in the naval environment.[37] Still, the brigade had shown itself to be an adaptable and agile construct. It was not, however, an ideal construct. Suitable in supporting a quick, localized intervention against an inferior foe, its use in sustained operations was not advised. In this regard, General Hunter and Lieutenant Charles Burne, RN, were especially scathing.[38]

Even if naval landing parties had shown better tactical acumen, other risks remained as they reduced the numbers available to stand watches afloat. The risk was realized in the early hours of 16 January 1901 when the cruiser *Sybille* grounded and was lost. With Captain Hugh Williams and a party presently holding a position ashore at Lambert's Bay to forestall a Boer force advance from Calvinia, Lieutenant Henry Holland cleared the bay owing to the onset of a gale. Returning to the anchorage following the storm's moderation, the ship foundered in the presence of strong currents.[39]

As the war progressed, the role of the fleet returned to normal proportions, with marines such as majors Archibald Paris and Frederick White detached for duty with the Army.[40] The former arrived in 1900 and, by 1902, commanded the Kimberley Column, a unit composed of irregular soldiers. During its operations, the troop was augmented with a battalion of Imperial Yeomanry, a battery of Royal Field Artillery, and elements of the Cape police. Paris' column might not have been as ill-prepared as that commanded by Baker Pasha in 1884, but it suffered limitations in broader officership and tactical training. That Methuen accompanied the column during its march from Vryburg made what followed only the more bitter. Attacked near Tweebosch on 7 March 1902, the British were routed with a severely wounded Methuen, Paris, and most others captured. However, Paris and a small band of mounted troops had been the last to surrender, yielding only in the face of sustained pom-pom fire. Emerging from the debacle with credit, Paris received a brevet promotion and a mention in dispatches.[41] Meanwhile, Frederick White, a veteran of Alexandria and Graham's operations in Sudan, arrived in South Africa in February 1900. Appointed a district commissioner, he commanded a reinforced company at Ladybrand the following September and subsequently served as an intelligence officer to Lieutenant General Sir Charles Knox.[42]

Still, the greatest service performed by the Royal Navy was isolating the theater of operations, thereby preventing a foreign intervention. With the Channel Fleet safeguarding the Atlantic and Mediterranean lines of communication leading to South Africa from Gibraltar, the East Indies Squadron performed a similar role off Africa's eastern coast.[43] Even if the threat of foreign intervention proved a chimera, others took note, including Abdülhamid II, the Sultan of Turkey. He believed the efficiency of the Mediterranean Fleet had preserved the greater peace.[44] Surrounded and with her lands coveted by others much stronger, the presence of that fleet played a unique role in Turkish calculations. Closer to the scene, the Royal Navy exercised local sea control by inspecting those ships entering Delagoa Bay. Any found carrying contraband were seized and processed through prize courts. Some, including Germany, castigated the heavy-handed treatment meted out to neutrals, and so she might, as the British control precluded any attempt to intervene more directly.[45]

When Lord Roberts reached Cape Colony in January 1900, he arrived without a plan of campaign.[46] An even more significant handicap, however, was an army lacking the typical structures of brigades, divisions, and corps. Even brigades suffered as they operated minus dedicated battalions.[47] Such a deficiency explains much about the course of immediate events. Yet, Roberts lacked neither hope nor ideas owing to the presence of Colonel Henderson, erstwhile professor at the Staff College. An expert on Thomas "Stonewall" Jackson, the Southern rebellion, and strategy in general, Henderson now served as director of intelligence.[48] That commission does not begin to capture the scope of duties encompassed for intelligence at this hour was very much about supporting the planning of future operations. To that end, commander and confidant spent their hours in conclave during the voyage south, weighing options and opportunities.[49] Befitting one versed in the American Civil War, the advance on Bloemfontein undertaken to relieve Ladysmith and Kimberley bore all the hallmarks of the Union advance on Richmond. Unfortunately, Henderson's body did not prove nearly as robust as his intellect in the forthcoming campaign.[50]

Given the cost and setbacks experienced, final success against the Boers did not temper the case for change and reform. Yet, the war had not been simply a litany of woe, though there was indeed a lot of woe. The British, operating against type, had raised, equipped, trained, and moved an army of proportions never before witnessed to a distant theater.[51] That problems had been exposed and setbacks had occurred is hardly remarkable. That some were not new, however, was probably the more salient issue. Thus, Salisbury, no more than Canute, could forestall the inevitable accounting, especially as the poor medical service rendered drew the attention of the queen-empress. Professor William Osler would address matters here while the financier Clinton Dawkins examined the organization of the War Office.[52] With members of the Dawkins Committee drawn primarily from the private sector,[53] efficiency in transacting War Office work offered the spur to their remit. Their agenda, however, soon broadened to encompass the employment of the reserves in South Africa.[54]

Elsewhere, the war demonstrated a need for more staff officers than presently existing. A self-evident corollary to a war of such proportions, it suggested some officers had not performed as expected. Attempts at wireless communications on the veldt proved disappointing, though the navy secured better results between its ships operating offshore and the Simonstown dockyard.[55] Meanwhile, the "stores scandal" pushed parliament to establish a Royal Commission in July 1905 under George Farwell to deal with the problems in military contracting. Exposing a climate of mismanagement and incompetence, though not personal corruption, clearly, the army still had much to learn about operational logistics.[56]

One change immediately forthcoming was the establishment of six corps, complete with staff and supporting arms, to replace the existing district structure. The war had been a marvel of improvisation and expansion, but the resulting force had been less effective than one presumably manned, equipped, trained, and staffed beforehand. In making his case, St. John Brodrick promised that if an expedition composed of three corps ever needed to be deployed a nucleus would remain at home upon which an efficient defense could be fashioned.[57] That was a claim too bold, for there could be no promise that the next crisis would merely mirror the last in scale, intensity, and length.

If the Boer War proved a nasty knock, it confirmed the Empire's ability to work in a common effort. Thus, beyond the employment of the British Army and the now-familiar naval brigade, the war witnessed the deployment of troops from Australia, New Zealand, and Canada. Additionally, a contingent drawn from British India had taken the field again. Its rapid creation and movement to South Africa had averted a greater disaster. The force was then sustained through the length of hostilities with units rotated at periodic intervals.[58] Surprisingly, though, neither naval nor marine officers served at Army Headquarters in South Africa while Lieutenant General Lord Kitchener commanded. The dearth continued in echelons below with only Lieutenant

Charles Hood, RMLI, serving as Major General Horace Smith-Dorrien's *adc*. This may say something about the state of the war at this point, but the absence is notable given the cooperation previously highlighted.[59] Still, the shortfalls and failures in South Africa became the spur for adopting doctrine within the British Army, or so believed Colonel Ladislaus Pope-Hennessy.[60] Like most first efforts, the results were mixed at best, of which more remains to be said. Finally, if a greater war never materialized in Africa, events halfway across the globe demanded a simultaneous commitment where British arms would be at the fore. Thus, this narrative now turns to China and the events commonly recalled as the Boxer Rebellion.

Seven

China and the Boxer Rebellion, 1900

It is all very well to have the Gospel of Christ at your head, but your influence will be greatly diminished if you must be followed by gunboats at your tail.[1]

Salisbury

If the cauldron of South Africa tested the mettle of countless officers later to serve in the First World War, then 1900s China offered a similar grounding for many a naval one. Admirals John Jellicoe, David Beatty, and Roger Keyes were at the fore of this fraternity. Still, others operating a tier below, including George Warrender, Christopher Cradock, and Richard Phillimore, proved no less prominent, if not so richly rewarded.[2] A British squadron operating in Chinese waters had been a feature of longstanding and so too standing garrisons in Hong Kong, Shanghai, and Wei-Hai-Wei. All supported British interests in an occupation highly reminiscent of affairs in Egypt, where sovereignty ostensibly residing with the Celestial Kingdom saw Westerners enjoy local immunity and directing much of the country's finances.

The antecedents of the Boxer Rebellion or the Third China War, as it is also known in British circles, need not concern us save factors such as race, religion, and comparative economic advantage underlined Britain's position in China and influenced how senior officials responded to events. That the reverse established the antecedents of the nationalist revolt remains a given.[3] Western influence was pervasive and only growing touching as it did the commercial, educational, cultural, governmental, and spiritual strands of Chinese society. Adding to this heady mix stood famine, with volatility a certainty. Granted, a China in turmoil was nothing new. Hence, the expectation turmoil would feature yet again underscored the rationale for the sizable British forces retained. Of course, that was not the sole reason for their presence, as protecting British interests against other interlopers remained.

Agitation in Shantung (Shandong) province in late 1899 at the hands of a group colloquially known as the Boxers and directed at the Church of

England presaged events. Protests via diplomatic note followed, but sensing matters were proceeding in an unknown and possibly undesirable direction, Sir Claude MacDonald, Britain's minister to China, requested the presence of the British China Fleet off Taku (Dagu) to guarantee the maintenance of communications to the capital some 90 miles to the southeast.[4] Similar requests from the several legations were transmitted concurrently to their respective capitals. In London, Salisbury generally supported the steps taken by MacDonald. However, the dual-hatted foreign secretary and prime minister emphasized the need to exhaust "other means of pressure" before mounting a naval demonstration.[5] Ongoing operations against the Boers may have been one reason for the cautionary note; yet another was to maintain harmony with Washington, which had recently promulgated an "Open Door" policy toward China in the wake of its war with Spain.[6] Events on the ground, however, would not conform to Salisbury's wishes.

Consequently, prudence dictated preparatory measures, moving the Foreign Office to seek the assistance of the Admiralty on 24 March 1900. Responding with alacrity, the cruisers *Hermione* and *Brisk* sailed for Taku, operating there until mid-April before returning to a regular routine.[7] Yet, matters were far from quiescent and prompted MacDonald to order a recently arrived marine detachment to remain at Tientsin (Tianjin) in mid-May.[8] Protestations to the Imperial government that more be done to protect Christian missions from Boxer transgressions were renewed, but MacDonald remained dubious of their efficacy. Accordingly, mounting a naval demonstration was raised anew. This met with a more positive response from Salisbury, reflecting that matters were seen as approaching a crisis.[9] Crucial was the intent and remit of the Chinese government. On 27 May 1900, MacDonald advised London that the next 24 hours would be pivotal. Responding, Salisbury immediately sanctioned augmentation of the legation's guard.[10]

Thus armed, MacDonald wired Vice Admiral Sir Edward Seymour for help. For the commander-in-chief, his duty was clear enough for supporting and protecting the legation remained the ultimate rationale of his squadron. As the diplomatic quarter was relatively self-contained and self-supporting, the implication of MacDonald's signal suggested immediate worries resided elsewhere. Indeed, word soon arrived from the British consul in Tientsin that several stations serving the double-track rail line to Peking were ablaze.[11]

While British diplomats mined the legation's walls and blockaded its entrances, Seymour ordered the *Algerine* and *Orlando* to Taku. The former embarked a platoon of Marines for service in Peking to join 300-odd troops provided by Russia, France, Italy, Japan, and the United States.[12] Reaching the Imperial City proved fraught as Chinese authorities refused to abet their mission. Only on 31 May, in the face of force majeure, did the Imperial government acquiesce.[13] This was cutting things fine, for talk filled the air that all foreigners found in Peking would be summarily executed the next day.[14]

Admiral Seymour now weighed what else stood exposed. In truth, with missionaries, customs officials, aid workers, engineers, and businessmen scattered across China, obligations exceeded resources. Appropriately, he resolved to safeguard European lives over protecting British property. Given the legation's location in the interior, keeping an avenue open to Peking remained a priority. Worries multiplied when the consul in Tientsin signaled the admiral directly that protection on that front was a must. Seymour sent a further contingent under Captain Edward Bayly from the cruiser *Aurora* to maintain an axis of communications with the seat of power while protecting those residing in Tientsin's foreign concessions to counter this new threat.[15] Seymour now gathered further elements of his squadron off Taku.[16] Presenting a problem not unlike Alexandria, three forts and their guns guarded the approach to Tientsin and Peking. Unlike in 1882, a foreign flotilla stood by to join any collective action required.[17]

As the senior naval officer present, Seymour beckoned his foreign counterparts to a conference. At the meeting on 5 June, he proposed creating a multi-national naval brigade to relieve the legations. This measure supported MacDonald's request for help—a plea repeated by his fellow diplomats to their chancelleries.[18] Indicative of the growing danger, MacDonald further signaled to the Foreign Office, "As the wire to Tien-tsin may be cut any moment, please send immediate instructions to the Admiral."[19]

Following the meeting of naval principals, Seymour reported to the Admiralty the steps taken to date. Their lordships gave Seymour the widest latitude to concert his actions with the other navies present. This guidance conformed to the tenor of the Foreign Office, who advised MacDonald, "The situation is difficult, and your discretion must be quite unfettered. You may take precisely what measures you think expedient."[20] Thus, both the Foreign

Office and the admiralty appreciated the time for London's close control was nearing its end. Seymour sensed this, too, that things were cascading beyond his limited means. Hence, he sought the assistance of the Hong Kong garrison. To prod matters along, he volunteered the *Terrible* as transport.[21] Seymour further signaled his intention to lead the international force being collected and that a senior Russian would be his chief of staff. To that end, he requested the approval of the Foreign Office.[22] Whether Seymour needed such approval given his guidance is debatable, but his request underscored the sensitivities inherent in allied action. Still, before sanction could be obtained, MacDonald signaled his situation had become desperate—and did so twice in case the point was in danger of being missed.[23] This warning prompted Seymour to act immediately—a measure the Foreign Office subsequently sanctioned.[24]

The request to employ the Hong Kong garrison moved the Foreign Office to appraise the War Office of the worsening situation. Appreciating the anti-Western sentiments expressed in North China might spread more broadly, the Foreign Office suggested employing Singapore's garrison. The 12 June attack on the legation and a simultaneous desire to limit Hong Kong's exposure owing to a lack of troops there motivated their reading of the situation. As it was, reinforcement of Shanghai and Nanking (Nanjing) was deemed essential, notwithstanding the British gunboats already operating on the Yangste (Yangtze).[25]

With the support of the War Office secured, William St. John Brodrick, the undersecretary of state for foreign affairs, believed further resources were necessary. Thus, he pressed the India Office and the War Office to backfill those troops so far co-opted.[26] Responding quickly, the former tasked the viceroy to prepare a brigade-sized force and acquire the necessary sea transport. Meanwhile, the War Office nominated Colonel Arthur Dorward, presently serving at Wei-Hai-Wei, as prospective commander of the military force.[27] Departing from Calcutta on 25 June, the first Indian troops sailed with 3 months' stores in ships chartered from the British India Steam Navigation Company. Reaching Taku 3 weeks later, they were followed by a second brigade, which made it to Hong Kong on 29 July.[28] Ultimately, India would contribute four brigades of infantry and one cavalry regiment to operations in China.[29]

In all this, MacDonald was no stranger to difficult situations. A career which had begun in the army with service in Egypt in 1882, duty as a military attaché quickly followed. Wounded at Tamai in 1884, henceforth his life assumed

China and the Boxer Rebellion, 1900   59

diplomatic proportions. His fellow ambassadors appreciated the pedigree and nominated him as their representative in what was becoming a dangerous affair.[30] Seymour, too, was very experienced in China, being present at the same Taku forts 40 years previously. Appreciating the dangers lurking, the commander-in-chief landed and proceeded to Peking with such troops as he could muster.[31] Commandeering three trains, the mixed force of nearly 1,900 Americans, Austrians, Germans, Japanese, French, Italians, and Russians, of which only half were British, steamed toward Tientsin and the legations. As second-in-command, Seymour secured Captain Bowman McCalla, commanding officer of the protected cruiser *Newark*.[32] By 11 June, the expedition had grown to over 2,000 and covered four trains.[33]

That Seymour elected to rely on the rail line to reach Peking rather than use the river was not unusual. The criticalness of the situation demanded reaching the legations promptly, and with the trains under the control of British engineers, coordinating their use was infinitely easier than securing junks and then cart transport for a river transit. Moreover, heavy silting had made navigation of the White River difficult.[34] Quickly reaching Tientsin and then progressing the 40 miles to Lofa, Seymour hoped Peking might be made by the evening of the eleventh.[35] Alas, events told otherwise.

Proving Seymour's reading of the situation had been correct, the relief force found the rails, bridges, and water tanks leading to Peking had been destroyed. It was now that the first skirmishes occurred, halting efforts at Langfang, 20 miles from their objective. The expedient of deploying a limited force of about fifty men was adopted to reach Anping, while repairs were made using a portion of the second track to repair the first.[36] Throughout 12–13 June, the party commanded by the *Aurora*'s Lieutenant Arthur Smith received increasing attention from the Boxers. Forced to withdraw to Langfang, Seymour could not advance or retreat in equal measure owing to the damaged lines. By force of effort over the next few days, his force repaired portions of the track only to see other segments sabotaged again. When another body of would-be rescuers reported the massing at Lofa, Seymour was forced to deal with that threat.[37] This points to the tenuous nature of using the rail line as the primary axis of advance: Ostensibly facilitating speed, it consumed troops to ensure the safety of stations, tracks, and towers, thereby reducing the size of the force able to advance.

With progress debarred by train, Seymour turned to the river. Adding to his worries, food and ammunition were running low. This necessitated the introduction of half-rations and attests to the problem of relying on a mixed-contingent hastily raised and indifferently supported. If their military skill and weapons were superior to that of the rebels, they nonetheless required sustenance. Indeed, the situation confronting Seymour was more dangerous than he realized, for in the intervening period since departing Tientsin, that city was itself besieged. This was not immediately understood, though the admiral knew things were becoming more dangerous as couriers sent to secure further transport and provisions had failed to return. In fact, from 13–26 June, Seymour knew little about what conditions were like beyond the confines of his command. Moreover, it now transpired that not all opposing him were rebels. Regulars from the Peking garrison, including cavalry and artillery, had joined the action at Langfang on 18 June.[38] This represented a significant escalation for prior thinking held that the Imperial government was beset and not belligerent, with a return to the *status quo ante* the desired end-state.

Understandably, Seymour now weighed matters with his foreign counterparts on 19 June. From this, a retreat following the contours of the river was ordered. With the wounded and artillery transferred to junks commandeered by German troops, progress was slow. Adept at handling small boats, the ways of the Chinese junks largely escaped the ken of naval ratings.

Withdrawing by day under fire and camping by early evening was the norm until action became general on the third day. Accordingly, after resting for a couple of hours, the retreat resumed in the early hours of 22 June 1900. Again, it was not long before Seymour's force was engaged by sustained rifle and artillery fire from the far shore, necessitating a sweep to clear the Hsiku arsenal.[39]

Having neutralized that danger, the Allies established themselves at the magazine, which afforded them a natural defensive position. That move came with another benefit. With ammunition and provisions nearly exhausted, a search revealed rice and modern ammunition aplenty. Seymour's force defended their hard-won position for 2 days while waiting for relief. That such was on the way was not assured as all efforts at getting messages through to Tientsin had failed to date.[40]

Fortunately, others surmised Seymour's plight. Vice Admiral Hiltebrandt,[41] the next ranking officer commanding the Russian Squadron, assumed the lead. Convening a council of war in the *Rossia*, the Allies resolved to attack the forts at Taku, guarding the seaward approaches.[42] These batteries included modern

Krupps and commanded the river and its roadstead. Prompting the decision to tackle the forts was word that rolling stock was being collected, suggesting the intervention of the Chinese Army was at hand. When news arrived that the forts were preparing for eventualities and that a fresh barrier of electric mines was covering the Peiho, Hiltebrandt struck. This was highly reminiscent of Alexandria in 1882, yet with a crucial difference: The Chinese Army did not wait for events to unfold. They opened fire on the Allied fleet while the ships and gunboats prepared to land a force under Cradock.[43]

Surprise forfeited, Cradock and 900 officers and men opted for a nighttime landing under heavy, if mostly ineffective, fire covered by the fleet's guns. The latter's 4-inch shooting under moonlight was little better. Following the expenditure of much ammunition, the ships fired intermittently until sunrise offered better prospects. Consequently, Cradock halted the attack lest losses become severe and waited for sustained fire to resume. Success followed, and the shooting of the German gunboat *Iltis* proved especially noteworthy, but permanently silencing the mobile field guns proved difficult. The attackers reduced the two northwest forts using dead ground and attacking from multiple points. This accomplished and employing the enemy's batteries with effect, those others situated on the southern bank fell too after limited resistance. When over, Chinese losses amounted to at least 450 dead. Friendly casualties were more modest but striking in that they occurred mainly in the supporting ships, with the Russian *Giliak* suffering ten killed and forty-nine wounded. Meanwhile, the *Iltis* lost eight dead, with a further thirty wounded in the brief action.[44]

Notwithstanding this success, the action broadened the lines of the crisis. The rebels may have been nationalists but were not the regular soldiers holding the Taku forts. Eliminating one risk, the measure was an act of war against a country the intervention was nominally meant to support and was viewed as such by those in Peking. Thus, a Chinese declaration of war followed, joined by the shelling of Tientsin's European quarter. In turn, the empress-dowager ordered the expulsion of all diplomats. With memories of the Cawnpore (Kanpur) massacre, MacDonald and company stayed put and vowed only to leave under European military escort.[45] Of course, the Gordon relief expedition offered another scenario. The siege proper of the Peking legations began.[46]

Unfortunately, Admiral Bruce could not act immediately as the British ships present had been denuded owing to the operations ashore. Thus, he awaited reinforcement from those ships sailing off Hong Kong and the Philippines.[47]

By 24 June, a relief force of 2,000 under the command of Major General Anatoly Stessel departed for Tientsin. Arriving the following day, they soon reached Seymour's force found a few miles to the north. Rescuers and the rescued then returned to Tientsin, but not before several villages along the way paid a fearful price.[48]

Seymour acknowledged the general failure of his efforts. Yet, lacking surprise, cavalry, mounted infantry, heavy guns, and being unable to alter his line of approach, it could have been so much worse. Others have criticized Seymour for failing to secure his line of communications first.[49] Given the immediacy of the situation and the few sailors and marines available, that option risked defeat in detail. Seymour adopted the only course available; that it proved insufficient must be counted a hazard of command. Indeed, the admiralty did not view matters quite so adversely. Recognizing the situation defined the plan adopted, they held Seymour had acted correctly. If unable to reach Peking, he had reached those Westerners living and working along the rail line.[50] Yet, the price had been dear. Of the 2,000 ratings and marines engaged through 26 June 1900, total casualties equaled 285, with the British share being sixteen killed and ninety-seven wounded.[51]

With would-be rescuers chastised and ensconced in Tientsin, those trapped in the legations were *in extremis*. Many sharp fights ensued that first week of July, but these focused on relieving Tientsin. If the Chinese lost heavily in these skirmishes, the underlying situation remained. On 11 July, the Chinese made a determined effort to seize Tientsin's train station, and though repulsed, the defending French and Japanese suffered over 150 casualties. Further reinforcements soon brought Allied numbers at Tientsin to over 12,000. Surrounding them, however, were over 20,000 Chinese rebels and Imperial troops.

The arrival of friendly regular troops marked the end of Seymour's command of the mixed naval and military force. Returning to the *Centurion*, he focused on the threat presented to the broader tapestry, particularly Shanghai.[52] This did not end the role of the 300 British bluejackets and marines remaining, nor of their mobile guns, which had featured prominently in the actions to date.[53] In short, command arrangements were being regularized for the period ahead. Thus, command of the naval landing party fell to James Burke, captain of the cruiser *Orlando*. Reporting to Edward Bayly, who served as the senior naval officer at Tientsin, all came under the tactical control of Brigadier General Dorward.[54]

Only a negligible maritime threat had allowed the *Orlando* to land 75 percent of its company during the crisis.[55] The naval risk was more significant than perceived, for the Imperial government was not the neutral agent believed.[56] Hiltebrandt's decision, highhanded and producing untoward results, received much subsequent criticism.[57] That, however, ignores the real dangers Seymour and his force—including many Russians—faced. It is easy to imagine the charges of dereliction that would have followed if all had stood pat—recall the rioting and massacre of Alexandria in 1882 when another Seymour initially demurred.

With northern China in revolt, the Admiralty deployed further ships to the theater and, just as importantly, more officers and ratings to man the ships whose crews were ashore.[58] Percy Scott recently arrived from active service in South Africa, felt chagrined that Bruce had not made better use of the *Terrible* and her complement of wheeled, heavy naval guns.[59] Personal feelings aside, others were landed from the *Algerine* and *Phoenix*, suggesting Bruce was mindful of sharing opportunities and honor across the fleet.[60] Meanwhile, Seymour's withdrawal became a fighting retreat, with Boxers operating on one flank and Chinese troops on another. The river's low level now hampered the withdrawal as the junks grounded frequently. Still, progress continued in the presence of numerous, sharp fights, including the one in which the admiral's flag captain, John Jellicoe, was seriously wounded.[61]

Yet, even before Seymour's involuntary retreat, it was assumed a more robust force would be required. Unfortunately, the immediate plight of those in Peking, to say nothing of others in Tientsin, had forced his hand. That force, a battalion of regular British infantry and a contingent of Indians, arrived in two stages. An advanced element embarked in the *Terrible* reached Tongku on 21 June, with the balance of the 2nd Royal Welsh Fusiliers following 4 days later in the commercial transport *Hansing*. Absent their essential wherewithal, those arriving first were provisioned by the fleet.[62]

In the meantime, an Allied proclamation announced that their mission was limited to securing the diplomatic community. Hard-pressed in Tientsin and elsewhere, the desire to forestall a broader action was palpable.[63] Meanwhile, Dorward and the locally recruited Chinese regiment made Taku on 26 June 1900. As with Seymour before him, Dorward assumed command of the miscellaneous national contingents and advanced anew toward Tientsin.[64] A colonel serving as the senior staff engineer at Wei-Hai-Wei, he had been a local brigadier general pending the arrival of Lieutenant General Sir Alfred Gaselee from India. Another substantive colonel, Gaselee, would bring 10,000 troops with him. Beyond these measures, London canvassed France, Russia, Japan, and the United States for further reinforcements. This became a delicate ballet as introducing large numbers of troops from competing powers threatened any return to business as usual.[65]

Advance against Tientsin proper was necessary if for no other reason than to forestall the constant shelling of its European settlements, while each passing day brought word of further depredations.[66] With combined numbers less than desired and because of the setback previously suffered, not all desired an early return to the offensive. This was the view of the Russians, and as they possessed the greatest number of troops and were awaiting the arrival of still others, it was a view that prevailed for the moment.[67] Such hard facts were brutal to accept, owing to the plight of those in Peking. With the rail lines cut and the rains expected, advancing a sizable force by way of the river was seen as equally impractical.[68] Seymour conceded a force of 40,000 would be required, while his American counterpart, Rear Admiral Louis Kempff, thought 80,000 was closer to the mark. While London may have desired a certain promptitude, such numbers were beyond its immediate ability to fulfill.[69] Proximity alone dictated the use of sizeable Russian and Japanese forces. Pulling the chestnuts of others out of the fire is rarely done without cost. Thus, Britain assumed the expenses of transporting Japanese troops to China.[70]

With numbers at last augmented, the assault began anew on the morning of 13 July when over 4,000 troops supported by the guns of the naval brigades advanced on multiple axes. Within 24 hours, Tientsin had been secured, but at a cost with losses in dead and wounded exceeding 750, a total easily surpassing that incurred by Seymour's relief force earlier.[71] Lack of effective planning and prior reconnaissance has been advanced as reasons for the severe losses suffered. When key officers understanding the plan of assault were lost, cohesion broke down. Yet, a subsidiary cause must be the emphasis in offensive action notwithstanding the losses incurred by some national contingents.[72]

Making Tientsin on 27 July, Gaselee assumed command of British forces. A brigade commander during the Tirah campaign of 1897, he was seen as a sound tactician. By his side was Sir Walter Hillier, an old China hand, now acting as a political adviser.[73] Securing an overall commander proved more problematic with national sensitivities at the fore. In the end, cooperation prevailed. With Gaselee acting as a sort of *primus inter pares*, relief of the legations remained the ultimate objective, though other considerations applied. The latter made cooperation difficult, especially with Gaselee's Russian and French opposites. Here, Gaselee's charter to secure Shanghai first, where substantial British interests were at stake, demonstrates the safety of the legations remained but one facet of the crisis. That some sought to avoid adding to present woes by accruing a financial loss in the city on top of any loss of life in China is a conclusion hard to avoid.[74]

Gaselee's detour delayed his reaching Tientsin by 3 weeks, as the *Alacrity* anchored at Shanghai on 26 July, where ferment was alive.[75] Gaselee estimated that 10,000 troops would be necessary to protect its European settlements. That was certainly more than Seymour could support from the fleet and a number more than London contemplated, for the Foreign Office was seeking to maintain a small footprint away from North China if only to remove a source of friction with those in revolt.[76]

Seymour and the *Alacrity* soon left Shanghai for Nanking to confer with the viceroy on 1 August. His departure indicated that affairs were heated but not yet hot. Still, the aim remained to work with local Chinese authorities and de-escalate matters where possible. Landing troops in Shanghai to serve as a backstop to the Local Defence Force was prudent, but if done highhandedly, it might tip matters adversely. Thus, Seymour sought to land a reduced force with the concurrence of Lin Kun Yi. To this the viceroy agreed, but in doing so, he presented demands of his own: the departure of all foreign ships and the limiting of British vessels to but a single ship at each port. Still, nothing was simple in China that summer, and the agreement secured seemingly evaporated the moment the *Alacrity* raised anchor, with Lin Kun Yi quickly reversing himself.[77] Such confusion was hardly limited to the Chinese, however. During the disembarkation of Major General O'Moore Creagh's brigade at Shanghai on 14 August, it was ordered to Wei-Hai-Wei. Proceeding thence, the brigade's orders were countermanded anew, bringing its return to Shanghai on August 18.[78]

As for Gaselee, determined to reach the legations, he threatened to advance with or without Allied support. That decided matters, for their absence implied a loss of influence when matters were settled.[79] With over 20,000 troops available, the force was also now better apportioned in artillery. The renewed advance began on 4 August. With over fifty boats under the charge of a naval transport officer moving the force's stores and equipment, the troops marched along both banks of the Peiho River.[80] The British, under Major General Sir

Norman Stewart, included a brigade of regular infantry augmented by the Hong Kong Regiment and elements of the original naval brigade screened by the 1st Bengal Lancers. The action became general the following day, with the brunt of the fighting and dying borne by the Japanese. At Peitsang, some 7 miles from Tientsin, they lost over 300 when tackling 8,000 Chinese regulars occupying multiple trench lines.[81]

Nonetheless, Gaselee pressed on toward Yangtsun (Yangcun), where flooding impeded further progress. This necessitated a return to Peitsang while an alternate course was found. Unfortunately, this required the construction of a bridge, but the delay engendered proved otherwise fortuitous, as Gaselee now reorganized his command with elements shifted between the two riverbanks.[82] When the advance resumed, multiple skirmishes were fought, though, in truth, the back of the resistance had now been broken. In the face of the intense heat and dust, the force rested on 7 August while it resupplied. With the advance renewed, Tungchow fell on 12 August. A final planning conference outlined the lines for the assault against Peking proper. Slated for 15 August, the event transpired sooner than expected when the Russians stole a march to be the first to enter the city. This found the other contingents flat-footed, but not unduly, as the Russian advance bogged down. Thus, it was Major Henry Vaughan's seven Rajputs who reached MacDonald on 14 August.[83] In the long interval, sixty-six foreigners had died in Peking.[84]

Thus, one crisis eased, but chaos abounded everywhere. If the Imperial government had fled, then the Boxers and the Chinese Army remained a worry, with communications to Tientsin still tenuous.[85] The lack of official control made it impossible to restore matters to the *status quo ante*. Still, a further problem remained the diffuse nature of the intervening powers as their desiderata were far from harmonious.[86] Clearly, making war had proved easier than establishing the conditions of peace. Follow-on operations to disarm the rebels would continue for months and, in a measure anticipating another war's end 45 years hence, national zones of occupation were created.[87] Suspected Boxers were shot on sight, and that excesses were committed can be assumed as contemporary accounts paint a portrait of wanton retribution, rape, confiscation, and outright theft.[88]

For Britain, these operations had occurred in an area far removed from her seat of power while coinciding with the South African War. Successfully projecting power to two distinct and separate theaters while retaining ample naval resources elsewhere speaks to a capability without peer. France and the United States might have aspired to such potentialities but could not equal them. In truth, Britain's maritime reach was deceptive, for a similar military capability did not match it.

Telegraphic communications had allowed London to be appraised and offer general guidance, but more substantive intelligence passed by letter took 6–8 weeks to reach authorities. Paradoxically, MacDonald's communications with London remained better than his links to Seymour, who operated within 40 miles of the British legation. Though couriers occasionally passed between rescuers and those to be rescued, delay was endemic. The issue became acute as Seymour advanced and the Chinese severed his physical and telegraphic communications to the outside world. Thus, any relief mission faced two discrete tasks: successfully reaching the legations while ensuring the security of their rear to allow for a subsequent withdrawal. Seymour understood this, which moved him in part to request the dispatch of an infantry battalion from Hong Kong on 13 June to protect his reward communications.[89]

Thus, local British officials were expected to employ judgment, recognizing what decisions needed to be referred home for resolution and what could be accomplished off their own bat based on previous orders, instructions, and guidance. Accordingly, the political nous of an officer weighed in his subsequent success in securing flag or general officer rank. This, too, applied to civilian officials. Perhaps unfairly, MacDonald was faulted by some contemporaries for being slow to read the nature of the threat. However, the arrival of the *Hermione* and the *Brisk* in March off Taku testifies he sought aid when matters appeared to be heading for a crisis. Where criticism can be leveled is in the late appeal issued to the War Office as matters escalated. Seymour, at last, raised the alarm, but his reasons for doing so were primarily parochial, relating to the detrimental effects that supplying landing parties had on the China fleet. If nothing else, the late notification to the War Office suggests a weakness in control and oversight married to a lack of standing operating procedures and reporting at the sharp end. An expedient employed in modern operations is to delegate coordination among lateral organizations, with the caveat that superiors be kept informed to allow their veto if the steps pursued fail to conform to their reading of the problem. Save for the direct signal made by William Carles to Seymour requesting support at Tientsin, such instances were notably rare. That changed on or about 8 August, when the War Office authorized the general officer commanding Hong Kong to communicate directly with the commander-in-chief, China.[90]

The timely dispatch of ships affirms the utility of naval forces and is a reminder that China in 1900 offered a highly beneficial maritime environment. Though the Chinese Navy never offered a serious threat, concern for the safety of their transports by St. Petersburg and Berlin prompted action against the Taku forts.[91] That success cemented control of the inner ring and allowed the build-up of forces to proceed. Meanwhile, the Royal Navy possessed an anchorage secure from attack at Wei-Hai-Wei. As the unrest escalated, it assumed a greater importance in the evacuation of refugees and wounded as the sanctity of Hong Kong could no longer be presumed. Thus, a temporary hospital was fashioned at Wei-Hai-Wei and soon became the vehicle for sustaining the troops operating in the interior.[92]

Ever a constraint facing both Seymour and Gaselee was command and control. At any moment, the possibility existed that non-British forces would cease to cooperate. Indeed, this concern arose during the attack on the Taku forts when the USS *Monocacy*, acting under national orders, limited her support. Tact and sound judgment at the sharp end reduced points of friction and treating convenient allies fairly proved key. Following the capture of four destroyers, which coincided with the assault on the forts, Admiral Bruce transferred one each of the vessels to the Russian, German, and French squadrons.[93] In an age when prize rules operated, the measure secured more than goodwill: It secured good fortune. Likewise, London recognized the value of coordinating its response. With numbers limited and danger seemingly everywhere, the Admiralty understood the wastefulness of keeping ships on station where those of friendly states were already present. Here, the French were most keen to formalize naval arrangements, though the Foreign Office resisted for the moment.[94] Conversely, Britain's decided military weakness moved the Foreign Office to concede command as the build-up of army forces gathered pace.[95]

Perforce, when communications were limited and languages varied, understanding affairs beyond one's immediate surroundings faced untold difficulties. Friendly fire incidents were noticeable for their rarity, though one observer held the general lack of action forestalled their occurrence.[96] Tactically, wireless communications proved disappointing, while telegraphic lines were easily cut. Meanwhile, visual communications were not always possible owing to weather and enemy action. Telephones between fixed positions proved useful, especially at Tientsin. There, Bayly controlled the indirect fire of artillery fire on 13 July from a signal tower, though couriers were the norm.[97] Normally, doctrine might have abetted matters, but in a composite force, such was lacking. That chaos did not reign owed much to common sense and prior cooperation experience. This, however, was not universal, with the rebellion becoming the first instance of the United States Army and Marine Corps working with foreign partners since their revolution.[98]

Fortunately, many officers spoke English and French, the latter language having been impressed upon British naval officers during their formative years of education and training.[99] As the campaign expanded, liaison officers were appointed to the national contingents and Chinese-speaking missionaries were seconded.[100] To wit, Clive Bigham, who had been serving as an extra attaché in the legation, joined the expedition after becoming trapped at Tientsin. Well-traveled across northern China, the expedition gained the services of a former grenadier now ensconced in intelligence duties. Eventually, Bigham joined the Russian contingent, where he observed Major General Orloff's campaign in Manchuria while traveling across Asia toward England during that hot, dry summer.[101]

Supporting the multi-national force was a most convoluted logistics chain. During Gaselee's advance, the British lines of communication became the responsibility of Major General Lorn Campbell. Mules transported from India provided the initial means of portage augmented by the watercraft secured by Commander George Borrett, *Centurion*'s first lieutenant and torpedo officer. Over time, supply arrangements were regularized, though recourse to commandeering mules, carts, and junks still occurred. Moltke, no mean authority in military matters, was impressed with the command of logistics displayed by the British force.[102] As for medical services, they were not severely tested within Gaselee's force, though one errant casualty was Colonel John Bookey, the principal medical officer, who was invalided early. Attached to each Indian infantry brigade were two field hospitals, while one British and three native hospitals deployed as second-tier support. A further amenity was the *Gwalior*, a hospital ship furnished by its namesake maharaja.[103] During the final advance, limited cases of dysentery appeared among the Indian and British troops, unsurprising given the filth of the Peiho, where bodies were being routinely disposed.[104]

Savage Landor, who had the opportunity to observe the rebellion, held that British sailors and marines were without equal, being finely led and approaching perfection. Allowing for ample national pride, the verdict does not appear unduly effusive when British efforts in supply, transport, and medical arrangements are contrasted with their foreign counterparts. Still, topographical intelligence of China's interior highlighted a recurring shortcoming in the period's British military operations. Given her ever-growing involvement in China, the failure did not stem from any lack of opportunity to acquire. George Lynch of the *Illustrated London News*, who covered British operations in South Africa and again in China, believed those serving on the veldt were of a better stripe. Though not a soldier, he possessed a keen eye. Of one thing, he was certain: The power of modern weapons made the defense the more potent form of war.[105]

Eight

Somaliland, 1901–1904: Chasing the "Mad Mullah"

If they wanted to break the power of the Mullah *permanently and effectively why did not the Government make their arrangements accordingly? Why did they continue to dribble out small bodies of troops which were cut to pieces by the overwhelming numbers arrayed against them? It was one of the most disgraceful, most lamentable, and most discreditable chapters in the recent history of this country, that brave soldiers and devoted men should be sent on expeditions for which they were not in the slightest degree equipped.*[1]

William Redmond

At the dawn of the twentieth century, instability in the Horn of Africa was not a new spectacle. British interests in the region, though, were greater than heretofore, and, so consequently, the risks now incurred. From Aden, where he became versed in the tenets of Islam, Muhammad Abdullah Hassan returned to his native land. Organized as British Somaliland in 1895, Hassan, now styled a mullah or religious dignitary, preached the faith. Initially finding few adherents, Hassan secured better results when he began preaching to his own tribe in a region straddling portions of Abyssinia and Somaliland. By 1899, his reach met the grasp of the British Empire. Proclaiming war against infidels, Hassan raided the Habr Yunis tribe and occupied Burao, thereby threatening the northern tier of British Somaliland. Maintaining only a token constabulary, little beyond the climate, the elements, and the inclination of other tribes faced Hassan.[2] Even if this was not all reminiscent of the Mahdī, a response was sure to follow, for the depredations now threatened control of a protectorate under British tutelage. In truth, the protectorate offered little by way of compensation, save its possession kept other interlopers from occupying an area astride the Gulf of Aden.

In time, Hassan received the moniker "Mad Mullah," but as "no Englishmen ever set eyes on him," perhaps the insanity resided elsewhere. In all events, final success would only be secured following the First World War when a last expedition abetted by disease and the Royal Air Force saw to matters.[3] In the meantime, limited, unsuccessful operations were conducted against an enemy possessing strong local knowledge and unmatched physical powers of endurance. These were led initially by Lieutenant Colonel Eric Swayne, beginning in 1900. By 1903, with affairs in South Africa and China squared, the time seemingly arrived to settle matters conclusively. Most troops in the first campaign were recently raised Somali levies commanded by seconded British officers assisted by three companies of the King's African Rifles (KAR). The tactical skills of the local levies suffered from a want of training, though the material was sound enough. The men were effective marksmen, good riders, and highly fit. As their officers did not speak the tribal languages of their charges, orders were translated by interpreters. Surprisingly, when regulars appeared following the South Africa War, a period of local training was often required before taking the field. Transfers, leave, and separation from service were now the root causes and highlighted the difficulties of sustaining unit military effectiveness following recent high-tempo operations.[4]

These operations were overseen by the Foreign Office, which had assumed responsibility for the region from India following the establishment of a protectorate on 1 October 1898. That oversight, though, remained of a general kind for a joint War Office and India Office committee provided operational guidance. Here, the War Office acted as the senior partner even if the troops employed were Indian, going so far as to task Calcutta which formations were to be used.[5] Liaison with Abyssinia and Italy was a notable feature of these operations in which the Royal Navy's East Indies Squadron played an essential part. The latter's contribution, if of a lesser nature than previously surveyed, nonetheless included force sustainment, medical support, and coastal observation. Success here proved fleeting, given the breadth of coast to be watched and the paucity of assets available. Thus, Hassan never lacked military necessities, with Djibouti proving a ready supply source, notwithstanding France's presumed cooperation.[6]

Early operations lacked practical cooperation with Abyssinia despite the presence of Major the Hon. Algernon Hanbury-Tracy and Captain Ralph Cobbold.[7] A root cause was that Abyssinia felt little compunction to follow British advice. Thus, their operations began before Swayne's force was ready.[8] Be that as it may, Swayne inflicted defeats thrice on Hassan and his forces. The

Foreign Office then peremptorily ordered Swayne to desist from entering the Ogaden. This was reminiscent of the response to Graham's early success in Sudan against Diqna, where an advantage secured went begging.[9]

Lack of water and hard marching took their toll on friendly forces, with success fleeting. One such effort witnessed a sharp action fought at Erego in October 1902, where Captain Alexander Cobbe did fine execution with his machine gun. Still, Swayne soon retreated to Bohotle.[10] It was now that the War Office assumed responsibility for operations, with the Foreign Office limiting itself to offering political guidance. To this end, a joint War Office and India Office committee (but absent Admiralty representation) guided affairs.[11] The omission was striking given the navy's role on the Red Sea littoral, and would yet play in coordinating British actions with its Italian opposite.

Locally, Brigadier General William Manning, the inspector general of the KAR but responsible for the lines of communication in Somaliland, replaced Swayne. The illness of the latter was given as the ostensible reason. It was now that the expedition was reconstituted as the Somaliland Field Force.[12] Returning to London, Swayne was seconded to the Foreign Office to advise on the next phase of operations. Reinforcements from India and South Africa followed, allowing Manning to employ regular troops in a manner that was unavailable to Swayne.[13] This bromide, if providing a more effective force, came with costs. Financial, to be sure, but also political, for the Somali tribes quickly resented the presence of Indian and Arab troops more than the depredations of Hassan. Thus, Manning aimed to limit their use to a supporting role; even then, the rising nationalist feeling did not abate.[14]

The British did not believe the unfolding campaign would end Hassan's raiding, but they did aspire to dent his prestige. Again, coordination with Abyssinia was pursued, and so was cooperation with Italy, the occupying power of southern Somalia. The last was facilitated in part by Sir Rennell Rodd and Lieutenant Colonel Edward Altham of the War Office's Intelligence Division during meetings convened in Rome following a joint reconnaissance of Obbia and Illig on the Somali coast by the cruisers *Pomone* and *Naiad*.[15] These surveys identified the possible sites for amphibious landings. For the navy, a protected, deep anchorage to handle cruisers was deemed critical. For the army, nearby sources of fresh water and grazing lands were needed. From the surveys made and the soundings taken, Obbia, an exposed anchorage in Italian Somaliland, was selected, though subsequent experience testified to the superiority of Elhur. Further surveys marked the best routes for laying rail lines to support an operation that would always be constrained by logistics and the weather. Meanwhile, tracks able to accommodate the wheeled transport of regular units were improved by engineers.[16]

The Indian troops included mounted infantry, artillery, engineers, and the Bikanir Camel Corps. A company of the King's Royal Rifles and another of mounted infantry arrived from South Africa.[17] The latter, in common with Wolseley's *voyageurs*, was sent on a 6-month deployment. A complicating restriction when using an Imperial element, but in the circumstances of a just concluded South African War, a welcome demonstration of political reconciliation. Owing to the seasonal monsoon, the troops landing at Obbia could not retire from that roadstead if the campaigning extended beyond April. Thus, Manning's force intended to march across the Somali interior via Bohotle to Berbera. As Italy desired to keep operations from extending southward, this movement at least had the merit of meeting an essential political constraint while demonstrating British authority to tribes along the axis of advance. The War Office issued instructions to that end to Manning on 19 December. Sailing from Aden on 1 January 1903, the general and his staff arrived offshore 3 days later before landing on 5 January.[18]

Meanwhile, a covering force sailing from Berbera under the command of Major Paul Kenna, a hero of Omdurman and the charge of the 21st Lancers, departed in the transport *Haidari* for Obbia.[19] Their task was to secure the anchorage, unload stores, acquire local intelligence, procure animal stock for transport, and develop a camp for a "flying column" of the Somaliland Field Force. In support of the landings made over an open beach, the Commander-in-Chief East Indies, Rear Admiral Charles Drury, deployed three cruisers under Captain Alexander Bethell.[20] Commander Harry Jones of the *Pomone* acted as the landing's beach master, assisted by Lieutenant George Bevan, the *Pomone*'s navigating officer. With an Italian transport ship forming part of the squadron, Captain George Hewett, RIM, served as liaison to that part of the force backed by Lieutenant Ernest Huddleston, RIM.[21]

What followed for Commander Edmund Pears of the *Perseus* was familiar enough, having done as much at Benin in 1897 while serving in the *Forte*. Following an initial insertion of the 1/KAR and 5/KAR, the off-loading continued intermittently over the next 6 weeks during daytime under extremely wet and difficult conditions, with troops, baggage, stores, and animals unloaded in that order. A limiting factor was the lack of boats or, perhaps, more correctly, suitable ones for Somali conditions. Thus, an immediate task was to scour the coast for surf boats to assist in the unloading. Though losses in stores were minimal, the subsequent wastage of camels was severe, with the time spent waiting aboard ship before landing judged the chief reason.[22]

Manning appreciated the efforts made, believing the difficulties were "probably without parallel in the history of the disembarkation of an expeditionary force."[23] Surely a stretch, but in substance, mirroring the verdict of the commander-in-chief, East Indies, who recorded that "having examined the landing place & been to Obbia, I consider it is impossible to exaggerate the importance of the work."[24] Beyond providing boat crews to negotiate the roughest of surfs, Manning sought naval support in long-haul communications. The establishment of a Marconi wireless network with stations at Obbia and Berbera aimed to facilitate the control of columns divorced by many miles while providing contact with London and Calcutta via Aden to be exercised. Alas, the promise remained unfulfilled as Lieutenant Arthur Silvertop's signalers could not overcome the poor propagation experienced. Thus, the naval telegraphists departed in May 1903. Fortunately, fixed communications via landline had been concurrently extended from Berbera to Bohotle.[25]

After coordinating the movement of the supporting Abyssinian force and following an initial survey of the interior by Colonel Alex Cobbe, Manning and the 1,100 troops of the "flying column" struck out for Bohotle via Galkayu on 22 February; on their heels, a column under the command of Major Johnnie Gough departed Bohotle for Galkayu on 3 March.[26]

With the enemy main force operating 150 miles west of Galkayu and roughly equidistant from the Abyssinian blocking effort, Manning's strategy required the compliance of the mullah to succeed. In style, the British advance repeated the pattern of operations followed by General Graham in Sudan, with the availability of water and camels constraining the number of troops deployed. Again, the terrain was broken and inhospitable, and the wells were often brackish. As in Sudan, the construction of defensive zeribas, though benefiting now with barbed wire, occurred as the column advanced. This allowed stores to be held at regular and protected intervals. As ever, it was the location of the wells that dictated the line of march. British forces, consisting primarily of companies from the Indian Army and the KAR, had discipline, training, and firepower on their side, but the Dervishes possessed that other invaluable quality: numbers. The risk remained that a small, isolated force might meet the enemy's main force and be overwhelmed. Such occurred at Gumburu on 17 April 1903 when Lieutenant Colonel Arthur Plunkett and 160 troops from 2/KAR supported by forty-eight sepoys of the 2nd Sikhs came to grief when facing 12,000 warriors.[27]

Responding, London offered further reinforcements. Manning declined these, avowing a sufficiency on hand. In truth, he probably worried a greater force would also bring a greater commander. Hassan, though, had his troubles too and, following his losses, looked to retire northeastward across the expedition's line of communications to reach Nogal. This was not unwelcome as it took the enemy away from the south and brought him into a region of British strength. Accordingly, Colonel John Swann, overseeing the lines of communication of the expeditionary force, was repositioned to intercept the enemy. He demurred, unwilling to risk the tenuous logistics of the expedition. A veteran of the recent intervention in China, where he had performed similar duties, his caution now testified to a need for more bayonets on the ground. The War Office often deferred to the local commander save when he demonstrated a lack of grip. Where Swayne had been supplanted following the debacle of Erego, now it was Manning's time to give way.[28] It was not the case that Manning's losses had been daunting so much as his efforts had been void of success.

Arriving in June were units from Aden and India, including three companies of the 1st Hampshires, the first British regulars to appear.[29] Coming too was Major General Sir Charles Egerton, a much-experienced campaigner to replace Manning. The former had been a mere supporting actor during Kitchener's Sudan operations, but his remit and ambitions were of a larger order when he reached Africa anew on 3 July.[30] He now found a force needing rest, replenishment, and pack transport, as many beasts had succumbed. Procuring others proved difficult for those imported lacked the stamina of those native to the area.[31] The deficiency in transport gave rise to poor diet, with some succumbing to scurvy. A contributing factor doubtless was the decision not to extend the rail lines into the interior. Cost was certainly a factor, but geography proved the more telling one as the seat of operations extended into areas under Abyssinian and Italian control.

Where Manning eschewed reinforcement, Egerton specified it as a condition for success. Engineers to improve the tracks and sink new wells, but also infantry to occupy critical points along the axis of operations. Key, though, was the provision of additional camels from India.³² A further reason for Manning's failure was the lack of a proper staff to plan, organize, and oversee operations. Egerton now brought a proper divisional headquarters organized per Indian *Field Service Regulations*. Possessing a strong intelligence branch, Egerton inherited the *Naiad*'s Lieutenant Ernest Carey, who became provost marshal to the Somaliland Field Force.³³

Unlike operations in Sudan and China, Somalia suffered from a dearth of navigable rivers. British fires might rend native ranks, but the first requirement was getting a force to the scene of operations. Absent internal waterways, improved roads and rail lines became the enablers to allow columns to be sustained and afforded possibilities for British weapons to be employed. While Messrs Gardner, Gatling, and Maxim provided superior firepower, none should gainsay the advantages of superior horsepower that Messrs Watt and Fulton contributed. Finally, where geography largely operated against a direct naval contribution, the employment of sappers assumed greater proportions. Unfortunately, their presence remained at a premium.

Though the navy provided only limited assistance to Egerton's operations conducted in the hinterland, it could offer a diversion in conjunction with the Italian Navy. Thus, at Obbia in November 1903, the cruisers *Porpoise*, *Perseus*, and *Galileo*, with the sloop *Merlin*, landed stores with the hope Hassan's spies would read it as something more foreboding. The partnership of the two navies, though, went beyond this limited foray as they routinely coordinated their actions off the African coast. Indeed, when an Italian officer (Lieutenant Carlo Graban) was killed at Durbo, Commander Ernest Gaunt and the *Mohawk* upheld Italian pride to the point of landing a party of bluejackets and marines. Demanding the forfeiture of arms and the surrender of tribal elders, when the negotiations collapsed, the third-class cruiser directed its guns on Durbo. In the ensuing engagement, Gaunt received a severe wound while Marine John Staunton succumbed.³⁴ Temporarily retiring, the British returned to torch the hamlet before the *Mohawk* set course for Aden.³⁵ Though Rear Admiral George Atkinson-Willes, the senior naval officer, acknowledged the bravery on display, he believed the action had exceeded standing orders. The Admiralty retained no such doubt, perhaps in part because Italy officially recognized Gaunt's heroism by awarding its Silver Medal for Military Valour. Not to be usurped, the Admiralty promoted Gaunt to captain for the initiative shown.³⁶

Egerton now sought a fresh naval demonstration followed by a landing at Illig, a fishing village 200 miles north of Obbia on the Nogal River in Italian Somaliland. The aim this time was to narrow Hassan's ability to secure resupply from the coast. It would also offer a degree of muscle where friendly strength was absent. Regrettably, Atkinson-Willes had to cancel the serial in the face of worsening weather and rising surf.[37]

In December 1903, a major concentration of the enemy was located at Jidbali by a mounted reconnaissance under the command of Colonel Kenna, leading to the action of 10 January, where the concentrated Somaliland Field Force engaged 6,000 Dervishes. Killing 1,000 of the enemy, total British losses equaled sixty-four.[38] Hassan, though, had escaped, retreating northward into the British Protectorate. This prompted Egerton to seek further cooperation with the Italians and the navy. The former was secured but arrived too late to be of use, but the support of the East Indies Squadron proved more forthcoming. The *Perseus* landed a company of troops at Las Khorai in late February.[39] Hassan and his forces proved elusive, however. By April, facing the familiar problem of broken transport and the onset of the rainy season, Egerton proposed concluding the campaign. That soon occurred, but not before a final stroke aimed at Illig occurred following the belated approval of Rome for the operation.[40]

Following a survey of the coast in February by the *Pomone*, it was learned Hassan and his main body were heading for Illig. This moved Atkinson-Willes to confer with his Italian opposite, Commodore Tommaso Bixio, at Aden before meeting Egerton at Berbera. A joint force consisting of the second-class cruiser *Hyacinth* and the third-class cruiser *Fox* embarked 125 men from the Hampshires on 15 April. Sailing with the Hampshires was Captain George Munn, Egerton's *adc*, to serve as a military adviser to Atkinson-Willes.[41] Reaching the Gallule River, the cruisers now joined the *Mohawk*, which had anchored off the roadstead on the morning of 20 April 1904. With a direct landing at Illig too treacherous, Atkinson-Willes elected to land some four miles away. Already on scene, the *Mohawk* showed its lights. If announcing the presence of a single ship, then Atkinson-Willes hoped that it would also mask the arrival of the *Hyacinth* and the *Fox*.

What followed offered a template for future practice. A covering force of 100 men departed the *Hyacinth* at dawn, reaching shore around 5 a.m. Led by Captain Horace Hood, a veteran of Keppel's Nile flotilla, they quickly moved inland to secure the dominating plateau. In a move reminiscent of Hewett in the Sudan and Seymour in China, Atkinson-Willes accompanied Egerton and the main force of 540 men in the follow-on landing. Thus, command of the flotilla devolved to the *Fox*'s Captain Frederick Pelham for a time. Indeed, with Hood and Commander Sidney Drury-Lowe of the *Hyacinth* and Commander Richard Phillimore of the *Mohawk* absent from their ships, one can imagine a very chagrined Pelham steamed offshore.[42]

Arriving in boats towed by the steam pinnaces of the flotilla, tows were slipped when approximately 30 yards from shore. In a running surf, the boats approached and anchored upon reaching a depth safe for disembarking. The pinnaces then collected their charges and returned to the cruisers offshore to begin the process anew. Additional boats were detailed for the collection of wounded or covered the landings with machine guns. Meanwhile, in conjunction with the landing of the covering force, the *Mohawk*'s boats offered a feint at a point where a known enemy post existed.

Marching roughly 4 miles to the village, a brief, sharp action against an enemy deployed behind stone zeribas followed. Supported by the 4.7-inch guns of the flotilla, the Dervishes soon retreated, allowing the main body to collect the weapons, stores, and animal skins left behind; the latter the medium of exchange for acquiring arms. Following a brief occupation, the village was torched, and the British retired to the sea from whence they came. Friendly casualties—all sustained by the naval contingent—amounted to twenty, with a lack of tactical acumen adjudged the chief cause. The action effectively marked the close of the fourth expedition directed against the "Mad Mullah."[43] Most troops soon departed Illig, but a party of fifty marines with four machine guns and Major Sydney Jackson's Hampshires remained as a garrison. At this point, Swayne returned to Somaliland to serve as consul general where he raised a troop from the local tribes and proceeded to irritate Egerton in the process.[44]

Collectively, these operations were dominated by factors of geography, climate, and political considerations. Of the last, the cost of conducting operations in a region where the economic and commercial prospects appeared poor proved a major constraint to commanders, if not always to planners.[45] Meanwhile, coordination with Abyssinia and Italy taxed operations externally while shifting tribal loyalties applied a similar constraint internally. Recognizing the controlling interests of the Foreign Office, a political officer of the Indian establishment, Captain Harry Cordeaux, ensured Egerton's operations worked in tandem with the administration of the protectorate.[46] Still, in the words of the 1907 *Official History*, "the campaign resolved itself into one of expediency, complicated by political considerations which placed no small difficulties in the way of the commanders by neutralizing their plans and preventing the campaign from being brought to a speedy and satisfactory conclusion."[47] It was a lesson others might have kept in mind.

Due to adverse conditions, the landings made at Obbia in January 1903 took over a month. Fortunately, immediate opposition by the enemy had not been among the barriers faced. Once ashore, further time was required before the advance could begin to arrange the camels, mules, and horses for additional service. In truth, animal transport represented an Achilles' heel in amphibious operations as they hindered rapid exploitation of the advantage gained. As operations progressed, transport issues prohibited the immediate return of the wounded to Berbera and Obbia. Securing the numbers and type of beasts required at the start of the campaign was the first obstacle to be overcome. The wastage of active service soon compounded matters. Thus, improvisation in supply and transport arrangements was endemic, leaving the *Official History* to conclude that equipping "a force with hastily improvised transport" was to incur grave risks.[48] With local intelligence cursory and the enemy retaining only irregular forces, the campaign waged in Somaliland was removed from any likely to be fought in Europe. The army was alive to this and trained accordingly. Thus, geography dictated strategy in a manner absent war against a first-class power where the defeat of the enemy's main force stood as the *sine qua non*. Where sources of fresh water were few, such an approach never sufficed. All this called for individual resourcefulness, initiative, and a significant degree of improvisation.[49] In all that followed, the legacy of this style of warfare is difficult to weigh. At a minimum, it fostered an ethos of getting on with the job, come what may, and doing the best possible with what was at hand.

Though the term was not employed then, operations in Somalia represented the application of the economy of force. The essential thing was to keep operations and, hence, costs within the bounds of reasonableness. As such, irregulars, paid a handsome wage by the standards of Somaliland, were infinitely cheaper than the employment of regular soldiers. Native bearers did not even receive that amount being paid in kind from the spoils of Hassan. Clearly, victory, if purchased at too dear a price, was to be avoided and represented a guiding principle in colonial campaigning; having spent roughly £2,300,000 in 1903–1904 in a failed attempt to eliminate Hassan, an equilibrium of sorts had been established.

As undersecretary for colonial affairs, Winston Churchill believed such a policy was foolish and inordinately risky. Instead, he argued for ceding the interior, building a wireless station to support communications with the outside world, and relying on reinforcement from Aden, India, and Britain. This would be infinitely cheaper and less risky than keeping weak, isolated garrisons at places having no intrinsic value.[50] This policy echoed Gladstone's Sudan policy, in which Britain was content to control the key points of ingress and egress anchored on the Red Sea. Moreover, it was a model infinitely adaptable to the needs of the West Indies and those dependencies found in the Pacific, where the cost of keeping penny-packet garrisons was deemed prohibitive. That model, too, proved insufficient and led Churchill to propose using naval airships acting in cooperation with ground troops to sanction Hassan in early 1914. A combined operation of a different sort, its application by Lieutenant Commander Frederick Boothby or anyone else, had years to await.[51]

Finally, operations in Somaliland did not require the establishment of a naval brigade and its attachment to the greater military force. The lack of rivers offers one explanation, though a military now equipped with crew-served weapons must be afforded the chief reason. Notwithstanding its absence, the services again demonstrated an ability to mount a joint operation against an inferior adversary. How successful amphibious operations might be against a more formidable adversary remained the great unknown. Events on the other side of the world suggested one answer.

Nine

The Russo-Japanese War, 1904–1905

It is not for us to ask for treaties; we grant them.[1]

Cranborne

Even in its day, the Russo-Japanese War was viewed as an object lesson to be studied.[2] Having its origins over control of Manchuria and Korea, the war's prominence owed something to the racial views prevailing where a rising Asiatic state had bested a European power. Clearly, to some contemporary professionals, that answer would not suffice, and no more than in Britain tied strategically to Japan now. Indeed, some feared Britain might be obliged to intervene. In the event, this failed to materialize, though preparatory measures had been initiated to ensure the safety of her interests in British India and China.[3] Here, the sizable forces still in South Africa were deemed the readiest and nearest at hand for reinforcing the subcontinent. To that end, the general officer commanding South Africa was ordered to prepare a force for movement, while the Admiralty determined the necessary shipping to move a force to India or Manchuria under convoy. The latter already held a British garrison, leading the Admiralty and War Office to consider whether augmentation could be accomplished more quickly through Atlantic Canada and thence by rail to a western port before sailing for China. A host of steps followed, including purchasing cold-weather clothing and pre-positioning supplies and fodder in South Africa while the Admiralty prepared the necessary measures to control merchant shipping. A further step saw the commander-in-chief, China screen German naval movements lest problems arise from that quarter.[4]

The rationale for these actions arose because a Russian attack against British interests could not be discounted. Demonstrating the alliance with Japan carried a dear price, other flashpoints remained. Thus, Russia might attempt to pass battleships of the Black Sea Fleet through the Dardanelles to strengthen its Far Eastern presence. If passage of these waters was governed by treaty, then the limits imposed remained a matter of interpretation. On his part, Balfour subscribed to the strictest of views, believing the eventuality would require severing relations with St. Petersburg. The question anticipated another to be faced 10 years hence when the neutrality of Belgium confronted another British prime minister. Moreover, with Russia aligned with France, the possibility of the latter becoming an enemy stood as the *Entente Cordiale* yet remained to be negotiated. Thus, a Mediterranean Fleet forced to engage the Russian Black Sea Fleet might also find itself dealing with a French squadron.[5]

A war employing the latest weaponry and seeing the greatest of military and naval actions was bound to garner British professional interest. Alignment with Japan, though, offered an unparalleled degree of access to all that unfolded. That access was never automatic and operated with decided limits.[6] Observers were attached to the principal higher military formations, but no foreign observers, including the British, served with the Japanese 4th Army. In this instance, the most that could be accomplished was to accept the inadequate Japanese reporting provided.[7] For Japan's three other armies, British lieutenant generals were attached to each numbered headquarters, and lesser officers were appointed to their associated infantry divisions and cavalry brigades. Hence, at least twenty British and imperial officers served with the Japanese Army.[8]

Conversely, five officers served with the Tsarist Army, including Captain Cresswell Eyres. The latter, a naval officer, was sent to St. Petersburg in April 1904 to observe the Russian fleet. At the invitation of General Kuroptakin, Eyres visited the front lines at Mukden (Shenyang) the following March, only to be captured by the Japanese.[9] Thus, numbers alone dictated that British accounting of Russian efforts would not be as fulsome as that from the other side of the hill. Mainly limited to corps-level observers, other limitations applied. To wit, General Sir Montagu Gerard died of pleuro-pneumonia and kidney failure at Irkutsk in July 1905 as he was proceeding home, while the Gurkha officer Major J. M. Home was invalided following the effects of battle in 1904. Otherwise, Captain Herbert Holman reached Manchuria only as the war approached its end.[10]

Four British naval officers and a Marine were attached to the Japanese fleet. The disparity in the numbers probably reflected nothing more than the concentrated nature of fleet operations compared to operations ashore. Certainly, the continued presence of Captain William Pakenham in Admiral Togo's flagship ensured that the direct observation of crucial naval events would not go unnoticed. He withstood the rigor of blockade duty before witnessing the action of the Tsushima Straits. That Pakenham enjoyed privileged access on a par afforded to Lieutenant General Sir Ian Hamilton may be inferred as Togo reported favorably on his conduct to the Japanese emperor.[11] That access was extended to Admiral Sir Gerald "Sharky" Noel, commanding the China Station, who wasted little time visiting Chinampo (Nampo) and Port Arthur (Lüshunkou) at the end of hostilities.[12]

Cresswell Eyres, however, remained the lone British observer to the Tsarist Fleet. Selborne, the first lord, responding to a parliamentary question, avowed he possessed extensive experience of Russia and was fluent in the language. Unfortunately, it has not been possible to verify these claims as his service record is silent on the matter; he certainly did not receive the allowances paid to an "official" interpreter.[13] No British naval officer was proficient in Japanese, though several served with the Japanese fleet. Nonetheless, the balance of British assessment in naval affairs remained biased toward Japan. Conversely, few attached British Army officers spoke Japanese. French, however, proved a useful common denominator save for Hamilton, who often conversed in German.[14] Otherwise, the Japanese provided interpreters with indifferent abilities. Over time, British access to Japanese military information grew, though preserving the secrecy of operations was deemed a "characteristic of Japanese military and naval procedure." So believed Captain Berkeley Vincent, and this view was confirmed by Hamilton, his reporting senior.[15] Here, establishing personal relationships became crucial, and to that end, Hamilton, watching affairs from 1st Army headquarters, touted his unique level of access.[16] In time, Japanese officers shared their plans and narratives and lectured British officers on the engagements fought. That was fortunate given the scale of operations and the few attachés present. British observers then appended adjoining commentary to these Japanese efforts—often through the lens of recent South African or Indian experience. Appropriate lessons were drawn, and, as such, the war confirmed or refuted orthodoxies enunciated in manuals such as *Combined Training*.[17] The war also seemingly confirmed the timeless verities derived from the Napoleonic era, the American Civil War, and the wars of German unification.[18] These would be categorized as principles for the British Army, but that awaited another day and another treatise: the *Field Service Regulations*.

Periodic summaries with annotated maps were forwarded to the War Office's Director of Military Operations and Army Headquarters Simla. Ever a problem was the tendency of observers to overidentify with their hosts. Only natural for those reporting on an ally, the bias also extended to those monitoring Russian forces.[19] Thus, the actual value of the reporting was not in the insight of the moment but in the collective and continuing analyses generated by officers coming from distinct combat arms based on their own professional experiences. Guided by a template of topics specified beforehand, these reports offered a standardized summary of the engagements fought. Unsurprisingly, most reports covered engagements solely occurring between opposing armies. Though joint operations featured, their prominence was most felt during the initial landings made in Korea and Manchuria, during the siege of Port Arthur, and in the serials removed from the main front.

Firsthand British reporting commenced in March 1904. Secondhand accounts of Japanese forces' initial transfer and landing had to suffice in the interval. Vincent provided the first British reports based on direct observation summarizing the landing of the Japanese Guards Division at Chinampo and then its subsequent advance to Ping-Yang (Pyongyang). His presence at the front was hastened by a fortuitous attachment to the Japanese Army for language instruction.[20] Otherwise, 2 months elapsed before Hamilton arrived in Korea.[21]

An early observation noted was the division of responsibility between Japanese naval and military authorities when executing a combined operation. Unlike British practice, it was more heavily weighted toward the military. When other than warships were employed, the Japanese Army selected the transports to be used, modified them as required, and then handled the embarkation and disembarkation of troops, animals, and equipment. The Imperial Japanese Navy, meanwhile, determined the points of loading and unloading, provided signalers for communications while at sea, and escorted the trooping convoy. Amenities and conditions were spartan in the ships, with space at a premium and conditions cramped for the rank and file. Nonetheless, as the passages were brief, few problems surfaced.[22] As such, direct comparison with British practice possessed decided limits, and the system's strength was not in the comfort and care afforded but in the clear delineation of responsibility.[23] Uniquely, most of the rail network in Manchuria remained under Russian control. Japanese forces were, therefore, sustained from the sea in a manner not unlike British custom. Here, the Japanese merchant fleet played a key role, with upwards of twenty hospital ships used to transfer the wounded from the theater of operations to permanent medical establishments at home. Employing a specialized unit without a British equal, it was the Imperial Japanese Army's responsibility to charter, modify, and man these hospital ships.[24]

British reporting of Russian operations suffered from a lack of observers, but more directly, because British officers were deemed suspect by St. Petersburg. This attitude is entirely understandable because of the growing formal relationship between London and Tokyo. Not always gaining access to Russian units, British observers resorted to obtaining intelligence from those attachés enjoying better facilities.[25] This information was supplemented with Russian reports and commentary where possible, and, as the doyen of foreign observers, Gerard secured courtesies and access outside the norm from General Kuropatkin. British reporting of Japanese forces overwhelmingly focused on operations, while its coverage of the other side of the hill focused on the technical and organizational. This included signals, transport, artillery, and the influence of weather on operations. British reporting on Russian Army operations did not address naval cooperation. Whether this reflected the bias of Indian Army officers who made up most of the agents reporting or reflected actual events on the ground cannot be determined. However, this writer leans to the former. Nevertheless, in the estimation of Gerard, one lesson stood out: "[I]t seems that days when Infantry was the Queen of Battles have now passed away, and that despite statistics and figures deduced from the percentage of wounds received, that artillery has now a preponderating influence on the battlefield."[26]

That the Imperial Japanese Navy was modeled on the Royal Navy and employed British-designed and constructed warships suggested an urgency for studying the Russo-Japanese War, if only to design and construct ships to a better standard. That the Imperial Japanese Army took the kaiser's army as its patron offered another vehicle for analysis.[27] Still, for a maritime power, the association of naval support with military operations had a particular resonance.[28] On paper, the Japanese Army was vastly inferior to Russia's. The margin was narrower at sea, but even here, Russia enjoyed superiority in local waters.[29] By seizing the initiative and executing a series of rapid amphibious operations, Japan trusted to negate the presumed superiority of the enemy. Russia understood the risk and dispersed its troops to protect vulnerable areas. Unfortunately, it could not be strong everywhere. Moreover, in ceding the initiative, Russia ceded much. Indeed, as early enemy efforts secured the

Korean peninsula and then witnessed the Japanese advance to the Manchurian border, one benefit to the initiative gained saw the Russians forestalled in directing efforts at Japan proper.

Though relations between Japan and Russia had been severed on 6 February 1904, the war had yet to start. All changed two days later when a nighttime torpedo attack by destroyers against the Russian fleet anchored off Port Arthur heralded what a royal proclamation had not. Surprise was complete. Indeed, the Russian admiral had been hosting a ball. The attack, though, failed to achieve the ends desired. On the morning of 9 February, Japanese heavy ships shelled the enemy fleet with indifferent results. That better results were not secured by Admiral Togo's ships owed everything to the gun batteries defending the anchorage as they kept the fleet from advancing closer. Successive bombardments by the Japanese fleet over the ensuing days failed to alter matters materially.[30]

From Sasebo, a Japanese brigade sailed in three transports, arriving off Chemulpo (Inchon) on 8 February. The 2,500 embarked troops acting as an advanced guard transferred to fifty-man sampans to land the following day. Void of immediate opposition, a first measure saw the seizing of the telegraph office to preclude the leakage of information.[31] Present within the harbor, though, was a Russian cruiser and a gunboat. Outmatched by the Japanese screening force, following a brief engagement, both scuttled. Most of the 20,000 follow-on troops came from the Japanese 12th Division, who then reached Seoul via rail.[32] Notably, the Japanese did not look to local sources of supply to sustain their foothold, being self-sufficient in all essentials, including lighters, launches, sappers, and workers.[33]

With the Russian Navy still a fleet in being, the Japanese landing contained a significant element of risk. Togo's answer was to mount a blocking operation at Port Arthur, thereby isolating the enemy fleet and allowing the build-up to proceed.[34] A successful fleet action, of course, would have achieved as much, but Vice Admiral Oskar Stark would not comply. The lesson was that an inferior force could defeat a superior through effective planning, preparation, and organization. Yet, the vital factor was the resolution to prevail once committed.[35] Thus, five merchant ships filled with coal dust and fitted with explosive charges were readied.

The theory was simple enough, but executing the stratagem proved more difficult. The effort of 23–24 February failed not for want of courage but owing to enemy fire, poor navigation, and obstructions. A subsequent bombardment, if inflicting damage on the besieged Russian vessels, proved otherwise inconclusive. When Russian shore batteries and ships gained the range of the attacking fleet, Togo was forced to disengage.[36] A second attempt ensued with the blocking ships now loaded with stones and concrete. On the evening of 26–27 March, the four merchantmen sallied forth. Again, the ruse proved only partially successful and for the same reasons.

Clearly, a greater blocking squadron was required if conclusive results were to be secured. In the meantime, Togo resorted to offensive mining to neutralize the Russian units both here and at Vladivostok.[37] The third attempt at blocking Port Arthur employed twelve *Marus* and formed a precursor to the landing of General Baron Oku's 2nd Army. Regrettably, a greater force only garnered a greater failure. Adverse weather was a factor, but the defenders' stout resistance must be accounted as the chief reason. Having witnessed two attempts already, surprise was a commodity in short supply when the Japanese tested Russian defenses anew on the night of 2–3 May 1904. Again, the courage of the Japanese seamen was never more resolute. Again, they proved unequal to the array of obstacles faced.[38]

Meanwhile, in Korea, the balance of the Japanese 1st Army under General Baron Kuroki continued to arrive through Chemulpo. By mid-March, an advance toward the Yalu River had begun. Thus far, the Japanese sustained their efforts through Chemulpo, yet acquiring a northern port became imperative for future campaigning. Eyeing Chinampo, presently ice-bound, the onset of warmer weather would allow for its use from mid-March.[39] By 1 May 1904, the First Army was positioned to cross the Yalu their advance having benefited from a series of anchorages along the Korean coast. This was no small benefit in a country where internal communications were poor. Still, as confirmed in Sudan, those on the march needed to lay a rail line to move supplies to areas not served by the sea.[40]

In Japan, unescorted transports were collected to support the dispatch of the 2nd Japanese Army to Chinampo, Korea. With local sea control established over the Yellow Sea, the Japanese Navy executed a series of feints near the mouth of the Yalu River to cover the main assault at Wiju (Uiju), Korea.[41] As for the 2nd Army, having reached Chinampo, it sailed anew for Manchuria. Again, access to the coast allowed these operations to be sustained. To that end, Togo employed the Yellow Sea's Elliot Islands (Changhai) as an advanced base.

On the morning of 5 May, in the face of no opposition, a 1,000-man naval landing party reached shore and established a covering position at Pi Tzu Wo, Manchuria. The troops of the 2nd Army quickly followed, but not their stores or field hospitals. Consequently, a period of consolidation followed before sustained operations began.[42] The presence of the Japanese 2nd Army threatened Port Arthur, but it did not support the efforts of the 1st Army and its advance from the Yalu. Until a junction of the two forces occurred, defeat in detail remained possible. Accordingly, a subsidiary landing made by Lieutenant General Baron Kawamura's 10th Division on 19 May at Ta-ku-Shan aimed to fill the breach and served as a spearhead for General Count Nodzu's 4th Army.[43] Following a diversionary feint, a naval landing party came ashore as a vanguard to the greater effort, and though Russian patrol craft had been encountered offshore, the landing met no resistance.[44]

While the beaches of Pi Tzu Wo afforded access, they offered little else as docks, derricks, and wharfage were absent. Following a greater action to secure Nan Shan (Jinzhou), Dalny (Dalian) was occupied without resistance on 30 May.[45] Further pressure from Nogi's Third Army over the next 3 months forced the Russians to yield their positions across the Liao-tung (Liaodong) peninsula, with the troops falling back upon Port Arthur. Both navies supported the seaward flanks of their respective armies during these operations, and, as had been true in South Africa, Japanese naval artillery consisting of 4.7-inch and 12-pounder guns were landed to provide fire support to the advance and investment.[46] Where matters differed from the veldt, the control of the sea remained contested. This was no better demonstrated than on 15 June 1904 when the Vladivostok Cruiser Squadron intercepted three Japanese ships ferrying troops. Two transports and 1,100 troops were lost in the ensuing engagement.[47]

Though the Japanese Navy had established an ascendancy, the risk of enemy mines demanded caution from its heavy ships. Meanwhile, the Japanese landward advance spelled danger to the Russian ships basking under the protection of Port Arthur's batteries. This moved these ships to accept a fleet action on 10 August lest they meet their demise while riding at anchor.[48] The Battle of the Yellow Sea proved tactically inconclusive as the Russian fleet returned to Port Arthur the next day. Strategically, this suited the Japanese as the enemy's squadrons remained divided between Port Arthur and Vladivostok, thus allowing Japanese sea control to remain intact.

Residing at the end of a peninsula, if Port Arthur was to be relieved, either the fleet contained within needed to assume a more offensive posture or the Russian Army had to deal the Japanese Army a decisive blow. Otherwise, time would eventually force the garrison's capitulation owing to a lack of supplies.[49] The Japanese 3rd Army suffered heavily and grievously in its advance, but the point remains: They advanced. Slowly, the redoubts ringing Port Arthur were reduced. From the sea, Japanese gunboats joined the cacophony of fire directed at the Russian positions.[50] Russian resistance was stout and gained many positions that had recently been lost. Unfortunately, local successes did not change the greater narrative, and while Japan's maritime interdiction of Port Arthur was never absolute, the defenders required more than the few supplies that entered. Ironically, the attacking force suffered even more from want with beriberi striking large numbers of Japanese other ranks. The contributing factor was a diet based on white rice and the absence of bread or meat.[51]

As Japanese forces sapped forward, siege artillery engaged Port Arthur, assisted by the commanding view, which was acquired at a high cost. One by one, Russian ships fell to the cannonade. In truth, by December 1904, their effectiveness had already been compromised. Nearly 4,000 ratings had been landed to assist in the defense of the bastion. With them came ammunition and over 140 guns from the ships' secondary armament. These measures owed everything to the poor landward defenses of Port Arthur. The demise of the fortress and the fleet it contained came the following month after a siege of 154 days, when over 24,000 Russian troops surrendered.[52]

The war continued, but the loss proved pivotal. With the Russian Second Pacific Squadron reaching Madagascar, some blockading Japanese ships returned to their dockyards for maintenance. Meanwhile, new landings occurred in northeastern Korea to rid the country of the remaining Russian forces.[53] As for the Russian squadron, it, too, had to address its own maintenance requirements after such a long voyage. To that end, Vladivostok beckoned, which, in turn, simplified Japanese naval strategy. It did not as yet simplify how the war was to be won. Being ice-bound in winter, Vladivostok was a less-than-ideal naval base, so the arriving Russian fleet faced a severe disadvantage.[54] Moreover, Japan's lines of communication were now inviolable from the sea. A war remained to be won, but the fulcrum of decision had shifted to the Japanese.

On its merits, the action fought at Mukden from 20 February to 10 March was not decisive save that the Russians had failed to alter the underlying

Japanese advantage. That benefit was accentuated by the defeat of the Second Pacific Squadron at the Tsushima Straits on 27–28 May 1905. The war, however, had never really been in doubt since the Battle of the Yellow Sea, which allowed the armies of Marshal Oyama to secure a series of victories culminating in Mukden. Togo's victory did, however, allow the subsidiary operation of seizing Sakhalin to be mounted in July. Again, a naval landing party facing no immediate opposition cleared the way with follow-on military forces consolidating the Japanese position. Over the next month, the island's mostly second-line troops were eliminated.[55] A minor operation, Sakhalin's seizure played an outsize role in the diplomatic negotiations underway. Japan demanded an indemnity; Russia demurred. Eventually, the wisdom of Solomon prevailed, with the peace agreement seeing the island partitioned.[56]

Japan supplanted Russia in Korea and Manchuria in a limited war fought for limited objectives. The cost, however, in blood and treasure had been high, which moved Japan to accede to terms. In retrospect, the greatest failure of Russia during the war was its failure to develop a credible threat against Japan proper. This need not be a large-scale invasion. Indeed, mining, naval bombardments, and raids were probably all that could be attempted. They would, however, have forced Japan to mind its homeland to the detriment of its greater aims. The absence of such a threat allowed the Japanese Navy to control the Yellow Sea and thence project a military force into Asia. In sum, Japan proper was uniquely vulnerable in a manner that European Russia was not. Why this never transpired may be explained by Russia's ill-preparedness for war, which was married to her failure in the higher direction of war, which saw naval and military activities as discrete events.[57]

As was true following the South African War, a British official history was prepared. Such a survey was not unique to Britain; Austria, Germany, and the United States did as much and confirmed that contemporaries believed the war possessed a particular saliency. The former army officer but now *Times* correspondent Charles à Court Repington,[58] however, went further. Drawing attention to the parallels between Great Britain and Japan, he argued for a single, national work to be written by a non-existent historical section of a still very new Committee of Imperial Defence.[59] That was a step removed from earlier practice where the services prepared histories separately. To that end, Colonel Wellscourt Waters, a credited observer to the Russian Army, was short-listed by Hugh Arnold-Forster to draft the War Office's accounting.[60]

Indeed, that officer's *Reports on the Campaign in Manchuria in 1904* had already appeared. Significantly, it had had little to say about combined operations.[61]

The Admiralty and the War Office continued to write separate histories. However, the historical section of the CID assumed responsibility for the general staff's treatment after the publication of its first volume.[62] The general staff recognized these efforts were premature insofar as Japan and Russia still had to release their official accounts. Nevertheless, they allowed the staff colleges to begin considering the problems the war exposed.[63] That they were premature is not to avow they were presumptuous: When the CID's *Official History* appeared, these earlier efforts were quoted verbatim and at length.[64]

The CID joint history possessed two strengths over those offered by the services. Firstly, they provided critical commentary on the events surveyed. This attribute was expressly lacking in the first monographs owing to the lack of substantive treatment then available by the belligerents. Secondly, written nearly a decade after the war and in the knowledge of powered flight, they could comment on facets not apparent to the first chroniclers. Those advantages, however, also meant that many of the lessons on offer would be eclipsed by the larger conflagration to come. Nonetheless, when the official history was published, it suffered several faults. Perhaps inevitable as a first foray in joint history, they never achieved the synthesis a consolidated telling promised as naval and military operations continued to be analyzed discreetly. A further drawback was that only the series' first two volumes had appeared before 1914. The third volume, though written before the war, was not published until 1920, owing to a delay in producing its maps while the First World War raged.[65] Meanwhile, for all the effort expended in describing the progression of the conflict, key operational enablers—command, control, and intelligence, for instance—were handled only in passing. Appropriate operational and tactical lessons received scant attention, including the mechanics of launching an amphibious landing and the role of economic warfare (blockade and contraband control). In short, the *Official History* offered a skewed accounting of the war. Japanese success appeared rather all too easy, if not even pre-ordained.[66]

Even in its treatment of strategy, the *Official History* can be faulted. The failure to stress the war's limited nature looms as its most significant shortcoming. Excepting the Baltic Fleet's (Second Pacific Squadron) misstep at the Dogger Bank, both protagonists limited combat operations to Korea, Manchuria, and the surrounding seas—the Japanese attack on Sakhalin proving a notable exception.⁶⁷ Discussion of why this occurred and, indeed, the larger political context of the war was avoided. Just as the navy and the army would have benefited from a history that probed beyond operations and tactics, the CID would have been better served by an accounting that remembered that war is a continuation of policy. Of course, that is seen clearly with hindsight and in the knowledge of the war yet to come. Those writing remained professionals, not prophets.

Still, as Hamilton's *A Staff Officer's Scrap-Book* demonstrates, these forays were not the sum total of discourse.⁶⁸ That work, if unofficial, was published by Edward Arnold, a house that served the India Office much as the Stationery Office supported the Imperial government.⁶⁹ In turn, George Aston, that most thoughtful of marines, penned his *Letters on Amphibious Warfare* while serving with the South African Defence Force. If an unofficial treatment, it, nevertheless, was used officially. *Letters on Amphibious Warfare* touted the advantages accruing to the power able to project military power ashore using the examples of Chile in 1891, the Sino-Japanese War of 1894–1895, the 1898 Spanish-American War, and, lastly, the Russo-Japanese War. As customary for a serving officer, the War Office vetted the manuscript before its publication. Drawing upon official and unofficial sources of information, Aston's work also benefited from his interview with Major Tanaka of the Japanese general staff.⁷⁰

As for the lessons distilled, the war, more than anything else, demonstrated the power of the offensive. A smaller army, though suffering greater casualties, dictated the pace of operations and secured its ends owing to the superb morale of its infantry supported by effective artillery fire. Still, local maritime superiority had been the essential precursor, allowing a field army to be landed and sustained in a theater lacking infrastructure. Indeed, the remoteness of Manchuria and Korea from European Russia contributed to Japan's maritime advantage. That the Japanese Army landed in one neutral nation (Korea) to attack a foreign army occupying a second (China) and functioned as the aggressor throughout were lessons perhaps best left for other general staffs to ponder. Japan, though, had demonstrated thoroughness in staff procedure even if the details of how Japanese staff managed things escaped the eyes of British observers. The results, however, spoke for themselves.⁷¹ Throughout, Japan had played for high stakes and won. For many, that alone proved to be the most significant lesson on offer.

Of relevance to this study, the war confirmed that ammunition expenditure had been immense, and so too the casualties arising. Further, the vulnerability of heavy ships to mining during inshore operations was shown to be all too real. Thus, a weaker power might refuse battle and rely instead on area denial weapons to protect its coast. Admittedly, minor ships were no less vulnerable, but their value did not equal that of heavy ships, which backstopped the effectiveness of all other types. Additionally, naval artillery, even when outranging its shore counterpart, inflicted appreciable damage to the latter only by happenstance. Effective at hitting buildings and outworks, destroying a gun emplacement was altogether another matter. The Russo-Japanese War testified to the limits of heavy ships when facing a fleet that would not sail. Subjugating Port Arthur and the fleet therein required not only command of the sea but control of the surrounding territory as well. Tellingly, an amphibious operation had been executed while command of the seas had yet to be gained. Indeed, such an operation had acted as the precursor to the fleet action eventually fought. The combined operation carried out need not be an opposed landing with the norm to avoid that trap if possible. This allowed troops, animals, and stores to be landed and then raised to the numbers required for the ensuing campaign. It also negated having to remove those wounded in the initial effort. Finally, a succession of different landings was recommended lest a single descent be met by a concentrated response.

How far affairs in East Asia represented what would occur in the future could not be known. Rare had it been for Great Britain to wage war absent allies; rarer still to employ an army of the size demanded in Manchuria. Coalition warfare inherently imposed compromises in policy and strategy among co-belligerents in a manner alien to Japan or Russia in the present conflict. Strategically, contemporaries saw the war as a watershed moment, even if the implications remained nebulous. More definitive were the tactical and operational lessons presented. Yet, would British officers be as bold as their Japanese counterparts? Manifestly, they were not likely to be as cautious as their Russian opposites. What lessons were drawn from the Russo-Japanese War and the campaigns recounted are now ripe for assessment.

Ten

Assessment

What seest thou else
In the dark backward and abysm of time?

Shakespeare, *The Tempest*

The operations surveyed are instructive for the light they shed on Britain's higher direction of war no less than in her amphibious operations practice. Collectively, if demonstrating the two services functioning well together at the tactical and operational levels, then the results secured owed as much to goodwill as to good planning. Always abetted by a dose of good luck, the element of time often proved key. Kitchener's success in Sudan from 1896 owed everything to method unconstrained by time. Conversely, the repeated setbacks experienced in South Africa in 1899 may be summed up in the adage a day late and a dollar short, where deficiencies abounded and with improvisation a hallmark. Heralding Kitchener as a past master in the art, Lieutenant General Ian Hamilton also believed improvisation in South Africa had been "a great source of weakness."[1] From the perspective of China, Edward Seymour might well agree, and so, too, a no-less-chastened Wolseley in 1885.

Operationally, no deficiency was felt more keenly than the want of transport. Notwithstanding the use of larger ocean-going vessels allowing whole units to be moved, any landing represented but the first step to a more significant effort.[2] Before the advent of the internal combustion engine, exploitation by the landed force rested on rivers, canals, railways, and largely unimproved roads. Their absence acted against the speed required by the limited numbers initially employed in a landing to secure first aims. Even when British forces landed in areas under their control, such as in Natal, the infrastructure might not be equal to the requirement. Moreover, even if adequate roads existed, an expedition's animals required a recovery period following their voyage. Unsurprisingly, a desired enabler was to secure a nearby railhead to support the follow-on operations contemplated. This step had featured in Egypt, and its absence in Sudan was a strong reason why operations failed when attempting to reach General Gordon. Again, Admiral Seymour sought to exploit the railway in China, and so too, Japan following upon its landings at Chemulpo. This begs the question of whether contemporaries thought beyond the needs of an initial landing and considered the manner of exploitation. Leaving a considered reply to a subsequent discussion, Wolseley was one officer who certainly appreciated the problem, though not always to a successful conclusion. Contemporaries recognized the importance of railways in the abstract, though not always tying it to the requirements of amphibious landings. In the wake of South Africa, Lieutenant Colonel Sir Percy Girouard believed the War Office required a standing railway capability if only to effect better military planning.[3] The need, though, remained more than an ability to plan.

The operations conducted in Sudan, Burma, and China relied on improvised transport in a manner absent from Egypt, South Africa, and Somaliland. Indeed, riverine operations represented the epitome of improvisation, for while horses, camels, and oxen were amenable to ready purchase, the specialized boats to support the unique needs of an expedition were not so easily procured. In truth, riverine operations and the operational seam exposed were the Scylla and Charybdis of joint operations.

With time, the critical factor, the most fundamental problem, remained to secure a decision that action of a kind was required. Here, the health of Gladstone became an ever-present factor from the winter of 1883 onwards, albeit never a controlling one. So also, the schedule of parliament and cabinets, which ran to a cycle, divorced from outside events.[4] Of course, the initiative of ministers remained, but even the boldest of these still required the sanction of parliament to spend funds. Had a more robust structure of governmental control existed, then the element of time might not have weighed quite so heavily. However, the seasonal prorogues of parliament meant some actions failed to receive timely scrutiny as members scattered to constituencies, the continent, or their courtesans. This was true in January 1882, when the dual note was issued to Egypt. It featured again in January 1884 when Gordon departed for Egypt and, thence, to Sudan.[5]

A close corollary to the above remained that the ultimate aims of British policy were rarely defined. Thus, officials fashioned responses without an evident appreciation of what would ensue. The arrival of warships off Alexandria in

May 1882 may have been prudent, but it occurred within a greater context. For the British Mediterranean Squadron and the Ottoman Empire, that context included the recent killing of Commander William Selby of the composite gun-vessel *Falcon* by Albanian shepherds while hunting ashore at Artaki the previous February. Subsequently, Ottoman authorities arrested Commander Harry Grenfell, the captain of the *Cockatrice*, for assault.[6] For Egyptians, it was the recent French occupation of Tunisia. As the revolt possessed an intense nationalist ardor, the presence of foreign warships stirred local passions even more, with rioting soon the result. The bombardment of Alexandria by the British—and not the French, who had been playing the stronger bat up to then—exemplified a tendency to think for the moment.[7] By any calculation, the act was premature, with General Alison and his forces still in Cyprus and forming no part of the military plan as then drafted.[8]

Necessarily, actions subject to parliamentary scrutiny tend to induce delay; no bad thing if a peril is avoided. The risk becomes if time—a factor ever so crucial in military affairs—is lost. Admittedly, democracy offers its perils as competing priorities and agendas operate. The standing presence of capable on-scene forces might mitigate matters, but only to a point. Having forces at hand might have only bought additional time for debate and not necessarily led to a speedier conclusion. Brackenbury, for one, lamented the delays occurring in London that kept those in Sudan from reaching Gordon promptly. Arriving late in the season, they found the Nile more challenging to navigate.[9] Without denigrating the efforts of Butler and his whalers, the calculation that a Nile advance was not practicable above the Third Cataract had been proven essentially correct. Certainly, not in the time permitted.

The dispatch of Gordon occurred after the demise of Hicks and Moncrieff but before that of Baker. Those setbacks demonstrating the limits of British officership over another's armies might have prompted a degree of soul-searching in Cairo and London. They did not. This suggests these failures were deemed as owing as much to the quality of those leading as those being led. Moreover, it remained that others, such as Admiral Hewett and Major Hunter, were largely successful in their concurrent missions to reduce Egyptian liabilities.[10] Of course, distance and indifferent communications did not abet understanding, and the range of problems faced by those in England was always greater than that of Egypt and Sudan. If Gladstone and company can be faulted for willing the ends but not willing the means—at least in a prompt manner—then a measure of understanding must be allowed for their announced policy was one of imperial restraint. Hartington and Wolseley knew this, and inherent in their repeated advocacy of actions against the tenor of that policy was that only limited and belated measures would ensue as Gladstone fought to hold his cabinet together.

A complaint previously voiced was that naval and military commanders in joint operations were frequently at odds with each other. The sympathy and cooperation exhibited between Seymour and Wolseley in 1882 proved sufficient and workmanlike, but it was hindered by formality. This stemmed partly from personality differences, but mainly, it represented the gulf in ethos separating the services. Notwithstanding his experience of the navy, Wolseley chaffed at the support rendered. Excepting Hewett and Beresford, Wolseley viewed the fleet as an appendage of the army and held the Admiralty and naval officers in a negative light. Ever more was this displayed in 1884.[11] While the relief of Khartoum was a more difficult proposition than the defeat of Urabi, Wolseley's view possessed a certain merit. To wit, the War Office sought the appointment of a marine to Wolseley's staff for liaison purposes, much as Rawson had handled coordination with the fleet following the attack on Alexandria. Originally vetoing the request, Northbrook finally yielded, though insisting a junior officer fill the role.[12] The not-too-subtle message offered was that the Admiralty feared a more senior one might prove too independent and too knowledgeable and compromise the prerogatives of Admiral Lord John Hay, the commander-in-chief, now operating in the shoes of the departed and ennobled Seymour.[13]

Closer though were the ties of Graham and Hewett with the former fulsome in his praise of an admiral who accompanied the 1884 expedition for a portion of its march. Clearly, Hewett proved one officer adept at working with his military brethren. Meanwhile, Graham employed the same officer as his naval *adc* in his campaigns of 1884 and 1885. Lieutenant Claud Lindsay had distinguished himself during the landings at Suez in August 1882, and his solo reconnaissance ahead of the naval landing earned the praise of Hewett. Seen as intelligent, efficient, and resourceful, Hewett touted Lindsay's merits to Graham, and by all accounts, Graham concurred; he specifically requested Lindsay during his final campaign.[14]

As the general officer commanding, Wolseley had broad scope in selecting officers. With many sharing the experience of previous campaigns and not a few possessing ties of marriage and birth, these links produced a cadre of intimate, if not always collegial, associates. Meanwhile, the presence of others merely reflected Wolseley's currying political favor.[15] This might include Beresford, an intimate of the prince of Wales, yet other evidence testifies to his holding a positive view of that officer. Still, differences remained. Lieutenant General Sir Edward Hamley, commanding the 2nd Division, did not see eye-to-eye with Wolseley on the outlines of the 1882 campaign. The root causes were Hamley's personality, seniority, and relegation to a supporting role when forced to trail a false coat in front of Aboukir. Seen as Britain's leading expositor on military affairs, Hamley probably held himself superior to Wolseley in the ways of strategy.[16] While commandant of the staff college, Hamley brooked no opposition to his views, a trait not unknown in Wolseley. Their dispute anticipated the Fisher-Beresford feud of the next century, both illustrating the proportions *amour propre* could assume in disputes. Tellingly, Hamley did not feature in Wolseley's final campaign.[17]

Conversely, Wolseley lamented the presence of Herbert Macpherson commanding the Indian contingent. Here, the sin was his inferior rank. A substantive colonel and local major general, his relative inferiority in an expedition where general officers appeared penny a pack made Macpherson a problem of a different sort: How to employ an officer and a force residing beyond the direct remit of Horse Guards without infringing the sensibilities of more senior British Army officers. Counting him a friend of longstanding and one of the ablest present, Wolseley nevertheless wished "the Indian Government had consulted the War Office before they had made these military arrangements, which place me in a difficult and disagreeable position."[18] Wolseley's lament is one a future commander would come to appreciate. Thus, employing an imperial force alongside a British one brought its own set of challenges. A situation mirrored when marines were employed ashore in conjunction with the army. Both instances would foster change in the years ahead to ensure interoperability.[19]

Whatever Wolseley's subsequent failings, the 1882 campaign showed British arms at their operational best. Infantry battalions and artillery batteries were loaded with all their equipment in single transports. Owing to the numerous horses involved, cavalry regiments were necessarily divided across two ships, but the system proved otherwise sound with flats and horse boats accompanying the troopers. The synchronization of the commercial armada from seven different ports owed everything to prior planning married to the performance of modern telegraphy. Prior reconnaissance had been thorough, and engineering support was expansive, including the provision of locomotives and rolling stock from home. Moreover, coordination with the navy was superb. Even the absence of the French proved a blessing as the operational seam removed paid handsome tactical dividends notwithstanding the political problems exposed.[20]

Events in Sudan offered an altogether different story in 1884. Here, the absence of Evelyn Baring in England between April and September did not abet matters. Telegraphic communications proved spasmodic and recourse to messenger equally so. Wolseley's appointment demanded an officer possessing judgment, tact, and the trust of civil authorities. If those qualities were rarely evidenced, the fault was not his alone. The problem exposed not an operational seam between the two services but something more severe: a chasm governing the overarching object of the enterprise between the political authority and the military. This strategic failure was so fundamental to all else that it raises a counterfactual rarely considered: What would have followed if General Wilson had found a very much alive Gordon? The answer, of course, is impossible to know, but it is by no means certain that a greater crisis would not have arisen.

A further point worth underscoring is that the several operations surveyed were executed against foes of the second, if not third rank, in military proficiency. Risks could be taken simply because the operational capabilities of the enemy were so constrained. All were anchored on maritime dominance, whether exercised by Britain alone or in association with allies, as proved in China. That dominance then sustained the ground operations ensuing, as resources were drawn from Britain, India, and now, the broader empire. Only such benign environments allowed for denuding the Mediterranean Station and the East Indies Squadron as naval forces were concentrated to support operations ashore. Nonetheless, the successes realized in each of these efforts often obscured the underlying risk or ignored the benign European diplomatic climate that allowed the operations to proceed.[21]

In the wake of Alexandria's bombardment stood Alison, Wolseley, and the greater expedition. With the War Office and India earmarking the forces to be deployed, the Admiralty and the Bombay government gauged the number and type of civilian vessels required to move the forces deployed from England and India.[22] Some of these were readily available, as Britain routinely conveyed military units from the home establishment to distant imperial holdings. Now, it was a question of retasking the appropriate ships. Where immediate resources were lacking, the difference was made good by charter. Ships were modified to meet unique military requirements in berthing arrangements and allow for transporting horses, mules, and munitions. These modifications did not render the vessels assault ships in the modern sense of the meaning, but they did make them something more than the generic transports they had been. In all, nearly seventy ships were employed to move the forces sailing from England and Ireland to Egypt in 1882.

To this end, military landing officers and naval transport officers coordinated the loading and unloading of the 40,000 troops deployed.[23] When the cabinet sanctioned the dispatch of a force from Britain in July 1882, the Admiralty immediately appointed the requisite transport officers, with all coming under the authority of Captain Harry Rawson.[24] They, in turn, embarked in the *Thalia*, an armed troopship, but now, for all practical purposes, a tender dedicated to supporting Wolseley's follow-on landings. As such, she carried the specialist workers, materials, and equipment to repair the piers and rail lines to sustain operations.[25] With the military force embarked in either Admiralty troopships or ships taken up from trade, small craft, whether accompanying the force leaving England or acquired elsewhere in the Mediterranean, served as lighters for transferring men, animals, and stores to shore once Egypt was made. Always a problem in such evolutions was the proper stowing of stores, such that the last loaded before departure represented the first needed on the receiving end. Not for the last time had the issue been manifest. Nonetheless, Goodrich believed the July landings stood as a model of execution, with the two services understanding their unique roles.[26] The opposition then had been cursory, and how all would have fared in the face of stiffer resistance, Goodrich did not venture to weigh.

In its essentials, the preceding template worked well for the next 30 years and changed only when the tactical situation became more problematic. Even then, the above did not disappear; newer appliances and methods merely augmented it. In 1882, the military drew its initial supplies from Britain and India but looked to Egypt to meet its longer-term needs. A key exception was the fodder for animals, which continued to be supplied by England.[27] In 1884, British logistics benefited from Thomas Cook and Son's existing operations on the Nile. If chartered tourism was their proper *métier*, their availability offered capacity and local familiarity—at a price. Though using a commercial company presented a unique set of management problems, there can be little doubt that those problems were more manageable than if an inshore logistics force had to be created from scratch, as the experience of the Nile whalers demonstrated.[28] Finally, rotating personnel between home and abroad developed a vital side benefit: that accomplished in peacetime remained only to be exploited in war.

Together and before 1882, the services together had established the tonnage required to move a force of a given size over a set distance. With ships previously identified by the Admiralty's director of transport, all that remained was to inspect, contract for their use, and complete any necessary fittings before their loading and sailing. Administratively, the key billet for moving a force by sea was the principal naval transport officer, assisted by any number of naval transport officers with beach masters and assistant beach masters, who rounded out the naval personnel contributing to an amphibious movement.[29] Meanwhile, the size of any naval brigade was determined by the quantity and type of ships on hand, but whatever its scale, the personal weapons employed were of a standard kind across the several fleets. Following the campaign to relieve Gordon, the War Office sought to define a standard type of naval brigade to make future planning more predictable. To that end, Colonel Richard Harrison, RE, a veteran of the 1882 and 1884 campaigns, and Commander Tynte Hammil prepared a recommended table of organization and equipment for a naval unit supporting a military force's communication lines. Warming to their task, the hallmark of their proposal was its flexibility to support a greater requirement than the 100 miles of support initially posited by the War Office.[30]

Manifestly, some were attempting to learn from recent experience, yet limitations remained. Drawn from the fleet and not a dedicated establishment, the tactical performance of a naval brigade often failed to match that of a corresponding military unit for shipboard routine told against the fitness of the sailors when having to march at length. General Graham, if generally laudatory of the naval brigade supporting his operations from Suakin, testified that the pace of advance suffered owing to the toll the marches had exacted on the bluejackets.[31]

Though India had sent forces to China in 1860, their deployment to the Mediterranean in 1878, when war with Russia threatened, had occurred in a climate of controversy. One fear, if only imagined, held that any government willing to employ Indian troops outside of Asia or Africa might employ such means at home at a later date against Britons. Meanwhile, others argued that a Christian nation should not deign to use Islamic soldiers against Christian Russia.[32] Such niceties overlooked that Britain, as a maritime power, retained limited military means in any crisis. Thus, implicitly, the development of colonial armies needed to mirror the development of the British Army if interoperability was to ensue and logistics were not to break down. In 1882, an Indian contingent composed of long-service regulars had been equal to the task. In 1885, a willing but ill-trained New South Wales formation remained untested in the briefest of campaigns.[33] Such might not always be so. With the conditions and terms of service present throughout the many forces of the crown far from congruent, the way ahead promised to be fraught with difficulties. Significantly, Wolseley expressly selected graduates of the staff college or those displaying marked ability in earlier campaigns for service on his staff when on active service.[34] Absent a standing expeditionary force with a corresponding staff, the practice possessed an advantage perhaps not always appreciated by his critics.

As the navy lacked a staff college and would not establish one for another 30 years, Seymour lacked a cadre of similarly trained officers. Indeed, the very idea of a staff to support an admiral was alien to the ethos and style of command exercised within the Royal Navy. This orthodoxy can easily appear as hidebound conservatism, yet it reflected that naval warfare was of a substance unlike that waged between armies. At sea, lines of communication did not need to be controlled, nor was there a need for extensive written orders, save for the execution of an amphibious landing. Indeed, focused on the imperatives of fleet action, the last exception escaped the ken of most naval officers of the period. Having staff officers, however, was but part of the equation for departmental organization mattered, too. In this regard, the Admiralty's position vis-à-vis the War Office stood on firmer ground with Brett, for one, doubting the latter's efficacy. Here, the worry remained that affairs were being optimized for peacetime administration rather than fitting the demands of war. To wit, many holding positions of authority would yield their desks to fill command and staff positions in any expedition, leaving behind unprepared civilians and second-rate officers to manage. Time would demonstrate this central truth.[35] Accordingly, more than the abolition of purchase, establishing the staff college was probably the most critical measure adopted in professionalizing the army.

Complicating these operations had been the store of topographical intelligence, which remained extremely limited, if not wrong. This was not a new problem. It had featured during the Russian War and led to the creation of a topographical and statistical department within the War Office.[36] Still, with the source of the Nile only discovered in 1858 and much of the Sudanese interior remaining unexplored, maps, at best, approximated geographical reality. This alone made river advances difficult. As an example of where matters stood, Lieutenant Edward Montagu-Stuart-Wortley carried three separate charts that placed features in opposition to each other in 1884.[37] Where finding fresh water represented the difference between life and death, every trek became a risk, whether calculated or otherwise. When the Foreign Office nominated Walter Miéville as a consular officer in 1882, they recommended he contact the Royal Geographical Society to ascertain the best times for traveling to his post. That agency pleaded ignorance, advising that the available literature was unreliable. Better for him to interview those in London who had experience of the region. This, Miéville did. Concluding that the heat of summer and overall lack of water argued against departing Suakin in March, Miéville waited until autumn before journeying. Significantly, this was Wolseley's concern in 1884, who similarly lamented the quality of intelligence available.[38] That said, Majors Henry Colvile and Alfred Turner drafted detailed topographical reports on Sudan while attached to Wolseley's staff that were still being referenced 2 decades later.[39]

Improvisation featured in all that was accomplished. Following the landings at Alexandria, Captain William Tucker, RMA, mounted a captured Krupp gun on a railcar and "did great execution among the enemy" at Kassassin. Captains Wilson and Fisher of the navy did much the same with machine guns and then did one better by mounting a heavy gun.[40] That two senior officers were absent from their ships speaks to the permissive maritime environment present. Only such a condition permitted the display of initiative by senior naval officers in joint operations. Be it Seymour and Hoskins at Tel-el-Kebir, Beresford on the Nile, Woodward on the Irrawaddy, or Seymour again at Tientsin, senior officers routinely vacated their commands to support operations ashore.[41]

Certainly, one area where the support of the fleet featured time and again was in the provision of crew-served weapons. This was true in 1882 at Alexandria and Tel-el-Mahuta and remained the case during Sudan and Burma operations. They feature again in South Africa and China, though they were absent in those operations directed against the "Mad Mullah." In the case of the last, the rearming of the army must be afforded the chief reason. The British advantage in these operations did not always come from superior technology. Against the Mahdi, the British faced Krupp guns deemed more equal to their own. Thus, superior training and fire discipline frequently proved the difference. Conversely, units hastily co-opted together and operating on unfamiliar ground risked defeat if cohesion collapsed. Here, Graham singled out the Black Watch as one unit fighting with more *élan* than effectiveness.[42]

Contemporaries viewed the bombardment of Alexandria as a signature occurrence, as instances of a fleet attacking fixed defenses were rare. This was the view of Goodrich, and it was one George Clarke later came to appreciate, too. For the former, the most apparent lesson was the advantage fortifications enjoyed when situated above the area being defended, as this made observing the fall of shot by the attacking squadron extremely difficult and told against the flat trajectory of naval fires. A close second was the almost infinite ability of defensive works to be strengthened and prepared to a standard whereby they could withstand the largest of naval rifles firing whatever manner of projectile and fuse. Designed to engage other warships, the ironclads of the 1880s worked against type when attacking positions ashore. Goodrich's answer was to build a hybrid warship able to meet both tasks or employ ships purposely designed to engage fortifications. Ideally, these vessels would be armed with guns possessing the characteristics of howitzers and mortars with their high trajectories. Notwithstanding the weapon employed, the use of protected vessels paid dividends, as the ability to accept a degree of punishment was a *sine qua non*.[43]

Coming from a knowledgeable, independent witness (albeit one retaining sympathetic views), Goodrich's observations are of value as they anticipated many problems that would confront the Royal Navy in the years ahead. His conclusions were not infallible, but they were reasoned. Thus, he argued that ships should approach within the limits of prudence and anchor rather than fire while steaming. His ultimate remark, though, minced no niceties: *"vessels are not yet and never will be able to fight on even terms with forts."*[44] Goodrich faulted the lack of troops on hand to deal with the consequences of the bombardment, for from that failure stemmed the looting, violence, and destruction subsequently arising. Allowing that foreknowledge of what transpired could not be expected, officers needed to absorb the lesson for the sake of future actions.[45]

Though intended for an internal audience, Goodrich's report quickly became public, with Vice Admiral Philip Colomb quoting from it in his *Essays on Naval Defence*.⁴⁶ Of course, the Admiralty, too, attempted to cull lessons from the recent intervention. Thus, ships participating in the action forwarded their assessments of what worked and what remained to be corrected. Unsurprisingly, the quantity and type of ammunition available proved a common criticism. Two, though, went further and penned a joint report which concluded:

> [T]he appearance of all the batteries justifies the statement that our fire was accurate, but, at the same time, accurate as it was, the batteries appear to have been silenced more because the men were driven from their guns than because the guns were actually disabled or the earthworks demolished.⁴⁷

Goodrich viewed Britain's ability to project military force to a distant shore as a powerful weapon made even more potent by steam engineering. No longer were expeditions at the mercy of fickle winds and unkind currents. Rather, a nation's entire seaboard stood at risk, rendering the defense against seaward assaults the harder still.⁴⁸

Alas, Goodrich proved too optimistic for the counters to be faced would not stand idle. Bringing a force to the proximate scene of battle was not the same as getting it ashore, and the last mile, represented by the transfer from ship to boat, would prove the crux of the problem. Currents, sea state, winds, and gradients remained as significant obstacles. At Suakin in February 1885 and, owing to a lack of berthing facilities, camels transported from India were dropped over the side and expected to swim to shore. Only a becalmed ocean and the absence of immediate opposition permitted such methods.⁴⁹

Necessarily, British operational capability worked within a broader strategic context. The campaigns surveyed were feasible propositions, but the limited size of Britain's military forces required judgment on the part of statesmen on their execution. When it appeared war with Russia might arise in 1885, obligations were quickly discarded. A lesson drawn was having acquired a significant portion of Asia, and in the process of claiming more, Britain needed a military of greater proportions, for not all defense issues were answerable by maritime dominance.⁵⁰ Not for the last time, these operations demonstrated that beginning a campaign—even seemingly a victorious one—was no guarantee of ultimate success. That waged in upper Burma suggested an India capable of waging a joint campaign with only minimal oversight from London. Yet, the success achieved took longer than anticipated, notwithstanding securing the immediate object. Meanwhile, those waged in North Africa upset the region's political status quo. Great Britain was not free to disengage without sacrificing that which prompted her interventions in the first instance: the safety of the Suez Canal and the solvency of Egypt. A calm of sorts had been restored, but not sound finance, with the situation now worse owing to the claims arising by others for the losses incurred at Alexandria. Britain's political, financial, and military involvement only deepened when further military disasters ensued. That commitment came with steep political and strategic costs, for the price of making good Egypt was to acquiesce to French and Italian actions elsewhere. This only created more significant turmoil at the expense of the Ottoman Empire. More troubling, Britain's occupation of Egypt threatened her maritime orientation by turning her into a "Continental State," or so held Sir William Harcourt, the home secretary, in November 1884.[51] The truth of Harcourt's claim would be tested not in quiet English fields but in other realms not always painted red on the map. In the interim, the services aimed to capture the lessons of recent experience, and attention is now turned to this aspect of the story.

Eleven

Joint Operations and the Educational Response, 1882–1914

> [I]t may be said without exaggeration, that, on a large scale, there can be no British war strategy that is either purely naval, or purely military, it must always be 'amphibious' in the sense that it must consider the armies and fleets of both sides.[1]
>
> George Aston, 1914

From the sixteenth century, one truism dominated British military thinking. To wit, the army need not weigh fighting at home. After the loss of its Norman holdings, geography made this possible. Strategy and empire, however, made it essential. This points to the vital importance of the maritime equation in every British strategic problem. As an industrial stalwart dependent on imported raw materials and lacking in domestic foodstuffs, the defeat of the Royal Navy would spell calamity of the highest order. Secure at sea, no enemy dare come. Absent that command, not even the greatest of armies under a modern Marlborough could forestall the ensuing starvation and ruination. The validity of this centuries-old assumption would be challenged in the years before the First World War, yet from that proposition followed one incontrovertible truth: Strategically, the British way of warfare was inherently maritime.

Operationally, this need not be as the routine of mounting operations along the Indian frontier demonstrated. Still, India might be counted as the exception, only proving the rule. Capturing the point, the War Office noted in 1909:

> It has often been truly said that a navy alone cannot bring a war to a successful termination, and never has done so in the history of the world. The only possible exception to this might be in our own case, if a foreign navy held supremacy at sea....

No other country with which we may be at war depends for its existence on sea-power, and the mere destruction of their fleets can only be the preliminary step to enforcing their submission. It is for this reason that combined naval and military operations are certain to be undertaken in our next war.[2]

Admittedly, others, including France, Japan, and the United States, might conduct amphibious operations. Still, Britain, by virtue of its wealth, industry, shipping, and geography, was unique in what it could attempt and to what it could aspire. Simply put, amphibious operations retained a saliency in British warfare largely unknown by others.

A staff college built upon a reformed senior division of the officer training establishment at Sandhurst dated from 1858.[3] Chartered to develop officers in staff duties and the art of command, to some, the very name evoked a misnomer.[4] Entrance required passing a series of examinations or securing a nomination for the 2-year course. During the period under review, quotas limited the number of officers from the separate corps and line battalions so that aspirants competed within a pool of similar candidates. As artillerists and engineers matriculated to Woolwich based on the superiority of earlier examination results, the previous testifies only a limited form of meritocracy existed. This was considered essential lest the staff be dominated by a single arm and, with it, a single point of view. The restriction on officers attending from the same regiment reduced a burden on the parent formation but operated against the Royal Marines in an untoward manner, given its size.

For those desiring the fullest of careers, attendance at staff college was thought a must in the years preceding the First World War. So believed Captain William Marshall, who would not attend Camberley, however, owing to the onset of war in South Africa. Rising to general officer rank, Marshall's lack of staff experience would continue to cloud an otherwise excellent record.[5] Another holding attendance essential was Arthur Nicolson of the Foreign Office. Possessing only mediocre academic credentials himself, including time in the *Britannia*, he nonetheless appreciated why his son Frederick sought to leave Lord Hardinge and India for Camberley.[6] Yet, the British Army knew of its priorities for the officer experienced in campaigning secured promotion and preferment over those who had not.[7] So marked was this quality that officers on leave, such as Horace Smith-Dorrien, regularly volunteered for active service while commanders invariably searched elsewhere for suitable able hands, including the staff college.[8]

Until the Boer War, the army was never so much educated as trained. Trained to a high standard, to be sure, but the emphasis remained fixed on rote learning with higher mathematics, chemistry, musketry, field craft, riding, and ballistics at the fore. Wolseley deprecated its current lines, and only when the institution started examining war's broader lines (i.e., strategy) and elucidating its underlying principles did matters begin to fit officers for future duties. Training now migrated into the realm of education with a Rubicon crossed. Field Marshal Sir William Robertson believed these principles fostered a common viewpoint among officers and made everything that followed much easier.[9] That may be crediting too much for even a well-read officer such as Charles Townshend, who lacked the motif of passed staff college or *psc*, accepted that principles governed military affairs.[10]

It remained that officers, having once secured the *psc*, were expected to return periodically to regimental duties. At one level, this allowed another to fill a vacancy in the leaving officer's wake and tied the general staff—established in 1906—to the greater service. Yet, some viewed the custom as a *bête noire*, for it returned officers at the hub of affairs to mundane duties.[11] Meanwhile, others believed it made it much harder to develop true specialists in the higher direction of war. So held Esher, who lamented, "There is not one man on the Army Council, and very few among the Directors of the W.[ar] O.[ffice], who have ever attempted to think about the work they have now to do before they were appointed to their present duties."[12] Accordingly, the staff college could never be a panacea while manning policies continued as before. In sum, the system was imperfect, as any directed toward a practical end must invariably be.

Attending staff college required an officer to pass an entrance examination or secure a nomination. As a rule, few officers passed these examinations outright, and, indeed, according to one source, few cavalry officers would have entered Camberley otherwise.[13] In 1908, only 20 percent of aspirants managed to pass. More often, an officer doing sufficiently well in his papers addressing strategy, tactics, mathematics, languages, law, administration, engineering, topography, and geography was deemed to have "qualified" and awaited one of the coveted nominations. That the weight of assessment was skewed toward a candidate's understanding of strategy suggested the future lines of student discourse. That the examinations favored skills acquired at Woolwich suggests why recourse to nomination existed. Otherwise, most staff officers would be drawn from the ranks of gunners and the sappers.[14]

Before the Boer War, Camberley made only limited forays into the science of amphibious operations for the simple reason that naval officers did not yet attend. At the same time, the attendance of marines was limited to one officer per class. Still, under Colonel Henry Hildyard, an officer of naval antecedents, and Colonel Frederick Maurice, attempts were made.[15] When the future Chief of the Imperial General Staff (CIGS) Henry Wilson sat his final examinations in November 1893, he had to address the role of naval supremacy in the war against Denmark.[16] Four years later, while studying staff duties, Douglas Haig prepared a mobilization plan for an expeditionary force. That same year, an exercise focused on the recapture of Sudan was also undertaken, which anticipated Kitchener's efforts the following year. Such theoretical work was matched by excursions to the coast where qualifiers prepared plans nominally representing the landing of a force on an enemy shore.[17]

Major John Gough's much-delayed attendance at Camberley coincided with the Russo-Japanese War. Emphasizing its seminal importance, weekly assessments of its progress were prepared by staff and students alike.[18] The Marine George Aston, however, lectured with a broad brush. Thus, surveys of the Spanish-American War, the Chilean War of 1891, and the 1894–1895 Sino-Japanese War were featured.[19] Not neglecting recent British experience, Wolseley's Egyptian campaign and the South African War were addressed, and so was the peacetime serial conducted at Clacton in 1904. Some lessons remained eternal, with the tactical loading of the transporting fleets being perhaps the foremost.[20] Aston was at pains to emphasize the shared nature of amphibious operations and, from this, the shared risks inherent in their execution. Thus, command of the sea might still be contested, requiring an expedition to be moved under conditions of significant risk. Moreover, that risk did not reside merely at sea, for once knowledge of a force's departure had been gained, moves to reinforce vulnerable areas must be expected by the enemy. Thus, maintaining the secrecy of pending operations was vital lest the limited force available for an assault be overwhelmed when matters came to conclusions.[21] Once committed, secrecy would be lost, and from this stemmed the need "to ensure the utmost speed attainable in the operation, because every minute lost may increase the strength of the opposing force."[22]

Just as important as what Aston had to say about amphibious operations was his pronouncement on naval demonstrations and bombardments. From Graham's operations in the Sudan littoral, Aston knew firsthand the limitations of naval artillery. Even against soft targets, aiming was difficult, and the appropriate ammunition often lacking. Thus, indifferent results resulted. Against prepared strong points, more of the same followed with success only secured once a military force landed and took the position from the rear.[23] By 1913, qualifiers and naval officers alike were adjoined to ensure the bombardment of those positions guarding the beaches and the approaches during the assault.[24] Better yet, if that wisdom had been formally accepted in the nascent doctrine crafted.

The Naval War Course

The navy, too, had its priorities in the nineteenth century, of which command at sea while a captain remained the essential element for reaching flag rank. Unfortunately, having more officers than seagoing billets with many ships relegated to the Reserve Fleet, the period found many officers on the beach drawing half-pay until a vacancy afloat arose.[25] The Naval Defence Act of 1889, which *inter alia* specified a "Two-Power Standard," brought a measure of relief, but so too did the growing complexity of naval warfare as ashore technical training establishments such as the *Excellent* and the *Vernon* followed. Concurrently, the era witnessed the first sustained thought on the purpose, role, and application of naval power. In the United States, this saw the creation of a naval war college to advance the study of naval strategy, a move Great Britain would emulate. Thus, from at least 1896, the Royal Navy offered a fleet tactics and strategy course sandwiched between courses in signals, gunnery, and torpedo work.[26] In 1900, the admiralty introduced a war course for captains and commanders. Operating under the aegis of the Royal Naval College Greenwich, the 8-month course was truncated in 1904 and then moved to Portsmouth in 1906, with the curriculum eventually subsuming the course in fleet tactics and strategy. Additionally, a limited course in strategy was taught at Devonport to reach more officers. Reflecting the interest joint operations began to assume, British Army officers began attending the war course in 1905.[27]

As with many innovations, too much was attempted initially and too much was proclaimed of the results achieved. Such is the nature of progress. The service was trying to correct a vacuum in professional education where the higher direction of war and the underlying tenets governing naval strategy were, heretofore, strangely absent in the career progression of most officers. Progress, however, proved stilted, with the need to man the seagoing fleets being a prime factor. The establishment of the war course did not provide the first practical steps of tying military and naval higher education together so much as cement the limited advances in mutual training so far made. It would be too much to say jointness was yet the product, for the doctrinal underpinnings of both services remained separate and uneven. Still, a beginning was being forged, and that the curriculum of the war course would, in time, be subject to oversight from the Committee of Imperial Defence offers evidence that its parameters extended beyond the confines and needs of the naval service.[28]

The creation of the war college followed upon the heels of a report drafted by Rear Admiral William Henderson, which examined the American response to the ongoing naval revolution.[29] In turn, Captain Henry May largely shaped the initial lines of instruction. An early proponent for creating a school for tactics, May had been present at Alexandria in 1882 before commanding the naval brigade at Suakin. His professional fortunes soon suffered, though, when he was held responsible for the loss of a confidential manual and then the grounding of his ship. Misfortune had also befallen Henderson, lending credence to the Shavian twist, "Those who can do; those who can't teach." Command of a ship not being May's forte, he migrated to the ordnance committee before arriving at Greenwich in September 1900. Truly, cometh the hour, cometh the man, and henceforth, until his untimely death in 1904, May found his calling. Indeed, past misdeeds were forgotten when he secured flag rank in September 1902.[30]

The fact that naval officers were already lecturing at Camberley by 1901 and that reciprocal visits were returned suggests that one impetus for establishing the war course was to advance the scientific study of combined operations.[31] This was more than raids, feints, and blocking operations executed with the army against minor objectives. It encompassed operations to seize, hold, or place at risk a prize of great value to an enemy. It also entailed extracting any force upon an operation's success or failure. The last was vital, for possessing a relatively weak military, Britain dare not undertake a combined operation if destruction of the military force ensued. Re-embarkation need not be an outright admission of defeat—only an admission that present circumstances were not opportune. This was a lesson of the Peninsular War when Sir John Moore had retired upon the coast more than once to begin the threat anew.[32]

Fresh from service in South Africa, Lieutenant Colonel Edward May, a well-published military writer, lectured on the principles of imperial defense to those studying at both venues.[33] Though May's lecture notes have not been traced, his *Principles and Problems of Imperial Defence* appeared contemporaneously and offer the likely strands of his thinking. Unsurprisingly, the centrality of seapower, the underpinning of maritime commerce, and the utility of combined operations appear at the fore in his writing. With its imperial and commercial interests, that reckoning required a navy supreme against all comers. It also needed a military capable of supplementing the navy and, *just as* essential, a maritime arm capable of supplementing the army.[34] As an island nation at the heart of a global empire, the British Army, unless repelling an invasion, only counted in the calculations of others if it could be placed on a distant shore. Thus, unlike that pursued by continental powers, British strategy necessarily had to be joint. That was surely correct, but British strategy also operated in a political and diplomatic context. In appreciating the need for the services to work together operationally, Edward May discounted the possibility the nation might have to do the same with others.[35]

If recognizing the potential of combined operations, May also appreciated its limitations. Against a European power, Britain could hardly expect to prevail because of the limited force that could be landed, the obstacles to be overcome, and the rapidity with which a defender could meet the point of attack. At best, an amphibious operation on the periphery was possible, but the disadvantage here was it would not likely hold hostage what an enemy viewed as vital. Even if such opportunities existed, it remained possible more would be expended than secured in the process. This led May to conclude only against a second-rate enemy could a combined operation be executed with profit.[36]

The curriculum of the war course encompassed maritime warfare in the broadest sense of its meaning. Lectures on strategy and tactics informed by historical experience were at the core of the war course. Whether surveying the Dutch Wars, those of the Napoleonic Era, or more recent events in Asia, they remained but a gateway to understanding the utility of combined operations. Pearce Higgins and the Reverend Thomas Lawrence, both prominent jurists of the first rank, offered further subjects in international and maritime law. In truth, Lawrence had a record of lecturing young naval officers on the subject predating the war course.³⁷ Supplementing this legal grounding were discourses on economics and supply by Douglas Owen.³⁸

The presence of Lawrence, Higgins, and Julian Corbett confirms that the best instruction sometimes flowed from outsiders. Yet, knowledgeable officers as instructors were the norm. Captain Richard Foster, RMA, secured his military *psc* at Camberley in late 1913 and then went to the War College to serve as an instructor. The appointment ended soon enough with the approach of war.³⁹ Meanwhile, if Corbett varied the case studies employed through the years, the lasting principles elucidated remained the essential norm. Beginning with a general lecture on the principles of naval strategy, he then surveyed the application of British maritime power through the years to inform his instruction. He quickly settled on combined operations as the salient feature of the British approach to war. This style of warfare contrasted with how continental powers traditionally achieved their aims. Corbett sought to assess its continuing utility by examining the present and the near future. Of course, the prior record testified that combined operations had not always been crowned with success. Accordingly, Corbett sought to understand why and to assess the inherent versus the accidental reasons this proved so. His analysis concluded that combined operations were executed for two primary purposes. Firstly, it served as an adjunct to securing command of the sea, and, secondly, it represented a military operation aimed at occupying the attention of a portion of an enemy's army. From this review, Corbett fastened on a critical difference separating naval warfare from its military counterpart: Navies retained the freedom to deny battle absent operations on land.⁴⁰

Historical examples anchored his analysis, but by itself, this was insufficient. As technology advanced and navies adopted the newer means afforded, the risk was always latent that that which had proven successful and adequate earlier would no longer suffice. Thus, even if Corbett could not predict the future, his lectures surveyed the evolving nature of naval warfare to assess the continuing viability of combined operations. Accordingly, the picture painted encompassed the dawn of modern experience from the Elizabethan period to the transitory period of the Crimea War through the latest expression reflected in the Russo-Japanese War. Corbett concluded that combined operations remained viable with two crucial caveats. The landed force must carefully select its theater of operations, finding ground that supported its defense and cohesion while remaining distant from an enemy's fulcrum of power "to produce as much exhaustion of his offensive power as possible by imposing on him long lines of communication." It also needed to remain a combined operation in the truest sense of the word and not merely morph into a continental style of operation. Too often, this occurred as the naval and military authorities failed to maintain cohesion in their respective strategies.[41] The last might have prompted Corbett to espouse the principle of unity of command and, with it, the appointment of a single overseer to oversee any combined operation. This he never did. Instead, he championed the British method of retaining separate naval and military commanders and viewing the alternative as continental orthodoxy.[42]

Corbett was far from a solitary voice regarding the utility of combined operations. Others, including Aston, Colonel Charles Callwell, and Lieutenant Colonel Wilkinson Bird, espoused its utility with all codifying broadly accepted precepts. As a sometime professor at Camberley, Aston turned his lectures into profit in the guise of *Letters on Amphibious Wars* and then *Sea, Land, and Air Strategy*. Here, he especially noted the importance of finance and its influence on strategy.[43] Meanwhile, Callwell, held to be "a very able theorist," discoursed at length on amphibious operations.[44] His identification of maritime preponderance, a situation where operations occurred when the command of the sea remained disputed, and its relationship to military operations tied the strategies of the two services in a manner unequaled by Clausewitz, Mahan, or Corbett.

Modern readers will appreciate the condition described as one of sea control finding full expression in Callwell's *Military Operations and Maritime Preponderance*. That work appearing in 1905 remained the most fulsome treatment on the question of amphibious and inshore operations to appear in print before the First World War.[45] Meanwhile, Bird, a much-wounded veteran of the South African War, recognized that amphibious operations allowed the initiative to be seized and could compel an adversary to disperse his forces to protect that which stood at risk from the sea. Properly executed, a combined operation offered the concentration of a superior force against a portion of the enemy.[46]

By its very nature, a combined operation was a complex undertaking drawing on the resources of the navy, army, and probably the merchant fleet as well. The variety of coastal fortifications increasingly made any attempt more difficult in the modern period, and this argued for care in considering possible serials. Still, one problem was evidenced repeatedly in such operations: the requirements of the two services were never congruent. Never mutual, their differences meant that the nature of command was shared between naval and military authorities. This, too, was at variance from continental practice, especially its German variety, where a single commander was designated. Here, command need not devolve to the senior military officer, though it most often did. The essential principle was that it must not be weakened. Corbett did not testify which method was the more desirable offering that Britain had met with success under both command examples. However, her recent experience was with the shared/joint model, which recognized the increased size and complexity of modern combined operations. More significantly, he reflected that amphibious assaults were more likely to be met with success when a local commander had the flexibility to alter the line of operations and was not unduly managed from above.[47]

Corbett omitted direct discussion of this problem and drawing any conclusions from this failure would be speculative. Perhaps the best explanation was that Britain had not resolved the amount of control to be exercised from the center, and he refrained from voicing a solution that others would eschew.[48] With Corbett providing historical and strategic context, naval and military officers addressed the actual mechanics of a combined operation. This included the type of ships required for embarking the stores, animals, and personnel, along with their subsequent forming into convoys. Getting all ashore required the establishment of comprehensive landing tables, and how to arrange and administer that which had been disembarked was covered. Umpires reviewed drafting of orders and instructions for their adequacy and shortcomings. At Camberley, a common approach was to investigate an example theoretically in the classroom before testing matters in the field. Here, one may cite the excursion held in March 1910 on the River Lees as a typical example.[49] Just as importantly, practical demonstrations were featured, such as those held on the Isle of Wight.[50] The officer leaving would not be an expert on mounting a joint operation. Still, he would be in a much better position to appreciate the complexities involved and the pitfalls to be avoided.[51]

Such addressed the "joint" aspect of the British experience, but this did not address the navy in battle *per se*. Hence, from 1912, Corbett began to lecture on Trafalgar, offering four lectures on Nelson's famous victory. Here, not all the lessons enunciated were received with universal acclaim. Aston, for one, took him to task on the primacy of fixed objectives contrasted to defeating the enemy fleet as the primary goal of a British fleet. To Corbett, the destruction of the enemy fleet remained but a means to an end, arguing that the possession of Sicily conferred supremacy over the French Mediterranean squadron during the Napoleonic period and guaranteed the safety of India.[52] This was anathema to many. It was, though, consistent with an approach that sought to define a general theory of war and subordinated the place of naval strategy within it. It was also consistent with the utility of combined operations, which has as its immediate object the securing of a geographic feature.

Aston dissented. He held that the primary objective must remain the destruction of the enemy's fleet, just as the destruction of the opposing army must remain the aim of ground operations. This remained true even when that fleet was escorting a convoy of transports carrying an invasion force. His view would find full expression in *Sea, Land, and Air Strategy* with a chapter dedicated to analyzing the strategies appropriate for land and naval warfare.[53]

Between Corbett and Aston stood the views of Callwell, who accepted the destruction of the enemy fleet as the ideal and represented the *sine qua non* of the superior naval power. Still, Callwell recognized that dockyards and fortresses were enablers to any fleet. To this end, capturing or destroying an enemy's supporting fleet infrastructure was another means of furthering maritime preponderance. Though examples existed of naval action alone securing success against a fixed position, incompetence, the poor morale of defenders, or the obsolescence of the defenses often explained victory in these instances. This was far from the norm, and only an amphibious operation offered the realistic prospect of defeating such positions.[54]

Captain Hereward Wake also railed against Corbett's teachings. An infantryman from the King's Royal Rifle Corps and a former *adc* to Lord Roberts in South Africa, Wake sat the War Course in December 1908. Where Cato the Elder is reputed to have ended his perorations with "*Carthago delenda est*," Wake invariably closed his letters to Lieutenant Reginald Plunkett with an *ad hominem* attack on Corbett. Exactly what of Corbett bothered Wake is difficult to establish, though the suspicion remains it was his touting schemes against the German coast. Many believed these were ill-considered, ill-advised, and ill-arranged—if arranged at all. Alternatively, it could be Wake held Corbett too readily dismissed Britain's vulnerability to invasion.[55] More definitely, he believed the root of the problem remained the lack of a proper staff within the naval service, married to a tendency to espouse the benefits of combined operations without ever seriously practicing their execution. Here, Wake believed Rear Admiral Lewis Bayly was especially guilty. Time would demonstrate the validity of this failure, and Wake remained sympathetic to joint action—just not all the schemes the navy floated. As for Plunkett, that naval officer adopted portions of his friend's arguments when writing for *The Naval Review*.[56]

Admittedly, the divergence expressed by Aston and Corbett remained essentially one of degree married to the use of specific historical examples. Having acquired an empire of global proportions, Aston believed England was no longer free to pursue a pure maritime approach in war. Even here, he proved undogmatic and accepted that a purely naval attack with second-line units against an enemy strong point might have value. This might witness ships passing through a narrow channel covered by fixed strongpoints if the object awaiting at the end was of the greatest value.[57] The rub, as ever, was to find the proper balance between risk, aim, and capability. Fortunately, the example of Japan in her recent war with Russia offered salutary lessons. The key remained the establishment of a unified command. The nascent CID did not constitute such an agency—of which, more hereafter—leaving Aston to argue for creating a joint agency possessed with executive authority in times of war. Until then, sailors and soldiers had to "think amphibiously."[58]

The above verdict was rendered during a lecture at the Royal United Services Institution. In the discussion afterward, the commonalities and differences remaining received full display. Clearly, it was easier to espouse general principles than to define the steps to be adopted in specific situations. It was also easier to see the shortcomings of the present than to identify suitable palliatives. Brigadier General Sir Henry Rawlinson, a leading light in bridging the divide between the services, was instrumental in bringing Aston to Camberley in August 1904 as an instructor and welcomed the participation of naval officers to inform the curriculum's attempts at addressing combined operations.[59] Indeed, to Aston belongs the credit for initiating the joint staff rides conducted. Rawlinson saw these as a waypoint in unifying naval and military control. Indeed, finding officers who understood both services demanded a special school in Rawlinson's eyes. That was too bold for the moment, and it would take the greatest of wars and another 20 years before his proposal culminated in the establishment of the Imperial Defence College.[60]

Having long sent marines to Camberley, it was perhaps natural the military would benefit from attending a reciprocal course. Though not as fulsome as the regime taught at Camberley, the war course, even for a military *psc*, widened horizons by examining problems from the perspective of the other service. The actors behind the innovation were Colonel Henry Wilson, the assistant director of staff duties, and Edmond Slade, the captain of the war college.[61] Thus, Captain Wilfrid Spender, the army's youngest staff officer, soon attended in company with the Cheshire Regiment's Captain Warren Anderson.[62] Future sessions saw four or five army officers and roughly thirty other naval participants join three or four flag officers.[63] Paying homage to the keenness of officers attending and the nature of problems being investigated, Spender only lamented the brevity of the course, believing the schemes weighed were rushed. Better results would only be secured if the navy established a counterpart to Camberley.[64]

That remedy awaited, but the presence of military officers at the war course and the attendance of naval officers at Camberley evidenced a desire to foster ever-closer links between the services. This was a step removed from 1882 when the War Office avowed a marine could never serve on the general staff. Certainly, Hugh Arnold-Forster, the secretary of state for war, desired as much in 1905.[65] To this end, and only after several false starts, Aston's posting to Camberley followed to fill a new professorship in imperial defense and naval strategy.[66] A further measure saw the setting of a common problem between Camberley and the war college. Thus, during the spring 1908 war course, a preliminary joint exercise in February was followed by staff rides in April and May. The sapper, Captain Graham Bowman-Manifold, was one recently minted *psc* who presumably took something positive away from the experience.[67] Still, if Captain Arthur Vyvyan is any judge, too much should not be read into these first efforts. Understanding the advantage gained, naval officers readily appreciated the cursoriness of joint instruction in 1913, with so much more remaining to be done on the practical side.[68]

Where Corbett spoke to strategy and the utility of combined operations, Aston addressed the operational and tactical factors at play. That he did is largely unremarkable, for he had done as much already in his study of the Benin expedition for the naval intelligence department.[69] Thus, in "Imperial Strategy: Scheme No. 1," qualifiers working in pairs were asked to define the effort required to subjugate a minor island (Hampshire) held by an unnamed enemy, which might then serve as a base for follow-on operations.[70] Though the locale was fictitious, the exercise mirrored others underway to be executed in a future war.

Sending officers to another service's school was more than simply making a more proficient individual. Nor was it the case of fostering a better understanding of the other arm's point of view, though this was undoubtedly a benefit. Increasingly, the chief reason was seen as uniting the doctrine of the services. The last was not an easy proposition when the very concept of doctrine lacked congruency. Here, Rawlinson was one officer desirous of developing the closest cooperation between the services. To this end, he invited Corbett to Camberley. This was not without risk, and so he warned:

> I think it would be well if you could let me have just a rough syllabus of what you propose to say, for though I quite agree to laying before the students at this College both sides of any question, still at the same time I think it hardly advisable to demonstrate to them the uselessness in European war of Naval and Military Co-operation.[71]

This was prudent, for with Aston already lecturing on imperial and naval strategies, there was little need to air differences that might exist in naval circles. More fundamentally, though, the military was beginning to think about deploying a force to the continent. Thus, Rawlinson needed to know Corbett's views beforehand:

> We fully realize that so far as the British Empire is concerned in European war, where Naval objectives in the first instance must be paramount, and it seems almost probably that it may be necessary to call on the Army to co-operate in order to completely attain these objectives; moreover, even when the enemy's Naval bases have been captured or destroyed, we think that the employment of land forces will be obligatory, in order to bring our opponent, whoever he may be, to complete submission, even though these armies may not be wholly composed of British troops.
>
> What are your views on these matters?[72]

Though a reply has not been traced, it may be assumed Corbett's answer proved satisfactory for his lecture "The Army in Relation to Gaining Command of the Seas" followed in due course. This raises the question of how closely the instruction imparted at Camberley mirrored that being expounded within naval circles. Beyond ensuring a commonality of subjects, of which combined operations were at the fore, a host of topics unique to each service remained. Nevertheless, both services concerted their instruction when dealing with a common subject. To this end, the instructors of both venues attended a four-day conference in 1912 where presumably current problems and possible fault lines were discussed.[73]

A central and unique feature of war course instruction remained the war game. Its emphasis on the naval encounter at the tactical level did little to foster inter-service cooperation, but its strategic variant demonstrated the possibility of raids, feints, and invasions. Of course, a perennial problem remained establishing the political context, which gave rise to the war in the first case.[74] Thus, whether the operations suggested would suit the needs of strategy on the day was very much a leap in the dark. Established to weigh questions of maritime strategy and naval tactics, war course instruction probably remained more effective regarding the latter. This is because it remained the one avenue subject to purely naval influences and control.

Traditionally, British strategy was inherently maritime, economic in outlook, and combined in execution. This was Corbett's reference point but not necessarily the reference point of others who fixated on the tactical encounter. The legacy of Trafalgar may have been one reason, but the ongoing competition in warship construction *vis-à-vis* Germany must be reckoned as another. Simply put, this competition conditioned officers to weigh the ultimate test. The traditional reference point of British strategy increasingly held less sway for some, including Henry Wilson. His tenure as commandant of the staff college was a critical moment, and while the study of combined operations continued, it was ever more relegated to a second tier behind the support of France in a continental war.[75]

Until a *Manual of Combined Naval and Military Operations* appeared, a standard treatise announcing the shared doctrine of the services was absent. Certain orthodoxies were accepted, however, notwithstanding whether one studied at Camberley or sat the war course. The precepts accepted as mutual were the value of surprise, the ability to engage the enemy after landing, and the need to stow the transports tactically such that what was required first upon landing was readily available.[76] That manual will be examined in due course, but its absence, at least at the working level, did not prove a significant barrier to progress.

A Staff College for India

India consumed military forces, be it the British Army or the now-unified Indian Army. Removed from institutions such as the staff college, the Aldershot Military Society, and the Royal United Services Institution, maintaining currency in doctrine with the home establishment was always problematic. The founding of the United Service Institution of India attempted to ensure officers serving in Asia did not atrophy professionally and sending a limited number of officers each year to Camberley helped.[77] Yet, distance and expense meant any benefit gained could only be a salting of the actual need. Manifestly, a local setting was a must for the gap in intellectual pursuits to be narrowed. Nonetheless, creating a new venue offered both promise and concern. Beyond improving the intellectual grounding of officers, the worry a chasm would inevitably be opened between the home and Indian establishments appeared palpable.[78] To preclude this possibility, the director of staff duties, Doveton Hutchinson, sought "to arrange one standard, one curriculum, one examn., etc. for the 2 colleges, English & Indian."[79]

That fear failed to sway Kitchener, who viewed establishing an Indian staff college as a necessary enabler to his greater reforms. Positing that Camberley was simply incapable of producing the number of officers required by India and with the experience of South Africa firmly shaping his views, this argument was hard to refute. Previously, three or four Indian Army officers matriculated each year to Camberley. Notwithstanding their talents otherwise, the total produced was too few to meet the requirements of modern war.[80] Expanding Camberley might have been an alternative save many served in India owing to their straitened fortunes. Unfortunately, studying at Camberley required one to possess more than talent, where private costs could easily exceed £200 a year.[81]

Ultimately, Kitchener prevailed in his wish to establish an Indian staff college, and the first instructors posted were a balanced lot drawn from the several arms of the Indian Army. If this ensured an alignment in the curricula between the two schools, then an immediate problem presented itself. The close associations which had developed between the war course and Camberley were not so easily transferred to the new school. This made the study of combined operations problematic or so believed Repington, now a military correspondent for *The Times*.[82] Of course, Indian instructors would have familiarity with combined operations, but the real issue was developing intimacy of thought across the services through close work and association. That was one potential pitfall to be negotiated, but another remained: the new school would, of necessity, focus on the problems of India and the latent threat presented by Russia.

While a permanent site was readied, the first class of twenty-four officers convened on 1 July 1905 at Deolali.[83] Things did not start well as the qualifiers loathed Major General Alfred Bayly, the commandant. A favorite of Kitchener's and much experienced of the staff, Bayly was not himself the product of a staff college education. This alone would have been fuel for domestic critics.[84] An immediate corrective saw Colonel Thompson Capper, an officer deemed brilliant and very much a staff college product, appointed instead.[85] Meanwhile, Brevet Lieutenant Colonel Henry Drake was seconded as a professor in 1907 and remained at Quetta until 1912. A graduate of Camberley, that officer of the Royal Marine Artillery had previously served as an instructor in the army's southern district, where the joint training between the services was concentrated.[86]

The Indian Army's requirement for more trained staff officers was an unfulfilled and longstanding requirement. The Liberal politician Duncan Pirie, a veteran of the Egyptian campaign, questioned the scarcity in 1897 when only thirty of 142 Indian Army staff officers held the *psc* designation. The Tory Lord George Hamilton, the secretary of state for India, conceded that the numbers were substantially correct, though British Army staff officers trained at Camberley also served in India.[87] Given the need for officers to alternate between staff and regimental assignments, the shortfall would not be alleviated if matters continued as presently ordained. Thus, Kitchener is to be credited with advancing matters. As for the fear that a separate venue would produce officers of divergent abilities, this was doubtlessly so. This, though, was more than just a question of curriculum. The ethos of the two armies was not as one; it was also largely irrelevant. Failure to train officers to *a* standard would simply mean untrained officers would be employed in the future. This posed a greater risk than not having trained an officer at all.

Meanwhile, the Indian staff college did not ignore the subject of combined operations. Unable to attend Corbett's lectures or hear Japanese veterans expound upon their recent war with Russia as was occurring at home, they otherwise persevered.[88] The presence of Wilkinson Bird ensured the teaching of strategy and combined operations were never neglected.[89] More than that, however, Capper, Bird, and twenty qualifiers in 1907 traveled to Manchuria to survey its battlefields accompanied by Japanese escorts. From this, Bird would publish a history of the campaign based on his lectures, while the sketches produced by Captain Alexander Glasfurd, one of the tour's qualifiers, were published to a broader audience in 1910 and then incorporated into the *Official History*.[90]

Significantly, combined operations featured again that year for the Indian Staff College when Capper directed a staff ride at Karachi with the support of Captain Algernon Heneage and four officers of the East Indies Squadron. While the exact lines of the ride have been lost, it remains that Commodore George Warrender touted the benefits accruing to both parties.[91] As for Manchuria, the Indian Staff College would visit its battlefields at least once more before the onset of war when Lieutenant Colonel George Barrow led a tour in 1914.[92]

Thus, combined operations came to be at the heart of the services' higher-level education efforts. This was the lesson Corbett had fastened onto and one reason why the Russo-Japanese War achieved such prominence within the war course, at Camberley, and now, at Quetta. As a witness to that war, Capper was most attuned to its lessons and lacking the support of a Corbett, an Aston, or a Callwell, he sought officers with equal experience to inform Quetta's curriculum. This led him to Major Berkeley Vincent, one of India's official observers of the Russo-Japanese War. Kitchener acceded, though how closely he weighed the appointment as he prepared to leave India for the last time is unknown.[93] Others, including Henry Wilson, saw only trouble and seized the moment to terminate Vincent's appointment.

A recent Camberley *psc*, Vincent was not unknown to Wilson. Indeed, there was a history as Vincent had questioned the sanctity of the former's pronouncements while at Camberley and saw too much of the "hail fellow well met" in the commandant. That both were Irish, though of differing stripes, offered a further variable.[94] With service in South Africa, China, and Manchuria behind him, Vincent had more direct knowledge of modern war than Wilson. That experience informed Vincent's views about the utility of artillery, mounted infantry, the *arme blanche*, and the place of the offensive in war. Commissioned into the Royal Field Artillery, Vincent, in time, migrated to the 6th Inniskilling Dragoon Guards.[95] Lieutenant General Sir Douglas Haig, chief of staff to Sir O'Moore Creagh, also found him wanting. Questioning him on the role of cavalry as sanctioned in the *FSR*, Vincent's replies had failed to impress one not known to brook views at variance to his own.[96]

Officially, Wilson argued that Vincent, a marginal student at staff college, could not possibly instruct others. Wilson's rationale begs whether an officer rated so poorly deserved the *psc* in the first place.[97] Some, such as Edward May and Lieutenant Colonel Hugh Jeudwine, had taught at Camberley without the benefit of prior attendance, indicating qualifications other than academic merit applied in selecting instructors. Concern regarding Vincent might appear parochial, save that the creation of the Indian staff college had been itself an act received warily by Wilson, overseeing military education and training at the War Office.

Capper conceded that Vincent possessed decided limitations. Yet by experience, training, and inclination, he remained the most potent candidate available to expound on cavalry, horse artillery, and the lessons of the Russo-Japanese War while also covering staff duties.[98] Indeed, his witness of Japanese amphibious operations made him uniquely qualified on that score alone.[99] This was too much for Wilson:

> The news about Vincent's [appointment] is confirmed. It leaves us all in a rather breathless condition. We cannot think who is responsible for the selection. I suppose my report on him was seen. We can scarcely believe it unless indeed which seems likely, the opinions in Simla of a Camberley Staff College report is that it is not worth the paper it is written on. In this, as in every case, it represents the opinion, the unanimous opinion, of the whole Staff here. Eleven of us. I feel inclined to ask for permission to be relieved from reporting on officers of the I.A. [Indian Army] in future as it appears to me to be rather a waste of time. The personal part of all this is a very small matter. What we all feel is that the selection & appointment of Vincent is by far the worst thing that has happened to the Quetta S.C. up to date. For this reason we are most awfully upset about the business. And don't think I have any down on Vincent. In some appointments he would do admirably but Quetta – good Lord.[100]

Wilson's views on mounted infantry and cavalry were ironically closer to Vincent's. The conflict appeared most pronounced on the merits of the offensive, which Vincent held paramount against the "defensive-offensive" touted by Wilson. Beyond this stood Vincent's relationship with Ian Hamilton, which Vincent believed made him a marked man. The last suggests that the issue dividing Wilson and Vincent remained more personal than doctrinal. Throughout the episode, Wilson saw Vincent as his own Dr. Fell, leading him to employ Haig, a known conservative on the question of cavalry, as a useful foil.[101]

If nothing else, the episode suggests the Indian staff college remained something of a poor relation to certain home authorities. Be that as it may, Quetta filled a pressing need for an Indian Army never blessed with a surfeit of staff officers. It also allowed a limited number of imperial officers to be trained, including Captain Thomas Blamey, the future field marshal.[102] In sum, the Indian staff college can be viewed as a military version of the navy's war staff course. Established in the shadow of its more noted counterpart, its reach clearly exceeded its grasp, with the first challenge merely gaining acceptance and establishing a measure of gravitas.

On the Nature of Combined Operations

Invasion and re-embarkation represented the pinnacle of combined operations as understood by British officers before 1914. Both evolutions were complex, fraught with risk, and required the presence of highly developed lines of communication. Withdrawal in the face of the enemy was a task not to be undertaken lightly, for rout could soon overtake retreat if cohesion broke down. Even if that misfortune did not transpire, loss of men and material was all but a certainty. To reduce the dangers, any plan for landing needed to be accompanied by a corresponding one accounting for re-embarkation if circumstances necessitated it. This might be viewed as planning for failure at one level, but Britain's limited army demanded as much.[103]

Associated with these two evolutions were the lesser serials of reconnaissance, feints, raids, and blocking operations. More limited in time and space, their logistical requirements were similarly reduced. Hence, the presence of lines of communication represented the dividing line between invasions and the lesser tasks of combined operations.[104] Behind all stood the enablers of intelligence, loading, and force sustainment. All required much thought beforehand concerning the object to be obtained, the forces necessary to execute, and the drafting of the required orders and instructions to bring clarity and coherence to the problem. Much of this was not unique to combined operations. Combined operations, however, aggregated these issues in a manner absent traditional assaults, introduced the complexity of multi-service coordination, and began from a less-than-ideal base anchored as it was on a vulnerable fleet tethered to a fixed locale. Though the actual site of a landing might be unknown to a defender, gathering the required forces by the assaulting force meant strategic surprise was rarely present. Moreover, once any force had landed, the defender usually enjoyed the advantage of superior communications as any objective worth assaulting could be assumed to have sufficient transportation links to make it of value in the first instance. Thus, without supporting air or strong artillery fires, the defending army enjoyed an advantage if the initial assault could be defeated or held in check.

Thus, success against a first-rate military power appeared problematic. Fortunately, American success in its war against Spain, but especially Japanese success in Manchuria, offered convincing testimony that a maritime strategy anchored on combined operations was not an approach to be discarded lightly. Captain Thomas Jackson's reports from the Japanese Fleet did not sugarcoat the difficulties, yet success remained distinctly possible. To wit:

> Attempts to block the entrance to Port Arthur by sinking vessels in the fairway took place on February 24th, March 27th, and on the morning of May 3rd. Vice Admiral Togo reported, after the last attempt, *as follows*, "As five out of eight blocking vessels entered the harbour mouth successfully and sank, the harbour entrance appears to have been completely blocked to the passage of cruisers and larger vessels."

> In selecting a landing place for the Army which was only sixty miles from Port Arthur the Japanese recognized that they were committing, what was termed by a Naval Officer on the staff of the Minister of the Navy, an "*impertinence*," and by a high Military Staff Officer "*un coup audacieux*." They hoped that the harbour was sufficiently blocked to prevent large vessels passing out, but could not obtain any definite information on this point. They considered that it was possible for destroyers to pass, and they assumed that a torpedo attack on the transports was a certainty. Accepting this, they took steps to minimize the danger as far as possible. Every available Japanese destroyer and torpedo boat, about sixty in all, was stationed either off Port Arthur or between that place and the anchorage. As is shown in the plate [not reproduced], they protected the anchorage with booms and nets, laid dummy mines, arranged a system

of patrolling boats, and anchored protecting ships in suitable positions for covering the transports....

The disembarkation commenced on May 5th. A party of seamen, under the command of Captain Nomoto, were the first to land, and, owing to the tide being at the ebb, they were obliged to wade about a thousand metres (*1094 yards*) before they could reach the beach. They effected the landing at 7.22 a.m., and at once occupied the high land commanding the beach. The troops commenced to land at 8.5.[105]

Harmonizing instruction, if a worthy goal, faced practical obstacles. The conditions of service remained one, but the operational experience and requirements of the British and Indian armies, never mind the Royal Navy, were hardly congruent. Telephones, wireless, and motorized vehicles were commodities more typically seen in Britain than in India. Accordingly, imparting the nature of staff duties when the establishments were not as one technically soon separated practice from theory.[106] In July 1909, Aston learned the navy would stop sending officers to Camberley. Through a judicious approach to Richard Haldane, the secretary of state for war, who then pigeonholed Reginald McKenna, the first lord, Aston succeeded in forestalling the measure.[107] What prompted the proposed change has not been traced. It may have been an Admiralty facing other unfulfilled requirements, thought the investment a poor one. More cynically, perhaps the Admiralty believed it was losing control of its strategic thought if not of British strategy.

The last may have been key for as good as the Admiralty was at administration, Aston conceded the War Office's general staff were better at formulating strategy. Others would hold as much in time, forcing the navy to adopt an Admiralty war staff to rectify matters.[108] That measure would eventuate over the winter of 1911, but more limited steps were pursued in the interim. Thus, the Admiralty modified its war course to cover staff duties. That was a false start as the present course already had been truncated and time was not available to cover the array of existing subjects while adding staff duties to the mix. The solution ultimately adopted was the inauguration of a separate war staff course covering the principles of strategy, tactics, joint operations, the strategic distribution of fleets, commerce protection, coastal defense, staff duties, the naval intelligence system, international law, Admiralty organization, mobilization, and logistics. Recourse to historical examples highlighted the salient features of each, and the driving force behind these was Fisher, supported by Captain Charles Ottley and Captain Maurice Hankey of the CID.[109]

Michael Howard avows that "It was neither the Boer War nor the American Civil War nor even the Franco-Prussian War that European military specialists had in mind when their armies deployed in 1914: it was the fighting in Manchuria in 1904–05."[110] This is undoubtedly correct. Accordingly, British officers cast their nets wide to garner lessons that, if minimally appropriate for Europe, might say something about fighting in other locales of which the empire could claim a surfeit of diversity. Here, attention coalesced on the Dardanelles and Asiatic Turkey, where British interests intersected with those held by others. At Camberley in 1907, Captain Archibald Montgomery wrote at length on the "strategical routes and centres in Asiatic Turkey" while those attending the Indian staff college weighed how to defeat the Ottoman Empire. A solution offered in the last example was to instigate riots in Egypt, dispatch reinforcements from Britain to restore order, and then employ the situation created as cover to divert the force to the Dardanelles.[111] Consideration of the ruse testifies that for contemporaries, the problem remained of securing strategic and tactical surprise against an objective where immediate forces were lacking.

Meanwhile, Lieutenant Charles James sat the 4-month Japanese war course in Tokyo in 1908 before proceeding to sea for 3 months in a Japanese destroyer.[112] This can be seen as a reciprocal measure insofar as Commander Kiyokazu Abo, a veteran of the recent Japanese campaign and now the naval attaché in London, sat the British naval war course in late 1906.[113] This was followed by Commander T. Matsinra, who participated in the next session with its now routine Portsmouth-Camberley staff ride. This saw the entire war course paired with the thirty-eight staff college's senior division officers in May 1908.[114]

If the services cast a wide net when examining the historical record of combined operations, the problem of gauging their relevance to the British condition remained. This was never truer than when surveying the American experience against Spain. A continental power, the United States pursued amphibious operations against islands where geography allowed the object to be isolated and, thus, action contained. Conversely, the usual experience of Britain, an island power, was to project power against a distant shore not so readily isolated. True enough in Crimea, Egypt, Sudan, China, and, most recently, South Africa, this worked when the presence of an opposing navy was not a limiting factor. The viability of such operations where naval opposition could be expected was at the heart of the diverging views that began to take form at the War Office and the Admiralty. However, a contributing factor to the schism was the navy's lack of a proper staff system.

Coordinating the dictates of strategy and developing mutual sympathy were the primary reasons the education of naval and military officers became intimate, but successfully conducting an amphibious operation demanded more. It also demanded a thorough understanding of the procedures and administrative habits of the other service. The creation of the 10-month war staff course in April 1912 may have been primarily a measure for developing officers for the nascent Admiralty war staff. Still, it also reflected the necessity of ensuring officers understood the needs and limits of cooperation. As was taught at Camberley and Quetta, emphasis on staff duties, organization, and administration were at the fore. Yet, a significant difference existed: The navy's needs were not congruent with the army.

Officers completing the war staff course were noted as being best suited for operations, intelligence, administrative duties, or able to execute all tasks.[115] This followed the custom of the military staff college. When securing his *psc* in 1894, Captain John Rose, RMA was "thought energetic and keen" but lacked "force of character."[116] Meanwhile, General Rawlinson believed Captain St. George Armstrong of the Royal Marine Light Infantry was best fitted for intelligence work, an unsurprising observation insofar as Armstrong came to the staff college following years of experience in intelligence duties.[117] Ever the problem, though, was what to do with the officer trained at another service's school and in another service's ways. This challenge stood acute for the marine, who was neither fish nor fowl. Many would be seconded to the army or a colonial offshoot, and while this marked time toward a pension, it did not necessarily make for the fullest career. Some, such as Aston, managed it better than others, yet even he faced impossible barriers. Talent only counted for so much; it was asking much of the War Office to employ a marine at the highest levels when so many of its own officers lacked for promotion.[118]

Together, the services understood the imperative of studying the higher aspects of war and, to that end, took the first concerted steps in fashioning interoperability across the services. Given the equities and the costs involved, progress proved methodical and evolutionary rather than rapid and revolutionary. If time had been unlimited, resources had been unconstrained, and the need to operate fleets and maintain armies had not weighed so heavy, the payoff would have been greater. In establishing its war course, the navy was attempting to ensure senior executive officers shared a common understanding of naval warfare. Given the highly selective nature of Camberley and Quetta attendance, this was an infinitely broader sweep than what the army attempted. In contrast, the war staff course served a more limited purpose—certainly, more limited than that pursued by the army. Both, however, failed to educate sufficient staff officers before 1914.[119]

Such, though, is the nature of education. Some are educated and successful. Some are educated and fail. Others are not educated to a standard yet may succeed through innate ability. Wolseley, surveying his four *adc*'s in 1884, believed Major Frederick Wardrop far superior to the rest even though he lacked the cache of the *psc*.[120] Difficulties stood in the way of progress, with not all being amenable to control by the Admiralty and the War Office. Indeed, not all were amendable to the control of London. Thus, the war in 1914 found Britain and the empire ill-prepared. Snook's conclusion that the late Victorian Army was a more professional organization than generally credited is surely correct, and the same may be claimed for the Royal Navy. So much, however, depended on the day, and always deficiencies remained.[121]

What all appreciated was Britain's way in war was inherently maritime; else, why spend so much time studying combined operations? The irony, of course, was that the more empire one acquired, the more continental in outlook matters became, for not all threats could be mastered from the sea. This conundrum resided at the heart of the British situation in 1914. While the empire may have been cast as one on cartographers maps, reality offered it as but a loose confederation of disparate entities. Fashioning a coherent strategy and supporting doctrines of war in such an environment demanded much, indeed, too much. Needs must, however, and the services persevered and, to that end, adopted their first formal joint treatise. Thus, *The Manual of Naval and Military Combined Operations* is now ripe for review.

Twelve

Toward a *Manual of Combined Naval and Military Operations*

Owing to the custom that prevailed in the eighteenth century of embarking battalions of the line on board men-of-war, to act as Marines, it is probable 150 years ago the British Army, as a whole, was better fitted to take part in over-sea operations than in the present day.[1]

Charles Telfer-Smollett, 1905

The issuance of a *Manual of Combined Naval and Military Operations* in 1911—circumscribed as it was—can be seen as a seminal moment in the development of amphibious warfare doctrine. Codifying precepts in a previously lacking manner provided an established point of departure for further progress. It did not yet represent settled joint doctrine because the *Manual* remained an imperfect product, leaving much unsaid. A revision in 1913 advanced matters, but only in 1925 would the work approach true joint doctrine when the services, now three in number, adopted its corporate and underlying tenets.[2] This is not to avow that reflection had been lacking previously, but those efforts had tackled cooperation in a general manner or lacked official standing. To wit, no evidence has been traced that the *Manual* before 1914 represented anything more than the War Office's view of joint operations issued with the concurrence of the Admiralty. Absent Admiralty blessing as an "Official Use" or "Confidential Book" publication, it remained for others, including the Royal United Services Institution (RUSI), to keep the topic alive in professional circles.[3]

Here, the Russo-Japanese War offered a spur for progress.[4] To that end, RUSI, for its annual essay competition in 1905, set the topic "The Best Method for Carrying Out the Conjoint Practice of the Navy and Army in Embarkation and Disembarkation for War, Illustrated by the Experience of the Past." Lieutenant Colonel Charles Telfer-Smollett claimed the prize of a gold medal and thirty guineas. Tragically, that officer died in a motoring accident in 1912. More fortunate proved to be Major George MacMunn, who earned a creditable second on the heels of an earlier paper recognized by the United Service Institution of India titled "The Influence and Application of Sea Power in Expeditions Based on India."[5] Indeed, the last anticipated much that would appear in the *Manual of Combined Naval and Military Operations*, suggesting the precepts touted now had matured to the point of doctrine.[6]

Turning to the measures adopted post-1882, practical exercises duly occurred. These demonstrated the landing of an attacking force and defending areas at risk from enemy assault. Necessarily, these evolutions suffered from a want of scale owing to the size of peacetime forces and the demands of economy. Bombardments, if occurring, were limited to the firing of a few representative rounds with lesser ships approximating more capable units. Heavily scripted and conducted to minimize difficulties, these often witnessed second-line forces cooperating with their frontline counterparts and served as a vehicle for imparting basic field training or proving new concepts. Still, testing the lines of an opposed landing featured infrequently, if at all. As such, those conducted off Milford Haven in 1886 and Dover in 1890 possessed pronounced limitations.[7]

During the latter, the second-class battleship *Audacious*, the gunboats *Mistletoe*, *Magnet*, *Grappler*, and *Rattlesnake*, and accompanying tugs landed a force of cavalry, infantry, and engineers in a serial intended to represent the disabling of forts by an army corps.[8] Superficially, if recalling Seymour's attack on Alexandria, then that reflected more coincidence than intention, for the primary aim was to demonstrate the centralized fire control of the forts. Of course, a further benefit was the serial offered a chance for the navy and the army to work together. The risk, however, was ever-present that those participating might assume a degree of efficacy not warranted. Indeed, this was the view of General Sir Andrew Clarke, who held "Foolish 'manoeuvres' of this class serve only to spread erroneous impressions, to add to the confusion of ideas already so prevalent, and to teach tactical lessons which may one day have to be unlearned at the price of blood and disaster."[9] This is ever a problem where not all participants are privileged enough to understand a training serial's real import.[10]

One purpose of the 1899 naval exercises was to demonstrate wireless communications in a tactical setting.[11] That was ably shown—perhaps too well—for propagation results were not equal in the following year minus the presence of Guglielmo Marconi. Yet, something else was confirmed: the vulnerability of shore signal stations. Here, that located at Bere Island near Berehaven, Ireland, where a party from the gunboat *Niger* landed and "severed" its associated telegraph cables. If the exercise confirmed the advantages of wireless communications, it had also shown the exposure of British cables—a point confirmed during the previous year when the United States had severed French and British cables when fighting Spain.[12] Thus, if tactically, the landing had represented little more than the forays made previously against custom houses and post offices, then strategically, it portended something greater.[13]

On the Mediterranean Station, Vice Admiral Sir John Fisher and General Sir Francis Grenfell, the commander-in-chief, Malta, conducted parallel exercises. Again, testing the utility of electronic communications in fleet operations, their broader purpose demonstrated the landing of a military force. This posited a main assault supported by a divisional feint. Boarding cruisers and proceeding to sea from Malta, those making the assault came from the Sherwood Foresters. Transferring to steam launches preparatory to the landing, a brief bombardment by heavy ships and cruisers preceded a landing, followed by the insertion of over 2,400 naval personnel. In principle, the exercise tested the feasibility of making an opposed landing. The onset of worsening weather and the fleet's limited shooting make drawing definite conclusions problematic. Still, certain precepts are discernible. Firstly, a covering force seizing the high ground and reducing immediate enemy strongpoints would precede the landing of the main force. Secondly, naval personnel would be employed in association with the military effort.[14]

Using a covering force can be seen as a natural progression from the employment of an advance guard to cover the progress of a main body on the march in a traditional military operation with due allowance for the unique tasks required in an amphibious landing. The landings of November certainly marked a practical improvement from the more limited serial conducted in April. Then, troops and attached personnel did not embark and land, with the exercise assuming their safe insertion. Following 3 days of "war," the raiding force re-embarked (actual) under the guns of the fleet.[15] All participating could claim a measure of satisfaction—the defenders for the resistance offered and the attackers for successfully masking the point of their withdrawal and then skillfully exiting. Beyond a chance for the two services to train together, extracting a landed force in contact with the enemy stands out as the serial's most significant feature.

The war in South Africa offered valuable lessons in the loading, moving, and landing of a force on a distant shore where the supporting infrastructure was indifferent. It also presented a benchmark for gauging the casualties to be endured in the face of modern weaponry. Of course, such calculations could only serve as an approximation, and it remained that some lessons might not apply more generally. Here, the role of mounted infantry comes to mind. Not part of the peacetime establishment, they might not be available to participate in an amphibious operation. Instead, the employment of cyclists as part of the attached troops of an infantry division was worthy of consideration. Not requiring any alterations in shipping, they might allow a force to move that much quicker.[16] This was an important consideration, as maintaining the security of any operation was viewed as a necessary precursor to success. Moreover, synchronizing the arrival of infantry and cavalry was no easy matter, given their differing transport needs. Thus, cyclists seemingly reduced one aspect of the problem, though others remained.[17] In short, the South African War was a useful point of departure in setting the problems to be solved. The ensuing exercises also informed the debate about the susceptibility of Britain and colonial outposts to invasion.

Here, the views of the War Office generally offered that a large-scale landing by an enemy force against static protection might be overcome. This did not argue that British forces could achieve the same. However, it suggested that operations of more substance than administrative landings remained feasible. In 1901, Edward Altham believed Malta was vulnerable "to a determined attack of a *powerful* landing force, threatening a landing at many points and throwing as large as force as possible upon the north-west of the island" with the supporting naval force meeting Malta's coastal batteries on equal terms. This was mere conjecture, but it remained an informed view of the demonstration provided by Fisher and Grenfell. More worryingly, recent French naval exercises in the Mediterranean had tested making a landing against a defended port.[18]

Noel's serial of 1900 indicates the navy practiced landings periodically. These evolutions represented the exception, and not the rule, in naval exercises typically focused on fleet action. To Fisher and the Mediterranean Fleet belong the credit for adding naval landings to the routine of exercises. Though details are sketchy, one occasion witnessed the disembarkation of 12,000 men with guns in 19 minutes—a feat Fisher looked upon with some pride.[19] Unsurprisingly, Fisher pressed for greater cooperation between the services in their training upon his return home. To that end, in late 1903, he suggested a joint exercise employing 50,000 troops. That was heady stuff, indeed. Still, the plea found favor as the War Office soon allocated £170,000 to test whether 30,000 troops could be landed and sustained in the face of present naval defenses. Designed partly to gauge Britain's ability to meet a raid, just as importantly, these serials were meant to provide practical experience in executing an amphibious landing. The record shows these exercises were ordered when war with Russia became a distinct possibility, and the reinforcement of India appeared pressing.[20] Doubtlessly, that worry proved one spur to action, but the record is clear Fisher had already been thinking along such lines before the onset of the Russo-Japanese War.

Others had, too, including Commander George Ballard and Sir John French. In the case of the former, he desired to see better cooperation at the tactical level such that an opposed landing would become a feasible proposition of war. Reviewing the lines of recent foreign amphibious operations in China and Chile at a meeting of the Aldershot Military Society, Ballard argued a campaign plan developed beforehand remained essential. Recognizing that this was far removed from the wealth of recent British experience, French concurred and then expressed the wish that *"we may ultimately hope even to see the two [services] merged into one great national service."*[21] Too much must not be read into Sir John's affirmation beyond the apparent conclusion that much practical work remained to be accomplished.

While commanding at Portsmouth, Fisher tested the ability of submarines to meet an attack delivered by heavy ships and destroyers against a defended port. The results were judged promising as the attacking force was deemed to have lost four battleships in a March 1904 exercise.[22] These exercises can be seen as part of an increasingly complex set of joint serials testing the offensive and defensive capabilities of the services when considering the shortfalls identified by the Mowatt Committee in 1900.[23] That worry only increased with Britain now aligned with a Japan engaged against Russia. In response, the CID now proposed a series of combined exercises.[24] Demonstrations, staff rides, and exercises duly followed, including the Channel Fleet's attack on Gibraltar.[25]

Meanwhile, in Britain, Field Marshal Wood aimed to conduct a serial in which troops, guns, wagons, and animals embarking at Portsmouth would descend upon an open beach at Bournemouth. The exact reason why the navy could not support this request is not documented, but Wood accepted the counteroffer of a more limited demonstration.[26] Wood now recast the exercise run by Brigadier General Percy Lake to emphasize the drafting and issuing of corps, division, brigade, and battalion orders in an amphibious evolution. This saw three separate displays on 19 April 1904 of the fleet's ability to land guns, horses, and wagons using flat-bottomed boats, a 42-foot launch, and rafts.[27]

Before proceeding with the practical part of the work, Commander Wilfred Henderson of the *Excellent* discussed the mechanics of landing a corps. His accounting did not lack detail, but it had been prepared without the assistance of the army. As such, it overlooked important military factors, prompting General Lake to argue that cooperation between the services had to start at the beginning of any enterprise. Lake also questioned the scale of the naval escort posited by Henderson, believing it was rather large. As naval personnel would form the necessary beach parties to assist with the landing, securing the numbers required demanded the use of numerous vessels. In truth, this argued for a dedicated force divorced from the needs of the seagoing fleet.[28] Absent such a body, Lake understood the demands of higher naval strategy might negate the operational feasibility of any landing as the ships necessary might not be forthcoming. It also highlighted a further fundamental consideration: Could a landing proceed before the command of the sea had been established? Both George Clarke and Admiral of the Fleet Sir Geoffrey Hornby believed the ability to send an expedition safely overseas constituted the very essence of command of the sea.[29] That left unsaid many lesser operations. Eventually, received wisdom accepted the degree of command necessary to support an operation was directly tied to an expedition's ultimate objective. Raids and feints might proceed, but an invading force with its exposed lines of communication undertook severe risks in its absence.[30]

Henderson conceded all this and held landings in Europe were unlikely until the question of that command had been settled. This reflected admiralty thinking even though the ongoing war over Korea and Manchuria might have suggested otherwise. That it did not owe everything to the passivity of the Russian Pacific Fleet, which permitted Japan to land a force at a place of her convenience. This had been a scene absent immediate enemy opposition, a precursor Henderson held to be vital given the increased ranges modern weapons enjoyed and which a defending force would likely possess. Thus, where previously rowed boats carrying troops might pass the zone of danger in under a minute, modern firepower would tell much sooner and be much more effective than hitherto.[31]

This, too, the army accepted, for it was simply too small to engage in violent and sustained combat. Henderson also posited a further lesson: Voluminous orders, if providing granularity, came at the expense of clarity. Less detailed orders were more easily digested but left the possibility for misunderstanding. Thus, all pointed to the closest collaboration aforehand between the army and the navy, with Henderson offering "that with liberal help from the navy, the success of such an operation as the landing of an army on an open beach is, humanly speaking assured; but that without it, or if such help is present only in a limited degree, it will be a lengthy, not to say dangerous operation."[32] Finally, this tactical exercise without troops proved the need for an amphibious equivalent to the *Field Service Regulations*. Differences in views would always exist, but an authoritative treatise stood as a must.[33]

Beyond the necessity of avoiding immediate resistance ashore and the presence of effective sea control, Henderson believed fair weather a must as this abetted the transfer of soldiers, kit, transport, and animals from ships to shore. Meanwhile, effective sea control was more than just ensuring the force's safety during transit. It needed to be held and maintained for the duration of operations. As the crews of civilian transports were not adept in small boat work, lighters, barges, and hoppers would have to be manned by naval ratings. With crew members potentially absent from their ships for days, it was now when the supporting fleet faced its greatest danger. It was this vulnerability that required the prior negation of the enemy fleet.[34] Not specified by Henderson and Lake were two further elements understood to be vital in amphibious operations: speed and secrecy. These factors were so critical that their absence in the preceding represented not so much an oversight as a commonplace. Certainly, these factors received due attention in staff college instruction.[35]

That June, a second serial ensued. This saw the transport *Soudan* embark two companies of the Sherwood Foresters, thirteen horses, and two guns at Southampton before disembarking that force near Spithead. Beyond being a modest, practical test, the exercise demonstrated a new boat for landing across an open beach.[36] The balance of the summer saw II Corps involved in the usual round of training exercises on the Salisbury Plain.[37] September, however, brought a full-scale demonstration approximating Wood's original idea for a combined exercise. Against the backdrop of an ongoing war between Blue representing Britain and an unspecified Red, a follow-on landing against Red ensued. The strategic setting posited the previous defeat of the Red fleet and an earlier landing at Sussex. Thus, the landings beginning on 8 September at Essex represented either a supporting feint for the imaginary main force operating in Sussex or a threat to the Red capital.[38] Preparatory to the onset of the exercises, supply depots deemed neutral were created to support the logistics of those participating, while engineers laid telegraph lines to support the control of the exercise.[39]

The attacking force came from Lieutenant General Sir John French's I Corps. Marching from Aldershot to Southampton, the troops boarded ten ships preparatory to beginning their "war" at midnight on 6–7 September.[40] The essential step had not passed without incident when many of the chargers had stampeded.[41] Eventually, Rear Admiral Sir Wilmot Fawkes' Cruiser Squadron escorted the convoy to Clacton-on-Sea. Early on the seventh, the transports anchored, allowing the invading troops to be transferred to launches. First reaching shore were marines and engineers to construct the pontoons to serve the infantry coming an hour later. In short, what was being tested was an unopposed landing across an open beach.[42] French's force of nearly 12,000 men, forty-two guns, and 2,700 horses soon marched the 16 miles toward Colchester to dispose of the defending Red force.[43] Significantly, Blue began their advance before the ships had completed unloading. Such boldness was rewarded as Colchester quickly succumbed. This represented only an intermediate objective. Maldon, 20 miles distant, remained the ultimate aim as its capture would allow Blue to unload directly onto its piers, thereby facilitating force sustainment.[44]

Farm crops limited the lines of approach, and when the exhaustion of the troops became a factor, a day's truce followed.[45] Such unrealities are inescapable in peacetime serials where the numbers engaged are limited, the safety of personnel key, and minimizing damage to property assumes prominence—never mind the presence of bathers on the beach.[46] How these influenced matters cannot be determined, though Repington held at least one decision critically preferred Blue at a critical moment.[47] More certainly, Blue did not have to negotiate the mines and barbed wire, which were sure to have been present in a real war.

General French had had his way up to this point, but a severe setback allowed Major General Arthur Wynne, commanding Red, to redeploy his 6,000 troops toward Colchester. Thus, Blue was forced to retire upon the prize so recently won.[48] It was now that the weather intervened. Not a serious factor during the initial landings even though seven horse boats and some stores had been lost, it now precluded the withdrawal of Blue from Clacton and Holland-on-Sea at the appointed hour.[49] Severely pressed by Colonel Edmund Allenby's Red cavalry, the exercise conveniently terminated before the former could embarrass General French.

To one correspondent, all this demonstrated just "how rather difficult a task the invasion of England really would be" even if British command of the sea had been lost. Under actual war conditions, Blue would have been defeated, notwithstanding the good achieved in the intervening days.[50] Indeed, so bad had the weather become thought had been given to re-embarking only Blue's infantry with the cavalry returning to their garrison over land.[51] In the event, the re-embarkation occurred across the beaches on 13–14 September and fulfilled a key objective of the exercise of redeploying "an expedition driven back to its original landing place on the beach."[52]

Possessing the keen eye of a military expert, Repington's observations were more than the musings of an errant scribbler being further informed by his many contacts among the participants. One recently returned from Manchuria offered that British wagons and equipment were unequal to that of the Japanese Army, where lighter types were employed.[53] Two others observing these proceedings were Colonel Albert d'Amade of the French Army and the staff college's Aston. What the former took away has not been traced, though this was not his first experience observing the British Army in the field, having witnessed the South African War. Present at Gallipoli years later, it would not be d'Amade's last opportunity either. Aston, meanwhile, offered that the affair had shown the need for stowing the transports such "that what you want to land first is to be found on top."[54]

The services marked the salient lessons arising at a follow-on conference held months later. Attending for the War Office were Major General Plumer (quarter-master general), Brigadier General Henry Lawson (director of movements and quarterings), Colonel William Kincaid (assistant quarter-master general, Aldershot command), and Colonel Edward May (assistant director of military training). Representing the Admiralty were Vice Admiral George Boyes, Ret. (director of transport), Captains Charles Madden (naval assistant to the controller), George Ballard (assistant director of naval intelligence), and Commander Lionel Halsey. Foremost, the venue captured the factors governing a combined operation. This included the respective responsibilities of the services, the procedures required, and the manner of embarkation and disembarkation. Otherwise, a further inter-service working group dealt with the many technical issues arising. While a new pattern of horse-boat eventually followed, maximizing the use of present resources animated their recommendations.[55] In short, solutions entailing the expenditure of funds were eschewed. On balance, the conference's most significant contribution was to specify the critical assumptions governing joint operations, though tellingly, they were unable to reach an agreement on the nature of "command." Here, the need for an invading army to avoid immediate contact with defending troops stood paramount.[56]

The Admiralty could, however, assert the timing governing any operation executed. Summarizing the naval position, Battenberg, the director of naval intelligence, had recently written:

THE principle which must guide our naval strategy in such a war is "Concentration of effort against our main objective."

The *main objective* is the enemy's fleet, which ours must endeavour to "take, sink, burn, or destroy," according to the old phraseology of the navy.[57]

Only then would the environment exist for the navy to support the execution of subsidiary operations, of which an overseas expedition formed but one. On the surface, this appeared as a concession of the first rank by the War Office. In truth, reality said something less. As an island empire, the British Army could not pursue an overseas expedition without the assistance of the navy. Thus, the War Office accepted naval requirements must prevail. Events, however, would demonstrate such decisions remained the preserve of cabinets.

The representatives agreed that the aim of landings must be limited to match the means available. Consequently, an attack against "the main territory of Continental Power" was eschewed, meaning "the objective of the expedition would probably be a colony or colonies of the Power with which we are at war." As for the scale to be attempted, two divisions of infantry and a brigade of cavalry were posited. Finally, it was assumed the necessary planning would be done jointly by the Admiralty and the War Office in association with the designated senior naval officer and the general officer commanding the operation. The last was particularly important for the commanders-in-chief of stations, fleets, and squadrons lacked the staff to perform detailed mission planning. For that matter, so too did the Admiralty. It was assumed that after the required preliminaries, the respective commanders would sail together to refine their plans.[58] These caveats were not definitive, but they were reasoned and represented an attempt to place realistic constraints around planning a joint operation. Collectively, the conference report anticipated much that subsequently appeared in the *Manual of Naval and Military Combined Operations.*

The following year, the experimentation scene moved to Ireland, where a cavalry brigade under Brigadier General Michael Rimington undertook the primary steps associated with making an amphibious landing.[59] Employing the hired transport *Kansas* and the cruiser *Donegal*,[60] the "general idea" saw an all-arms raid directed at a vital rail link. Occurring under cover of darkness, beyond demonstrating the weaknesses of existing boats, the serial can be seen as proving the concept of operations of employing a covering force. Due to moonlight, the defending force successfully met the main force, but better results were secured by the simultaneous feint offered. Accordingly, one critic suggested matters would have been better served by redirecting efforts toward the secondary objective.[61]

This was food for thought which a yet unpublished *Manual* would not address. Still, this is not to avow guidance and practical measures were otherwise lacking. Already, the positions of naval transport officer, military transport officer, beach master, assistant beach master, and deputy beach master had been codified. However, the scope of their duties and authorities remained opaque, as Lieutenant Seymour Fortescue had found, to his chagrin, in 1885 at Suakin.[62] At home, the position of naval transport officer was apt to be filled by a recently retired officer. Rowland Berkeley serving at Southampton offers a case in point rendering support to the exercises held in 1904. Indeed, the tendency to employ unemployed officers in transport duties extended to the apex of the service with George Boyes, retired since 1896, serving as the Admiralty's director of transport while John Hext had long occupied a like capacity in India.[63] The system worked well in peacetime, but as many holding their appointments retired owing to age or medical infirmity, the risk remained ever-present that the stress and pace of war might prove too much at a later date. Such proved the case in 1897 with Commander Reginald Heriz during the Benin expedition.[64] In the interim, those appointed attended short courses and became conversant in the governing regulations. To that end, an interdepartmental committee met and revised those regulations in 1903.[65]

In the meantime, the Admiralty kept a register of vessels suitable for transport duties, which, by 1914, stood at roughly 2,000 ships.[66] The record suggests Australian authorities had not gone quite as far, though they, too, followed the organizational nomenclature when deploying their expeditionary force in 1914.[67] Meanwhile, the Admiralty laid the groundwork for deploying a specialized brigade to support power projection operations. Employing infantry battalions drawn from the principal home ports and employing a body from the Royal Marine Artillery, the "advance base force" would allow the fleet to operate at a distance removed from the service's dockyards.[68]

More pressing than conducting a large-scale amphibious exercise was the planning to execute one in the event of war. France aligned with Russia, and Russia at war with Japan presented fresh worries. With Russian naval reinforcements from the Baltic passing through the Mediterranean and Red seas around September 1904, a port call at Madagascar was presumed. Occupying Diego Suarez made Russian reinforcement of its Pacific Fleet more difficult, but it also removed a latent threat to Britain's lines of communication to the Cape and India. Consequently, longstanding plans dating from at least 1890 were at hand. In 1897, those plans anticipated a *coup de main* by 24,000 Indian troops. The War Office intelligence division now queried the India Office whether a strike could be mounted if the need arose. Given existing defense shortfalls *vis-à-vis* Russia, the scheme was a commitment too far for India. The CID accepted this, noting that the defenses of Diego Suarez were more robust than previously allowed.[69] Indeed, the whole question governing French colonial ports prompted the CID to suggest the creation of a Secret Service.[70]

In 1911, a *Manual of Combined Naval and Military Operations* appeared. Codifying the duties and responsibilities of the two services, it provided the doctrinal context for the execution of one type of joint operation. Capturing the salient points as generally understood, much remained unsaid in this first primer. Most notably, the *Manual* failed to address riverine operations—a

Improvised logistics was a hallmark of the Gordon Relief Expedition including the use of hastily recruited non-military boatmen to operate craft that remained to be constructed. The problem would be replicated anew and highlighted that getting a force ashore was in many respects the easiest part of any joint operation with exploitation of the initial advantage gained still to be waiting. Source: Alamy 2PH318W

The Black Watch cheers General Wolseley as they advance up the Nile during the Gordon Relief Expedition. While the Nile afforded access, it did so only reluctantly with cataracts, an opposing current, and the distance to be covered to Khartoum presenting three barriers to the relieving force. Source Alamy BACFK5

Drawing upon the personnel of the Mediterranean Station, a naval brigade commanded by Captain Lord Charles Beresford supported the Gordon Relief Expedition. Reaching Khartoum too late to save General Gordon, from the experience the War Office sought to define a naval brigade standard organization to support future riverine operations. Source Alamy PT0JB6

The Battle of Abu Klea – William Barnes Wollen. In the advance to relieve General Gordon several sharp actions were fought including that at Abu Klea on 17 January 1885. Though prevailing, the mixed force of bluejackets, infantry, and cavalry—British and Egyptian—that had not trained together and suffering numerous breakdowns in their weapons came close to disaster. Alamy 2RBWP6R

Contemporary engraving originally appearing in *The Graphic*. Contemporaries viewed the conquest of Upper Burma in 1885 as a Navy-led and Army-supported operation. So it proved in its initial phase but a lengthy pacification effort was required before ultimate success followed. The minor military and constabulary operations occurring in the interior exhibited the familiar traits of movement across difficult terrain supported by tenuous river transport with campaigning limited to benign months. Source: Alamy FF4FGX

Not pressed for time the way Wolseley had been, Kitchener's reconquest of the Sudan was methodical, thorough, and supported by rail and river in a manner alien to the disastrous 1884-1885 campaign. British joint operations were at their best when the time to plan a campaign was afforded beforehand with improvisation kept to a minimum. Source: Alamy KW79JM

Frequently naval support did not end once a force was safely ashore but shifted to other means. Gunboats in Burma and Sudan provided tactical fires, performed reconnaissance, offered logistics support, and facilitated casualty support while offering a mobile headquarters to the military commander. Following their support at Omdurman in September 1898, gunboats steamed to Fashoda and provided the margin of difference in squaring matters on terms favorable to Britain and Egypt in the ongoing standoff with France. Source: Alamy JD98BF

With both the Transvaal and the Orange River State landlocked countries, amphibious operations did not feature significantly in the Second Anglo-Boer War. Naval support, however, was vital in isolating the theatre of operations thus precluding any outside intervention, cutting off the Boer Republics from outside material support, and providing crew-served weapons to British forces. Here 4.7-inch naval rifles modified for use ashore are manhandled by their crews across the Tugela River. Source: Alamy 2AG0GFY

ADMIRAL SEYMOUR'S RETREAT ON TIENTSIN.

Given the limited force that could be landed initially, British custom was to land at a point mutually beneficial to the requirements of the naval and military contingents but found some distance from the objective. Use of rail, river, canal, road, or track then facilitated the exploitation of the advantage won. Admiral Sir Edward Seymour's advance to relieve the Western legations in China in 1900 took advantage of the local rail line—unsuccessfully.
Source: Alamy KWD27B

The Russo-Japanese War was studied assiduously by the Royal Navy and British and Indian Armies in the years before the World War. Japan's successful amphibious operations conducted before local sea control had been secured were high-risk and highly profitable. Whether a certain Lieutenant General Sir Ian Hamilton, one of the British observers attached to Japanese forces, appreciated all the lessons on offer may be doubted. Here Japanese forces land horses at Chemulpo (Inchon), Korea. Source: Alamy D70HCA telling omission given recent British experience. That void stood the greater as it was a style of operation seemingly not covered in the standalone serials of the services. This had serious implications for Army Service Corps personnel training, but it also told against a navy focused on blue water requirements.[71] Still, the appearance of the manual was a seminal occurrence for the codification of first principles, which allowed tenets to be tested, refuted, and then modified based on the experience of exercises or current operations.

The first practical steps toward drafting the *Manual* followed the joint exercises held in September 1904. In the new year, a joint committee reviewed those results with their report anticipating much of the language later adopted in the *Manual*.[72] Yet, even now, progress remained slow and stilted, leading the War Office to lament both services' cursory knowledge on the subject. Conditioning this view remained the lack of an official treatise.[73] Why progress remained lukewarm must be a conjecture, though the absence of key officers is certainly a strong consideration. Wood departed II Corps in December 1904, and Fisher migrated to the Admiralty shortly before him. Missing, too, was Admiral Fawkes, the senior naval officer guiding the Essex serials, who did not attend the 1905 conference that codified so much. As a previous adviser to the inspector-general of fortifications, Fawkes possessed a strong background on the naval side of the equation. Unfortunately, between the Clacton exercise and the conference convening, he had hauled down his flag as commander of the Cruiser Squadron, leaving it to Commander Halsey of the *Good Hope* to speak to the lessons garnered. Halsey was an excellent officer and would support the army the following year during a staff ride in Ireland. Thus, it would be too much to claim Fawkes' attendance was vital. It did, though, say something about relative priorities: Fawkes now chaired an Admiralty committee on officer entry-level education.[74]

In hindsight, 1904 represents a singular point in the story of British amphibious warfare development. With their naval antecedents and now command of the I and II corps, French and Wood exemplified the apex of a navalist school within the British Army. Meanwhile, wearing his flag as commander-in-chief, Portsmouth, and fresh from service with Esher and Clarke, Fisher stood out as *the* naval officer listened to in the corridors of power over things military. With Aston teaching imperial strategy at Camberley, the confluence of personality and moment is telling and abetting what chance brought together was Britain's strategic situation. Yet, it proved gossamer.

Never mind Wood's retirement or a Fisher transfixed on broader horizons once enthroned at the Admiralty. A moment had passed.

Of course, a further reality existed: Balfour and his Liberal successors were committed to reducing the estimates of the services following the South African War. That reality shaped the larger, ongoing argument on the role and size of the army. As for the *Manual of Combined Naval and Military Operations*, the 1911 edition posited that "oversea operations" required Britain to possess "command of the sea." That limiting caveat would be eschewed in the 1913 edition when the opening chapter merely specified the general naval situation necessary to allow an operation to be pursued. The later edition now explicitly raised the preliminary issues requiring resolution before any joint plan could be adopted. Notably, the issuance of separate orders for naval and military units was insufficient. Some manner of joint orders could be expected and how such orders were to be issued now featured. Implicit in the last was the preparation and adoption of a supporting communications plan, and, to that end, a common *Vocabulary Signal Book* to facilitate joint interoperability between ashore and afloat units followed. This publication was updated yearly and updated at intervals by addenda. Indeed, it was in the consideration, drafting, and issuance of orders that the 1913 edition more fully diverged from its 1911 counterpart, with six appendixes now offering sample orders for use.[75]

Unlike its earlier iteration, the revised edition understood landings might occur in the face of enemy resistance. Accordingly, it did not discuss the execution of administrative landings avowing "This manual deals only with operations oversea which involve a landing on an open beach and in circumstances when sea communications and disembarkation are liable to interference by the enemy's naval or military forces." Employing language more explicit and emphatic, it read in part:

> **Owing to the varied circumstances in which such operations may have to be undertaken, the instructions should be regarded as a general guide, being subject to such modifications by naval and military commanders as the necessities of any particular operation may demand.**[76]

The boldface type reminded commanders that their judgment remained vital. A more cynical reading would be that the War Office and the Admiralty were telegraphing that any failure in execution need not be attributed elsewhere.

Toward a *Manual of Combined Naval and Military Operations*   147

As for the object of a combined operation, three possibilities existed. Firstly, a landing might occur to secure a coastal fortress or to allow operations to be developed against the field armies of the enemy. Securing an area to allow an advance base or anchorage to be established to support subsequent fleet operations offered a second rationale for an amphibious landing. As minor vessels such as destroyers and submarines possessed limited ranges, the strategic mobility of the fleet was constrained by the ancillary craft that accompanied heavy ships on distant operations. Thus, establishing an advance base might serve as the precursor to permit a fleet action to proceed or allow a blockade or mine barrage to be maintained. Finally, a minor landing to deny the enemy an essential communications focal point, such as a harbor, port, or transmitter station, remained an option. Not specified in the *Manual*, a combined operation might be pursued to force a reluctant enemy to sally his fleet to meet the unfolding threat. Certain naval circles accepted this as a possibility to secure command of the sea. How far the military did remains unclear. Reluctant to try conclusions in the Baltic, whether the general staff objection remained more general cannot be claimed.

Notwithstanding the object to be obtained, both editions vowed the navy was responsible for transporting and sustaining the force at sea and ashore. The landing itself would occur in two phases. Firstly, a covering force would land under conditions of darkness to be followed, secondly, by the main force. Though not explicitly stated, most believed the latter should arrive at daybreak.[77] To guarantee success, secrecy was a must, leading to the employment of feints to confuse the enemy of true intentions. Beyond establishing the initial lodgment, the covering force would occupy those points from where artillery fires against the transport fleet must be expected, which might be several miles inland at dispersed locations. Given the number of areas to be secured and the limited hours of darkness available, inserting the covering force would likely require multiple ships.[78]

The object and presumed scale of resistance would define the size of the main force, while tides, gradients, depth of approach, currents, and the ability to shelter the transports from the elements did the same for the locale finally chosen. If the aim was to advance further inland, then landing near a railhead, river, or canal offered the best means of forward movement. Road networks offered the least advantage as wagons and vehicles required animals, fodder, and fuel. Surprisingly, these considerations were not featured in either prewar edition of the manual, though their bearing had influenced the decisions of

Wolseley and Seymour earlier. The omission testifies that the pre-1914 *Manual* remained, at best, a work in progress.

In parallel with the *Manual of Combined Naval and Military Operations*, the army's *Field Service Regulations* (*FSR*) and *Field Service Pocket Book* were revised to account for combined operations.[79] In turn, the *FSR*'s treatment amplified the tasks and responsibilities required of the services. Here, the greatest service performed by the *FSR* was to specify the key naval personnel involved in a combined operation with their corresponding military equivalents. Thus, the roles of the principal naval transport officer, naval transport officers, principal beach master, and their subordinates were amplified for the military reader. Ironically, a counterpart to the principal naval transport officer, the individual charged with managing the disembarkation at the scene of operations, was not explicitly specified in the *FSR*. Still, the most significant weakness remained a failure to address the how of any amphibious operation.[80] Meanwhile, the *Training and Manoeuvre Regulations* of 1913 acknowledged that "special 'exercises"—those conducted with the navy—might occur. In a work devoted to the minutia of military exercises, more might have been said about combined operations than simply landing a force across an open beach or against unprotected anchorages. That more did not appear indicates such serials remained the exception and not the norm on the cusp of war.[81]

In the prewar period, the navy's poor counterpart to the *FSR* remained the *Rifle and Field Exercises for H.M. Fleet*.[82] Dating from at least 1888 and revised anew in 1901, 1904, 1909, and 1913, the work would be revised and retitled the *Royal Naval Handbook of Field Training* following the war. Even then, Lieutenant William King-Hall scorned its usefulness in preparing a naval force for military duties.[83] As for the *FSR*, it documented the arrangements for forces on active service, thus allowing all to work to a common understanding.[84] That need was never more apparent than when the military depended on the navy during the execution of an amphibious assault. The wonder remains that the navy did not feel a corresponding need to develop a counterpart to the *FSR* to address their share of the equation. It may be the Admiralty believed its *Regulations for His Majesty's Transport Service* met any void. While these covered the general movement of men, material, and beasts, they remained largely silent on the how of execution.[85] To wit:

(i) The entire operations of landing and shipping troops, animals, guns, regimental stores, and stores (cargo), whether alongside wharves or piers, either Government or mercantile, or to and from a beach, will be controlled by the Navy, who will provide the boats, lighters and tugs, and any labour required in connection with the same. All other labour required will be found by the Army, except in cases where the circumstances render it desirable that the Navy should provide some or all the labour. The ultimate decision on this point will rest with Naval authorities.

(ii) The Navy will be responsible for the berthing of all ships, lighters tugs and boats; but the convenience of the Army must be considered as far as practicable in the positions allotted. For landings and embarkations the Navy will have full control of the entire beach up to the high-water mark, and of such further portions of the same, and of the piers and wharves as they consider necessary to enable them to control the work of the embarkation and disembarkation. Within these portions the military officers will carry out all instructions issued by the naval officer in charge, but beyond them the responsibility for the safety and transportation of men, animals, guns, vehicles, and stores on shore will rest with the Army.

(iii) While the foregoing are the general rules governing the division of duties between the Navy and the Army, it is to be clearly understood that each Service is working for a common object, and will render the other all the assistance which lies in its power.[86]

As a service publication, the above focused on the operational and tactical. Unsurprisingly, the weakness of strategic control would bedevil British practice for many years.

Meanwhile, over the course of April–May 1907, the staff college, in association with the war college, conducted another joint staff tour. Its summarizing report by Brigadier General Wilson again pointed to the need for a joint manual "for the use of both Services comprising the general lines on which a modern landing will take place."[87] That an officer forever associated with the continental commitment proved a chief advocate for a *Manual of*

Naval and Military Combined Operations must be afforded one of the ironies of history. As for the 1907 tour, marines representing "a part of the actual force" embarked in the cruiser *Terpsichore* before landing on the Isle of Wight, where their presence was deemed to have enhanced the exercise's utility from previous years. Speaking to the most salient lessons derived, Captain Edmond Slade of the war college identified three: 1) the necessity of surveying sites in peacetime which might feature as an objective in war; 2) landing the covering force at night to reduce the advantage a defending force derived from modern weapons; and 3) inserting of the beach party immediately following the landing of the covering force to prepare the way for the main force. To Henry Wilson, the tour demonstrated that "joint naval and military operations are among the most difficult of all our exercises when judged from a staff point of view." Calling attention to the difficulty of visual signaling between ship and shore, he believed the early establishment of telephonic communications essential.[88]

In July 1907, Major General Michael Rimington directed the exercises held by Scottish command that year.[89] This witnessed ships taken up from trade, embarking cavalry and supporting artillery. Landing from two ships on a rough shore in otherwise calm weather, the serial displayed that a cavalry regiment could be disembarked within 6 hours.[90] More expansive was the exercise occurring in 1910, where Captain Heathcoat Grant prepared the detailed naval transport requirements to support a raid in excess of 10,000 troops, including 2,500 horses. Employing regular and territorial soldiers, the event nonetheless displayed those artificialities common to the period's joint exercises: individual ships were meant to represent flotillas while only a portion of those engaged landed.[91]

Of course, not all amphibious exercises were joint. During the naval maneuvers conducted off Ireland in 1909, the cruiser *Arrogant* escaped the fires of the battleship *Bellerophon* to land a party at Crew Bay. First seizing Rosmoney Coast Guard Station, the party next captured Westport's rail station while the *Boadicea* entered the Shannon to land a force at Carrigaholt, County Clare where they subdued the post office.[92] Not to be outshone, in September 1912, General French, minus the navy, "landed" a corps-size enemy force (Red) under Lieutenant General Haig between Hunstanton and Wells, intending to reach London before the British troops (Blue) had time to mobilize.[93] Red forfeited the opportunity to deal a mortal blow to a Blue division moving across the open country as it meant disobeying its orders to hold a fixed position.

Brigadier General Lancelot Kiggell, the director of staff duties, faulted the rigidity of the orders governing operations as a priceless opportunity went begging.[94] Also observing the above was Captain Sidney Drury-Lowe, who was attached to French's staff for the exercise's duration. Drury-Lowe's military links date back to at least 1904, when he organized the landings made in Italian Somaliland while serving with the East Indies Squadron. More recently, he supported the territorial force in its summer serials before being attached to the staff college.[95]

During the 1913 summer naval maneuvers, 347 vessels fought in a scenario positing a German attack upon Great Britain. Such a collection of ships necessitated withdrawing units from the Mediterranean station to join their domestic counterparts. Hence, beyond testing the lines of amphibious operations, the exercise guaranteed the interoperability of the main fleets, now designated Red and Blue.[96] As the play unfolded, the Red fleet demonstrated a repeated ability to evade Blue and land troops over open beaches. Those landing on 26 July at Blyth represented a covering force embarked in twelve boats. Grounding approximately a half mile from shore, the three companies of 450 marines had to wade the remaining distance. Halfway to the beach, they were met by the machine gun fire of a defending Territorial cyclist unit. Although the after-action report did not assess the level of casualties sustained, it did speak to the tactical implications of immediate resistance. To wit, the covering force needed to reach its initial objectives rapidly or else face annihilation. These had to be known by all before disembarkation. Even then, coordinating the efforts of those coming from multiple vessels proved extremely difficult with communications across echelons and between ship and shore trying. In part, the covering force possessed too few signalers or runners to pass information and orders. It also possessed too few junior officers to command the reinforced companies organized for these landings. Finally, the covering force needed to be organized into fire teams to deal with any resistance met.[97] Forming the covering force from marines had long been advocated, given their length of tenure and familiarity with boats. As a general treatise drafted by the War Office, the *Manual of Combined Naval and Military Operations* did not go this far, probably because proposing such a prescriptive remedy would be seen as brazen.[98]

In addition to the several battalions of infantry borne in the Red Fleet's transports, military observers serving across the two fleets had monitored the unfolding action. Beyond extending a courtesy to the War Office, their presence demonstrates the steps being taken to develop sympathy and understanding between the services.[99] The director of staff duties had tasked these officers to register their observations of the fleet. Learning of this, the Admiralty's chief of the war staff, Admiral Henry Jackson, sought copies of their comments.[100] Exactly how many riders accompanied the fleet is not recorded, but ten reports deemed the most salient were forwarded to the Admiralty. Necessarily, their eyes had been cast wide afield, but their views on amphibious warfare are of most concern here. Major Francis Marshall offered that future expeditions would have to be escorted by destroyers, not heavy ships, owing to the submarine peril. Moreover, as a fleet would have its hands full dealing with that peril and still others and ships' companies no longer possessed a surplus of numbers, reserves of rating would have to be allocated. Ideally, these hands would be trained in peacetime for the duties performed in war.[101] From the *Achilles*, Major Henry Smith-Rewse posited that a trained staff officer should serve with the fleet commander.[102] That proposition stood little chance in the near term in a naval service only now coming to terms with the role and place of a war staff.

Captain Henry Alexander contrasted the methods of the respective Red Fleet admirals: George Callaghan and John Jellicoe.[103] Timing and initiative counted for much, leading Alexander to conclude "that a raid, although undertaken in the face of great numerical supremacy, has a good sporting chance of success, and I am satisfied that no strategist with a true conception of the results to be gained would hesitate to employ such raids in a war waged by a hostile naval power against this country."[104] To Captain Eric Seagrave, naval signalers were more adept than their army counterparts. Meanwhile, naval signalers expressed frustration at the length of army messages. Thus, Seagrave recommended the cross-posting of instructors to each service's schools of signaling to foster interoperability. Reflecting a difference in ethos and operating environment, army orders were not always endorsed by a unit's superior but sent on the authority of a subordinate staff officer. Received by a ship, the message, at a minimum, proved impolite as naval communications were always made from commanding officer to commanding officer. The unspoken risk remained the navy might not always act as desired.[105] Finally, Major Harold Street concluded that the views of the two services were at such odds that it was not enough to send naval officers to Camberley or have their military counterparts sit the naval war course. A recent attendee of the war course, he posited that the navy should appoint an officer to the directing staff of the military staff college, with the army doing likewise to the Royal Naval war college.[106]

What Jackson made of these observations has not been traced. Still, they indicated that the two services were working to learn from each other, notwithstanding the questions of greater policy separating them. With a professional foot in each camp, George Aston stood as a prime exemplar but so did others who began their career in one service only to migrate to another. Still, the previous grounding was not without benefit, even if it operated against the immediate expense of the senior service as it conditioned some to think more broadly about the nature of war in a maritime-centric empire. Thus, it is now appropriate to examine that portion of the story.

Thirteen

Deus Ex Machina: Reform from Above

A nation in case of war should have determined beforehand where to strike, and should be prepared to strike.[1]

Esher, 1910

In past wars the ubiquity conferred by sea power has ever given to a British military expedition a value out of all proportion to its strength. Sea power remains essential, but the improvement in land communications and the enormous growth of modern European armies have greatly lessened, if they have not as yet completely destroyed, the advantages this ubiquity once gave.[2]

Spencer Ewart, 1909

If nothing else was gained from the Anglo-Boer War, the need to reform the British Army was a task that Conservatives and Liberals seized with both hands. To wit, in the parliamentary election of 1900 both parties championed reform of the army.[3] This is not to claim the need for such had been absent earlier. Still, the test of large-scale military operations provided ready fodder for those arguing previous initiatives had been incomplete. Such investigations overseen by the Marquis of Hartington, Clinton Dawkins, and Sir Francis Mowatt spoke to problems ever of concern where public finance is involved. The recent war highlighted questions of more profound worry, and while previous efforts were not wasted, they tackled subsidiary problems or received an indifferent reception. Thus, the genesis of the Royal Commission for the War in South Africa, directed by the Earl of Elgin.[4] Taking evidence from October 1902 through June 1903, they possessed the broadest of remits, which seemingly went begging as no concrete recommendations ensued. Amply cataloging a litany of shortcomings, the void demonstrated the difficulties of securing consensus where so many equities were at play.[5]

Of course, a reason why earlier initiatives faltered was the ongoing military operations had drawn many key officers to South Africa. This was inevitable in an environment where the military establishment was maintained on modest lines—at least modest by continental standards. Yet, even if that bar had not been present, the inclination and habits of ministers married to the perceived limits of finance provided two further reasons for stasis. Reform aplenty there remained, though directed toward other priorities, be it church disestablishment, education, Irish Home Rule, or the expansion of the franchise. Absent perceived immediate need, partisans expended their limited political capital on propositions guaranteed to cement their power.

If the Boer War exposed operational and tactical shortcomings, it also highlighted Britain's vulnerabilities in defending a global empire when already committed to action in a distant theater. "Splendid isolation" was fine if Britain could define the parameters of her aloofness. Unfortunately, imperial obligations often said otherwise, as events in South Africa had shown. This was a strategic problem of the first order, and its realization forced Britain to find partners elsewhere.[6] Japan, in the first instance, followed by France, aligned with Russia. Increasingly, the problem of Germany subsumed all others, though Britain always had more points of friction with France and Russia than with the former. This might have prompted Britain to find accommodation with Germany, and, indeed, attempts were made to this end, yet not to the point of abandoning the understanding already secured with France. Increasingly, then, Berlin's wants suffered as these tended to be aimed at the expense of Paris. This was a price willingly paid, for it secured British interests in Asia and Africa while maintaining the balance of power in Europe in the face of Germany's rising economic strength.[7] Granted, the German naval program remained, but Britain would have built dreadnoughts, nonetheless. Perhaps not as rapidly or as many, but British maritime supremacy demanded a fleet capable of meeting all comers.

The South African War had taxed British military prowess. Reform of the army duly ensued, which witnessed a reordering in the structures controlling the higher direction of war. Here, the most significant change saw the transformation of the Defence Committee into a Committee of Imperial Defence (CID) in December 1902. Dating from 1895, the Defence Committee refereed disputes between the services and the treasury. Helpful in that regard, Balfour believed its examination of strategic problems suffered to the detriment of effective long-term planning.[8] That was not entirely correct, as the Defence Committee's charter was highly elastic.[9] More to the point, the

Defence Committee had not been used as fully as it might have been. That was a criticism of Salisbury more so than of Devonshire, who chaired that body, though Balfour was too polite to say as much in public.

With meetings rare and senior officers speaking even rarer, Devonshire conceded the Defence Committee had not been all it could have been and believed two critical innovations were required to make the body successful. Firstly, its secretariat had to be strengthened. Secondly, and more vitally, the prime minister had to take charge of its proceedings.[10] This Balfour accepted, but the new prime minister eyed two further problems: the baleful influence of the treasury and the absence of professional advice at the summit of consideration. His proposed reform of the Defence Committee received an unhappy reception from the Liberal benches, and that it had not been socialized with parliament beforehand nor covered by primary legislation had not assisted matters.[11] That the announced changes came at the expense of collective cabinet responsibility and strengthened the hands of prime ministerial authority only raised the ire of such Liberal stalwarts as Sir Henry Campbell-Bannerman and Mr. John Morley.[12]

War Office (Reconstitution) Committee

Reginald Brett, M.P., in time, became Brett the civil servant, with his influence and prominence only growing. Possessing tact, charm, and intellect, as a courtier, he quickly earned a reputation as a fixer able to steer difficult problems to satisfactory conclusions. His experience in public works led to his appointment to serve on a committee investigating the construction of military barracks. Success in that regard found him soon by Lord Elgin's side and charged with investigating the army in the wake of the South African War. If the deliberations of the last bore little tangible fruit, then they certainly bloomed handsomely for Esher as Balfour now tapped him to examine War Office administration. His ties to the king and political outlook were qualities of no mean importance when the question to be faced concerned the war office, where interests and opinions abounded.[13] Working with Esher on this vexed matter were a newly installed commander-in-chief, Portsmouth, (Admiral Sir John Fisher) and the governor of Victoria (Sir George Clarke, later styled as Lord Sydenham of Combe), with Lieutenant Colonel Gerald Ellison acting as the body's secretary. All were strong players in their own right and not given to viewing subjects with a neutral eye.[14]

Selborne, the first lord of the Admiralty and Salisbury's son-in-law, had sought to keep Fisher off the committee. His serving could only place the Admiralty in an invidious position with the War Office. In the event, Balfour believed otherwise.[15] Meanwhile, Clarke's appearance transpired when General Sir Francis Grenfell refused to serve.[16] Clarke, however, possessed a history and, in the mind of some, not a wholesome one. Fisher, though, touted his expertise. Of his brilliance, few could argue passing as he did first into and first out of Woolwich.[17] As for Ellison, he was viewed as highly capable, presently drafting what would become the *Field Service Regulations*. Perhaps too capable, as the adjutant general fought to keep him tethered to current duties. Lieutenant General Sir Thomas Kelly-Kenny's obstruction proved wasted; it was not forgotten as Esher claimed his scalp when an army council replaced the army board.[18]

Professor Brian Bond avows that Esher's efforts were without equal in the matter of War Office reform. That verdict may be accepted notwithstanding the subsequent orders-in-council issued to round off the sharper edges of what had been created.[19] Animating all was the necessity of separating administration from command.[20] Even this did not seem to go far enough in Balfour's eyes as he deemed the very name "war office" problematic and not in keeping with the times nor the views of the self-governing dominions. Better was the proposed re-establishment of the Defence Committee as the CID equipped with a proper secretariat to evaluate the significant issues facing Britain. These were always "combined operations" and required balancing naval and military strategies.[21]

How far the underlying problems in defense being addressed were structural rather than ministerial may be pondered. To Esher and company, that problem was not a major worry for "New measures demand new men."[22] The most that can be said is that while strong and gifted personalities may make any system work, a solid edifice to advance matters is necessary for the rest of us. With that in mind, what was created bettered what had previously sufficed. Nonetheless, criticism was not long in coming, fueled by the eclipsing of parliament by the press once more as the findings of Esher's *Second Report* appeared. That the findings seemingly had been reached minus evidence to support the conclusions advocated "caused the government considerable embarrassment."[23]

Esher and company seconded Balfour's proposed changes to the Defence Committee, which offered the prime minister a level of political cover.[24] Unfortunately, one not serving on the present commission, though of the reforming kind, was the secretary of state for war, Hugh Arnold-Forster.[25] Unsurprisingly, Arnold-Forster and Esher clashed during the implementation phase. Partly, this reflected the former's desire to paint with a broader brush than Esher.[26] Partly, it stemmed from the moves, subtle or otherwise, of Esher. Not content with proposing, he sought to dispose by influencing the personnel changes necessary to bring all to fruition.[27] Exercising "power without responsibility—the prerogative of the harlot throughout the ages"—if applied by Stanley Baldwin at another moment, might well have been said of Esher now. Certainly, Arnold-Forster thought as much, telling Esher, "I think in your position of great power and little responsibility you sometimes overlook or forget what are the burdens you impose upon me, who have to endure the whole of the personal application of your recommendations."[28]

That Esher acted with Balfour's blessing can be assured. Yet, only a year previous, Arnold-Forster had penned a memorandum anticipating much that was now recommended.[29] This included a revised Council of Defence formed by subject matter experts divorced from ministerial responsibilities to be augmented by a strengthened secretariat to record its findings.[30] Arnold-Forster worried about the absence of a common doctrine across the services and the lack of formal links between the Admiralty and War Office. More explicitly, for a maritime empire, the intelligence department of the Admiralty was staffed woefully, while a trained force to support the maritime operations Britain must be expected to execute in war did not exist. Certainly, that force was not the Royal Marines, whose composition stemmed more from an accident of history than a purposeful design.[31] Ironically, given the preceding, Arnold-Forster rejected establishing the army's principal operational command at Portsmouth, believing it would inevitably place its commander in an inferior position to his naval counterpart.[32]

As it happened, the question of officer education and training was very much alive within the Admiralty. Selborne now sought to tie the marines closer to the navy. Finance alone must have been why he sought to distance them from their military ties for the ongoing expansion of the navy demanded ever more personnel of ever greater technical competence. As presently trained, marine officers could not solve that pressing problem, but they did represent an untapped pool of potential with closer integration eliminating the vestiges of War Office control.[33] Highly regarded as a military force, their long service and the esprit that comes with it produced a superior specimen even if rarely training in more significant numbers than a company. Maintained from a central depot, the Royal Marines did not face the logistical problems of the army's decentralized regimental regime.[34] Indeed, short-service enlistment was viewed by one observer as a bar to developing expertise in amphibious operations as time only permitted the imparting of rudimentary training.[35]

Enter the Committee of Imperial Defence

Though a regular participant, from November 1903, Balfour began chairing the CID. The immediate genesis of the change was the resignation of Devonshire over the issue of free trade.[36] Balfour now shaped the CID's membership to fit the problem under consideration. This would allow colonial participation and became a vehicle for examining critical issues across party lines.[37] Thus, the attendance of the political heads of the Admiralty and War Office as *ex officio* members ceased. Adding a permanent secretariat in April 1904 brought a degree of regularity and order to an agency that necessarily trimmed the sails of those departments and committees overseeing imperial policy. Yet, the creation of a permanent secretariat did not go uncontested. Balfour, for one, remained to be convinced, while others deprecated the idea of Clarke as its principal occupant. Esher, however, prevailed in the change.[38]

More than anything else, the changes suited the needs of Balfour, who consistently took a strong hand in strategic matters. While the CID did not replace the cabinet, the remit of the latter necessarily suffered for recommendations arising from an organ chaired by the prime minister were not readily dismissed. In time, the CID secretariat approached in status the planning section of a nascent joint staff for succeeding secretaries did not limit their toil to the coordination of issues, but began forwarding position papers of their own creation. This challenged an unwritten rule of military and naval administration that held plans should be prepared by the agency executing the operation. For the moment, it was argued, executive action remained with the cabinet and the departments.[39] The edicts of Esher, who remained outside the cabinet and the War Office in removing and appointing officers, suggested matters were not quite so simple.

Esher's influence did not end there, as Kitchener touted his work when reshaping the Indian Army.[40] This soon put him at odds with Curzon, and as the viceroy had a stormy relationship with the former commander-in-chief, General Sir Power Palmer, the fault could not be ascribed solely to Kitchener. Whatever the merits of Kitchener's proposals, increasing the scope of India's commander-in-chief promised to reduce the authority of the viceroy. To a man of Curzon's bearing, this was poisonous, and as the viceroy possessed experience of India, which Kitchener lacked, the change was presumptuous to a degree.[41] As for Kitchener's reforms, the record again proved mixed. Hardinge, a later viceroy, lamented the ensuring chaos within the military department.[42] More positively, Kitchener rationalized the number of garrisons, thereby reducing overhead costs. Eliminating the Indian staff corps, all officers now served in an Indian Army with units renumbered to bring order to their nomenclature where none seemly existed. Upsetting many, the principle was sound enough.[43] As for the position of the commander-in-chief, just as it was being abolished in the British Army, its Indian variant was strengthened with administration and command placed in the hands of a single officer.[44]

Though the underpinnings of the British and Indian armies remained different, the desire remained they should share a strategic view such that coordination in wartime would be enhanced. Salisbury anticipated as much in 1882 when he claimed India stood "as an English barrack in the Oriental Seas from which we may draw any number of troops without paying for them."[45] The Indian Army now accepted the divisional structure for out-of-area operations, of which over a dozen were conducted between 1857 and 1914.[46] Implicitly, this assumed Indian troops engaged in large-scale operations would probably act under British Army control as the latter retained a corps structure.[47]

Notwithstanding Kitchener's efforts, the CID viewed the logistical arrangements of the Indian Army as an area of concern. Nominally able to mobilize eight divisions, shortfalls meant only four divisions were readily available.[48] On a more positive note, India prepared war establishment tables, which allowed planners to calculate the transportation requirements for moving a unit of a given size via road, rail, river, or ocean. This was no slight advantage as long as units mobilized to a set pattern.[49] To be sure, the Imperial service troops maintained by the princely states remained a further concern. Commanded by Indian officers, they trained under the guidance of British officers and thus remained outside the direct remit of Simla.[50] Numbering roughly 18,000 troops in 1911, they were an Indian variant of the militia possessing many of the same benefits and not a few of the same ills. Their equipage depended on the largess of their benefactors with their understanding of army procedure and the deeper aspects of war cursory.[51] To offset such shortfalls, Special Service officers from the Indian establishment filled out these units when deployed for British service.

The Admiralty's influence within the CID was at its apex from its gestation. Nicholas d'Ombrain concludes the body "was a success because the Admiralty liked it."[52] More correctly, the Admiralty liked it as far as the ox being gored belonged to the War Office or India, for their issues consumed the first deliberations of the CID. However, a poor showing in South Africa forced the War Office to embrace reform with both hands. If the impetus for change was to recast the army into a more effective service, then a corollary benefit saw the War Office exerting a growing influence in CID deliberations.[53] Partly doctrinal and institutional, the creation of a proper staff system within the war office employing highly effective officers trained to a common standard resulted. The prize gained was increased service influence, as reflected in the reports and memoranda submitted to the CID by the general staff, which soon outpaced naval contributions.[54]

Still, another reason for the War Office nascent ascendency resided in the changed strategic setting. It remained that the most intractable strategic problems facing Britain and India were of a military nature. Defending India, Canada, and Egypt had their maritime dimensions, but that was not where problems were manifest. Thus, the naval problems looming reflected the long-term nature of foreign shipbuilding programs. Given sufficient resources, Britain would prevail on the day. Of course, that is an oversimplification, but at this hour, naval analysis often yielded to the mere bean-counting of competing fleets. Conversely, military problems were inherently complex owing to geography, differing force structures, and the presence or absence of allies. In electing to maintain the foremost navy, Britain was under-resourced to meet other first-rate powers on equal terms on land. Compounding matters was the need for stringency to pay for the Boer War, to be sure, but for Liberals to meet the expense of social reform.[55]

War Office reorganization, if desirable for better administration, supported a change every bit as significant: defining the purpose of the army. This had been a vintage concern made no easier by the separate conditions of service for the regular, militia, yeomanry, and volunteers. Of importance to this accounting were their varied obligations for overseas service. Unlike all naval personnel, the posting of militia, yeomanry, and volunteers overseas was eschewed.[56] The anomaly owed something to the principle of voluntary enlistment, but more significantly, it owed something to the social standing of those leading part-time units. Manifestly, Britain's position as an island allowed the tradition to continue beyond the point of safety, notwithstanding the empire acquired along the way. Wolseley saw the conflict as one between ends and means and argued the army must be ready to conduct amphibious operations.[57]

Officially, the War Office continued to avow that the British Army was the handmaiden to a maritime-oriented approach. Balfour endorsed this view when he chartered a permanent subcommittee to consider joint action by the services in 1905.[58] This was a natural outcome of the recently held joint exercise at Clacton. It was also a natural outcome of the striking force posited by Arnold-Forster and Esher. Fisher was one animating spirit for just such a committee, though not a lone one.[59] Grimes touts the spark of Captain Charles Ottley, who understood that planning and organizing a joint operation on the fly when the enemy was Germany could only lead to disaster.[60] Summerton, meanwhile, avows the backdrop of the Moroccan Crisis had prompted Arthur Wilson, then commanding the Channel Fleet, to posit that British support to France against Germany could not be limited to naval means alone.[61] Both are correct, yet the War Office had already been arguing as much because of Britain's treaty obligation to Japan. With that agreement now under revision, Major General James Grierson, the director of military operations, noted that the "arrangements for combined action must be frequently revised." Lansdowne, the foreign secretary, concurred.[62] Fraser, meanwhile, avows that Clarke was the guiding hand for the new agency with the measure taken to buttress the nascent CID in anticipation of the Liberals coming to power.[63] Surely, that is to credit a benefit of secondary importance. The motive force for establishing the subcommittee was to concert Admiralty and War Office planning in the wake of the Moroccan Crisis and to revise plans developed earlier to support Japan.

Both Ottley and Clarke appreciated that planning in the disjointed hands of Fisher and Lyttelton was hardly a formula for success. Meanwhile, the responsibility for preparing joint plans fell between two stools. The director of naval intelligence lacked the authority to prepare such plans on his own accord, meaning those fashioned so far lacked standing. This was the strongest argument for creating a select committee under the auspices of the CID, as it would force the two services to concert their efforts in a previously absent manner.[64] Thus, upon the extension of the Anglo-Japanese Treaty in July 1905, meetings followed over the next 6 months. Ostensibly chartered to weigh assisting Japan in the event of a new Asian war, action supporting France against Germany needed to be assessed given the understanding existing between Britain and France. Here, the Admiralty proposed blocking the Elbe estuary or sending the Channel Fleet into the Baltic to cover landings against Schleswig-Holstein. Both the general staff and Admiral Beresford looked dimly at these proposals. That Britain possessed only 100,00 deployable troops and these lacked organic artillery seemed to suggest their prompt destruction if the attempt were made. Instead, the general staff argued that an equal force should be sent to France or Belgium.[65] Meanwhile, Japan would strike at German possessions in China.[66]

The suggested descent on the German coast was a product of Fisher's fertile imagination. By threatening Berlin, the move would pose the gravest situation to a German Army already committed to a headlong thrust against France. All this was too much for the general staff. Indeed, it was too much for some naval officers. Landing a force in the Baltic assumed a neutralized German Fleet. It also assumed a force landed there could be maintained over the winter months.[67]

The senior service's loss of sway within the CID continued notwithstanding Ottley, fresh from attending the Second Hague Conference, replacing Clarke, an Army officer with pronounced maritime leanings, as secretary in October 1907.[68] His *The Navy and the Nation*, penned in association with the journalist and historian James Thursfield, posited that every strategic question ultimately resolved upon Britain's maritime standing as this made all else possible.[69] Ottley would depart in 1912, ostensibly after reaching the statuary limit of service. In truth, his departure followed when he failed to secure a better financial package than the £2,000 a year he had been receiving. Having been allowed to retain his allowances as a naval *adc* to the King as secretary, pushing the envelope in emoluments was not new to Ottley.[70] Henry Asquith, the prime minister, evidencing little desire to enter a bidding war, now thanked Ottley for his services.[71] Filling the gap was a marine with a strong intelligence background and presently serving as an assistant secretary: Captain Maurice Hankey. Hankey's subsequent quarter-century of service has obscured the legacies of Clarke and Ottley and, though eventually having all the influence of his predecessors and more, his accession benefited the War Office and its strategic view in the near term as Hankey initially focused on narrow issues.[72]

Increasingly, military strategy focused on deploying an expeditionary force to Europe. This was a change of the greatest importance, for while previous planning accepted that military forces were available for offensive operations, the scenario typically envisioned raids against an enemy's colonial possessions or naval bases. France served as the primary consideration; hence, plans for taking Martinique, Dakar, Saigon, and Diego Suarez were specified, and surveys of their defensive arrangements were then undertaken.[73]

In the case of Martinique, British Army officers surveyed the island in 1894. In late 1897, Fisher, while commanding the North American and West Indies station, tasked the corvette *Cordelia* to investigate the feasibility of a *coup de main*. After recalling previous expeditions against the island, Captain Maurice Bourke's paper suggested a force of 5,000 troops arranged for extended operations would be necessary.[74] Whether the assault could succeed was another matter. Major Henry Drake of the naval intelligence department believed that the scale of force required would preclude any chance of surprise.[75] As the island possessed excellent docking facilities and was viewed as a powerful enabler for forces operating in the Caribbean, revisions to the scheme followed.

Revisiting the question in 1903, Captain Prince Louis of Battenberg believed Martinique's isolation was its greatest weakness. Possessing none of the means that modern fleets required beyond what had been previously stored, these must eventually expire. The same remained true in the case of Diego Suarez, Dakar, and Saigon, with the director of naval intelligence arguing that their capitulation must follow the defeat of the French Fleet. Thus, plans for their direct assault were misguided, leading Battenberg to conclude that "there is no need to keep any troops specially ear-marked at home for these over-sea expeditions. By the time they become possible, the army for home defense should be able to provide all that is needful."[76]

This view only gained traction once France became an ally in all but name. Conceptually, such operations remained to be done against other powers such as Spain.[77] Progress faltered, and here, two reasons may be adduced. Firstly, unless the serial furthered the maritime strategy of the war posited, the Admiralty believed it represented a dispersion of effort. Secondly, the advent of the submarine had now strengthened the means of local resistance. In the future, a military force must land at a distance removed from a serial's true objective.[78] These realities weakened the case for joint operations. Confirming these essential truths, in 1914, the war orders for the distant fleets stressed concentrating their dispersed ships in the first instance before engaging enemy vessels with thoughts of joint operations secondary. All this freed the War Office to focus on making war in association with France.[79]

Why it was thought Britain's minuscule military contribution counted for so much in the balance moved the issue beyond the realm of strategy. The creation of an expeditionary force, if adopted for reasons of high policy, justified a larger army—or at least a larger role in policy formulation—which meeting an invasion of Britain could never secure. Officially, an undefeated Royal Navy made invasion an impossibility. Unofficially, room for doubt certainly existed, and while the issue resides outside the scope of this review, the problem presented led Britain to conduct a series of combined exercises of value beyond determining the level of effort required to meet the risk.[80] Sending a force to Europe to fight alongside France implied providing an army of the greatest number of combat units to maximize British influence in the overall strategy adopted. This meant the adoption of more rifle battalions over service troops in the regular force, with the administrative tail coming from second-line forces upon mobilization.[81] Operationally, the ability of the army to deploy and land as a self-contained entity in a non-European setting became less.

More immediately, in December 1905, Esher chaired a committee weighing whether combined naval and military operations against Germany were feasible. These could either be raids against the main German ports or the occupation of nearby islands as the first step toward landing on the mainland in an operation conducted by the British unilaterally or in cooperation with the French. Alternative schemes vetted included sending a force to the continent if Belgian neutrality was compromised.[82] Given the presumed distances from the points of embarkation to the corresponding facilities in France where such a force would land, this called for the exercise of local sea control and an administrative transfer of troops, while a Baltic operation presumed either the defeat or neutralization of the German High Sea Fleet. Arguing for operations in Belgium or France was that administratively and militarily, these were the easiest and least risky to execute and would result in British forces coming into action sooner.[83]

It was one thing to weigh a raid, the seizure of an advanced base, or even a landing against a power of the second rank. Still, it was quite another to consider an operation against Germany, the foremost military power. Preliminary discussions between the naval intelligence directorate and the directorate of military operations proved inconclusive. These had seen Captain George Ballard and Colonel Charles Callwell wrestle with the problem. Known as an intellectually gifted officer, Callwell proved a little too supportive of Admiralty Baltic intentions.[84] Certainly, he had been more supportive than others in the operations directorate, including Major Disney Fasson. Hence, the intervention of Esher to resolve matters.[85]

Unfortunately for Esher, Balfour had just resigned as prime minister—he was again the motive force behind establishing a committee to weigh overseas operations. With the Liberal Campbell-Bannerman now in harness, an election soon ensued. In the early twentieth century, these ran at a more sedate schedule such that the Liberals did not secure a majority until early February 1906. This does not mean Esher was marking time, but resolving the underlying issues necessarily awaited the resolution of the political vacuum. Eventually, Esher sided with the War Office and the CID confirmed this stance.[86] This was not to Fisher's liking, and when Esher conceded that the general staff was not on a par with the Admiralty, Fisher's patience must have been tested even more. Meanwhile, to Clarke, the third member of the triumvirate examining War Office organization, Esher despaired that their efforts had only created a "Frankenstein's monster" to the detriment of the CID. Writing privately to Edward VII, Esher shared the central problem exposed:

> The marked characteristic of this meeting of the Committee was the ease with which the Admiralty carried their point, and the failure of the War Office to carry theirs. This result was not due to the action of the War Minister, which was all that could be desired, but to the weakness of the General Staff.[87]

One victim of the change in administrations was the body to weigh combined operations. Esher emphasized its essentialness to Campbell-Bannerman, advising, "No similar enquiry has ever been made into our joint naval and military requirements of the Empire for offensive-defensive purposes."[88] The argument failed to move the prime minister, and that the committee lapsed should not prove surprising: A similar fate had befallen the short-lived Colonial Defence Committee once Disraeli had exited the political scene.[89]

The present failure, however, came with a cost: It left Fisher free to pursue planning outside the bounds of enunciated strategy.[90] This was prudent at one level, for nothing is ever truly settled in military planning. Still, it created a disjointed strategy by separating the Admiralty from the CID and the War Office and, doubtlessly, shaped the attitudes of those involved when a later crisis arose. Most clearly, this was found in the continued planning for Baltic operations in any German war and the subsidiary operations to be made against German colonies. Repington, for one, held these plans were not the equal of those serials prepared when France was the presumed enemy. This is correct as half of the equation remained missing in the Admiralty's calculations as Ballard, Slade, and Corbett from the war college pursued Fisher's preferred lines of inquiry. A junior member supporting this work was Hankey, who had previously assisted Ballard when the latter was the naval member of General John Owen's Defended Ports Abroad Committee.[91]

Meanwhile, the War Office continued to assume the deployment of a force to Europe, with Haldane authorizing Grierson to begin talks with the French. Tellingly, the decision came when Campbell-Bannerman and the cabinet were out of town and fixated on the pending election. These discussions focused on the administrative transfer of four brigades of cavalry, two corps of infantry, and a single division of mounted infantry to Boulogne, Calais, Dieppe, and Le Havre, with their subsequent deployment directed to support either French or Belgian forces as circumstances dictated. As the planning was unofficial, correspondence between the Admiralty and the War Office referring to the lines of any deployment was eliminated.[92] These talks proved a watershed as they brought the British and French armies into closer touch. With the Admiralty entertaining alternate strategic views, the risk presented by the bilateral staff talks was manifest. At a minimum, naval representation should have been afforded in so far as every military problem was inherently a maritime problem for Britain. Of course, all this is easily seen in hindsight.

Ultimately, a prime benefit of the War Office reorganization fostered by Esher and implemented by Haldane was that it allowed multiple strategic problems to be pursued concurrently. This is not to avow that the product of War Office deliberations evidenced a superior strategy, but the change certainly facilitated a superior process. Too often, common problems were being held in abeyance owing to Admiralty disagreement or indifference abetted by poor staff operations.[93] This was the view of the War Office, and it remained at the heart of the charges Admiral Beresford was leveling concurrently to the prime minister in 1909. At the working level, Major Hereward Wake captured the barriers hindering progress in joint planning in a thoughtful letter to his friend, Lieutenant Reginald Plunkett. The heart of the problem remained the lack of a "general staff" at the Admiralty "to settle broad questions of policy, strategy and training, a body of officers who are trained, as far as human foresight can do it, to think correctly and think alike." This was far from the case, and as a consequence, long-term planning in the joint arena was proving impossible. Other problems existed, too, in Wake's eyes, but this was the key failing from which all other existing maladies followed.[94]

The mismatch in differing strategic approaches featured anew in August 1911, with the Admiralty offering the prospect of executing a Baltic landing and the war office positing the deployment of an expeditionary force to France. Naval authorities argued that a division-size force would tie down those troops manning the German coast and probably force the High Sea Fleet to sortie to meet the danger posed. This suited British naval strategy, but allowing for the best outcomes in the Admiralty's case, the question naturally followed: Then what? The central tenet of the war office case for a military commitment to the continent was that notwithstanding the fruits garnered in the maritime realm, the position of France—hence, the balance of power—could not be preserved by naval action alone. Here, history testified conclusively: Nelson's victory at Trafalgar did not stop Napoleon in central Europe; it only prevented the invasion of England.[95]

The presentation of Brigadier General Henry Wilson, a naturally loquacious officer, benefited materially from his in-depth study of the German problem. Concluding France aligned with Russia must be defeated, redemption remained possible if Britain intervened militarily on the continent as long as three conditions existed. Firstly, British mobilization had to be congruent with the French Army. Secondly, the entire field army "*must* be sent at once." Finally, Britain would have to sustain the expeditionary force throughout the war.[96] In the ensuing discussion, General Wilson did not claim to have all the answers. Still, he spoke with a specificity absent Reginald McKenna, the first lord of the Admiralty, and Admiral Wilson, the first sea lord.[97]

Facilitating Henry Wilson's case was the fact the actions described only addressed the necessary initial steps. Mobilization, movement, and deployment were quantifiable actions, and as the expeditionary force was of limited proportions, they were more decidedly so. The naval case remained more circumspect. Mobilization and deployment, to be sure, followed by blockade. The last never offering quick results begged the question: What next? A landing on Heligoland, with or without the aid of the military, formed the essentials of the naval plan, with these securing the bases required to maintain a close blockade of the German coast.

Referencing the Japanese landings at Port Arthur, Field Marshal William Nicholson, the CIGS, doubted whether the navy retained the means to achieve as much. As an observer of the Manchurian War, Nicholson spoke with a degree of authority not to be dismissed.[98] More to the point, the offerings of the first sea lord had not been coordinated with the general staff. Thus, Admiral Wilson's foray proved more aspirational and circumstantial than concrete and convincing.[99] Not helping was his habit of offering blanket assertions as if they were facts. As the problems being weighed were set against the backdrop of a new Moroccan crisis, such bald statements did not wear well. It also did not sit well that the navy was attacking the earlier decision to support France on the main front. Historians frequently cite this conference as a watershed moment as it demonstrated the inferiority of Admiralty planning. It indeed moved Asquith to replace McKenna with Winston Churchill, and soon, Admiral Wilson gave way to Sir Francis Bridgeman. That view is not wrong, but it remains incomplete as the dynamics of the Liberal Party cannot be ignored.

McKenna and the ever-burgeoning naval estimates went against the tenets of Liberal orthodoxy. Now, it transpired the admiralty was not even in accord with established strategy. It did not help that McKenna objected to sending the army to the continent.[100] Thus, McKenna's position became untenable politically, and though his successor would yet demonstrate a knack for profligate naval spending, that remained for the future. The Churchill of 1911 was an economizer in naval armaments. Indeed, 2 years earlier, he had threatened resignation over the Admiralty's expanding appetite.[101] Asquith was betting Churchill would be a better first lord and McKenna a better home secretary. As for Admiral Wilson, the former Etonian was no fool,[102] but he sometimes took a foolish line toward the CID, which he feared was usurping the role of the Admiralty.[103] More fundamentally, Admiral Wilson equated naval strategy with national strategy and assumed defeating an enemy's maritime strength remained the true path to victory. This was dubious because the centrality of the sea varied from state to state.

Like his predecessor, Arthur Wilson did not look sympathetically upon establishing an Admiralty war staff. Asquith tolerated this stance in the face of a press campaign calling for the creation of a proper staff so long as the Admiralty was seen to be master of its brief.[104] Recent CID meetings, however, confirmed all was not in order with Haldane, the secretary of state for war, threatening resignation if matters were not put right.[105] The demise of McKenna at the Admiralty was soon followed by Arthur Wilson and almost the entire board of Admiralty that November.[106] The departure of the first did not preordain the departure of the second, but the experience of 1904 when the issue was reform of the War Office had shown that pouring new wine into old bottles is rarely advised. Admiral Wilson did not help his cause by disdaining the grafting of military ways upon the navy.[107]

The arrival of Churchill also marked another watershed: Near-term planning for executing a Baltic descent receded. Naturally combative, the reservations of the new First Lord reflected his understanding of the intended theater, the underwater threats to be negotiated, and the strength of the German Army concluding, "Great Britain can never violate German territory even after the defeat of that Power at sea, her Army not being organised or strong enough for such an undertaking."[108] Of course, Churchill being Churchill, no avenue of attack could long reside on the back burner, and he too would, in time, press for consideration of Baltic gambits.[109]

This reduced one area of Admiralty--War Office friction, but others remained. Arthur Pollock, the editor of the *United Service Magazine*, called for the creation of a joint staff as a natural byproduct for an "amphibious power" explaining, "So long as the Navy and the Army are administered in water-tight compartments, there must not only be something lacking in respect to perfect cooperation, but also be waste of money owing to un-necessary duplication of financial and other business."[110] The plea for a joint staff remained too bold, but no minister could turn a deaf ear to economy. Rather than seek new funds, Churchill curtailed the emoluments of officers to meet the cost of establishing an Admiralty war staff.[111]

Notwithstanding the establishment of staff systems within the war office and the Admiralty, problems in joint planning remained. A byproduct of Esher's War Office Reconstitution Committee had seen the termination of the Joint Naval and Military Committee on Defence, where bilateral problems had heretofore been investigated by senior officers working in harness. That body had been upgraded in 1894 under the auspices of Henry Campbell-Bannerman to facilitate the planning of joint strategy in war. The true import of the present change was not appreciated, with even Ottley avowing that the usefulness of that agency had been circumscribed because issues were typically handled via interdepartmental minutes.[112] Unfortunately, minutes, however good at capturing an agreed position, rarely capture the protagonists' arguments beforehand. One benefit of the prior body was that its secretary served *ex officio* as the naval adviser to the inspector-general of fortifications, becoming an insider in joint service deliberations in the process. To this billet, the Admiralty posted officers closely associated with the army. This included Captain Cecil Colville, who served on the Nile and in Sudan, and Captain Lowther Grant, who had fought his guns with the Highland Brigade in South Africa.[113]

In strengthening control at the center, the effectiveness of the board of Admiralty suffered—or so Cranborne now styled the Marquess of Salisbury following the death of the late prime minister.[114] D'Ombrain posits that the height of the CID's success occurred with the creation of a body to consider overseas operations. That is assuredly so, but the failure that followed owed less to the inattentiveness of the War Office, as d'Ombrain suggests, and more to the inattentiveness of Balfour's successors.[115] Both Campbell-Bannerman and Asquith remained transfixed on issues closer to Liberal orthodoxy: social welfare, free trade, reform of the lords, and Irish Home Rule. These inclinations made George Clarke worry whether the CID could survive Liberal governance. His concern was not baseless as the CID had met eighty-two times under Balfour but would convene a mere forty-seven times under the Liberals until the onset of war in 1914.[116]

Of course, strategic planning continued, but the fulcrum had returned to the Admiralty, the War Office, or elsewhere. Certain regions came under the auspices of the Foreign Office, while others fell under the government of India or the Colonial Office. Militarily, this division of responsibility was echoed by the War Office, which assumed responsibility for operational planning and gathering local intelligence for some areas while the Indian Army headquarters oversaw matters elsewhere. To that end, the Indian Army established its own Intelligence Department in 1890, focusing on India, East Africa, and Asia. Meanwhile, overseeing collection on Europe, West Africa, and the Americas fell to the War Office. Such parsing was never absolute, and here Mesopotamia afforded a prime example as the area found north of a line running from Aqaba to Basra came under War Office consideration, with the balance falling to Simla.[117]

Nevertheless, due to operational factors, Britain's ability to conduct combat operations in 1914 was uneven. Not all establishments were at full strength, and even those with the nominal numbers desired, the level of proficiency was often less than what the conditions of active service demanded. This was true for British formations, especially for imperial establishments where the demands of frontline service were always a distant, future consideration with support in aid of the civil power the immediate problem. In theory and from 1909, British dependencies accepted an obligation of mutual defense.[118] Theory, though, did not match capability. Thus, much effort was spent on non-warfighting activities, whether suppressing local unrest or dealing with natural disasters and famines. For imperial formations, a further complication proved to be the quality of their arms, which were obsolescent, if not obsolete. Consequently, acquiring and rehoning basic skills to maintain a cadre of semi-trained units was necessary. Though this was largely achieved, it made acquiring advanced skills, including proficiency in combined operations, problematic.

The War Office understood all this and sought to match capabilities to requirements. Logistical matters made this essential if forces were to be moved from one theater to another in wartime. Further complicating the question was that the War Office controlled few of the garrisons stationed outside Britain. To its credit, it did not doubt the difficulties posed:

> Forces which are raised by one State, or a federation of contiguous States, governed by one will and organised on one system, possess the great advantages that spring from unity of organisation and direction; but where, as in the case of the British Empire, the forces available for employment in war are separated by intervening oceans, are administered by different Governments, and are primarily constituted to meet varying requirements, the difficulties of combining them for concentrated action oversea are seriously increased.[119]

All this might be thought insurmountable, but promise existed too. Given the very breadth of the empire, forces from one region might reach another area sooner than an expeditionary force mounted from the United Kingdom.

Specifically, units from India might reach Egypt in a crisis and be backfilled by Australian troops to ensure the subcontinent's needs were not compromised.[120]

The above was less of a problem for the Admiralty because the dominions and colonies maintained only rudimentary naval establishments before 1914.[121] When these finally appeared, the Admiralty desired to see all act as part of a single imperial force. This went against the drift of local political sentiment, though training to a common standard was accepted.[122] This was all to the good; however, complications soon ensued when local authorities attempted to control squadrons within their limits. Here, the case of South Africa may be cited. The new union retained responsibility for local defense. It worked hand-in-hand with the Colonial Office, the War Office, and the CID to prepare plans for defensive and offensive operations.[123] Here, planning against German South-West Africa implied the control of naval shipping along the Cape of Good Hope to the consternation of the Admiralty. Such teething problems were addressed at the Imperial Conference of 1911 when a framework for internaval cooperation in peacetime and control during wartime was agreed upon.[124]

In accepting external defense obligations in 1909, the dominions only acknowledged a practice of some standing. South Africa had been the most recent demonstration of this, with Canada, Australia, and New Zealand each raising forces to fight in the war. Following the Imperial Conference of 1909, General French visited the principal dominions to harmonize their military establishments.[125] Whether these forces would serve overseas depended on the circumstances arising. Still, the critical thing was dominion establishments were being trained and equipped to meet an imperial obligation. This cooperation required concrete measures to effect, but it also implied closer political ties between London and the self-governing dominions. This was less of a problem seemingly for colonial forces as they were governed directly by London, but here considerations of race arose. When the West African Frontier Force (WAFF) was raised in 1897, it was understood that it would not deploy in "white men's wars." In 1906, this guidance was adjusted so that:

> the strength of the colonial forces should be fixed at the minimum force required to insure the maintenance of internal order and to deal with risings of the native population, and that the question of maintaining them at a strength sufficient to place them on an equality with the

colonial military forces maintained by foreign Powers in an adjacent territory should be disregarded.[126]

Thus, the employment of locally raised forces in expeditionary warfare presented a host of difficulties—political, to be sure—but also operational, given their dependence on levies, porters, and camp followers. Those who lament the length of tail-to-tooth in modern militaries would do well to consider its variation in *fin de siècle* Africa, where ratios of four to one were typical.[127] One additional variance should, however, be noted: the presence of political officers in support of operations. Wolseley deprecated their presence as they represented an untoward seam when British forces operated alongside them.[128]

A more fundamental issue remained: the existence of several types of small arms. By 1913, the War Office had migrated to the Mark VII pattern of .303 ammunition. This did not suit the needs of colonial forces as their rifles and machineguns fired the Mark VI version and could only employ the latest type if the weapons were resighted. As the War Office did not retain stocks of the Mark VI ammunition, initiating production again was not a trivial matter in terms of cost or time.[129] Of course, other considerations were at play. A genuine fear of providing native troops with too many weapons of the most modern type existed.[130] The conclusion must be tentative, but surely a lesson of the Indian Mutiny was that trust in non-British elements extended only so far. This was one reason Indian battalions served in East Africa in peacetime, and the practice was mirrored in West Africa, where a battalion of the West India Regiment served.[131] Moreover, with its linked battalions, the post-Cardwell Army made such deployments a necessity as insufficient British forces existed to meet all requirements. Thus, Indian formations routinely saw service in Aden, Singapore, and Hong Kong while offering an independent, reliable body of armed troops thought immune to local influences. Though Simla held such deployments made these formations better prepared for active service, this was not altogether true. They were often composite units raised by culling non-commissioned officers and other ranks from different units.[132]

Gauging the effectiveness of British Imperial and colonial forces on the eve of the World War must be done with care. Roberts held the musketry of Indian troops superior to their British counterparts—so much so—he would not allow open competition between the two for fear of demonstrating the latter's weakness.[133] This may say more about the readiness of British troops in India than anything else. On the eve of the South African War, Wolseley lamented the effectiveness of British formations on the subcontinent, believing them riddled with drink, fevers, and venereal disease.[134] Another, not nearly so vicious in his assessment, believed the militia, yeomanry, and volunteers fighting had displayed pronounced limitations in training and discipline. The problem was never the troops so much as the system "which forces us to employ such untrained men in the field," according to Grierson.[135]

Yet another barrier existed within the WAFF and the KAR: the lack of a permanent cadre of British officers. Relying on seconded officers who would eventually return to their parent establishments or staff duties precluded developing officers steeped in the traditions and ethos of their present formations. If effective in small unit tactics, then the price paid was a lack of officers able to see the larger picture. Ultimately, this worked to the advantage of the civilian hierarchy of the Colonial Office, where a sense of cost consciousness prevailed. Little is gained in assessing whether an opportunity was lost in not establishing a King's African Army, yet it must be the case that the local defense schemes developed before the First World War suffered owing to the professional inadequacies of those preparing them to say nothing of the steady cheeseparing of the Colonial Office.[136] Unwittingly, another problem was evidenced. As the officers assigned to colonial forces held temporary appointments and faced half-pay in Britain if involuntarily returned early, the pressure to report that which was acceptable became manifest. Brigadier General William Manning, the first inspector-general of the KAR, felt the wrath of civil displeasure when he reported on the unit's military inefficiency. His findings after 5 years of service, including action against the "Mad Mullah," reflected a mature view. His superiors disagreed and guaranteed Manning's future reports would not be so nearly expansive.[137]

Because of their overall underdevelopment, the threat from either German East Africa or German South-West Africa was not considered an immediate worry. However, this might change over time, with the British position at the Cape being tenuous at best.[138] With that thought clearly in mind, General Lord Methuen, the general officer commanding, argued capturing German South-West Africa would solidify Britain's imperial position by uniting all union elements in a common effort in the event of war.[139] The harshness of German governance was considered a weakness that could be exploited, yet the lack of consistent reporting against defined criteria made the intelligence picture presented uneven. As many reporting were not trained staff officers and were working to the needs of the civil government, topographical, economic, political, and meteorological data predominated.[140] These supported operations within British protectorates but did little to support action against locales controlled by others.

Hence, the need for better information grew. The British representative residing at Dar es Salaam began reporting on local military conditions in 1913. From the reports covering German East Africa surviving, it may be adduced that guidance had been promulgated to focus on this area as a collection target. A report discussing the newly constructed wireless transmitter at Dar es Salaam features and, so too, a fuller report on German East Africa filed by the KAR's intelligence officer. The genesis of the former resided with Captain Chetwode Crawley, RMA, who had identified the characteristics of the transmitter, the defensive means covering the port while offering one manner for how the station might be destroyed from the sea.[141]

Topographical intelligence was a key enabler in weighing whether a combined operation was feasible. Experience demonstrated that these reports needed to be prepared by qualified officers able to consider the strategic, tactical, and environmental factors governing any operation. Tides, prevailing winds, beach gradients, and defensive works were essential considerations, but so were roads, rail lines, rivers, canals, and port facilities to allow for sustainment and exploitation. These implied surveys conducted by sappers and probably ones who had graduated from the staff college as well. Few serving in Africa could claim such qualifications.

As for the forces raised in the colonies and protectorates, a start had been made in the years before the First World War. The fact that more was not achieved reflected the cost of meeting present needs, which always had to be balanced against future financial liabilities. The Colonial and Foreign Offices always prized efficiency over effectiveness. In truth, much the same can be said of the War Office. Necessarily, if Britain were ever to conduct raids, feints, or opposed landings with local forces, a degree of supplemental training would be required first. Finally, there was an inherent conflict over the defensive needs of a protectorate and that of an empire. The CID and the CDC might acknowledge the dilemma, but with forces primarily raised and funded locally, it was not a situation that was easily resolved.

Throughout, the Indian Army represented an imperial reserve. Indeed, given the climatic conditions prevailing in most colonial areas, its troops were deemed especially useful. As internal security was always a concern in India this reserve was not unlimited. Still, unlike the forces of the home establishment, the Indian Army, with one crucial exception, often exceeded its authorized levels.[142] That exception was the number of British officers carried in its regiments of cavalry and infantry battalions. Nominally set at twelve officers, this figure was not met in 1901 or the following years. Owing to leave, training, and secondments, the truer figure was closer to eight. This hindered developing unit proficiency, leaving General Sir Arthur Palmer, the commander-in-chief, India, to warn, "it is no economy to keep up a native army during times of peace which, owing to its being under-officered, will be unfit efficiently to meet the numerous demands on the outbreak of war."[143]

When mobilized, the Indian Army became a potential field force of four divisions with ancillary units. Not facing the legal constraints of the home establishment when deploying overseas, it appeared to offer a rapid expeditionary capability. Its reserves were paltry, with 24,000 authorized in 1899 but only 17,000 troops then mustering. Expansion was problematic given the near lack of British officers, who, in 1914, stood at only forty.[144] With its diverse language requirements and the centrality of continuous personal contact in officer and native soldier relations, this was not a shortcoming amenable to an easy solution. Artillery, too, remained an arm underrepresented within the Indian establishment. A legacy of the Mutiny, domestic units made do with inferior types.[145] Thus, the Indian Army, if of sizable proportions by British standards, possessed definite limitations. In a sense, everything was in the shop window. Composed of long-serving soldiers with a modest reserve, its ability to sustain casualties and retain cohesion in anything other than minor operations appeared dubious.

Nonetheless, Simla was further expected to provide forces for other at-risk areas. Thus, in May 1906, Kitchener advised India could send a division to Egypt to meet a Turkish threat originating from the Sinai. Of course, Britain's interest was in the vulnerability of the Suez Canal, notwithstanding that both Egypt and the Sinai were *de jure* Turkish territory. Presumed inviolate if the Royal Navy (or its partners) controlled the Mediterranean Sea, an attack from the landward side was deemed difficult as infrastructure was so poor.[146]

Turkish occupation of the Sinai threatened to remove this barrier and, if a rail line followed, would make subsequent overland operations feasible. Into the summer, reinforcement of Egypt proceeded apace, with 2,500 troops joining the 3,700 already on hand. That was one measure, but others under consideration included seizing several Ottoman Aegean islands (i.e., Mitylene, Lemnos, Imbros, Rhodes, Samothrace, Chios, and Thasos), having a capital ship pass through the Turkish Straits and anchor off Constantinople, or a joint operation against Haifa or Acre. Warming to the task, George Clarke further posited a blockade of the Red Sea, supporting an Arab uprising in the Hejaz and the occupation of Basra by Indian forces.[147] Sir Edward Grey, the foreign secretary, believed such steps might be reserved for another time.[148]

Further measures under consideration included intercepting those ships making for Turkish ports, though a British fleet off Constantinople was deemed the most effective counter.[149] Barring such a bold move were the guns defending the straits, which were calculated at six 13-inch, twelve 11-inch, five 10.3-inch, forty 9.4-inch, six 8.2-inch, and thirty-four 6-inch guns. Found on both the European and Asiatic sides, these totals did not account for any mobile batteries present. Further landings posited included landing an Indian Army force on the Fao peninsula, where a British-controlled cable from Bushire was present with operations to control the Shatt-al-Arab following.[150]

If the immediate issue was a Turkish threat to the Suez Canal, General French posited a broader problem. The Ottoman Empire was increasingly aligned with Germany. Limited naval action could not forestall a Turkish move against Egypt, and the loss of minor islands in the Aegean was nothing to Britain's loss of advantage in Egypt. The only remedy was to ensure a British military force of sufficient means existed at the scene of worry to defeat an Ottoman advance and to preclude a simultaneous uprising of sympathetic locals. The force estimated to achieve these twin aims amounted to 150,000 troops, or the entire expeditionary force now being contemplated for duty in France if war with Germany arose from that quarter.[151] Endless difficulties were possible to imagine, but all turned on whether the navy could force the Dardanelles.[152]

Fisher was in high dudgeon over any scheme to force the Dardanelles, which led him to boycott the CID meeting on 26 July 1904. Esher, however, believed the points raised merited examination.[153] Clarke, a firm believer in a Dardanelles gambit, questioned whether any study would advance matters, telling Esher:

It follows that the importance of the Dardanelles question is greatest, & that it should be most carefully studied. If, therefore, as a result of our meeting, we study such it will be a great gain. Can we? Do we ever study anything thoroughly? Do we know how to study a question of this kind? Grierson's branch will turn out copious words. Ottley will produce some ingenious phrases. J.F. [John Fisher] would settle it all in a sentence or two; but his hasty imagination might be as unfortunate as that which has saddled us with those *Invincibles* and costing us little short of £6,000,000 & commending themselves to nobody.[154]

Tweedmouth, the first lord, believed the navy could force the straits. Ottley, the director of naval intelligence, held otherwise, referencing the example of Port Arthur from the Russo-Japanese War. Then, Japanese military casualties had been prohibitive and more than Britain's small military would allow.[155] Grierson believed that landing on Gallipoli's northern shore and taking the forts from behind was the only practical way of guaranteeing the fleet's passage through the straits. With opinions divided, the CID tasked the Admiralty and the War Office to weigh the problem anew.[156]

Though the minutes avow both were to investigate the "whole question," what followed was not a joint appreciation but rather a report prepared by the War Office (principally, Callwell) supported by Ottley's comments.[157] When the War Office appreciation appeared in December, it held a naval operation by itself was to be deprecated.[158] Accepting that the fleet might appear off Constantinople after losing several second-line units, their presence guaranteed nothing as the Sultan could retire into the country's interior. The fleet would then risk a return passage against an enemy even more prepared and alert than during its ascent. The ensuing retreat and loss of prestige spelled a risk of the highest order for an empire always protected on the slimmest of margins. Yet, the general staff went further. If a military operation against the entire Gallipoli peninsula made in conjunction with a naval attack spelled the most complete and effective means of destroying Turkish power, then it did not follow such a plan was sound as defeat of the Turkish Army could not be guaranteed declaiming, "However brilliant as a combination of war, and however fruitful in its consequences, such an operation would be, were it crowned with success, the General Staff, in view of the risks involved, are not prepared to recommend its being attempted."[159] What the general staff did advance was a joint strike by four divisions against Haifa as the best means of defending Egypt.[160]

The general staff postulated that the recent experience of opposed landings offered no guide as to whether such a venture might succeed, though its view discounted the potential. Instead, they argued for an administrative landing absent enemy opposition. This would allow the landed force the time and the space to ready itself for future operations. To achieve this at Gallipoli, the fleet would have to provide a shield such that Turkish effective opposition could not be mounted. The likelihood of this was held remote by Lyttelton. Moreover, securing the necessary surprise, given the preliminaries required, made a successful attempt nearly impossible. Even if feints succeeded in drawing off a portion of those defending, the Dardanelles would remain a requirement of the first magnitude not to be neglected by Turkey and argued for not attempting. In commenting on the previous, Ottley also drew upon Japan's recent experience against Russia and noted these efforts only employed minor gunboats, whereas the British could call on heavier warships. Thus, the present opportunities for a combined operation appeared feasible if Britain had no other option. Emphasizing the hazards and difficulties of any action, the need remained "to frequently practise joint naval and military manoeuvres such as the rapid throwing on shore of a military force in the presence of an enemy, under the cover of the guns of the fleet."[161] Ultimately, the CID accepted that a landing on the Gallipoli peninsula and the fleet's passage through the Dardanelles were not feasible propositions.[162] An unintended consequence of the conclusion was the ongoing acquisition of intelligence to reconsider the matter anew at a later date lapsed.[163]

Now, however, the problem of the German Navy and its rapid growth in northern waters intervened. The Admiralty looked to redistribute its ships on foreign stations, including the Mediterranean, to meet this threat. The Foreign Office and the War Office argued otherwise, leading to a conference in Malta in early 1912 to receive evidence from the area's senior officers.[164] Clearly, one motivation for such a rebalancing was finance. Yet, technology offered another. Recent improvements in wireless communications allowed timely intelligence to flow between London, Cairo, and Delhi. In many respects, the situation would mirror the problem of Singapore at another hour, with Kitchener now playing the part of a proto-appeaser when he called for an entente with Constantinople to alleviate the dangers.[165] The realignment had implications for the future as the protection of Egypt came to be anchored on the support of India. In a war with Germany, this need not be worrisome. Yet, the issue would become graver if the conflict included Austria and Italy—Germany's partners in the Triple Alliance. To meet such a contingency, Kitchener, now British agent and consul-general, sought three divisions from India.[166] This went against the grain of civilian thinking in India. More irksome was the thinking of Major General Douglas Haig, the Indian Army chief of staff. He posited sending a three-division force with attached cavalry to Europe or Mesopotamia in the event of hostilities with Germany or the Porte. Hardinge, the viceroy, was having none of that and took umbrage that Simla and the War Office were planning as much behind his back.[167] Hardinge's intervention merely moved matters *sub rosa*; contingency planning did not stop. Simla continued to refine the tables of organization for deploying any number of expeditionary forces to satisfy differing requirements. This included the number and type of animals to be taken on active service, the requisite stores of fodder, and the ancillary clothing and equipment for theater-specific deployments.[168] This is not to claim detailed operational plans existed in the summer of 1914, but neither was Simla working from a clean slate.

Meanwhile, whether the Dardanelles could be forced remained a matter of conjecture. In 1911, against the backdrop of continuing Ottoman difficulties, Churchill held its passage in wartime remained an impossibility under prevailing conditions. This furthered the case for reducing the Mediterranean Fleet to a cruiser force with its heavy ships returned to home waters.[169] Still, Egypt's boundaries were only one irritant in British relations with the Porte. The Shatt-el-Arab and the Fao peninsula represented another. Here, the Ottoman claim of the entire Shatt-el-Arab posed an obvious peril to the oil exported by the Anglo-Persian Oil Company. Slade, the erstwhile director of naval intelligence and now commanding the East Indies Squadron, warned of the dangers lurking and suggested a blockade of Hodeida to reduce Ottoman control of southern Arabia. If Slade did not explicitly call for an Arab revolt, then the implication remained to be drawn.[170]

In this instance, a CID subcommittee of the great and good examined the problem. It found that Britain had little legal basis for denying Turkish sovereignty claims and that the best arrangement was to secure an understanding through bilateral negotiations. These duly followed, but agreement proved elusive, for the Ottoman Empire soon found herself at war with Italy.[171] A further desire was to safeguard British shipping concessions operating on the Tigris and the Euphrates rivers, which were now economically threatened by the advance of the Baghdad railway. Protecting Britain's greater commercial interests in the Persian Gulf area was a key strand of diplomacy. This applied no less to the Anglo-Persian Oil Company, which sought fresh concessions in Mesopotamia. That the primary beneficiary of Anglo-Persian oil production was the Royal Navy only made British securing interests in the region more compelling.[172]

Clearly, harmonizing policy, to say nothing of force structure and capabilities, across the multiple offices having equities in imperial and colonial policies was no easy matter. The officers on attachment were sensitive that their ultimate career prospects were tied to the War Office and not the Foreign and Colonial Offices. Goodwill and reasonableness were required across the board; this was not always forthcoming. Ultimately, responsibility resided with the prime minister who, in turn, depended on the CID with specific problems devolved to subordinate committees and, in the case of colonial strategic policy, to the CDC, itself to be restyled as the Overseas Defence Committee (ODC). Officially, the entire structure was advisory, though taskings issued by the CID carried weight if only because they reflected the concurrence of the prime minister. If generally suiting the needs of peacetime administration, what would follow if operations against a first-class world power ever arose was left undefined. The system also required that problems affecting the equities of more than one department be referred to the CID system for adjudication—something not always done when one agency's financial considerations or interests were paramount. Thus, while the CDC weighed the level of regular forces garrisoning colonial possessions, it did not always contemplate the changes being made by colonial administrations to their locally raised establishments, though the two were inexorably linked.[173] Why this gap in practice existed is unknown, but as the CID concerned itself with the broad principles of defense policy and let permanent and *ad hoc* sub committees investigate and formulate recommendations, it could be the Colonial Office viewed the matter as technically being within its existing lines of authority.[174]

Since 1904, British policy had been to maintain the *status quo* in Europe and, to this end, had reached an accommodation with both France and Russia.[175] Reducing points of friction in Central Asia and Africa with these two powers alleviated immediate worries, but it did not spell relief. Invariably, the concern remained that a fresh combination of powers might present a danger of the highest order. To this end, Germany, in tandem with Russia, remained an acute worry for British naval superiority in northern waters.[176] Thus, detente with France and Russia had its limits of usefulness.[177] More fundamentally, alignment with France and Russia altered Britain's most basic strategic assumption: Command of the sea was *the* supreme issue. This was not immediately appreciated for the simple reason the original basis of the accord was to resolve outstanding political and economic issues between the three powers. Very quickly, however, that aim fomented difficulties with Germany. Always implicit in the entente was a willingness to side with France over Germany to the point of a military alliance, if necessary. As such, the War Office soon began planning for a European commitment and assuredly so after the First Moroccan Crisis.

If new strategic choices offered other possibilities, changing tactical realities made their mark, too. To the general staff, amphibious operations had not lost their usefulness, but they had become more difficult. Thus, "It is only of very recent years that naval and military authorities have come to recognise the tactical principle that under modern conditions an opposed landing is one of the most difficult operations of war."[178] That verity stood company with another demonstrated in South Africa and Manchuria: Frontal assaults conducted at the point of the bayonet were not apt to succeed. The latter proposition suggested the employment of flank attacks, the ultimate expression of which remained an amphibious operation. Now, however, the theory of amphibious warfare as a strategic enabler met the reality of present tactical conditions.

How far a view registered when the question was one of defending isolated imperial outposts was deemed true when Britain was the power initiating action may be judged by considerations to occupy Turkish islands and send a naval force through the Straits at the same proximate moment. Difficult, yes, but British maritime strategy was predicated on commanding the seas in war such that access maintained in peace continued as before. This guaranteed the commercial lifeline of Britain, but it allowed an expeditionary force to be sent when and where required, with reinforcement of India and Egypt being two considerations at the fore of contemporary planning. Indeed, save for Canada and India, all threats to the broader empire were inherently maritime, and a policy that failed to offer a robust exposition of naval power projection spelled doom to the very nature of the British Empire—and so it ultimately proved though taking another war to demonstrate.[179]

The CID accepted Balfour's proposal for a dedicated committee to prepare options for combined operations against potential enemies. In truth, it had little choice. The initiative had originated with Fisher, who sought to present a *fait accompli* upon the next government while drawing "the War Office out of its present quagmire."[180] By keeping such measures continuously up to date, plans would be available for rapid execution upon the outbreak of war. The importance attached to this effort can be gauged by the body's limited and focused membership: the prime minister, the first sea lord, the director of naval intelligence, the chief of the general staff, and the DMO, along with subsidiary officers from the Admiralty and War Office responsible for strategic war planning. Absent were the political heads of the services and representatives from the Foreign, India, and Colonial Offices. As the CID would approve the contingencies prepared, their opportunity to shape these plans remained for a subsequent date. Unfortunately, the assumptions and details previously weighed by the drafters rarely accompanied their products.[181]

At this proximate moment, Lyttelton led a conference of senior officers at Camberley to weigh a host of pressing and contentious subjects. Presently directing the war course, Slade expounded on the "Co-operation between the Navy and the Army in Over-sea Expeditions."[182] Whether a plan would ever be employed remained for another day. Still, his offering suggested the number and types of forces required, the requisite shipping to be reserved, and the probable timeline for their undertaking from warning order to execution. As to what evolutions were studied, the record is mostly silent. An initial investigation weighed a joint assault on the Dardanelles.[183] Other evidence posits a contingency requiring inland water transport. The scenario is unnamed but would be in keeping with operations occurring in Africa, Mesopotamia, or even China, where instability and rising nationalism remained continuing worries. Significantly, plans for executing noncombatant evacuation operations in the case of China and Constantinople were prepared. In the case of the latter, small arms were to be held by the legation for distribution to British subjects until the fleet arrived and made a naval landing to protect the route of exit. In a more permissible environment, the ambassador would charter a ship and simply evacuate those at risk. Beyond demonstrating that the lessons of the Boxer Rebellion and recurring Armenian massacres were very much in mind, these schemes highlight the shared and distributed responsibility for preparing plans covering potential joint operations.[184]

The evidence suggests the Admiralty did not support those efforts at strategic planning as fulsomely as might be expected. In this, it was no more or less guilty than the War Office, where specific courses of action were naturally preferred over others. Given the rapidity of the attacks on Yap and New Guinea in 1914, their prior consideration by the committee is suggested. Yet, it is equally feasible that the Admiralty and the War Office had developed plans off their own bat without yet securing the formal approval of the CID. Whether to neutralize a foreign station—even a German one—was not always a straightforward proposition. A committee reviewing overseas cable installations recommended leaving those at Yap unmolested, as the Germans and the Dutch jointly owned them. However, it was left to the Admiralty to weigh the overall merits of cutting.[185] They left the cable alone and focused instead on the co-located wireless transmitter. Indeed, whether to interrupt or maintain cable and wireless communications was a question where the interests of the Admiralty and the War Office frequently parted company—much depended on the nature of any future war and the circumstances arising. Still, the apparent ease of their cutting by local forces guaranteed these measures would always feature in contingency planning.[186]

The Admiralty issued orders and instructions to its overseas fleets and squadrons specifying the forces to be employed and the early actions to be accomplished in a war with Germany. One set of orders was operative if Britain fought alone, while another applied if Britain was allied with France against Germany. These operations, though, did not aim to subjugate a defended port or tackle an area robustly defended. Nor did they require the employment of the most modern warships. These units were reserved for use with the main fleet to secure command of the seas, and given their increasing cost, they could not be risked on dangerous secondary enterprises—or so the Admiralty held in 1905. If such had to be overcome, the preferred manner was to land a military force, for naval gunfire alone probably would not suffice. Here, the operative word is *military*, for the Admiralty by now deprecated employing its forces ashore.[187] The irony remained that the War Office believed in the efficacy of naval gunfire in support of joint operations in a manner alien to the admiralty.

In the wake of the South African War, a host of changes ensued. Some might have occurred notwithstanding this electrifying jolt, but the catalyst of war once again demonstrated existing deficiencies. Reform of the Defence Committee, now styled the CID, followed, and so too changes in War Office administration. If failing to suffer the abject lessons of the veldt, the navy necessarily implemented its own series of innovations. The creation of the Admiralty war staff and the founding of a war staff course followed not because of failure but because the risk of failing the next time could not be countenanced. Cooperation between the services was long accepted as a *sine qua non*. Pure naval strategy might not require the cooperation of the military, but the maritime strategy that Britain espoused assuredly did. The changes mainly implemented addressed systemic and institutional issues. Systems and institutions, however, rely on people and are typically the product of compromise. Rarely are they ideal. Fitting at one moment, seldom do they remain so over time. What had been fashioned was better than what had preceded it. That it was insufficient was mostly assumed. George Aston and Henry Rawlinson held as much in 1907, and Asquith felt the same way in 1912.[188] Just how so would be resolved by the test of war and it is to that story this study now turns.

Fourteen

Came a New War: Executing Expeditionary Warfare

Our frontiers are the coasts of the enemy and we ought to be there 5 minutes after war is declared![1]

Vice Admiral Sir John Fisher, 1899

In the summer of 1914, Admiral Sir Henry Jackson stood poised to assume command of the Mediterranean station following his tour at the Admiralty as chief of the war staff.[2] An officer of pronounced abilities, Jackson would never supplant Admiral Sir Berkeley Milne. Why this proved to be can be adduced to a minute drafted on 21 July by Vice Admiral Sir Doveton Sturdee. Though a general European war was not yet inevitable, Sturdee believed existing Admiralty plans suffered by their passivity and said as much when endorsing a paper that argued for reconstituting the Committee on Combined Operations. The author of this pivotal minute remains unknown, though Rear Admiral Arthur Leveson, the director of the operations division, or a principal subordinate may be presumed. Battenberg, the first sea lord, quickly sounded Hankey on the question before forwarding the docket to Churchill. Beyond acknowledging the paper, Churchill registered no view to the initiative, but given all that followed, his concurrence may be assumed.[3]

In the ordinary course of things, the paper would have been aired at a meeting of the Committee of Imperial Defence (CID). Indeed, a minute to that end had been drafted. Events now intervened. Here may be cited the issue of Ireland with a conference at Buckingham Palace then underway in a last-ditch attempt to forestall a seemingly inevitable civil war. At this point, the Austro-Serbian dam soon swept all aside. With most ministers out of town, Asquith, Grey, Lloyd George, and Churchill convened in an unofficial colloquium at Haldane's London home.[4] Ironically, the CID remained quiescent, but not so Hankey. Fearing Britain was about to forsake its traditional maritime strategy by sending the army to France, he approached Asquith about reconstituting the

Committee on Combined Operations.[5] The prime minister promptly acceded, and as Hankey had framed the problem as one "which might have a definite effect on the result of the war," a braver man than Asquith would have been required to deny the proposal.[6] Left unsaid was who should lead the body. As Hankey had also cleared the proposition with Haldane, it would not be surprising if the former war minister and close confidant of Asquith had been mentioned as a candidate. Jackson was near at hand, and his choice came minus the baggage of a Haldane appointment. Jackson, moreover, was conversant with current Admiralty thinking on the question of combined operations.[7]

Hankey's initiative was not misplaced, but it would have far-reaching and untoward consequences. A prudent step, if taken in peacetime, establishing the body on the cusp of war was brash to a degree and misdirected. Surely, weighing the greater strategic situation in a reasoned joint appreciation now that enemies and allies were being clarified was the first order of business. So believed Churchill, in a reasoned minute submitted to Asquith on 31 July, which pressed for creating a war staff–general staff body to examine joint action against Germany.[8] Unfortunately, this did not occur. Instead, a Committee on Combined Operations in Foreign Territory was chartered as a specialist subcommittee of the CID. Lacking a senior minister or the presence of an Esher to guide its proceedings, Jackson's committee became a narrow, technical body concerned with the execution and not the rationale of joint operations.[9]

Manifestly, the execution of amphibious operations at the start of a major war could never be reduced to the narrow and technical. The fulcrum of power remained with those who studied and owned any subject, for the power of veto exercised by a superior agency is essentially a negative power, leaving what is to follow vacant. This had been the experience of the cabinet in the face of the CID; it would be the war council's and the cabinet's experience in the face of the Committee on Combined Operations. Make no mistake, Jackson was viewed as a thoroughly proficient officer. Fisher, years before, had touted his merits, regretting only his lack of present seniority in joining the flag list immediately. Jackson remained a very practical seaman, an early advocate of employing wireless telegraphy in fleet operations, and an expert in gunnery fire control. That was no small accolade in a service that prized common sense and competence as much as material progress. Noted as thorough and careful rather than brilliant, the portrait was a fudge to preclude his being thought too clever by half.[10]

Serving with Jackson were two senior army officers: Ian Hamilton and the "dug-out" Charles Callwell, late director of military intelligence and a leading light on amphibious operations. Meanwhile, Aston, deemed the foremost naval expert on combined operations and presently the assistant director of operations, completed the naval contribution to the committee.[11] Rowland Sperling of the Foreign Office's Western department and Sir George Fiddes of the Colonial Office, with expertise in finance, the Far East, and Africa, rounded out the agency's principals with the contribution of General Edmund Barrow limited to those times when the interests of India arose.[12]

Thus, the collective intellectual merits of those serving were of a high order. Capable staff officers, both Aston and Callwell, possessed a strong record of publication. More than this, though, Aston bridged the differing schools of thought dividing the War Office and the Admiralty on combined operations. Ottley had sung his praises as a future Commandant of the staff college and a subsequent DMO. Hankey went even further, believing Aston might become CIGS. Of course, that was never likely given his naval antecedents, but it does testify to his overall merits.[13] Aston's *Letters on Amphibious Warfare*, based on his Camberley lectures, had soon been followed by *Sea, Land, and Air Strategy*.

During the previous year, Aston had sat on several naval committees, including one with Rear Admiral Bayly, where potential blocking operations, raids, and amphibious landings were examined. Zeebrugge was one possibility surveyed, and earlier work on defending critical points of vulnerability gave Aston a strong sense of the centrality of cable and wireless communications in supporting military and naval operations and their association with economic warfare.[14] Notwithstanding the importance of this work, Aston was merely marking time.[15] This all changed with war appearing imminent, and on 2 August, a signal ordered Aston to the Admiralty.[16]

Meanwhile, Callwell's primer, *Small Wars*, had secured a broad audience in Britain and beyond and eventually received the imprimatur of the war office.[17] If that work remained strangely silent on amphibious operations, then the subject assumed prominence in *The Effect of Maritime Command on Land Campaigns Since Waterloo* and *Military Operations and Maritime Preponderance*.[18] Rather than accept a lesser position, Colonel Callwell resigned in 1909. Thus, his surprise was complete when he was recalled and gazetted as a temporary major general as he filled Henry Wilson's shoes as the DMO.[19]

Hamilton lacked the *psc* moniker, having abandoned his cramming for the staff college to be by General Roberts' side in 1882; he lacked little else, however. An observer of the Russo-Japanese War, his two-volume *A Staff Officer's Scrap Book* soon appeared. Subsequently, Hamilton commanded Southern command, where a notable feature of his tenure was the exercise of combined operations. These serials were meant to represent opposed landings, and, in the exercises' after-action conferences, the views of naval officers featured.[20] Meanwhile, Edmund Barrow was a seasoned campaigner and experienced staff officer, though not a product of Camberley or Quetta. From Marlborough and Sandhurst, he was gazetted to the 102 Regiment of Foot (Royal Madras Fusiliers) before joining the Bengal Staff Corps. In the fallout arising from the Curzon-Kitchener contretemps, Barrow had the misfortune of being viewed as Curzon's man, and this taint probably worked against his reaching the very summit of the Indian Army. Thoroughly sound, his Indian experience was not necessarily the ideal grounding for weighing the measures now under consideration. In a sense, this was true for all the military members; hence, the support of the Foreign and Colonial Offices remained a vital contribution.[21]

Rowland Sperling could lay no claims to authorship, but he did have a talent for languages and had worked the foreign office side in French colonial questions.[22] As for Fiddes, an old African hand, he had served as Field Marshal Roberts' political secretary in South Africa. On that score, the charge that he had been single-handedly responsible for the Boer War hung in the air.[23] That claim was a disservice to Milner, Chamberlain, and Kruger, but more assuredly, it can be said that Fiddes was highly knowledgeable of Nyasaland and West Africa. A member of that group who believed oil existed in Nigeria since returning to London, his duties included overseeing the East Africa Protectorate.[24]

Notwithstanding the enemy faced, certain strands of strategy were set in stone, or so avowed the war orders governing the actions of the navy. Guaranteeing Britain's use of the seas stood as the first consideration. A second strand sought to deny the same to any foe.[25] As guiding precepts, they could not be bettered. Yet, a host of difficulties, pitfalls, and traps remained lest one walked a path best not followed. Having decided to support France on 2 August, Britain then temporized about committing its troops to the continent, arguing reinforcement of India and Egypt had first call on its resources. More positively, the British Fleet would guard the French coast.[26] Officially, this view was accepted as a brief, sharp war was thought likely. Unofficially, the French

Army pressed for a fuller commitment using the offices of Colonel Henry Yarde-Buller, the British Military Attaché in Paris, to argue their corner.[27]

Concurrently, Germany learned that the British Fleet would defend the French coast.[28] This moved Britain closer to Paris and away from Berlin, but it was a measure within Germany's power to forestall if the underlying cause giving rise to the measure ceased. As for a land commitment, London believed such fore-square support would only embolden Russia and France in the present crisis in their stance *vis-à-vis* Austria and Germany. Thus, while the chance of peace remained, Britain sought to preserve it. This was laudable, but it was also necessary given the existing split in Asquith's cabinet on supporting France to the point of war. Though a binding commitment was missing, those most closely associated with the CID held the staunchest views on supporting France now: Asquith, Churchill, Crewe, Haldane, Grey, Runciman, and McKenna. Not all could be classed as Liberal Imperialists. Still, the earlier charge that creation of the CID operated at the risk of cabinet government on the surface appears to have been vindicated. Of course, what truly carried the day was the lifeline offered by Bonar law, who put the Tories on the side of intervention. This halved the parliamentary problem at a stroke, leaving Asquith to manage his cabinet colleagues.[29]

Wasting no time and working to a frantic pace, Jackson et al. convened on 5 August 1914 sans Sperling, who missed three of the four initial sessions. This was little better than Hamilton, who only appeared at the opening session. Present, though, were others, including the inspectors-general of the WAFF and the KAR—Brigadier General Charles Dobell and Colonel Reginald Hoskins, respectively. Conveniently, the pair were in London on the outbreak of war. Others attending the committee included Colonel Alister Dallas from the War Office and Hankey, the redoubtable secretary to the CID. Collectively, they proposed extending operations to East Africa to deny Dar es Salaam to German cruisers and raiders. This would protect British shipping in the Indian Ocean while screening the East African Protectorate. As for the troops required, they looked to India, though the war office feared Egypt's reinforcement might suffer.[30] Other possibilities included attacking German South-West Africa, Togoland, and the Cameroons in Africa, along with Yap, Rabaul, Samoa, Palau, and Nauru in the Pacific.[31] Here, two aims were at work. Firstly, the severance of German wireless and cable communications made the transmission of local intelligence by the enemy impossible. This action would also benefit British communications as enemy jamming would prove more difficult. Secondly, the enemy would be denied anchorages to support their attacks against British trade.[32] Given the technical backgrounds of Jackson and Aston, their sponsorship of these initiatives may be assumed. Accordingly, the cruisers *Minotaur* and *Newcastle*, steaming in Chinese waters, sailed forthwith for German-controlled Yap and temporarily subdued its wireless station on 11 August; a Japanese raid on 7 October settled matters permanently.[33] Meanwhile, Australian forces occupied New Guinea and the surrounding islands of the Bismarck archipelago, and New Zealand troops occupied Upolu in German Samoa. Significantly, these actions occurred absent actionable intelligence on the present whereabouts of enemy cruisers.[34]

The proposed operations were in conformance with a maritime-oriented strategy, which always assumed Britain would retain the initiative in a brief, sharp war likely to end in a negotiated settlement. That hypothesis would be sorely tested by the extent of German progress in Belgium and France in the months ahead. Thus, the decision to send an expeditionary force to the continent in conformance to an understood but loose agreement with France followed on 6 August. This measure had been worked out in detail since the time of the First Moroccan Crisis. Revised periodically, including only the previous month, for the Admiralty, it meant detaching the mobilized second-line ships of the Second and Third Fleets to shield the passage of the BEF, which began on 9 August.[35] The deployment of five infantry divisions and another of cavalry was completed by 23 August, prompting Kitchener to announce that a further 100,000 troops would be raised, trained, and made available for overseas service.[36]

If the experience of the South African War was any guide, raising new divisions would present a host of future problems. Operating at the expense of existing territorial formations, the new armies would be deficient in artillery and specialist troops for months, if not years.[37] Understanding this, Kitchener moved to supplement the BEF by grafting an Indian corps onto it. This reversed a cabinet decision to limit Indian troops to second-line duties outside the main theater of war. It also operated against India's four remaining divisions as their artillery augmented the expedition heading to Europe: Lieutenant General Sir James Willcocks' Indian Expeditionary Force A.[38]

Time would see the commitment of the BEF as fundamentally altering British strategy; that, however, remained for the future. Of more immediate concern, the commitment of colonial forces required the arrangement of trooping convoys escorted by appropriate heavy ships not presently serving at the point of origin. This need was not contemplated in 1903 or 1910 when planning anticipated sending ships singly and unescorted on routes protected by Britain's overall umbrella of naval supremacy. Thus, the *Goliath*, a pre-dreadnought battleship serving at home, became one of several ships tasked to meet this emerging requirement.[39] A corollary problem was securing the safe transfer of the territorial force divisions being sent to the subcontinent from Britain to replace the regular units recalled.[40]

Presently, a further topic arose, though it is not featured in the minutes of the Committee on Combined Operations: Gallipoli. To this end, Callwell submitted a paper to the Admiralty summarizing the difficulties of an operation directed to that end. His cautionary message was eviscerated, however, when he suggested landing 60,000 Greek troops on the peninsula as part of a broader effort.[41] What spurred Callwell's memorandum was an offer by Venizelos, the Greek prime minister, to align his country with Britain and France. Grey argued against acceptance, believing it would spur Sofia and Constantinople to side with Berlin.[42] For the Admiralty, until the naval situation in the North Sea became more apparent entertaining commitments requiring ships from home waters was unsound. This was their view regarding operations against Togoland. Indeed, it had been their view in the years before the war when the subject was sending an expeditionary force to the continent.[43] Forsaken then, their view fared little better now concerning German Togoland. A surprise raid on Yap was one thing. Even supporting administrative landings in German South-West Africa demanded a commitment that went against the whole. More was this the case for any Gallipoli venture.

All this belies Corbett's claim that the initiation of operations against German colonies "had been thoroughly gone into in all its aspects, and decisions taken on well-considered strategical-grounds."[44] That was true only in the sense that the case for subduing these holdings had been examined in detail before the war; a fresh examination based on present realities was eschewed. Unknown then, however, were the actual circumstances giving rise to the present war and the current strategic situation. Of one thing, general staff planners of 1908 readily appreciated: "the capture of the German Colonies promises no results commensurate with the cost of the expeditions and will do nothing toward the solution of the deadlock which an Anglo-German war seems likely to reach at an early stage."[45]

The problem of committing an expeditionary force to the continent featured at the first meeting of the war council, essentially a select subcommittee of the CID, on 5 August.[46] With Asquith in the chair, the tenor of this meeting was that of experts wrestling with a technical question. Namely, where to deploy and not whether to deploy an expeditionary force. Those attending came overwhelmingly from the War Office or represented the senior officers of the force being mobilized. Surprisingly, neither Callwell, the director of military operations, nor Admiral Jackson attended the conference, though Ian Hamilton did. This was deeply troubling. Only 5 days earlier, it had been decided to pursue a naval strategy in the event of hostilities.[47] That decision was not explicitly overturned, but it was in danger of being compromised, for the act of sending an expeditionary force stood not alone from the deliberations of the Combined Operations Committee. Every decision taken needed to be measured against its place in Britain's greater war effort. Little purpose was served in insisting that proposals should only be considered that did not require forces destined for the main theater if the lines of that commitment remained unresolved.[48]

Had Hamilton continued to attend sittings of the Combined Operations Committee beyond its first session, liaison with the war council, which was immediately focused on the dispatch of the BEF, might have been made. Otherwise, Callwell might have joined the deliberations of the war council while keeping one foot in Jackson's camp. Neither event transpired. Beyond this, though, some supporting the Combined Operations Committee would find employment in the schemes they helped define. Their familiarity with the plans under review may explain this, or it could be that they were briefing plans formulated in the War Office, the Colonial Office, and the Admiralty, of which they had their department's lead. Another less charitable conclusion is that the operations contemplated afforded them an avenue for active service with the main army otherwise occupied. Thus, Hoskins departed for Africa to return to the KAR with operations in East Africa pending. This may be thought only natural, but the War Office was at that moment recalling officers seconded to colonial establishments to round out second-line formations. A corresponding effort saw 800 officers on home leave from India assigned to the BEF or tasked to train the new armies.[49]

Here, officers of Dobell and Hoskins seniority were at a disadvantage in finding employment in the main theater. Offering themselves to the schemes under review would have been a natural reaction, though whether the schemes became a vehicle for seeking employment cannot be claimed. Surviving evidence merely suggests; it does not clarify. In the meantime, those other proposals hanging fire and under evaluation by the appropriate offices awaited their turn. Dobell was named prospective commander for British operations in the Cameroons on 14 August. Consideration of operations here had been deferred on 5 August as they were believed to be beyond the ability of local forces. In the interim, France had been approached about cooperating in an invasion. She quickly agreed, and a meeting was convened at the Admiralty to flesh out matters on 15 August.[50] Those attending included Jackson, Dobell, and Capitaine de Vaisseau Comte de Saint-Seine, the French naval attaché. With Dobell confirmed as overall commander a week later, his plan for seizing Victoria, Buea, and Duela was endorsed by the CID and War Council soon after. Thus armed, he departed for West Africa on 31 August.[51]

Until the navy had secured Cameroon's nearby waters, it was intended to hold active operations in abeyance. Indeed, speculation was rife that at least one German cruiser was in the area and that the approaches to Duala were being mined.[52] The hiatus did not occur simply because the Nigeria Regiment had already initiated action against the German colony. This act conformed with the prewar defense scheme for Nigeria. Still, it did not help that the governor general and the presumed commander-in-chief, Sir Frederick Lugard, was absent, with responsibility devolving to Colonel Charles Carter of the Nigeria Regiment. Unfortunately, misfortune at the hands of the enemy followed when a dawn counterattack routed the Nigerians.[53] If the recent amalgamation of Northern and Southern Nigeria was a contributing factor, then fighting a style of war removed from the regiment's normal constabulary duties must be held as the more significant reason.[54]

Returning to the broader story, by the middle of August, a limited campaign against German East Africa to secure its ports had been approved, in addition to the raids against German Pacific territories in the Pacific and the Cameroon operation pending. This evidenced prompt action, but did it simply reflect opportunity over sound strategy? Indeed, in endorsing these plans, the cabinet believed only a limited effort would be required.[55] What follows in a further volume addresses the subject conclusively,[56] but, at a minimum, it can be said that if plans had been concerted earlier in one form or fashion, then their appropriateness to the circumstances of August 1914 had not. This presumably was where Foreign Office input was desired, yet Sperling, an infrequent participant, only attended two of the first nine sessions and did not debut until 8 August. His presence was immediately felt as the Foreign Office secured France's assistance in the campaign directed at Togoland. More prompt was the action of Captain Frederick Bryant on the Gold Coast, who advanced without orders and occupied Lome with two companies of the WAFF.[57]

Having secured the agreement of France, Saint-Seine attended the committee's eighth meeting with an immediate offer of naval assistance following. Originally, Dobell's concept of operations envisioned an administrative landing at Duala, but a combined operation in association with local naval forces had become necessary.[58] Again, no time was wasted as Dobell's combined Anglo-French force seized Duala, a base supporting Germany's small African naval squadron, the following month in a highly touted move deemed the "best run show" of the war.[59] What followed was trickier still, but orders for subjugating the entire Cameroons were promulgated within days.[60] This duly transpired only after a further 17 months of campaigning by a combined French, Belgian, and British force. Through it all, Dobell worked very well with his naval opposite Captain Cyril Fuller, whose cruiser the *Cumberland* had until the month before been a training ship for officer cadets. Paradoxically, the backbone of Dobell's command was French and came from those contingents garrisoning equatorial Africa and Senegal.[61] The cooperation exhibited between Dobell and Fuller was a commodity that had not always been featured in previous joint actions. An esteemed officer, Fuller, not unlike Dobell, displayed a solid ability to work alongside the French. That was a prized skill, for the aspirations of the two allies diverged rapidly once the goal of defeating the enemy had been achieved.

Beyond its powerful wireless transmitter and offering access to the sea, the Cameroons had little strategic value.[62] This, however, did not limit further operations with Dobell now ordered to gain the entire colony.[63] Beginning in October, a series of combined operations north, south, and southwest of Duala ensued.[64] Here, Cameroon's inland waters proved critical, with the *Cumberland*'s executive officer, Commander Lawrence Braithwaite, at the fore in directing the small flotilla of armed craft.[65] These operations demanded further resources. To that end, additional elements of the Indian Army arrived. If the execution of out-of-theater operations appeared independent, their separate demands in sustainment and finance inexorably linked them.

Elsewhere, the Union government accepted that operations against German South-West Africa should be pursued.[66] The initial thoughts of Jackson and company were to reduce the wireless stations found at Swakopmund and Lüderitzbucht. Still, this effort expanded on 9 August to an attack on the new, powerful transmitting station at Windhoek, which was held to communicate directly with Berlin. Significantly, a German military railway connected the two locations.[67] In effect, the revised proposal called for the subjugation of the entire colony. As for the committee's knowledge of the colony, this was extensive courtesy of Colonel Frederic Trench's attachment to the German military during the operations pursued in 1905–1906. Of course, a further reason for these operations was to forestall any German stoking of anti-Union sympathy courtesy of the thousands of Boers living in the colony.[68] Ironically, British actions now provoked that very crisis as Christian Beyers, the commandant-general of the Union's defense force, resigned. Open rebellion soon followed, led by Colonel Salomon Maritz and Christiaan de Wet. Notwithstanding the uprising, South Africa signaled its concurrence to the intended operations against German South-West Africa. A brigade soon landed at Port Nolloth on 31 August, followed by a highly successful naval raid against Lüderitzbucht, which fell on 20 September 1914.[69] The last had been a worry before the war as its bay was large enough to host the entire German Fleet.[70] Securing the greatest of gains at the cheapest of costs, the campaign stands unique as more than 250,000 square miles came under Union control for the loss of 140 lives from all causes. Still, requiring 50,000 troops and 11 months, perhaps Germany's loss was not so one-sided after all?[71]

In Egypt, the Indian Sirhind Brigade was retained to stiffen the defense of the Suez Canal while the balance of the Lahore Division under Lieutenant General Henry Watkis continued with Indian Expeditionary Force A to Marseilles to join the BEF. With the arrival of Force E under Major General Charles Melliss in November, the Sirhinds, at last, departed for the Western front.[72] Meanwhile, another Indian force, IEF C, was readied for Zanzibar and the East Africa Protectorate to fulfill the prewar plan to meet a German thrust. In turn, a third element, IEF B, again from India, was being organized to conduct offensive operations against German East Africa.[73] The foray against German East Africa was to be a limited operation. Belgium now proposed a joint operation to reduce the threat facing the Congo following British actions against Dar es Salaam. Expanding the campaign's objectives, Britain would likely have reached this decision minus the prompting of Brussels.[74]

From the beginning, the command and control of overseas operations presented many problems, for a simple, direct line did not flow from Westminster through Whitehall to the forces deployed. Thus, while cabinets and councils might ordain, they did not control. The distances involved offer a partial reason why. Still, the diffusion of executive authority across multiple agencies, be it the Foreign Office, Colonial Office, India Office, Admiralty, or War Office, was the more telling reason. At one level, this level of devolution made perfect sense. Politically, East Africa and Mesopotamia were problems of more saliency to India and nominally freed the War Office to focus on affairs of direct interest to Britain proper. Still, authorities in India did not operate in a vacuum receiving policy direction from the India Office in London. How closely those in London understood the situation in India and on the ground in Mesopotamia and Africa would be significantly tested, as routine status information on the strength, disposition, and readiness of deployed forces did not flow to the War Office. This made reaching informed decisions about future courses of action based on present difficulties largely a matter of conjecture.[75] That the CID, no less than the general staff, acquiesced in this is none to their credit.

Of course, Jackson and his compatriots lacked executive authority, but they were deemed subject matter experts, each influential within their departments. As such, their recommendations carried weight with those charged with considering actual proposals. As to whether the options proposed suited the needs of broader strategy that remained for others to decide. This did not occur. Instead, the war council and the cabinet approved proposals on the narrow lines of their apparent feasibility. Here, the Foreign and Colonial Offices can be faulted. By mutual agreement, war among Europeans in Africa was deprecated. This was codified by a treaty that stipulated that those European powers at war with each other would not affect the neutrality of central Africa.[76] While London need not assume such niceties would continue after the violation of Belgian neutrality, whether active operations should proceed in Central Africa remained another matter.[77] Here, Berlin's failure to guarantee the integrity of French African colonies in late July played its part. Indeed, Berlin's stance on the question had provoked the sharpest of British rejoinders at a time when Grey was attempting to still troubled waters, for it implied the end of France as a great power—a prospect Britain committed to the maintenance of a balance of power in Europe could not suffer.[78]

With a formal British response pending, the cruiser *Astraea* shelled Dar es Salaam. Two weeks later, Berlin relayed via the United States that they would respect the neutrality of equatorial Africa if the Allies did likewise and then suggested as much for East Asia.[79] Having ignored their obligations toward Belgium, faith in German paper guarantees retained decided limits now. To be sure, Uganda's prewar defense scheme assumed the violation of neutral African areas. Thus, the British naval action was in keeping with the tenor of the military plan. Manifestly, it conformed to the broader aim of securing command of the sea. Hence, the British attitude was, to a degree, self-serving. Whether it was yet wise might have been weighed at greater length.

On balance, establishing the Committee on Combined Operations in Foreign Territory was not an ill-advised move, but its focus and life were, in all events, too narrow and brief. With its last meeting occurring on 6 November, it would remain for others to reap the whirlwind. Common in many *ad hoc* bodies, its participants retained other responsibilities. As such, a few quickly departed, and others tackled different problems in further committees. This included Jackson.[80] Invariably, when others reaped what had been wrought, they operated at a distinct disadvantage as continuity in thought suffered. The problem mirrored what was also occurring within the CID, the board of Admiralty, and the general staff and spoke to a fundamental flaw in Britain's higher direction of war.

As a non-executive body, the withdrawal of the CID in wartime had been anticipated, though uncertainty existed about what would rise Phoenixlike in its place. The emasculation of the War Office as many staff officers departed for France had long been a feature in previous campaigns, though no less problematic now. The board of Admiralty did not suffer a like fate, but its authority was severely undercut by creating a new agency: the War Staff Group. Composed of the first lord, the first sea lord, Vice Admiral Sir Henry Oliver (chief of the war staff), Arthur Wilson, Sir Graham Greene (secretary to the board), Admiral Sir Frederick Hamilton (second sea lord), and Commodore Charles de Bartolomé (naval assistant to the first sea lord), it neutered standard Admiralty procedure—a point accentuated by the lapse of the second sea lord's participation.[81]

As for Aston, his tenure ended on 25 August when he was ordered to command a marine brigade being readied for Ostend. Being charitable, the *Official History* opined that the brigade, if accomplishing little, gave "confidence for what the new force might achieve under more favourable conditions."[82] Committed anew at Dunkirk, Aston now broke down, requiring the dispatch of Colonel Archibald Paris to Belgium to fill the void. In mitigation, it must be allowed that confusion was endemic with planning cursory, command arrangements *ad hoc*, and the force ill-fed, ill-equipped, and, most assuredly, ill-trained. Norman Macleod, a private secretary to the Admiralty's civil lord, observed things firsthand at the Admiralty, and predicted misfortune and was not wrong. Witnessing the machinations of the first lord, the essential problem remained a fertile mind lacking balance and consistency. Indeed, Macleod held Churchill was incapable of conceiving a grand scheme and carrying it to fruition as he "begins no end of things, threatens Heads of Depts with dire penalties if his plans are not carried out – then falters & delays giving a decision."[83] For the principals involved, that censure in the operation did not follow owed something to the presence of Churchill at these events as the orders of the first lord would have been central to any officer's defense.[84]

Colonel John Rose replaced Aston at the Combined Operations Committee, but he soon departed, too, when appointed to the South African Expeditionary Force in late October.[85] His departure coincided with the winding up of the Committee on Combined Operations. Planning for amphibious serials did not end; it merely shifted locale. Mesopotamia now featured, with General Barrow seeking the navy's cooperation working through Rose to that end before the latter's transfer to the Cape Station.[86] Otherwise, Churchill met with Jellicoe and his principals at Loch Ewe to review the war in northern waters. Tabled was a proposal backed by Sir Arthur Wilson for seizing Heligoland. Highly reminiscent of what had been suggested in 1911, the idea received no more support from Jellicoe than had been the case with Haldane. With losses in heavy ships likely severe and requiring the violation of Norwegian and Danish waters, Jellicoe indeed questioned Wilson's sanity, believing one capable of advocating such a plan was capable of touting anything.[87]

Britain issued an ultimatum to Germany and declared war on Tuesday (4 August), ordered an expedition to East Africa and the reinforcement of Egypt from India on Wednesday (5 August) before deciding to send an expeditionary force to the continent on Thursday (6 August). Kitchener, the redeemer of

Gordon and presently home on leave, was sworn to the privy council and became secretary of state for war. The appointment was warmly received and perhaps warmest of all by Repington, who had broached the idea in *The Times* 3 days earlier.[88] Forsaking party whip and lacking War Office experience, Kitchener possessed stature. The greater point remained that his career had been giving orders to others, though known as "K of Chaos," clearly not always to desired ends.

Tellingly, Britain's decision for war and where first measures were to be pursued occurred while Asquith retained the War Office portfolio in addition to being the first lord of the treasury and prime minister. It must be the case that Asquith had more than enough on his plate before weighing the recommendations coming fast and furious from Jackson's body. Of course, Asquith soon yielded responsibility of the War Office to Kitchener, an officer singularly lacking in Whitehall and War Office experience. That many senior members of the general staff were vacating present duties to join the BEF to be replaced by officers lacking any understanding of prewar assumptions and prior arrangements only spelled further problems. Hardly abetting matters, the CIGS, General Sir Charles Douglas, was soon overworked and then overwhelmed. Thus, Britain's machinery of wartime government, if less than ideal in August 1914, rapidly fell below even that modest standard.[89] Consequently, the actions proposed by Jackson et al., no less than the decision to send an expeditionary force to the continent, did not receive the scrutiny required and left unsettled the primacy of pursuing either a maritime or continental strategic approach. This failure was central to the problems later experienced. Presciently, Jackson warned of these risks in late August, though whether his minute made any impression is unknown.[90]

The serials undertaken were in keeping with prewar plans to deny the enemy communications to his overseas territories and eliminate access to local bases, all the while abetting the defense of Egypt and the empire. Accordingly, they were an extension of the naval blockade against Germany to areas beyond the North Sea and had been posited by the Admiralty in 1906.[91] Demanding few naval resources beyond the employment of those mostly older warships already on station, their execution did not always come to the war council for consideration.[92] Whether that was wise remains to be discussed, but it was indicative of a style of governance owing more to strong officials than strong structures. Accordingly, the Admiralty, Colonial Office, and the War Office could and did act at cross-purposes as they failed to coordinate their collective efforts. Higher order taskings offer one explanation for why this occurred, but more prosaically, both services failed to share their operational signals with the Colonial Office.[93]

Meanwhile, Jackson's committee evaluated other proposals. These included a combined operation against Zeebrugge, a landing at Borkum, and an assault on Alexandretta. Given their anticipated scale, complexity, and cost, all were referred to the Admiralty or the War Office for further investigation.[94] For those sanctioned, such as the one against Dar es Salaam, the conclusion must be that they went forward because they were viewed as easy to accomplish, demanded little in resources, and retained a link to the broader war against Germany. This was a mistaken reading for both the Admiralty or the War Office would yet have to raise the ante of support. In the case of the navy, to meet the expanding scope of military operations. For the military, to secure what had been ordained. Why closer attention was not paid to these serials by the war council reflects that all were fixated on the continent and the North Sea. In truth, Kitchener paid little attention to out-of-area operations and, when he did, to a negative result.[95] China is a case in point. Here, he scaled down the British contribution for seizing Tsingtao (Qingdao) to the 36th Sikhs so that several other battalions could be returned to the "real theater of war." This was not necessarily a wrong ordering of affairs, but an ordering taken unilaterally without cabinet sanction. Such acts exasperated Callwell, the DMO, who rarely featured in the war secretary's decisions.[96]

In the meantime, naval forces in the Mediterranean and the Indian Ocean began a series of local raids against Dar es Salaam and Syria to further the greater maritime strategy and support Egypt's defense. These were sound and only limited liabilities so long as they remained raids, but the transition to permanent operations, whether through the vehicle of administrative or opposed landings, became a different kettle of fish. Here, the record speaks of the British adopting such measures all too readily. This may have reflected the view that the war would be short. Accordingly, the desire to remove latent difficulties near British obligations became strong. It may be the case that some were initiated to force enemy cruisers operating outside of European waters to defend German colonies, thereby permitting their defeat in battle. In truth, all these reasons were at play in some measure.[97]

At the end of 1914, the BEF stood at over 150,000 troops and represented roughly 14 percent of the Allied forces fighting in France and Belgium.[98] In the background, three new armies totaling eighteen divisions had been authorized on 21 August, though a decision on their use remained open. Lloyd George held these to be the best forces ever raised by Britain as their ranks were filled by artisans and educated, middle-class soldiers. Witnessing stalemate in the main theater, the chancellor now argued the time was right for employing these forces elsewhere rather than seeing them impaled on France's barbed wire. Where that elsewhere should be remained for the general staff to say, though Lloyd George suggested the Balkans, Turkey, or Syria as possible alternatives.[99]

Lloyd George was neither a military man nor a militarist in the spirit of the first lord. Yet he was asking a vital question at an appropriate moment: How much of the war should Britain and the Empire assume, and where were efforts best made? Tradition suggested that either a continental or a peripheral approach held merit. Both featured at different times, and both met with success. Yet, such previous continental interventions had not seen deployments on the scale the new armies offered. Thus, wholesale augmentation committed Britain to a course of action without precedent.[100] Already, Esher had argued that the demands of the BEF were compromising the ability to execute an amphibious strategy. That was so, but Britain's ability to manage a traditional maritime war against Germany was no longer a given. Partly, this reflected the changes in the circumstances of naval warfare arising from the declarations of Paris and London, which compromised Britain's traditional ability to enforce economic measures against an enemy.[101] Yet, it also stemmed from the new facts on the ground Germany had created in Belgium and France.

Esher accepted Lloyd George's premise that a return to peripheral operations was warranted. Argued in successive meetings of the war council, the operations contemplated included the Dardanelles, Borkum, Zeebrugge, Alexandretta, and East Africa.[102] Ultimately, a maritime strategy prevailed, and it is easy to appreciate why. With stalemate existing on the Western front, fresh operations in that theater offered little promise. Further afield, however, the story appeared different. Extending the war to the Balkans and the Mediterranean would be done to secure new allies. Even if the moves did not lead to Germany's defeat, they at least promised to isolate her and would render the economic warfare being waged more effective.[103] Admittedly, Lloyd George did not argue for abandoning support in the main theater—only that its scale of support be curtailed. Yet, in accepting an enhanced peripheral strategy, the danger existed that Britain might not be strong enough to prevail across the board. That was one problem. Another remained that where positive results might be secured, they probably would not be decisive. They would, however, offer cheer to the home front that something positive was being achieved.[104] The more fundamental problem was that the war council would not settle on a preferred strategy. Electing to pursue fresh peripheral operations, further efforts in France were also authorized. A naval attack on the Dardanelles was approved to be followed by a campaign in the Balkans. The intended moves would not end the stalemate on the Western front, but they would offer relief to Russia and likely bring Italy into the fray on the side of the *Entente*. Moreover, Turkey's defeat would facilitate operations on the Danube against Austria-Hungary.[105] In support of the last, the war council directed the Admiralty to order twelve river monitors for shipment to Salonika.[106]

Meanwhile, if the landing at Basra in November 1914 had the avowed object of guaranteeing British access to the Persian Gulf, it soon generated other considerations. Having conceded control of the straits to Russia as the price of British action on that front, the Admiralty and the War Office desired to offset that loss by securing lower Mesopotamia. This led Kitchener to eye Alexandretta (Iskenderun), a prize meeting with agreement in Admiralty circles.[107] That ploy never advanced owing to France's sensitivities regarding matters of Syria. Hindsight suggests the failure to attempt was a major unforced error given the ongoing commitment in Mesopotamia.[108]

In time, out-of-theater operations came to be viewed as side shows, and while that judgment retains validity, it masquerades that not all ploys were of equal value. Callwell later accepted that those undertaken could be divided into the necessary, the excusable, and the "unjustifiable and mischievous" based on the resources they demanded and their link to Britain's greater maritime strategy.[109] His reading, if correct, obscures that Britain could no longer pursue a purely maritime strategy. This tension had been latent and stood unresolved since the middle of the last century.[110] Fundamentally, this speaks to a failure to reach an agreed grand strategy. That was one problem; indeed, it was the paramount one. Yet, even if that circle had been squared, Britain's operational grasp remained unequal to its reach. Just how so is considered from the vantage point of three critical campaigns in the forthcoming *British Amphibious Operations of the First World War*.

Bibliography

Official Papers

Australian War Memorial, Canberra.
  AWM 4, Imperial Force, Unit War Diaries: 1/1/1, 1/1/3, 1/8/4, 1/25/9.
British Library, India Office Records, Military Department Library:
  Army Headquarters India, War Diaries, IOR/L/MIL/17/5: 3243.
  Arabia, Syria, Turkey, Cyprus, IOR/L/MIL/17/16: 22.
National Archives, Kew, Richmond, Surrey.
  Admiralty 1, Correspondence and Papers: 6640, 6641, 6723, 6777, 6795, 6835, 6888, 7170, 7357A, 7367B, 7417, 7840, 7859, 8211, 8272, 8386/213, 8710/138, 8880, 8884, 8997.
  Admiralty 116, Naval Staff Memoranda: 34, 45, 208, 900B, 930, 931, 984B, 1169, 1214, 3111, 3132.
  Admiralty 137, Historical Section: 6, 452, 899.
  Admiralty 144, Channel Squadron and Fleet Correspondence: 28, 31.
  Admiralty 174, Navy Board and Admiralty, Plymouth Dockyard, Correspondence and Papers: 377.
  Admiralty 186, Admiralty Publications: 10, 592, 605, 608, 610, 612, 618, 621, 622.
  Admiralty 196, Officers' Service Records (Series III): 14, 15, 16, 20, 36, 37, 38, 39, 40, 42, 43, 61, 62, 86, 87, 88, 89, 125, 137, 141, 143.
  Admiralty 203, Admiralty and Ministry of Defence: Royal Naval Colleges, Dartmouth and Greenwich: Correspondence and Papers: 100.
  Air Ministry 10, Air Publications and Reports: 1206.
  Cabinet 1, Cabinet Office, Miscellaneous Records: 31.
  Cabinet 2, Committee of Imperial Defence and Standing Defence Sub-committee, Minutes: 1.
  Cabinet 6, Committee of Imperial Defence, Defence of India Memoranda: 3.
  Cabinet 17, Committee of Imperial Defence, Miscellaneous Correspondence and Memoranda: 95.
  Cabinet 19, Special Commissions to Enquire into the Operations of War in Mesopotamia (Hamilton Commission) and in the Dardanelles (Cromer and Pickford Commission), Records: 26.
  Cabinet 21, Cabinet Office and predecessors: Registered Files (1916 to 1965): 3, 60.
  Cabinet 24, War Cabinet and Cabinet Memoranda: 2, 3, 4.
  Cabinet 37, Cabinet Papers: 12/5, 12/6, 12/8, 12/12, 12/16, 12/18, 12/22, 12/25, 12/27, 13/36, 13/37, 13/40, 14/11, 16/59, 40/64, 44/27, 45/49, 50/38,

50/56, 50/63, 51/105, 53/71, 55/196, 63/145, 63/146, 63/166, 65/35, 69/38, 69/43, 70/62, 74/14, 78/115, 87/36, 105/27, 108/136, 112/106, 115/39, 119/47, 128/30, 162/32.
Cabinet 38, Committee of Imperial Defence Minutes and Memoranda: 2, 3, 3/53, 4, 5, 7, 8, 9, 10, 11, 12, 13, 14, 15, 16, 17, 18, 19, 20, 28, 29.
Cabinet 41, Cabinet Letters in the Royal Archives: 35.
Cabinet 42, War Council and Successors, Minutes and Papers: 1, 6.
Cabinet 53, Committee of Imperial Defence: Chiefs of Staff Committee: Minutes and Memoranda: 14.
Colonial Office 417, High Commission for South Africa Correspondence: 430.
Colonial Office 445, Niger and West Africa Frontier Force and West Africa Frontier Force Original Correspondence: 31.
Colonial Office 534, Record of the Colonial Office, 1905–26: 3, 4, 5, 12, 17.
Foreign Office 1, Political and Other Departments: General Correspondence before 1906: 30.
Foreign Office 84, Slave Trade Department and successors: General Correspondence before 1906: 1618.
Foreign Office 800, Private Offices, Various Ministers' and Officials' Papers: 48, 91, 102, 106, 107, 166, 342, 345, 353, 357, 359, 375.
War Office 25, War Office, Register of Royal Engineers: 3917/7.
War Office 28, Adjutant-General Records: 302.
War Office 32, Registered Files (General Series): 3094, 6106, 6108, 6109, 6112, 6113.
War Office 33, Reports, Memoranda and Papers: 40, 322, 344, 569, 644, 2982.
War Office 95, First World War and Army of Occupation War Diaries: 5117/2, 5235/6.
War Office 106, Directorate of Military Operations and Intelligence Papers: 39, 40, 46, 47, 48.
War Office 279, War Office and Ministry of Defence, Confidential Print: 8, 18.

Official Publications

Bean, C.E.W. *The Story of ANZAC from the Outbreak of War to the End of the First Phase of the Gallipoli Campaign, May 4, 1915*. Sydney: Angus & Robertson Ltd., 1941.
Clarke, Francis Coningsby Hannam. *Staff Duties: A Series of Lecturers Addressed to the Officers of the Staff College*. London: Her Majesty's Stationery Office, 1884.
Corbett, Sir Julian S. *History of the Great War, Naval Operations, Vol. I*. London: Longmans, Green and Co., 1920.
_____. *Maritime Operations in the Russo-Japanese War, 1904–1905, Volume 2*. Annapolis: Naval Institute Press, 2015.
Correspondence Respecting the Insurrectionary Movement in China. London: Her Majesty's Stationery Office, 1900.
Correspondence Respecting the Disturbances in China: China No. 1. London: His Majesty's Stationery Office, 1901.

Correspondence Respecting the European Crisis: Miscellaneous No. 6. London: His Majesty's Stationery Office, 1914.
Correspondence Respecting Reorganization in Egypt, No. 2. London: Harrison and Sons, 1883.
Edmonds, J. E. *Military Operations France and Belgium, 1914: Antwerp, La Bassée, Armentières, Messines, and Ypres October-November 1914*. London: Macmillan and Co., Limited, 1925.
Field Service Pocket Book. London: His Majesty's Stationery Office, 1914.
Field Service Regulations, Part I, Operations, 1909. London: His Majesty's Stationery Office, 1914.
Frontier and Overseas Expeditions from India, Vol. V, Burma. Simla: Government Monotype Press, 1907.
Further Correspondence Respecting the Affairs of Egypt, No. 1. London: Harrison and Sons, 1885.
Further Correspondence Respecting the Affairs of Egypt, No. 22. London: Harrison and Sons, 1883.
Further Correspondence Respecting the Cholera Epidemic in Egypt: 1883, Commercial No. 39. London: Harrison and Sons, 1883.
Further Correspondence Respecting Events at Peking: China No. 3. London: His Majesty's Stationery Office, 1901.
Further Correspondence Respecting the Affairs of China: China No. 3 (1912). London: His Majesty's Stationery Office, 1912.
Gleichen, Count. *The Anglo-Egyptian Sudan: A Compendium Prepared by the Officers of the Sudan Government, Vol. I*. London: His Majesty's Stationery Office, 1905.
Gooch G.P. and Temperley, Harold. eds. *British Documents on the Origins of the War, 1898–1914, Vol. 1, The End of British Isolation*. London: His Majesty's Stationery Office, 1927.
_____. *British Documents on the Origins of the War 1898–1914, Vol. III, The Testing of the Entente 1904–6*. London: His Majesty's Stationery Office, 1928.
_____. *British Documents on the Origins of the War, Vol. IV, The Anglo-Russian Rapprochement, 1903–1907*. London: His Majesty's Stationery Office, 1929.
_____. *British Documents on the Origins of the War 1898–1914, Vol. V, The Near East: The Macedonian Problem and the Annexation of Bosnia, 1903–9*. London: His Majesty's Stationery Office, 1928.
_____. *British Documents on the Origins of the War, 1898–1914, Vol. VI, Anglo-German Tension, Armaments and Negotiation, 1907–12*. London: His Majesty's Stationery Office, 1930.
_____. *British Documents on the Origins of the War, 1898–1914, Vol. VIII, Arbitration, Neutrality and Security*. London: His Majesty's Stationery Office, 1932.
_____. *British Documents on the Origins of the War, 1898–1914, Vol. X, Part II, The Last Years of Peace*. London: His Majesty's Stationery Office, 1938.
Goodrich, Caspar F. *Report of the British Naval and Military Operations in Egypt, 1882*. Washington, DC: Government Printing Office, 1883.

Hansard.
History of the Third Burmese War, 1885–1886–1887, Period I, History of the War Prior to the Annexation of the Country. Calcutta: Superintendent of Government Printing India, 1887.
History of the Third Burmese War, 1890–91, Period VI, The Winter Campaign of 1890–91. Simla: Central Printing Office, 1893.
Jeffrey, Keith. *The Secret History of MI6.* New York: The Penguin Press, 2010.
Jose, Arthur W. *The Royal Australian Navy 1914–1918.* Sydney: Angus and Robertson, Ltd., 1941.
London Gazette.
Maurice, J. F. *Military History of the Campaign of 1882 in Egypt.* London: J. B. Hayward & Son, 1887.
Navy List.
Official History (Naval and Military) of the Russo-Japanese War, Vol. 1. London: Harrison and Sons, 1910.
Official History (Naval and Military) of the Russo-Japanese War, Vol. II. London: Harrison and Sons, 1912.
Official History (Naval and Military) of the Russo-Japanese War, Vol. III. London: His Majesty's Stationery Office, 1920.
Official History of the Operations in Somaliland, 1901–04, Vol. I. London: Harrison and Sons, 1907.
Official History of the Operations in Somaliland, 1901–04, Vol. II. London: Harrison and Sons, 1907.
Official History of the Russo-Japanese War. Part II. From the Battle of the Ya-Lu to Liao-Yang, Exclusive. London: Harrison and Sons, 1908.
Official History of the Russo-Japanese War. Part III. The Siege of Port Arthur. London: Harrison and Sons, 1909.
Reports by Mr. Villiers Stuart, M.P., Respecting Reorganization in Egypt, Egypt No. 7. London: Harrisons and Sons, 1883.
Russo-Japanese War. Joint Report by Major G. H. G. Mockler and Captain H. C. Holman, D.S.O. War Office, General Staff, 1906.
Russo-Japanese War. Medical and Sanitary Reports from Officers Attached to the Japanese and Russian Forces in the Field. London: Eyre and Spottiswoode, 1908.
Russo-Japanese War. Part I. London: Harrison and Sons, 1906.
Russo-Japanese War. Reports from British Officers Attached to the Japanese and Russian Forces in the Field, Vols. I and II. London: His Majesty's Stationery Office, 1908.
Russo-Japanese War. Reports from Officers Attached to the Japanese Forces in the Field, Vol. 1, 1905.
Statistics of the Military Effort of the British Empire during the Great War 1914–1920. London: His Majesty's Stationery Office, 1922.

Private Papers

Churchill Archives Centre, Cambridge.
    Viscount Esher Papers.
    Admiral of the Fleet Lord Fisher Papers.

Lieutenant Colonel Adrian Grant Duff Papers.
Sir Robert Rhodes James Papers.
Reginald McKenna Papers.
Admiral Sir Reginald Aylmer Ranfurly Plunkett-Ernle-Erle-Drax Papers.
Imperial War Museum, London.
Lieutenant Colonel Kenneth Henderson Papers.
Vice Admiral Wilfred Henderson Papers.
Captain Hughes Campbell Lockyer Papers
Norman Macleod Papers.
Major General Ladislaus Herbert Richard Pope-Hennessy Papers.
Field Marshal Sir Henry Hughes Wilson Papers.
Liddell Hart Centre for Military Archives, King's College, London.
General Sir Archibald Alison Papers.
Major General Sir George Grey Aston Papers.
Admiral Sir Alexander Edward Bethell Papers.
Major General Sir Thompson Capper Papers.
Sir Julian Corbett Papers.
Brigadier General Sir James Edmonds.
Brigadier General Philip Howell Papers.
Major General Sir Frederick Barton Maurice Papers.
Field Marshal Sir Archibald Amar Montgomery-Massingberd Papers.
Middle East Centre Archive, St. Antony's College, Oxford.
Major General Sir Percy Cox Papers.
National Army Museum, London.
Lieutenant General Sir Gerald Francis Ellison Papers.
Lieutenant General Sir Aylmer Hunter-Weston Papers.
Privately Held.
Lieutenant Harold Bedwell, RN.

Secondary Sources

Journals
The British Medical Journal.
The Geographical Journal.
The Great Circle.

Newspapers

The Broad Arrow: The Naval and Military Gazette.
The Spectator.
The Times.

Dissertations and Theses

Caswell, Liam. "Born Soldiers Who March Under the Rising Sun: The Russo-Japanese War, Britain's Military Observers, and British Impressions Regarding Japanese Martial Capabilities Prior to the First World War." Master's thesis, Dalhousie University, Halifax, 2017.

Grimes, Shawn T. "War Planning and Strategic Development in the Royal Navy, 1887–1918." PhD diss., University of London, 2004.
Snook, Mike. "Wolseley, Wilson and the Failure of the Khartoum Campaign: An Exercise in Scapegoating and Abrogation of Command Responsibility?" PhD diss., Cranfield University, 2014.
Summerton, Neil William. "The Development of British Military Planning for a War Against Germany, 1904 – 1914." PhD diss., University of London, 1970.

Books

Adye, John. *Recollections of a Military Life*. London: Smith, Elder & Co., 1895.
Archer, Thomas. *The War in Egypt and the Soudan: An Episode in the History of the British Empire, Vol. III*. London: Blackie & Son, ca. 1886.
_____. *The War in Egypt and the Soudan: An Episode in the History of the British Empire, Vol. IV*. London: Blackie & Son, ca. 1886.
Ardagh, Lady. *Life of Major-General Sir John Ardagh*. London: John Murray, 1909.
Arthur, George, ed., *The Letters of Lord and Lady Wolseley 1870–1911*. London: William Heinemann, 1922.
Asquith, H. H. *The Genesis of the War*. London: Cassell and Company, Limited, 1923.
Aston, George. *Letters on Amphibious Wars*. London: John Murray, 1920.
_____. *Memories of a Marine*. London: John Murray, 1925.
_____. *Sea, Land, and Air Strategy: A Comparison*. Boston: Little, Brown and Company, 1914.
_____. *Secret Service*. New York: Cosmopolitan Book Corporation, 1930.
Atkinson, C. T. *The Royal Hampshire Regiment, Volume One, To 1914*. Glasgow: Robert Maclehose & Company Limited, 1950.
Atlay, J. B. *Lord Haliburton: A Memoir of His Public Service*. Toronto: William Briggs, 1909.
Barrow, George de. S. *The Fire of Life*. London: Hutchinson & Co., 1942.
Bates, Darrell, *The Fashoda Incident of 1898: Encounter on the Nile*. Oxford: Oxford University Press, 1984.
Batten, Simon. *Futile Exercise: The British Army's Preparations for War 1902–1914*. Warwick: Helion & Company Limited, 2018.
Beckett, Ian F. W. *A British Profession of Arms: The Politics of Command in the Late Victorian Army*. Norman: University of Oklahoma Press, 2018,
_____. *Johnnie Gough, V.C.: A Biography of Brigadier-General Sir John Edmond Gough V.C., K.C.B., C.M.G.* London: Tom Donovan, 1989.
_____. *The Victorians at War*. London: Hambledon and London, 2003.
Beresford, Lord Charles. *The Betrayal: Being a Record of Facts Concerning Naval Policy and Administration from the Year 1902 to the Present Time*. London: P. S. King & Son, 1911.
Bigham, Clive. *A Year in China, 1899–1900*. London: Macmillan and Co., Limited, 1901.
Bird, W. D. *A Précis of Strategy*. London: Hugh Rees, Ltd., 1910.
_____. *Lectures on the Strategy of the Russo-Japanese War*. London: Hugh Rees, Ltd., 1909.

Bloch, I. S. *Is War Now Possible? Being an Abridgement of the War of the Future in Its Technical, Economic and Political Relations*. Aldershot: Gregg Revivals, 1991.
Bond, Brian. *The Victorian Army and the Staff College, 1854–1914*. London: Eyre Methuen, 1972.
Bradford, Edward E. *Life of Admiral of the Fleet Arthur Knyvet Wilson Bart., V.C., G.C.B., O.M., G.C.V.O.* London: John Murray, 1923.
Brice, Christopher. *The Thinking Man's Soldier: The Life and Career of General Sir Henry Brackenbury 1837–1914*. Solihull: Helion and Company, Ltd., 2015.
Burne, Lieutenant [Charles Richard Newdigate Burne]. *With the Naval Brigade in Natal, 1899–1900*. London: Edward Arnold, 1902.
Busch, Briton Cooper. *Hardinge of Penshurst: A Study in the Old Diplomacy*. Hamden: Archon Book, 1980.
Butler, W. F. *Sir William Butler: An Autobiography*. London: Constable and Company Ltd., 1911.
_____. *The Campaign of the Cataracts*. London: Sampson Low, Marston, Searle, & Rivington, 1887.
Callwell, C. E. *The Effect of Maritime Command on Land Campaigns Since Waterloo*. Edinburgh: William Blackwood and Sons, 1897.
_____. *Experiences of a Dug-Out 1914–1918*. London: Constable & Company Limited, 1920.
_____. *Field-Marshal Sir Henry Wilson Bart., G.C.B., D.S.O. His Life and Diaries, Volume I*. London: Cassell and Company, Ltd., 1927.
_____. *The Life of Sir Stanley Maude*. London: Constable and Company Ltd., 1920.
_____. *The Memoirs of Major-General Sir Hugh McCalmont K.C.B., C.V.O.* London: Hutchinson & Co., 1924.
_____. *Military Operations and Maritime Preponderance: Their Relations and Interdependence*. Edinburgh: William Blackwood and Sons, 1905.
_____. *Small Wars: Their Principles and Practice*. London: Harrison and Sons, 1906.
Childers, Spencer. *The Life and Correspondence of the Right Hon, Hugh C. E. Childers 1827–1896, Vol. II*. London: John Murray, 1901.
Churchill, Seton. *General Gordon: A Christian Hero*. London: James Nisbet & Co., Limited, *ca.* 1900.
Clarke, George S. *Imperial Defence*. London: The Imperial Press Limited, 1897.
_____. and Thursfield, James R. *Navy and the Nation or Naval Warfare and Imperial Defence*. London: John Murray, 1897.
Colborne, J. *With Hicks Pasha in the Soudan*. London: Smith, Elder, & Co., 1885.
Colomb, P. H. *Essays on Naval Defence*. London: W. H. Allen & Co., Limited, 1896.
_____. *Naval Warfare Its Ruling Principles and Practices Historically Treated*. London: W. H. Allen & Co. Limited, 1895.
Colvin, Auckland. *Making of Modern Egypt*. London: Seeley & Co. Limited, 1906.
Connor, John. *ANZAC and Empire: George Foster Pearce and the Foundations of Australian Defence*. Cambridge: Cambridge University Press, 2011.
Coombes, W. C. and Wilkie, J. B. *The Commission of H.M.S. Naiad 1901 – 1904: Cape, East Indies and Mediterranean Stations*. London: Westminster Press, 1904.

Corrigan, Gordon. *Sepoys in the Trenches: The Indian Corps on the Western Front 1914–15*. Stroud: Spellmount, 2006.
Cromer, Earl. *Modern Egypt, Vol. I*. New York: Macmillan, 1916.
_____. *Modern Egypt, Vol. II*. New York: Macmillan, 1916.
Crosthwaite, Charles. *The Pacification of Burma*. London: Edward Arnold, 1912.
d'Ombrain, Nicholas. *War Machinery and High Policy: Defence Administration in Peacetime Britain 1902–1914*. London: Oxford University Press, 1973.
Daggett, A. S. *America in the China Relief Expedition*. Kansas City: Hudson-Kimberley Publishing Company, 1906.
Dane, Edmund. *British Campaign in Africa and the Pacific 1914–1918*. London: Hodder and Stoughton, 1919.
De Chair, Dudley. *The Sea is Strong*. London: George G. Harrap & Co. Ltd., 1961.
de Cosson, E. A. *Days and Nights of Service with Sir Gerald Graham's Field Force at Suakin*. London: John Murray, 1886.
Delaney, Douglas E. *The Imperial Army Project: Britain and the Land Forces of the Dominions and India 1902–1945*. Oxford: Oxford University Press, 2020.
Dilke, Charles Wentworth and Wilkinson, Spenser. *Imperial Defence*. London: Macmillan and Co., 1892.
Durand, Mortimer. *The Life of Field-Marshal Sir George White, V.C., Vols. I and II*. Edinburgh: William Blackwood and Sons, 1915.
E. C. H. [Ernest Charles Holtom]. *Two Years' Captivity in German East Africa being the Personal Experiences of Surgeon E. C. H., Royal Navy*. London: Hutchinson & Co., 1918.
Elton, Lord. *General Gordon*. London: Collins, 1954.
Esher, Reginald Viscount. *To-Day and To-Morrow and Other Essays*. London: John Murray, 1910.
Fay, Sam. *The War Office at War*. East Arsdsley: EP Publishing Limited, 1973.
Fitzroy, Almeric. *Memoirs, Vol. I*. London: Hutchinson & Co., 1920.
Fitzmaurice, Lord Edmond. *The Life of Granville George Leveson Gower, Second Earl Granville, K.G., 1815–1891, Volume II*. London: Longmans, Green, and Co., 1905.
Fortescue, Seymour. *Looking Back*. London: Longmans, Green and Co., 1920.
Foster, R. F. *Lord Randolph Churchill: A Political Life*. Oxford University Press, 2011.
Fraser, Peter, *Lord Esher: A Political Biography*. Barnsley: Pen & Sword Politics, 2013.
Fraser, Lovat. *India Under Curzon & After*. New York: Henry Holt and Company, 1911.
French, Viscount. *1914*. London: Constable and Company, Ltd., 1919.
Fritzinger, Linda B. *Diplomat Without Portfolio: Valentine Chirol, His Life and* The Times. London: I. B. Tauris & Co. Ltd., 2006.
Furse, George Armand. *Military Expeditions Beyond the Seas, Vol. II*. London: William Clowes & Sons, Limited, 1897.
Galloway, William. *The Battle of Tofrek*. London: W. H. Allen & Co., 1887.
Gardiner, A. G. *The Life of Sir William Harcourt*. London: Constable & Company Ltd., 1923.
Gatacre, Beatrix. *General Gatacre: The Story of the Life and Services of Sir William Forbes Gatacre, K.C.B., D.S.O. 1843–1906*. London: John Murray, 1910.

Geary, Grattan. *Burma After the Conquest. Viewed in Its Political, Social, and Commercial Aspects, from Mandalay*. London: Sampson Low, Marston, Searle, & Rivington, 1886.

Glasfurd, A. I. R. *Sketches of Manchurian Battle-Fields with a Verbal Description of Southern Manchuria: An Aid to the Study of the Russo-Japanese War*. London: Hugh Rees, Ltd., 1910.

Gleichen, Count. *With the Camel Corps Up the Nile*. London: Chapman & Hall, Limited, 1888.

Godley, Alexander. *Life of an Irish Soldier: Reminiscences of General Sir Alexander Godley G.C.B, K.C.M.G*. London: John Murray, 1939.

Godwin-Austen, A. R. *The Staff and the Staff College*. London: Constable and Company, Ltd., 1927.

Gooch, John. *The Plans of War: The General Staff and British Military Strategy c. 1900–1916*. Abingdon: Routledge, 2016.

Grant, James. *Cassell's History of the War in the Soudan, Vol. I*. London: Cassell & Company, Limited, *ca.* 1887.

Guinn, Paul. *British Strategy and Politics 1914–1918*. Oxford: Oxford University Press, 1965.

Hamilton, Angus. *Somaliland*. London: Hutchinson and Co., 1911.

Hamilton, Ian. *The Soul and Body of an Army*. London: Edward Arnold & Co., 1921.

_____. *A Staff Officer's Scrap-Book During the Russo-Japanese War. Two Volumes*. London: Edward Arnold, 1906.

Hardinge, Lord. *My Indian Years 1910–1916*. London: John Murray, 1948.

Harris, Robert Hastings. *From Naval Cadet to Admiral: Half-a-Century of Naval Service and Sport in Many Parts of the World*. London: Cassell and Company, Ltd., 1913.

Harrison, Richard. *Recollections of a Life in the British Army During the Latter Half of the 19th Century*. London: Smith, Elder, & Co., 1908.

Henderson, G. F. R. *The Science of War: A Collection of Essays and Lectures, 1891–1903*. Edited by Neill Malcolm. London: Longmans, Green, and Co., 1912.

Hertslet, Edward and Hertslet, Edward Cecil. eds. *British and Foreign State Papers, 1881–1882*. London: William Ridgway, 1889.

Holland, Bernard. *The Life of Spencer Compton Eighth Duke of Devonshire, Vols. I and II*. London: Longmans, Green and Co., 1911.

Jardine, Douglas. *The Mad Mullah of Somaliland*. London: Herbert Jenkins Limited, 1923.

Jeffery, Keith *Field Marshal Sir Henry Wilson: A Political Soldier*. Oxford: Oxford University Press, 2006.

Jerrold, Douglas. *The Royal Naval Division*. London: Hutchinson & Co., 1923.

Johnson, Franklyn Arthur. *Defence by Committee*. London: Oxford University Press, 1960.

Jones, Spencer. *From Boer War to World War: Tactical Reform of the British Army, 1902–1914*. Norman: University of Oklahoma Press, 2012.

Judd, Denis. *Balfour and the British Empire: A Study in Imperial Evolution 1874–1932*. London: Faber and Faber, 2015.

Kelly, Saul. *Captain Gill's Walking Stick: The True Story of the Sinai Murders*. London. I. B. Tauris, 2019.
Kochanski, Halik. *Sir Garnet Wolseley: Victorian Hero* London: Hambledon Press, 1999.
Lamothe, Ronald M. *Slaves of Fortune: Sudanese Soldiers & the River War 1896–1898*. Woodbridge: James Currey, 2011.
Lee, John. *A Soldier's Life: General Sir Ian Hamilton, 1853–1947*. London: Macmillan, 2000.
Lees-Milne, James. *The Enigmatic Edwardian: The Life of Reginald 2nd Viscount Esher*. London: Sidgwick & Jackson, 1986.
Luvaas, Jay. *The Education of an Army: British Military Thought, 1815–1940*. Chicago: University of Chicago Press, 1964.
Lynch, George. *The War of the Civilisations being a Record of a "Foreign Devil's" Experiences with the Allies in China*. London: Longmans, Green, and Co., 1901.
Lyttelton, Neville. *Eighty Years: Soldiering, Politics, Games*. London: Hodder and Stoughton, 1927.
McMeekin, Sean. *The Berlin-Baghdad Express: The Ottoman Empire and Germany's Bid for World Power 1898–1918*. London: Penguin Books, 2011.
Macdiarmid, D. S. *The Life of Lieut. General Sir James Moncrieff Grierson, K.C.B., C.V.O., C.M.G., A.D.C.* London: Constable & Company, Ltd., 1923.
Malet, Edward. *Egypt, 1789–1883*. Edited by Lord Sanderson. London: John Murray, 1909.
Mallett, Bernard. *Thomas George, Earl of Northbrook, G.C.S.I.: A Memoir*. London: Longmans, Green and Co., 1908.
Marder, Arthur J. Ed. *Fear God and Dread Nought: The Correspondence of Admiral of the Fleet Lord Fisher of Kilverstone, Vol. I, The Making of an Admiral, 1854–1904*. London: Jonathan Cape, 1952.
Marshall, William. *Memories of Four Fronts*. London: Ernest Benn, Ltd., 1929.
Maurice, F. Ed. *Sir Frederick Maurice: A Record of His Work and Opinions*. London: Edward Arnold, 1913.
May, Edward S. *Principles and Problems of Imperial Defence*. London: Swan Sonnenshein & Co. Limited, 1903.
Melville, C. H. *Life of General the Right Hon. Sir Redvers Buller V.C., G.C.B., G.C.M.G. Vol. 1*. London: Edward Arnold & Co., 1923.
Milner, Alfred. *England in Egypt*. London: Edward Arnold, 1902.
Morley, John. *Life of William Ewart Gladstone, In Three Volumes—Vol. III (1880–1898)*. London: Macmillan and Co., Limited, 1903.
Morton-Jack, George. *The Indian Army on the Western Front: India's Expeditionary Force to France and Belgium in the First World War*. New York: Cambridge University Press, 2014.
_____. *The Indian Empire at War: From Jihad to Victory, The Untold Story of the Indian Army in First World War*. London: Little, Brown, 2018.
Nicolson, Harold. *Sir Arthur Nicolson, First Lord Carnock: A Study in Old Diplomacy*. London: Constable & Co. 1937.

Nisbet, John. *Burma Under British Rule—And Before, Vol. I.* Westminster: Archibald Constable & Co., Ltd., 1902.
Pownall, Helen. ed. *At Home and on the Battlefield: Letters from the Crimea, China and Egypt, 1854–1888 by Sir Frederick Charles Arthur Stephenson, G.C.B.* London: John Murray, 1915.
Pradhan, S. D. *Indian Army in East Africa.* New Delhi: National Book Organisation, 1991.
Preston, Adrian. ed. *In Relief of Gordon: Lord Wolseley's Campaign Journal of The Khartoum Relief Expedition 1884–1885.* Rutherford: Farleigh Dickinson University Press, 1967.
Preston, Adrian and Dennis, Peter. eds. *Swords and Covenants: Essays in Honour of the Royal Military College of Canada 1876–1976.* London: Croom Helm Ltd., 1976.
Repington, Charles à Court. *Vestigia: Reminiscences of Peace and War.* Boston: Houghton Mifflin Company, 1919.
Riddell, George. *Lord Riddell's War Diary 1914–1918.* London: Ivor Nicholson and Watson, 1933.
Roberts, Andrew. *Salisbury: Victorian Titan.* London: Weidenfeld & Nicolson, 1999.
Robertson, William, *From Private to Field-Marshal.* London: Constable and Company Ltd., 1921.
Roch, Walter. *Mr. Lloyd George and the War.* London: Chatto & Windus, 1920.
Royle, Charles. *The Egyptian Campaigns, 1882 to 1885.* London: Hurst and Blackett, Limited, 1900.
Savage Landor, A. Henry. *China and the Allies, Vol. I.* New York: Charles Scribner's Sons, 1901.
_____. *China and the Allies, Vol. II.* New York: Charles Scribner's Sons, 1901.
Scott, Percy. *Fifty Years in the Royal Navy.* New York: George H. Doran Company, 1919.
Seymour, Edward H. *My Naval Career and Travels.* New York: E. P. Dutton & Company, 1911.
Smith, G. Barnett. *General Gordon: The Christian Soldier and Hero.* London: S. W. Partridge & Co. Ltd., 1900.
Smith-Dorrien, Horace. *Memories of Forty-Eight Years' Service.* New York: E. P. Dutton and Company, 1925.
Stewart, A.T.Q. *The Pagoda War: Lord Dufferin and the Fall of the Kingdom of Ava, 1885–6.* Bangkok: White Lotus Press, 2003.
Steyn, Richard. *Milner: Last of the Empire-Builders.* Johannesburg: Jonathan Ball Publishers, 2022.
Symons, Julian. *England's Pride: The Story of the Gordon Relief Expedition.* London: Hamish Hamilton, 1965.
Thornton, James Howard. *Memoirs of Seven Campaigns.* Westminster: Archibald Constable and Co., 1895.
Townshend, Charles V. F. *My Campaign in Mesopotamia.* London: Thornton Butterworth Limited, 1920.
Trevelyan, George Macaulay. *The Life of John Bright.* London: Constable and Company, 1913.

Tulloch, Alexander Bruce. *Recollections of Forty Years' Service.* Edinburgh: William Blackwood and Sons, 1903.
_____. *A Soldier's Sailoring.* London: Jarrold & Sons, 1912.
Turner, Alfred E. *Sixty Years of a Soldier's Life.* London: Methuen & Co. Ltd., 1912.
Vaughan, H. B. *St. George and the Chinese Dragon: An Account of the Relief of the Pekin Legation by an Officer of the British Contingent.* London: C. Arthur Pearson, Ltd., 1902.
Verner, Willoughby. *The Military Life of H.R.H. George, Duke of Cambridge, Vol. II, 1871–1904.* London: John Murray, 1905.
Vetch, R. H., Ed. *Life, Letters, and Diaries of Lieut.-General Sir Gerald Graham V.C., G.C.B., R.E.* Edinburgh: William Blackwood and Sons, 1901.
Vibart, Henry M. *The Life of General Sir Harry N. D. Prendergast R.E., V.C., G.C.B. (The Happy Warrior).* London: Eveleigh Nash, 1914.
Villiers, Frederic. *Peaceful Personalities and Warriors Bold.* London: Harper & Brothers, 1907.
Vogt, Hermann. *The Egyptian War of 1882.* London: Kegan Paul, Trench & Co. 1883.
Waters, H.-H. *"Secret and Confidential": The Experiences of a Military Attaché.* New York: Frederick A. Stokes Company, 1926.
Watson, Charles M. *The Life of Major-General Sir Charles Wilson.* London: John Murray, 1909.
Weaver, J.R.H. ed. *Dictionary of National Biography 1922–1930.* London: Oxford University Press, 1937.
Wessels, André, ed. *Lord Roberts and the War in South Africa, 1899–1902, Army Record Society, Vol. 17.* Stroud: Sutton Publish Limited, 2000.
Whittall, W. *With Botha and Smuts in Africa.* London: Cassell and Company, Ltd., 1917.
Wilkinson, Spenser. *Britain at Bay.* New York: G. P. Putnam's Sons, 1909.
Willcocks, James. *From Kabul to Kumassi: Twenty-Four Years of Soldiering and Sport.* London: John Murray, 1904.
_____. *With the Indians in France.* London: Constable and Company Ltd., 1920.
Williams, E. T. and Palmer, Helen M. eds. *Dictionary of National Biography 1951–1960.* Oxford: Oxford University Press, 1971.
Williams, Rhodri. *Defending the Empire: The Conservative Party and British Defence Policy 1899–1915.* New Haven: Yale University Press, 1991.
Wilson, Charles W. *From Korti to Khartum: A Journal of the Desert March from Korti to Gubat, and of the Ascent on the Nile in General Gordon's Steamers.* Edinburgh: William Blackwood and Sons, 1886.
Wilson, James Harrison. *China: Travels and Investigation in the "Middle Kingdom"—A Study of Its Civilization and Possibilities Together with an Account of the Boxer War.* New York: D. Appleton and Company, 1901.
Wolseley, Viscount. *The Story of a Soldier's Life, Vol. I.* New York: Charles Scribner's Sons, 1903.
Wood, Elliott. *Life and Adventure in Peace and War.* London: Edward Arnold & Co., 1924.

Wood, Evelyn. *From Midshipman to Field Marshal*. London: Methuen & Co., 1907.
Woodyatt, Nigel. *Under Ten Viceroys: The Reminiscences of a Gurkha*. London: Herbert Jenkins Limited, 1922.
Wright, Thomas. *The Life of Colonel Fred Burnaby*. London: Everett & Co. 1908.
Wright, William. *A Tidy Little War: The British Invasion of Egypt 1882*. Stroud: Spellmount, 2009.
Wylde, A. B. *'83 to '87 in the Soudan, Vol. II*. London: Remington & Co., 1888.
_____. *Modern Abyssinia*. London: Methuen and Co., 1901.
Younghusband, George. *Forty Years a Soldier*. London: Herbert Jenkins Limited, 1923.

Articles

Anderson, Ross. "The Battle of Tanga, 2–5 November 1914." *War in History*, v. 8, no. 3 (2001): 294–322.
Anon. "Some Notes on the Early Days of the Royal Naval War College." *Naval Review*, v. 19, no. 2 (1931): 237–47.
_____. "The Staff." *Army Quarterly*, v. 1, no. 1, (1920): 25–35.
Arnold-Forster, H. O. "National Defence." *United Service Magazine*, v. 37, no. 954 (1908): 138–59.
Aston, G. G. "Combined Strategy for Fleets and Armies; Or 'Amphibious Strategy.'" *Journal of the Royal United Services Institution*. v. 51, no. 354 (1907): 984–1004.
[B]. "Army Service Corps," *United Service Magazine*, v. 35, no. 946 (1907): 673.
Baylen, J.O. "Politics and the 'New Journalism': Lord Esher's Use of the 'Pall Mall Gazette.'" *Victorian Periodicals Review*, v. 20, no. 4 (1987): 126–41.
Beach, Jim. "The British Army, the Royal Navy, and the 'big work' of Sir George Aston, 1904–1914," *Journal of Strategic Studies*, v. 29, no. 1 (2006): 145–68.
Beaver, II, William C. "Intelligence Division Library, 1854–1902." *Journal of Library History (1974–1987)*, v. 11, no. 3 (1976): 206–17.
Beckett, Ian F. W. "The Third Anglo-Burmese War and the Pacification of Burma, 1885–1895." In *Queen Victoria's Wars: British Military Campaigns, 1857–1902*, edited by Stephen M. Miller, 220–39, Cambridge: Cambridge University Press, 2021.
Behrman, Cynthia F. "The After-life of General Gordon." *Albion: A Quarterly Journal with British Studies*, v. 3, no. 2 (1971): 47–61.
Bloss, J. F. E. "The Story of Suakin (Concluded)." *Sudan Notes and Records*, v. 20, no. 2 (1937): 247–80.
Bowen, John Eliot. "The Conflict of East and West in Egypt." Part II. *Political Science Quarterly*, v. 1, no. 3 (1886): 449–90.
Brown, G. Thompson. "Through Fire and Sword: Presbyterians and the Boxer Year in North China." *Journal of Presbyterian History*, v. 78, no. 3 (2000): 193–206.
Bury, J.P.T. "Gambetta and Overseas Problems." *English Historical Review*, v. 82, no. 323 (1967): 277–95.
Carland, John M. "Enterprise and Empire: Officials, Entrepreneurs, and the Search for Petroleum in Southern Nigeria, 1906–1914." *International History Review*, v. 4, no. 2 (1982): 191–206.

Ch' ên, Jerome. "The Nature and Characteristics of the Boxer Movement—A Morphological Study." *Bulletin of the School of Oriental and African Studies, University of London*, v. 23, no. 2 (1960): 287–308.

Chamberlain, M. E. "The Alexandria Massacre of 11 June 1882 and the British Occupation of Egypt." *Middle Eastern Studies*, v. 13, no. 1 (1977): 14–39.

_____. "Sir Charles Dilke and the British Intervention in Egypt, 1882: Decision Making in a Nineteenth Century Cabinet." *British Journal of International Studies*, v. 2, no. 3 (1976): 231–45.

Christian, John L. "Anglo-French Rivalry in Southeast Asia: Its Historical and Geography and Diplomatic Climate." *Geographical Review*, v. 31, no 2 (1941): 272–82.

Colston, R. E. "The British Campaign in the Soudan for the Rescue of Gordon." *Journal of the American Geographical Society of New York*, v. 17 (1885): 125–265.

Crammond, Edgar. "The Cost of War," *Journal of the Royal Statistical Society*, v. 78, no. 3 (1915): 361–99.

Daly, W. M. "Omdurman and Fashoda 1898: Edited and Annotated Letters of F. R. Wingate." *Bulletin (British Society for Middle Eastern Studies)*, v. 10, no. 1 (1983): 21–37.

Dawson, R. MacGregor. "The Cabinet and Administration: The British War Office, 1903–16." *Canadian Journal of Economics and Political Science*, v. 5, no. 4 (1939): 451–78.

Deringil, Selim. "The Ottoman Response to the Egyptian Crisis, 1881–82." *Middle Eastern Studies*, v. 24, no. 1 (January 1988): 3–24.

Dockrill, M. L. "Lloyd George and Foreign Policy Before 1914." In *Lloyd George: Twelve Essays* edited by A.J.P. Taylor, 3–31, London: Hamish Hamilton, 1971.

Elango, Lovett. "The Anglo-French 'Condominium' in Cameroon, 1914–1916: The Myth and the Reality." *International Journal of African Historical Studies*, v. 18, no. 4 (1985): 656–73.

Elmslie, Frederick. "Lessons to be Derived from the Operations of Landing an Expeditionary Force on An Enemy's Coast in Past Wars, with Special Reference to Similar Operations on the Part of Our Army in the Future." *Journal of the Royal United Services Institution*, v. 37, no. 207 (1895): 437–82.

Eubank, Keith. "The Fashoda Crisis Re-examined." *Historian*, v. 22, no. 2 (1960): 145–62.

Ferguson, Duncan Stuart. "'Splendid allies' or 'No more deadly enemies in the world?'" General Sir Ian Hamilton, the British Military and Japan, 1902–1914." *Journal of the Royal Asiatic Society*, Third Series, v. 20, no. 4 (2010): 523–36.

Gooch, John. "Sir George Clarke's Career at the Committee of Imperial Defence, 1904–1907." *Historical Journal*, v. 18, no. 3 (1975): 555–69.

Hardy, H. C. "Taming the River Nile." *Scientific American*, v. 123, no. 21 (1920): 524 and 535–36.

Harrison, Simon J. "Skulls and Scientific Collecting in the Victorian Military: Keeping the Enemy Dead in British Frontier Warfare." *Comparative Studies in Society and History*, v. 50, no. 1 (2008): 285–303.

Helmreich, Jonathan E. "The End of Congo Neutrality." *Historian*, v. 28, no. 4 (1966): 610–24.

Henderson, W. O. "War Economy of German East Africa, 1914–1917." *Economic History Review*, v. 13, no. 1/2 (1943): 104–10.

Hess, Robert L. "The 'Mad Mullah' and Northern Somalia." *Journal of African History*, v. 5, no. 3 (1964), 415–33.

Hobbs, P.E.F. "The Best Organisation for the Land Transport of the British Army, having Regard Both to Home Defence and Over-Sea Expeditions," *Journal of the Royal United Services Institution*, v. 47, no. 304 (1903): 628–54.

Holt, P. M. "The Sudanese Mahdia and the outside World: 1881–9." *Bulletin of the School of Oriental and African Studies, University of London*, v. 21, no. 1/3 (1958): 276–90.

Hornik, M. P. "The Mission of Sir Henry Drummond-Wolff to Constantinople, 1885–1887." *English Historical Review*, v. 55, no. 220 (1940): 598–623.

Howard, Michael. "Men Against Fire: Expectations of War in 1914." *International Security*, v. 9, no. 1 (1984): 41–57.

Hunt, Michael H. "The Forgotten Occupation: Peking, 1900–1901." *Pacific Historical Review*, v. 48, no. 4 (1979): 501–29.

Hunter, F. Robert. "Tourism and Empire: The Thomas Cook & Son Enterprise on the Nile, 1868–1914." *Middle Eastern Studies*, v. 40, no. 5 (2004): 28–54.

Jeffrey, Keith. "An English Barrack in the Oriental Seas? India in the Aftermath of the First World War." *Modern Asian Studies*, v. 15, no. 3 (1981): 369–86.

[King-Hall, W.S.R.] "Notes on a Naval Battalion," *Naval Review*, v. 9, no. 3 (1921): 395–410.

Lambert, Nicholas. "British Naval Policy, 1913–1914: Financial Limitation and Strategic Revolution." *Journal of Modern History*, v. 67, no. 3 (1995): 595–626.

MacKintosh, John P. "Role of the Committee of Imperial Defence before 1914." *English Historical Review*, v. 77, no. 304 (1962): 490-5-3.

MacMunn, G. F. "'The Best Method for Carrying Out the Conjoint Practice of the Navy and the Army in Embarkation and Disembarkation for War, Illustrated by the experience of the Past.'" *Journal of the Royal United Services Institution*, v. 49, no. 327 (1905): 495–523.

Madsen, Chris. "Rear Admiral Henry John May and the Royal Navy War Course 1900–1904." *Northern Mariner*, v. 31, no. 3 (2022): 285–312.

Maude, F. N. "Report of the Royal Commission on the War in South Africa." *United Service Magazine*, v. 28, no. 899 (1903): 26–31.

MelIwraith, Malcolm. "The Egyptian Government and the Caisse de la Dette." *Journal of the Society of Comparative Legislation*, v. 1 (1896–1897): 386–422.

Montagu-Stuart-Wortley, E. J. "My Reminiscences of Egypt and the Sudan (from 1882 to 1889)." *Sudan Notes and Records*, v. 34, no. 1 (1953): 17–46.

Moore, Keith. "The Royal Society's War Committee on Engineering 1914–19." *Notes and Records of the Royal Society of London*, v. 62, no. 3 (2008): 315–9.

Murad, Hasan Qasim. "British Involvement in the Sudan." *Pakistan Horizon*, v. 31, no. 4 (1978): 60–81.

Offer, Avner. "The Working Classes, British Naval Plans and the Coming of the Great War." *Past and Present*, no. 107 (1985): 204–26.

Peers, Douglas M. "The Indian Rebellion, 1857–1858." In *Queen Victoria's Wars: British Military Campaigns, 1857–1902*, edited by Stephen M. Miller, 8–39, Cambridge: Cambridge University Press, 2021.

Plunkett, Reginald. "The Staff College." *Naval Review*. v. 3, no. 1 (1915): 84–103.

Pollock, A. W. A. "Naval War Staff." *United Service Magazine*, v. 44, no. 999 (1912): 481–4.

Quinault, Roland. "John Bright and Joseph Chamberlain." *Historical Journal*, v. 28, no. 3 (1985): 623–46.

Redway, G. W. "Staff College Papers, August, 1908." *United Service Magazine*, v. 38, no. 960 (1908): 179–83.

Rose, John M. "Lessons to Be Derived from the Operations of Landing an Expeditionary Force on an Enemy Coast in Past Wars, with Special References to Similar Operations on the Part of Our Army in the Future." *Journal of the Royal United Services Institution*, v. 39, no. 209 (1895): 671–720.

Spiers, Edward M. "Haldane's Reform of the Regular Army: Scope for Revision." *British Journal of International Studies*, v. 6, no. 1 (1980): 69–81.

Sydenham of Combe. "Sea Heresies." *Naval Review*, v. 19, no. 2 (1931): 222–36.

Telfer-Smollett, C.E.D. "The Best Method for Carrying Out the Conjoint Practice of the Navy and Army in Embarkation and Disembarkation for War, Illustrated By the Experience of the Past," *Royal United Service Institution Journal*, v. 49, no. 326 (1905): 357–96.

Towle, Philip. "Russo-Japanese War and the Defence of India," *Military Affairs*, v. 44, no. 3 (1980): 111–7.

Ukpabi, S. C. "The Origins of the West African Frontier Force." *Journal of the Historical Society of Nigeria*, v. 3, no. 3 (1966): 485–501.

Usill, Harley V. "Britain's Achievement in the Sudan." *World Affairs*, v. 110, no. 4 (1947): 290–2.

van de Ven, Hans. "Robert Hart and Gustav Detring during the Boxer Rebellion." *Modern Asian Studies*, v. 40, no. 3 (2006): 631–62.

Vincent, B. "Artillery in the Manchurian Campaign." *Royal United Services Institution Journal*, v. 52, no. 359 (1908): 28–52.

Walford, N. L. "The Effects of the Bombardment of the Forts of Alexandria, July 11th, 1882." *Journal of the Royal United Services Institution*, v. 27, no. 119 (1883): 145–205.

Wilson, H. H. "Staff Tours," *Journal of the Royal United Services Institution*, v. 52, no. 363 (1908): 661–79.

Wilson, K. M. "The British Cabinet's Decision for War, 2 August 1914." *British Journal of International Studies*, v. 1, no. 2 (1975): 148–59.

Internet Resources

Grey, Jeffrey. "White, Sir Cyril Brudenell (1876–1940)." *Australian Dictionary of Biography* via: http://adb.anu.edu.au/biography/white-sir-cyril-brudenell-1032 - Accessed 26 July 2023.

Leonhard, Robert. "The China Relief Expedition: Joint Coalition Warfare in China Summer 1900." Johns Hopkins University, Applied Physics Laboratory via: The China Relief Expedition Joint Coalition Warfare in China Summer 1900 - DocsLib – Accessed 10 March 2024.

Treaty of Portsmouth via https://mjp.univ-perp.fr/traites/1905portsmouth.html - Accessed 25 January 2023.

Winkler, Jonathan Reed. "Silencing the Enemy: Cable-cutting in the Spanish-American War," *War on the Rocks*. https://warontherocks.com/2015/11/silencing-the-enemy-cable-cutting-in-the-spanish-american-war/ - Accessed 16 March 2023.

Endnotes

Introduction

1. Adrian Preston, "Introduction," in Adrian Preston and Peter Dennis, eds., *Swords and Covenants: Essays in Honour of the Royal Military College of Canada 1876–1976* (London: Croom Helm Ltd., 1976), 12.
2. Sean McMeekin, *The Berlin-Baghdad Express: The Ottoman Empire and Germany's Bid for World Power 1898–1918* (London: Penguin Books, 2011), 35.
3. I. S. Bloch, *Is War Now Possible? Being an Abridgement of the War of the Future in Its Technical, Economic and Political Relations* (Aldershot: Gregg Revivals, 1991), lxx.
4. Ian F. W. Beckett, *The Victorians at War* (London: Hambledon and London, 2003), 4.

Chapter 1

1. Hartington cited in Bernard Holland, *The Life of Spencer Compton, Eighth Duke of Devonshire, Vol. II* (London: Longmans, Green and Co., 1911), 3.
2. Having only a single frigate, the Egyptian Navy proved a negligible factor.
3. The National Archives, Kew, Richmond, Surrey, hereafter, TNA, CAB 38/18, CID minutes, 26 May 1911.
4. Charles Royle, *The Egyptian Campaigns, 1882 to 1885* (London: Hurst and Blackett, Limited, 1900), 169.
5. Edward Hertslet and Edward Cecil Hertslet, eds., *British and Foreign State Papers, 1881–1882* (London: William Ridgway, 1889), 1139.
6. *Ibid*, 1149-59 and J.P.T. Bury, "Gambetta and Overseas Problems," *English Historical Review*, v. 82, no. 323 (1967): 292.
7. Edward Malet, *Egypt, 1789–1883*, edited by Lord Sanderson (London: John Murray, 1909), 208–10.
8. Afterwards, the Duke of Devonshire.
9. In May 1899, Brett assumed the style of Viscount Esher.
10. Earl Cromer, *Modern Egypt, Vol. I* (New York: Macmillan, 1916), 228-30 and Malet, *Egypt*, 225–6.
11. "Parliament Out of Session," *Times*, 6 February 1882, 11 and Selim Deringil, "The Ottoman Response to the Egyptian Crisis, 1881–82," *Middle Eastern Studies*, v. 24, no. 1 (1988): 7.
12. Richard Harrison, *Recollections of a Life in the British Army During the Latter Half of the 19th Century* (London: Smith, Elder, & Co., 1908), 251–3.

13. Viscount Esher Papers, Churchill Archives Centre, Cambridge, hereafter, CAC, ESHR/2/6, "Journal, 1881–1884," 36–9.
14. Alexander Bruce Tulloch, *Recollections of Forty Years' Service* (Edinburgh: William Blackwood and Sons, 1903), 244–58 and Alexander Bruce Tulloch, *A Soldier's Sailoring* (London: Jarrold & Sons, 1912), 200–01.
15. TNA ADM 116/45, E. Palmer to W. Hewett letter, 1 August 1882. More generally, see Saul Kelly, *Captain Gill's Walking Stick: The True Story of the Sinai Murders* (London: I. B. Tauris, 2019).
16. "England, France and Egypt," *Times*, 19 May 1882, 5.
17. Hermann Vogt, *The Egyptian War of 1882* (London: Kegan Paul, Trench & Co. 1883), 99 and "Crisis in Egypt," *Times*, 18 May 1882, 5.
18. *Hansard*, House of Commons debate, 15 May 1882, v. 269, cc669–70 and Royle, *Egyptian Campaigns*, 38.
19. Cromer, *Modern Egypt, I*, 270–1.
20. Royle, *Egyptian Campaigns*, 39–40 and 58–61.
21. Malet, Egypt, 395.
22. Bernard Holland, *Life of Spencer Compton Eighth Duke of Devonshire, Vol. I* (London: Longmans, Green and Co., 1911), 363.
23. Malet, *Egypt*, 416 and "Latest Intelligence," *Times*, 4 July 1882, 5.
24. "Death of Lord Granville," *Times*, 1 April 1891, 8; "Egyptian Crisis," *Times*, 25 July 1882, 6 and Malet, *Egypt*, 409.
25. Roland Quinault, "John Bright and Joseph Chamberlain," *Historical Journal*, v. 28, no. 3, (1985): 637 and Edmond Fitzmaurice, *Life of Granville George Leveson Gower, Second Earl Granville, K.G., 1815–1891, Vol. II*. (London: Longmans, Green, and Co., 1905), 266.
26. Spencer Childers, *The Life and Correspondence of the Right Hon, Hugh C. E. Childers 1827–1896, Vol. II* (London: John Murray, 1901), 88–90.
27. Caspar F. Goodrich, *Report of the British Naval and Military Operations in Egypt, 1882* (Washington, D.C.: Government Printing Office, 1883), 13–25 and James Grant, *Cassell's History of the War in the Soudan, Vol. I* (London: Cassell & Company, Limited, no date, but *ca*. 1887), 26.
28. Tulloch, *Recollections*, 260–1.
29. John Eliot Bowen, "The Conflict of East and West in Egypt," Part II, *Political Science Quarterly*, v. 1, no. 3 (1886): 457–67 and Vogt, *Egyptian War*, 19 and 44.
30. "The Crisis in Egypt," *Times*, 5 July 1882, 7 and Alfred Milner, *England in Egypt* (London: Edward Arnold, 1902), 14.
31. Goodrich, *Naval and Military Operations*, 10–12 and Vogt, *Egyptian War*, 17.
32. The attacking ships of the outer squadron were the *Alexandra, Sultan, Superb* and *Temeraire*. Their initial focus was on the batteries covering the northern face of Ras el Tin. The inner squadron, consisting of the *Invincible, Monarch* and *Penelope* attacked the guns known as the Mex Lines. The *Inflexible* split its fire between the two objectives.
33. *London Gazette*, 29 July 1882, no. 25133, 3567 and Grant, *War in the Soudan, I*, 31–2.

34. TNA ADM 116/208, Commander-in-Chief Mediterranean to Admiralty letter, 10 August 1882; Goodrich, *Naval and Military Operations*, 40–41 and Dudley de Chair, *The Sea is Strong* (London: George G. Harrap & Co. Ltd., 1961), 35. Beyond the *Alexandra*, those damaged were the *Condor*, *Sultan*, *Superb*, *Penelope*, *Invincible* and *Inflexible*.
35. Percy Scott, *Fifty Years in the Royal Navy* (New York: George H. Doran Company, 1919), 62.
36. "The Accidents of the Alexandra's Guns," *Times*, 24 July 1882, 8 and Vogt, *Egyptian War*, 38.
37. TNA ADM 1/6640, H. Childers to G. Wolseley signal of 28 September 1882; Goodrich, *Naval and Military Operations*, 37; Tulloch, *Soldier's Sailoring*, 238–45 and Vogt, *Egyptian War*, 157. Captain Neville Walford, RA, assisted by Captain George Clarke, RE, and Commander Henry May prepared a corresponding British report. See TNA WO 33/40, "Report on the Defences of Alexandria, and the Results of the Action of 11th July 1882" and N. L. Walford, "The Effects of the Bombardment of the Forts of Alexandria, July 11th, 1882," *Journal of the Royal United Services Institution*, v. 27, no. 119 (1883): 145–205.
38. TNA ADM 116/34, "List of Killed and Wounded in Engagement with Batteries and Forts of Alexandria on the 11th July, 1882."
39. Royle, *Egyptian Campaigns*, 69–73, 80 and 103 and Grant, *War in the Soudan*, I, 36.
40. Bowen, "Conflict of East and West in Egypt," II, 472–3 and Grant, *War in the Soudan*, I, 38.
41. Goodrich, *Naval and Military Operations*, 80.
42. Bright cited in George Macaulay Trevelyan, *Life of John Bright* (London: Constable and Company, 1913), 433.
43. J. F. Maurice, *Military History of the Campaign of 1882 in Egypt* (London: J. B. Hayward & Son, 1887), 6–7.
44. TNA ADM 196/36 (H. Andoe); Royle, *Egyptian Campaign*, 89 and 100–07 and Edward H. Seymour, *My Naval Career and Travels* (New York: E. P. Dutton & Company, 1911), 221–39 and J. Fisher to K. Fisher letter, 20 July 1882, Admiral of the Fleet Baron Fisher of Kilverstone Papers, Churchill Archives Centre, Churchill College, Cambridge, CAC/FISR/15/3/2/2.
45. Alison had been ordered to Cyprus in early July in anticipation of a move on Ismailia to protect the Sweetwater Canal; see TNA WO 33/40, G. Wolseley to A. Alison memorandum, 6 July 1882. Upon Malet's return, Seymour no longer exercised the role of a joint Commander-in-Chief. Thus, Wolseley and Seymour were required to cooperate in the subsequent operations in a manner absent during the initial intervention; see WO 33/40, H. Childers to G. Wolseley letter, 4 August 1882.
46. Childers, *Childers*, II, 92–3.
47. *Hansard*, House of Commons debate, 1 August 1881, v. 264, cc447–8. The Army (Annual) Act, 1884 attempted to clarify matters, though problems of dual control persisted owing to the separate administrative chain of command enjoyed by the Royal Marines; see TNA ADM 1/6795.

48. Wolseley cited in Childers, *Childers, II*, 115–16. During this period the Admiralty maintained two distinct corps: the Royal Marine Light Infantry and the Royal Marine Artillery.
49. *London Gazette*, 8 September 1882, no., 25145, 4164–72.
50. TNA WO 33/40, R. Thompson (War Office) to J. Pauncefote (Foreign Office) letter, 6 July 1882.
51. Cromer, *Modern Egypt, I*, 583.
52. Childers, *Childers, II*, 94–7 and Deringil, "Ottoman Response to the Egyptian Crisis," 16–7.
53. Halik Kochanski, *Sir Garnet Wolseley: Victorian Hero* (London: Hambledon Press, 1999), 136.
54. It was intended for French forces to hold Kantara and Port Said thereby "protecting the canal between Ismailia and Port Said." Absent, this became the primary task of the Indian contingent, see TNA WO 33/40, G. Tryon to R. Thompson letter, 25 July 1882 and G. Tryon to B. Seymour letter, 4 August 1882.
55. John Adye, *Recollections of a Military Life* (London: Smith, Elder & Co., 1895), 330–1; W. F. Butler, *Sir William Butler: An Autobiography* (London: Constable and Company Ltd., 1911), 220–1; "The Army Reserve and Militia," *Times*, 26 July 1882, 12; "Military Preparations," *Times*, 27 July 1882, 6 and "Ministerial Crisis in France," *Times*, 31 July 1882, 6.
56. Adye, *Recollections of a Military Life*, 333. Some of the animals were purchased in Syria by Lieutenant Colonel Lord William Seymour who then found himself appointed to the staff of Admiral Seymour, his cousin. Having begun his career as a naval cadet and seeing action in the Baltic during the Russian War, Seymour subsequently transferred to the Coldstream Guards. Thus, the appointment possessed a logic beyond mere nepotism. See "Death of Lord William Seymour," *Times*, 10 February 1915, 11.
57. William Wright, *A Tidy Little War: The British Invasion of Egypt 1882* (Stroud: Spellmount, 2009), 145.
58. Harrison, *Recollections*, 258.
59. TNA ADM 196/86 (E. Rolfe).
60. Neville Lyttelton, *Eighty Years: Soldiering, Politics, Games* (London: Hodder and Stoughton, 1927), 130–1.
61. TNA ADM 1/6641, "Journal of Operations," 2 and C. E. Callwell, ed., *The Memoirs of Major-General Sir Hugh McCalmont K.C.B., C.V.O.* (London: Hutchinson & Co., 1924), 209.
62. TNA ADM 1/6640, G. Wolseley to H. Childers signal No. 21 of 31 August 1882.
63. R. H. Vetch, *Life, Letters, and Diaries of Lieut.-General Sir Gerald Graham V.C., G.C.B. R.E.* (Edinburgh: William Blackwood and Sons, 1901), 233; George Arthur, ed., *The Letters of Lord and Lady Wolseley 1870–1911* (London: William Heinemann, 1922), 71–3 and Frederick Elmslie, "Lessons to be Derived from the Operations of Landing an Expeditionary Force on An Enemy's Coast in Past Wars, with Special Reference to Similar Operations on the Part of Our Army in the Future," *Journal of the Royal United Services Institution*, v. 37, no. 207 (1895): 465.

64. Goodrich, *Naval and Military Operations*, 107.
65. *London Gazette*, 8 September 1882, no. 25145, 4165–6.
66. *Ibid*, 4166–7.
67. Maurice, *Campaign of 1882*, 36–7.
68. Royle, *Egyptian Campaign*, 151.
69. "The Capture of Chalouf," *Times*, 1 September 1882, 6.
70. *London Gazette*, 6 October 1882, no. 25154, 4555; Milner, *England in Egypt*, 17; C. H. Melville, *Life of General the Right Hon. Sir Redvers Buller V.C., G.C.B., G.C.M.G. Vol. 1* (London: Edward Arnold & Co., 1923), 164 and Earl Cromer, *Modern Egypt, Vol. II* (New York: Macmillan, 1908), 466.
71. "Admiral Sir Arthur Moore," *Times*, 10 April 1934,' 9; Royle, *Egyptian Campaigns*, 159–64 and Arthur, *Wolseley*, 77.
72. "Sir Herbert Macpherson," *Times*, 21 October 1886, 7.
73. James Howard Thornton, *Memoirs of Seven Campaigns* (Westminster: Archibald Constable and Co., 1895), 204–08; Willoughby Verner, *The Military Life of H.R.H. George, Duke of Cambridge, Vol. II, 1871–1904* (London: John Murray, 1905), 251; Vogt, *Egyptian War*, 159 and 166 and *Times*, 17 July 1882, 6.
74. John M. Rose, "Lessons to Be Derived from the Operations of Landing an Expeditionary Force on an Enemy Coast in Past Wars, with Special References to Similar Operations on the Part of Our Army in the Future," *Journal of the Royal United Services Institution*, v. 39, no. 209 (1895): 715.
75. Vetch, *Graham*, 248 and TNA ADM 196/59 (H. Tuson).
76. "Sir Charles Holled-Smith," *Times*, 21 March 1925, 16.
77. Charles M. Watson, *The Life of Major-General Sir Charles Wilson* (London: John Murray, 1909), 234–5 and John Morley, *The Life of William Ewart Gladstone, In Three Volumes—Vol. III (1880–1898)* (London: Macmillan and Co., Limited, 1903), 145.
78. Thomas Wright, *The Life of Colonel Fred Burnaby* (London: Everett & Co. 1908), 215; Frederic Villiers, *Peaceful Personalities and Warriors Bold* (London: Harper & Brothers, 1907), 186–7 and *Correspondence Respecting Reorganization in Egypt, Egypt No. 2* (London: Harrison and Sons, 1883), 3.
79. "The Soudan," *Times*, 26 November 1883, 5.
80. TNA CAB 37/12/12, Northbrook minute, 8 February 1884 and Count Gleichen, ed., *Anglo-Egyptian Sudan: A Compendium Prepared by the Officers of the Sudan Government, Vol. I* (London: His Majesty's Stationery Office, 1905), 94.
81. "Latest Intelligence," *Times*, 10 November 1882, 3; "The Suakin-Berber Railway," *Times*, 19 February 1885, 12; *Further Correspondence Respecting the Affairs of Egypt, Egypt No. 22* (London: Harrison and Sons, 1883), 4–11 and *London Gazette*, 2 November 1882, no. 25162, 4880. From Aden, Major Archibald Hunter landed to perform similar work.
82. Frederick Hamilton-Temple-Blackwood.
83. *Hansard*, House of Commons debate, 9 November 1882, v. 274, cc1119–21.
84. *Reorganization in Egypt, No. 2*, 16–7.
85. *Ibid*, 15–6,
86. "Sir Evelyn Wood," *Times*, 3 December 1919, 18 and Evelyn Wood, *From Midshipman to Field Marshal* (London: Methuen & Co., 1907), 484.

87. Milner, *England in Egypt*, 140; "Railroad from Suakin to Berber," *Times*, 11 October 1884, 7 and Watson, *Charles Wilson*, 242.
88. By August 1883, the occupation had been reduced to roughly 7,000 troops with each soldier costing the Khedive £4 per month. See TNA CAB 37/12/6, H. Childers minute, 24 January 1884.
89. Milner, *England in Egypt*, 66–70.

Chapter 2

1. Buller cited in "General John Sterling," *Times*, 8 December 1926, 21.
2. "The Cholera," *Times*, 31 July 1883, 5.
3. On the epidemic and the British response see *Further Correspondence Respecting the Cholera Epidemic in Egypt: 1883* (London: Harrison and Sons, 1883); Helen Pownall, ed., *At Home and on the Battlefield: Letters from the Crimea, China and Egypt, 1854–1888 by Sir Frederick Charles Arthur Stephenson, G.C.B.* (London: John Murray, 1915), 281 and Milner, *Egypt in England*, 67. The number dying from cholera is unknown but probably greater than the official count of 58,369. See Auckland Colvin, *The Making of Modern Egypt* (London: Seeley & Co. Limited, 1906), 41.
4. Morley, *Gladstone, III*, 144.
5. R. E. Colston, "British Campaign in the Soudan for the Rescue of Gordon," *Journal of the American Geographical Society of New York*, v. 17 (1885): 150.
6. A. B. Wylde, *'83 to '87 in the Soudan, Vol. II* (London: Remington & Co., 1888), 226–7.
7. E. J. Montagu-Stuart-Wortley, "My Reminiscences of Egypt and the Sudan (from 1882 to 1889)," *Sudan Notes and Records*, v. 34, no. 1 (1953): 18 and *Reorganization in Egypt, No. 2*, 3. Dufferin reported to Granville in February 1883 that Hicks had been engaged by the Egyptian government without reference to himself or Malet. That, however, disguised the efforts of Montagu-Stuart-Wortley, Baker, and probably Wood.
8. J, Colborne, *With Hicks Pasha in the Soudan* (London: Smith, Elder, & Co., 1885), 1–9.
9. Royle, *Egyptian Campaigns*, 236–44; Fitzmaurice, *Granville, II*, 319; Butler, *Autobiography*, 266 and Milner, *England in Egypt*, 70–1.
10. *Further Correspondence Respecting the Affairs of Egypt, No. 1* (London: Harrison and Sons, 1883), 90–1.
11. Untitled leader, *Times*, 23 November 1883, 9.
12. *Correspondence Respecting the Affairs of Egypt, No. 1*, 125–30.
13. Holland, *Spencer Compton, I*, 411–2.
14. Bernard Mallett, *Thomas George, Earl of Northbrook, G.C.S.I.: A Memoir* (London: Longmans, Green and Co., 1908), 174–6 and Fitzmaurice, *Granville, II*, 320.
15. Cromer, *Modern Egypt, I*, 379–87.
16. *Correspondence Respecting the Affairs of Egypt, No. 1*, 95.
17. TNA FO 1/30, T. Speedy memorandum, 21 December 1883 and Admiralty to Hewett signal of 4 January 1883 (*sic*).

18. Walter Severn, "Abyssinia and the Soudan," *Times*, 30 November 1883, 7.
19. A subsequent letter from Gordon noted the intention of King John to advance against the Mahdi. Gordon though in extremis, advised the British not to make a treaty with the king as "he is an arrant humbug." See TNA WO 32/6113, Gordon letter, 4 November 1884.
20. *Hansard*, House of Lords debate, 5 February 1884, v. 284, cc3–7 and "General Gordon and the War Office," *Times*, 9 February 1884, 10.
21. Cynthia F. Behrman, "After-life of General Gordon," *Albion: A Quarterly Journal with British Studies*, v. 3, no. 2 (1971): 47.
22. At the fore of this campaign was W.T. Stead, editor of the *Pall Mall Gazette*. See Lord Elton, *General Gordon* (London: Collins, 1954), 326–7.
23. TNA CAB 37/12/16, Granville to E. Baring draft despatch, no date, but March 1884; CAB 37/14/11, E.[dward] W.[alter] Hamilton, "General Gordon's Mission in the Soudan," 21 February 1885 and Julian Symons, *England's Pride: The Story of the Gordon Relief Expedition* (London: Hamish Hamilton, 1965), 16–23.
24. With parliament in recess, most had dispersed. Those attending were thus those readily available. Not attending however was Lord Derby, the secretary of state for the colonies, who had remained in London. That the omission was deliberate must be reckoned a strong possibility. Meanwhile, Dilke though outside the cabinet played an outsized role in influencing Britain's policy towards Egypt in 1882. See M. E. Chamberlain, "Sir Charles Dilke and the British Intervention in Egypt, 1882: Decision Making in a Nineteenth Century Cabinet," *British Journal of International Studies*, v. 2, no. 3 (1976): 231–45.
25. Thomas Archer, *The War in Egypt and the Soudan: An Episode in the History of the British Empire, Vol. III* (London: Blackie & Son, ca. 1886), 53–4.
26. Morley, *Gladstone, III*, 177; Mallett, *Northbrook*, 176–7 and A. G. Gardiner, *The Life of Sir William Harcourt* (London: Constable & Company Ltd., 1923), 512.
27. "Egypt and the Soudan," *Times*, 28 December 1883, 3.
28. The gendarmerie having responsibility for policing the rural areas of Egypt was akin to a border patrol.
29. M. E. Chamberlain, "The Alexandria Massacre of 11 June 1882 and the British Occupation of Egypt," *Middle Eastern Studies*, v. 13, no. 1 (1977): 23 and *Reorganization in Egypt, No. 2*, 4.
30. "Sultan Murad and Sultan Abdul Hamid," *Times*, 6 September 1876, 3; Montagu-Stuart-Wortley, "Reminiscences of Egypt and the Sudan," 18 and *Hansard*, House of Lords debate, 26 October 1882, v. 274, c154.
31. Villiers, *Peaceful Personalities*, 12 and Cromer, *Modern Egypt, I*, 399–404.
32. TNA CAB 37/12/8, Hewett to Admiralty signal 0055 of 6 February 1884.
33. Royle, *Egyptian Campaigns*, 265; Melville, *Buller, I*, 172–3; "The Egyptian Crisis," *Times*, 7 February 1884, 10; "The Egyptian Crisis," *Times*, 9 February 1884, 10 and TNA ADM 196/36 (W. Hewett).
34. "The Egyptian Crisis," Times, 15 February 1884, 5; TNA ADM 196/61 (T. Bridge) and Wright, *Burnaby*, 221.
35. *Hansard*, House of Commons debate, 17 March 1884, v. 286, cc41–5.

36. *Ibid*, House of Lords debate, 5 February 1884, v. 284, cc18–29.
37. Also rendered as Osman Digma.
38. "News of the Week," *Spectator*, 22 March 1884, 1 and Grant, *War in the Soudan*, *I*, 46.
39. On Hewett's attitude, see Viscount Wolseley, *The Story of a Soldier's Life, Vol. I* (New York: Charles Scribner's Sons, 1903), 6–47.
40. Holland, *Spencer Compton*, *I*, 425–7.
41. *Ibid*, 429.
42. TNA CAB 37/12/5, A. Cooper-Key to Northbrook memorandum, 19 January 1884; "The Egyptian Crisis," *Times*, 7 February 1884, 10 and "Affairs at Suakin," *Times*, 19 February 1884, 10.
43. Wood, *Midshipman to Field Marshal*, 483 and Cromer, *Modern Egypt*, *I*, 440–1.
44. Cromer, *Modern Egypt*, *I*, 452.
45. TNA CAB 37/14/11, Hamilton, "General Gordon's Mission in the Soudan," 21 February 1885.
46. P. M. Holt, "The Sudanese Mahdia and the outside World: 1881–9," *Bulletin of the School of Oriental and African Studies, University of London*, v. 21, no. 1/3, (1958): 279; G. Barnett Smith, *General Gordon: The Christian Soldier and Hero* (London: S. W. Partridge & Co. Ltd., 1900), 110–4 and Seton Churchill, *General Gordon: A Christian Hero* (London: James Nisbet & Co., Limited, *ca*. 1900), 215–7.
47. Archer, *Egypt and the Soudan*, *III*, 57.
48. *Further Correspondence Respecting the Affairs of Egypt, No. 1*, 137.
49. "News of the Week," *Spectator*, 5 April 1884, 1 and TNA CAB 37/14/11, Hamilton, "General Gordon's Mission in the Soudan," 21 February 1885.
50. Cromer, *Modern Egypt*, I, 457n and Colvin, *Making of Modern Egypt*, 67–9.
51. "General John Sterling," *Times*, 8 December 1926, 21.
52. *London Gazette*, 27 March 1884, no. 25332, 1459 and Lady Ardagh, *Life of Major-General Sir John Ardagh* (London: John Murray, 1909), 173.
53. Royle, *Egyptian Campaigns*, 272–5 and *London Gazette*, 27 March 1884, no. 25332, 1456.
54. Where estimating opposing numbers remained more conjecture than concrete, Buller gave the enemy as numbering 9,000 while Lieutenant Colonel John Ardagh, Graham's director of intelligence, held the total to be less than 6,000.
55. *London Gazette*, 27 March 184, no. 25332, 1456.
56. Vetch, *Graham*, 268–72 and *London Gazette*, 2 May 1884, no. 25349, 1979.
57. Vetch, *Graham*, 381–2.
58. *London Gazette*, 27 March 1884, no. 25332, 1455.
59. Melville, *Buller*, *I*,187–8; Watson, *Charles Wilson*, 262 and William Galloway, *The Battle of Tofrek* (London: W. H. Allen & Co., 1887), 75.
60. TNA CAB 37/12/18, Granville to Baring signal of 25 March 1884; Cromer, *Modern Egypt*, *I*, 542 and Vetch, *Graham*, 275.
61. Cromer, *Modern Egypt*, *I*, 466.
62. Holland, *Spencer Compton*, *I*, 422 and 446 and Fitzmaurice, *Granville*, *II*, 397.
63. *Times*, 24 April 1884, 9.

64. TNA CAB 37/12/22, Wolseley to Hartington memorandum, 8 April 1884.
65. Holland, *Spencer Compton*, I, 450–1.
66. Pownall, ed., *At Home and on the Battlefield*, 283, Cromer, *Modern Egypt*, II, 53, Watson, *Charles Wilson*, 268 and J. F. E. Bloss, "The Story of Suakin (Concluded)," *Sudan Notes and Records*, v. 20, no. 2 (1937): 256.
67. TNA ADM 196/86 (W. Graham).
68. Untitled leader, *Times*, 2 May 1884, 9.
69. "Obituary – Lord Esher," *Times*, 23 January 1930, 17 and Esher Papers, CAC/ESHR/2/6, Brett to Wolseley letter, 14 November 1884.
70. Mike Snook, "Wolseley, Wilson and the Failure of the Khartoum Campaign: An Exercise in Scapegoating and Abrogation of Command Responsibility?" (PhD diss., Cranfield University, 2014), 17.
71. Colborne, *With Hicks Pasha*, 64–5.
72. Snook, "Wolseley, Wilson and the Failure of the Khartoum Campaign," PhD diss., 134.
73. "Routes for an Army from Cairo to Khartoum," *Times*, 15 May 1884, 3–4 and Morley, *Gladstone*, III, 164–5.
74. Royle, *Egyptian Campaigns*, 313 and Childers, *Childers*, II, 183–5.
75. *Correspondence Respecting the Affairs of Egypt, No. 1*, 99.
76. TNA CAB 37/12/25, Wolseley to Hartington memorandum, 14 April 1884.
77. Pownall, ed., *At Home and on the Battlefield*, 320.
78. TNA CAB 37/12/27, Lord John Hay notes, no date, but *ca*. May 1884; Esher Papers, CAC/ESHR/2/7, Brett to Hartington letter, 6 January 1885 and Samuel White Baker, "The Nile Expedition," *Times*, 23 August 1884, 8.
79. TNA ADM 196/38 (T. Hammill) and ADM 196/61 (R. Marriott).
80. "Death of Sir Charles Wilson," *Times*, 27 October 1905, 12 and Cromer, *Modern Egypt*, I, 537.
81. In the event, the depth of the Nile proved even less than anticipated. See Adrian Preston, ed., *In Relief of Gordon: Lord Wolseley's Campaign Journal of The Khartoum Relief Expedition 1884–1885* (Rutherford: Farleigh Dickinson University Press, 1967), 81 and Verner, *Cambridge*, II, 275.
82. "General Sir. F. C. A. Stephenson," *Times*, 11 March 1911, 11.
83. E. J. Montagu-Stuart-Wortley, "My Reminiscences of Egypt and the Sudan (from 1882 to 1899) (Continued)," *Sudan Notes and Records*, v. 34, no. 2 (1953): 173 and Holland, *Spencer Compton*, I, 439 and "Death of Sir Andrew Clarke." *Times*, 1 April 1902, 8.
84. Holland, *Spencer Compton*, I, 459–60 and Gleichen, ed. *Anglo-Egyptian Sudan*, I, 248.
85. TNA CAB 37/13/37, R. Molyneux to Admiralty signal of 20 July 1884; Holland, *Spencer Compton*, I, 473; Vetch, *Graham*, 275; Watson, *Charles Wilson*, 272 and Royle, *Egyptian Campaigns*, 314–5.
86. TNA ADM 1/6723, W. Hall, "Sir Samuel Baker's Suggested Relief of Berber and Khartoum from Cairo by the Nile Route," 7 May 1884 and Baker, "Nile Expedition," *Times*, 23 August 1884, 8.

87. Cromer, *Modern Egypt, II*, 366–71 and "Death of Lord Northbrook," *Times*, 16 November 1904, 6.
88. TNA CAB 37/13/40, Northbrook to Gordon letter, 8 October 1884; Childers, *Childers, II*, 185–6 and Verner, *Cambridge, II*, 265–77.
89. See especially Elliott Wood, *Life and Adventure in Peace and War* (London: Edward Arnold & Co., 1924), 153.
90. TNA WO 32/6109, Wolseley to Hartington letter, 11 September 1884 and Hartington to Wolseley letter, 17 September 1884.
91. Count Gleichen, *With the Camel Corps Up the Nile* (London: Chapman & Hall, Limited, 1888), 2–30 and Gleichen, ed. *Anglo-Egyptian Sudan, I*, 248.
92. Pownall, ed., *At Home and on the Battlefield*, 328.
93. W. F. Butler, *The Campaign of the Cataracts* (London: Sampson Low, Marston, Searle, & Rivington, 1887), 20 and 372–4.
94. TNA ADM 196/38 (J Baker). Baker's second name was Alleyne. Though no connection has been traced to Colonel Alleyne, the possibility must be afforded.
95. Melville, *Buller, I*, 195–206; Royle, *Egyptian Campaigns*, 315; TNA ADM 196/36 (F. Boardman); "Sir William Butler," *Times*, 8 June 1910, 9; Butler, *Autobiography*, 277–87 and Butler, *Campaign of the Cataracts*, 215 and 231.
96. TNA WO 32/6108, Wolseley to Hartington signal No. 78 of 22 November 1884 and *London Gazette*, 28 April 1885, no. 25465, 1913.
97. TNA WO 32/6106, "Report of Proceedings of Naval Brigade from 26 November last to 8 March 1885".
98. Verner, *Cambridge, II*, 288.
99. Preston, ed., *Relief of Gordon*, 67 and 93; Holland, *Spencer Compton, II*, 6 and Arthur. ed., *Wolseley*, 128.
100. Melville, *Buller, I*, 199–200.
101. TNA CAB 37/14/11, Hamilton, "General Gordon's Mission in the Soudan," 21 February 1885.
102. TNA WO 32/6112, Wolseley to Gordon letter, 7 November 1884; WO 32/6113, Gordon to [Kitchener] letter, 4 November 1884 and Gleichen, *With the Camel Corps*, 69.
103. Melville, *Buller, I*, 208–9; Preston, ed., *Relief of Gordon*, 67 and Charles W. Wilson, *From Korti to Khartum: A Journal of the Desert March from Korti to Gubat, and of the Ascent on the Nile in General Gordon's Steamers* (Edinburgh: William Blackwood and Sons, 1886), xvii–xxii.
104. Montagu-Stuart-Wortley, "My Reminiscences of Egypt and the Sudan (from 1882 to 1889)," *Sudan Notes and Records*, 39; Wilson, *Korti to Khartum*, 113 and 301 and Alfred E. Turner, *Sixty Years of a Soldiers Life* (London: Methuen & Co. Ltd., 1912), 99.
105. Wilson, *Korti to Khartum*, xxii–xxiii.
106. *Ibid*, 9–11.
107. Symons, *England's Pride*, 230.
108. *London Gazette*, 20 February 1885, no. 25444, 755 and Wright, *Burnaby*, 81, 135, and 218.

109. Wilson, *Korti to Khartum*, 32.
110. *London Gazette*, 20 February 1885, no. 25444, 755.
111. *Ibid*, 24 February 1885, no. 25446, 855.
112. *Ibid*, 853.
113. Deemed brilliant on the strength of his qualifying examinations, Wilson commissioned directly into the Royal Engineers without matriculating at Woolwich first. Specialising in topography, his duties soon took him into the realm of intelligence. Arriving in Alexandria in 1882, he expected to serve as Wolseley's liaison to the Ottoman Army being readied in Turkey. When Constantinople ultimately demurred sending a force, Wilson found himself appointed as an observer to Urabi's court-martial to ensure fair play ensued. Subsequently, Wilson served as the director of military education. See Watson, *Charles Wilson*, 203–34.
114. Verner, *Cambridge, II*, 286.
115. "British Victory Near Metammeh," *Times*, 29 January 1885, 5, Adye, *Soldiers & Others I Have Known*, 125 and Melville, *Buller, I*, 213–8.
116. Stewart received a special promotion to major general before succumbing on 16 February 1885.
117. *London Gazette*, 10 April 1885, no. 25460, 1667-8; Wilson, *Korti to Khartum*, 92-117 and Butler, *Autobiography*, 297.
118. Wilson, *Korti to Khartum*, 128–9.
119. *Ibid*, 287.
120. *Ibid*, 174–5.
121. *Ibid*, 263 and *London Gazette*, 10 March 1885, no. 25450, 1027–8. Wilson's period of field command ended soon enough, becoming instead director of military intelligence to Wolseley for the balance of the campaign.
122. Royle, *Egyptian Campaigns*, 394.
123. *London Gazette*, 10 April 1885, no. 25460, 1663–6; Esher Papers, CAC/ESHR/2/7, Brett to Hartington letters, 5 and 6 February 1885 and Royle, *Egyptian Campaign*, 400.
124. *Ibid*, 388; *London Gazette*, 25 August 1885, no. 25505, 4039 and "Sir Reginald Talbot," *Times*, 16 January 1929, 17.
125. Arthur, ed., *Wolseley*, 155.

Chapter 3

1. TNA CAB 37/44/27, Cromer to Salisbury letter, 5 June 1897.
2. *Hansard*, House of Commons debate, 19 February 1885, v. 294, cc873–9.
3. "War in the Soudan," *Times*, 12 February 1885, 3 and Preston, ed., *Relief of Gordon*, 133.
4. "Major-General D. A. Scott," *Times*, 6 February 1924, 13.
5. *London Gazette*, 20 February 1885, no. 25444, 753–64 and 25 August 1885, no. 25505, 4040–4; Vetch, *Graham*, 286–8; Thornton, *Memoirs of Seven Campaigns*, 237 and Thomas Archer, *The War in Egypt and the Soudan: An Episode in the History of the British Empire, Vol. IV* (London: Blackie & Son, *ca.* 1886), 233.

6. *Hansard*, House of Commons debate, 19 February 1885, v. 294, cc873–9 and Galloway, *Battle of Tofrek*, 311.
7. *Hansard*, House of Commons debate, 19 February 1885, v. 294, cc873–9.
8. *Ibid*, 11 August 1884, v. 292, cc483–4 and Holland, *Spencer Compton, I*, 478.
9. *Hansard*, House of Lords debate, 19 February 1885, v. 294, cc849–57.
10. *Ibid*.
11. *London Gazette*, 23 June 1885, no. 25483, 2867–68.
12. Thornton, *Seven Campaigns*, 219–21.
13. Wylde, *'83 to '87 in the Soudan, II*, 90 and Galloway, *Battle of Tofrek*, 110.
14. *London Gazette*, 23 June 1885, no. 25483, 2868.
15. E. A. de Cosson, *Days and Nights of Service with Sir Gerald Graham's Field Force at Suakin* (London: John Murray, 1886), 70–7.
16. George Younghusband, *Forty Years a Soldier* (London: Herbert Jenkins Limited, 1923), 41.
17. "Death of Sir John McNeill," *Times*, 27 May 1904, 8 and *London Gazette*, 25 August 1885, no. 25505, 4040–4.
18. On the culpability of others, including General Graham, see Galloway, *Battle of Tofrek*, 31.
19. *Hansard*, House of Commons debate, 9 April 1885, v. 296, cc1158–66.
20. Esher Papers, CAC/ESHR/2/7, R. Brett to Hartington letter, 10 March 1885.
21. R. F. Foster, *Lord Randolph Churchill: A Political Life* (Oxford: Oxford University Press, 2011), 196.
22. "Naval and Military Intelligence," *Times*, 2 June 1885, 6 and Galloway, *Battle of Tofrek*, 320–1.
23. The resignations were quickly withdrawn.
24. Wylde, *'83 to '87 in the Soudan, II*, 70; Melville, *Buller, I*, 250; Thornton, *Seven Campaigns*, 238 and Gardiner, *Harcourt*, 523–4.
25. De Cosson, *Days and Nights of Service*, 290.
26. The Liberals were defeated on an amendment to the Customs and Inland Revenue Bill during its second reading on 8 June with Gladstone resigning four days later.
27. *London Gazette*, 25 August 1885, no. 25505, 4039.
28. *Ibid*; Holland, *Spencer Compton, II*, 43–5 and Turner, *Sixty Years*, 147–8 and 164.
29. Gleichen, ed. *Anglo-Egyptian Sudan, I*, 252 and Ronald M. Lamothe, *Slaves of Fortune: Sudanese Soldiers & the River War 1896–1898* (Woodbridge: James Currey, 2011).

Chapter 4

1. "Burmah," *Times*, 2 November 1885, 5.
2. TNA CAB 37/16/59, Owen Burne, "Note on the relations between the Government of India and Upper Burmah during the present King's Reign," 10 November 1885; John L. Christian, "Anglo-French Rivalry in Southeast Asia: Its Historical and Geography and Diplomatic Climate," *Geographical Review*, v. 31, no 2 (April 1941): 279; Grattan Geary, *Burma After the Conquest. Viewed in Its Political, Social, and Commercial Aspects, from Mandalay* (London: Sampson Low,

Marston, Searle, & Rivington, 1886), 136–53 and *History of the Third Burmese War, 1885–1886–1887, Period I, History of the War Prior to the Annexation of the Country* (Calcutta: Superintendent of Government Printing India, 1887), 2.
3. TNA CAB 37/16/59, Burne, "Note on the relations between the Government of India and Upper Burmah during the present King's Reign," 10 November 1885.
4. *History of the Third Burmese War, I,* Preface, 2 and 19.
5. Mortimer Durand, *The Life of Field-Marshal Sir George White, V.C., Vol. I* (Edinburgh: William Blackwood and Sons, 1915), 308–9.
6. *History of the Third Burmese War, I,* 26–33; Henry M. Vibart, *The Life of General Sir Harry N. D. Prendergast R.E., V.C., G.C.B. (The Happy Warrior)* (London: Eveleigh Nash, 1914), 208–18 and *Frontier and Overseas Expeditions from India, Vol. V, Burma* (Simla: Government Monotype Press, 1907), 140–1.
7. TNA ADM 196/15 (R. Clutterbuck).
8. TNA ADM 196/38 (A. Carpenter).
9. TNA ADM 1/6777, "Report of Proceedings of Burmah Force," 27 November 1885.
10. A.T.Q. Stewart, *The Pagoda War: Lord Dufferin and the Fall of the Kingdom of Ava, 1885–6* (Bangkok: White Lotus Press, 2003), 80.
11. *Third Burmese War, I,* 37–8.
12. *Ibid*; "Burmah," *Times*, 23 October 1885, 5; TNA ADM 196/37 (R. Woodward) and Beatrix Gatacre, *General Gatacre: The Story of the Life and Services of Sir William Forbes Gatacre, K.C.B., D.S.O. 1843–1906* (London: John Murray, 1910), 83.
13. John Nisbet, *Burma Under British Rule—And Before, Vol. I* (Westminster: Archibald Constable & Co., Ltd., 1902), 85–8 and Vibart, *Prendergast*, 244–57.
14. Ian F. W. Beckett, "The Third Anglo-Burmese War and the Pacification of Burma, 1885–1895," in *Queen Victoria's Wars: British Military Campaigns, 1857–1902*, ed., Stephen M. Miller (Cambridge: Cambridge University Press, 2021), 220.
15. Charles Crosthwaite, *The Pacification of Burma* (London: Edward Arnold, 1912), 1–2.
16. "General Sir Harry Prendergast," *Times*, 26 July 1913, 9; Gatacre, *General Gatacre*, 84 and Durand, *Sir George White, I,* 321.
17. *History of the Third Burmese War, I,* 56 and "Burmah," *Times*, 21 January 1886, 5.
18. Durand, *Sir George White, I,* 351–2; Vibart, *Prendergast*, 271–6 and Crosthwaite, *Pacification of Burma*, 18.
19. *London Gazette*, 12 September 1890, no. 26087, 4933–8.
20. *London Gazette*, 22 June 1886, no. 25599, 2974–5.
21. *Ibid*, 2966.
22. Crosthwaite, *Pacification of Burma*, 48–9 and *History of the Third Burmese War, 1890–91, Period VI, The Winter Campaign of 1890–91* (Simla: Central Printing Office, 1893), Appendix II, xi.
23. TNA CAB 37/18/47, Dufferin, note, no date but October 1886.

Chapter 5

1. H. Kitchener dispatch, 30 September 1896, *London Gazette*, 3 November 1896, no. 26791, 6002.
2. *Ibid*, 25 August 1885, no. 25505, 4039.
3. Villiers, *Peaceful Personalities and Warriors Bold*, 192–4 and William C. Beaver, II, "Intelligence Division Library 1854–1902," *Journal of Library History, (1974–1987)*, v. 11, no. 3 (1976): 213.
4. J. W. Robertson, "Sir (Francis) Reginald Wingate," E. T. Williams and Helen M. Palmer, eds., *The Dictionary of National Biography, 1951–1960* (Oxford: Oxford University Press, 1971), 1066 and W.H.-H. Waters, *"Secret and Confidential": The Experiences of a Military Attaché* (New York: Frederick A. Stokes Company, 1926), 52–3.
5. *Reports by Mr. Villiers Stuart, M.P., Respecting Reorganization in Egypt, Egypt No. 7* (London: Harrisons and Sons, 1883) and "Irrigation Works of Egypt," *Times*, 20 November 1884, 3
6. H. C. Hardy, "Taming the River Nile," *Scientific American*, v. 123, no. 21 (1920): 524 and M. P. Hornik, "Mission of Sir Henry Drummond-Wolff to Constantinople, 1885–1887," *English Historical Review*, v. 55, no. 220 (1940): 606.
7. Harley V. Usill, "Britain's Achievement in the Sudan," *World Affairs*, v. 110, no. 4, (1947): 291.
8. Keith Eubank, "The Fashoda Crisis Re-examined," *Historian*, v. 22, no. 2 (1960): 145.
9. Hasan Qasim Murad, "British Involvement in the Sudan," *Pakistan Horizon*, v. 31, no. 4 (1978): 70.
10. Colvin, *Making of Modern Egypt*, 262; "Sir C. Scott-Moncrieff on 'The Nile,'" *Times*, 26 January 1895, 10 and *Hansard*, House of Commons debate, 14 August 1896, v. 44, cc853–87.
11. Field Marshal Sir Henry Hughes Wilson Papers, Imperial War Museum, London, diary entries 3, 4, 11, 12, 16, 17 and 20 March 1896, MISC/80, Reel 1.
12. Cromer, *Modern Egypt, II*, 89 and Gleichen, ed., *Anglo-Egyptian Sudan, I*, 213–4.
13. "The British Forces in Egypt," *Times*, 14 March 1896, 12.
14. *Hansard*, House of Commons debate, 5 February 1897, v. 45, cc1439–521.
15. Malcolm Mellwraith, "The Egyptian Government and the Caisse de la Dette," *Journal of the Society of Comparative Legislation*, v. 1, (1896–7): 387.
16. Darrell Bates, *The Fashoda Incident of 1898: Encounter on the Nile* (Oxford: Oxford University Press, 1984), 81.
17. TNA ADM 196/42 (S. Colville).
18. *London Gazette*, 3 November 1896, no. 26791, 6002–03.
19. Cromer, *Modern Egypt, II*, 88–90 and *Times*, 3 July 1896, 9.
20. A. B. Wylde, *Modern Abyssinia* (London: Methuen, and Co., 1901), 62.
21. John Adye, "The Expedition to Dongola," *Times*, 17 March 1896, 4.
22. Cromer, *Modern Egypt, II*, 94–5.
23. Lyttelton, *I*, 185–6.

24. *Ibid*, 102, Simon J. Harrison, "Skulls and Scientific Collecting in the Victorian Military: Keeping the Enemy Dead in British Frontier Warfare," *Comparative Studies in Society and History*, v. 50, no. 1 (2008): 290; Colvin, *Making of Modern Egypt*, 263 and Gleichen, ed., *Anglo-Egyptian Sudan, I*, 44 and 265.
25. TNA ADM 196/87 (C. Keppel) and *London Gazette*, 28 April 1885, no. 25465, 1916.
26. Montagu-Stuart-Wortley, "My Reminiscences of Egypt and the Sudan," *Sudan Notes and Records*, 178–9 and W. M. Daly, "Omdurman and Fashoda 1898: Edited and Annotated Letters of F. R. Wingate," *Bulletin (British Society for Middle Eastern Studies)*, v. 10, no. 1 (1983): 25.
27. Cromer, *Modern Egypt, II*, 106.
28. *Ibid*, 103–08.
29. G. P. Gooch and Harold Temperley, eds., *British Documents on the Origins of the War 1898–1914 Vol. 1, The End of British Isolation* (London: His Majesty's Stationery Office, 1927), 160.
30. During these events Marchand was promoted from captain.
31. H. W. Jackson, "Fashoda," *Sudan Notes and Records*, v. 3, no. 1 (1920): 1.
32. G. P. Gooch and Harold Temperley, eds., *British Documents on the Origins of the War 1898–1914, Vol. III, The Testing of the Entente 1904–6* (London: His Majesty's Stationery Office, 1928), 378.
33. Gleichen, ed., *Anglo-Egyptian Sudan, I*, 4.

Chapter 6

1. TNA CAB 37/50/63. J. Chamberlain memorandum, 6 September 1899.
2. *London Gazette*, 8 February 1901, no. 27282, 878.
3. *Ibid*, 26 January 1900, no. 27157 497 and 8 February 1901, no. 27282, 829–30 and 918.
4. André Wessels, ed., *Lord Roberts and the War in South Africa, 1899–1902, Army Record Society, Vol. 17* (Stroud: Sutton Publish Limited, 2000), 16–7.
5. TNA CAB 38/4, War Office, "The Strength of the Regular Army and Auxiliary Forces, having regard to Peace and War Requirements," memorandum, 1 May 1904.
6. TNA CAB 38/16, Edgar Crammond, "Paper on the Finance of War," 20 April 1910.
7. Edgar Crammond, "The Cost of War," *Journal of the Royal Statistical Society*, v. 78, no. 3 (1915): 361–2.
8. G. P. Gooch and Harold Temperley, eds., *British Documents on the Origins of the War, Vol. IV, The Anglo-Russian Rapprochement, 1903–1907* (London: His Majesty's Stationery Office, 1929), 513.
9. *Hansard*, House of Lords debate, 30 January 1900, v. 78, cc17–30.
10. Wolseley proposed increasing troop strength paying special care to the supply and medical requirements of a campaign likely to begin in the autumn. See TNA CAB 37/50/38, Wolseley to Lansdowne memorandum, 8 June 1899.
11. "The Aldershot Autumn Field Operations," *Times*, 2 September 1899, 10 and Wood, *From Midshipman to Field Marshal*, 561–2.

Endnotes 237

12. Untitled leader, *Times*, 22 August 1899, 7 and Gooch and Temperley, eds., *Origins of the War, 1*, 85–91.
13. *London Gazette*, 17 January 1902, no. 27398, 366.
14. *Ibid*, 13 October 1899, no. 27126, 6178.
15. Lieutenant General Sir Gerald Francis Ellison Papers, National Army Museum, London, NAM 8704-35-818-35.
16. "Lieut.-General Sir Herbert Miles," *Times*, 21 May 1936, 11 and Brian Bond, *The Victorian Army and Staff College, 1854–1914* (London: Eyre Methuen, 1972), 194.
17. Beckett, *Victorians at War*, 198.
18. TNA CAB 37/50/49, Lansdowne memorandum, 12 August 1899.
19. *London Gazette*, 26 January 1900, 497 and Spencer Jones, *From Boer War to World War: Tactical Reform of the British Army, 1902–1914* (Norman: University of Oklahoma Press, 2012), 19.
20. TNA CAB 37/50/56, Wolseley to Lansdowne memorandum, 24 August 1899 and Lansdowne to Wolseley memorandum, 27 August 1899. Roberts reported that at any given time roughly 3,000 troops were affected by a sexually transmitted disease. See Andrew Roberts, *Salisbury: Victorian Titan* (London: Weidenfeld & Nicolson, 1999), 731.
21. Richard Steyn, *Milner: Last of the Empire-Builders* (Johannesburg: Jonathan Ball Publishers, 2022), 114-5 and "The Military Situation in South Africa," *Times*, 11 September 1899, 6. On 20 October at Talana Hill, General Sir William Penn Symons and much of the Indian contingent came to grief in a costly tactical success.
22. Sam Fay, *The War Office at War* (East Arsdsley: EP Publishing Limited, 1973), 17; Wood, *From Midshipman to Field Marshal*, 559–63; *London Gazette*, 26 January 1900, 498 and 8 February 1901, 913 and C.E.D. Telfer-Smollett, "The Best Method for Carrying Out the Conjoint Practice of the Navy and Army in Embarkation and Disembarkation for War, Illustrated By the Experience of the Past," *Royal United Services Institution Journal*, v. 49, no. 326 (1905): 365.
23. "Admiral Sir R. H. Harris," *Times*, 26 August 1928, 12 and Scott, *Fifty Years in the Navy*, 104–05.
24. *London Gazette*, 8 February 1901, 829.
25. Following an inheritance, Lambton assumed the style Hedworth Meux by Royal license in 1911. See *London Gazette*, 12 September 1911, no. 28530, 6729.
26. "Naval and Military Intelligence," *Times*, 23 August 1899, 9; TNA ADM 196/39 (H. Lambton) Scott, *Fifty Years in the Navy*, 100–01 and "Admiral of the Fleet H. Meux," *Times*, 21 September 1929, 12.
27. TNA ADM 196/88 (L. Halsey) and ADM 196/88 (A. Walker-Heneage-Vivian).
28. *London Gazette*, 8 February 1901, 915.
29. *Ibid*, 921.
30. Scott, *Fifty Years in the Navy*, 103–08.
31. *Ibid*, 110–1.
32. *Ibid*, 134.

33. *London Gazette*, 12 March 1901, no. 27293, 1730–4.
34. Lieutenant [Charles Richard Newdigate] Burne, *With the Naval Brigade in Natal, 1899–1900* (London: Edward Arnold, 1902), 55.
35. *London Gazette*, 12 March 1901, 1755.
36. *Ibid*, 26 January 1900, 505; *London Gazette*, 30 March 1900, no. 27178, 2125 and "Battle of Graspan," *Times*, 30 November 1899, 5.
37. Burne, *With the Naval Brigade*, 112–4.
38. *Ibid*, 125–7 and Jones, *From Boer War to World War*, 122.
39. *Hansard*, House of Commons debate, 21 March 1901, v. 91, cc702–03 and "Latest Intelligence," *Times*, 12 January 1901, 5 and "Wreck of the Sybille," *Times*, 23 January 1901, 13.
40. The *Beagle*, however, landed a detachment at Mossel Bay in October 1901 as a precautionary measure against Boer incursions.
41. *London Gazette*, 11 April 1902, no. 27424, 2414–5 and 17 June 1902, no. 27443, 3970 and TNA ADM 196/61 (A. Paris).
42. TNA ADM 186/61 (F. White).
43. TNA CAB 38/2, translation of "Possibility of Oversea Invasion," *Marine-Rundschau*, June 1902.
44. Fisher Papers, CAC/FISR/3/1/1758, J. Fisher to A. White letter, 8 August 1902.
45. "The Seizure of Foreign Ships," *Times*, 10 January 1900, 5; Gooch and Temperley, eds., *Origins of the War, I*, 243; G. P. Gooch and Harold Temperley, eds., *British Documents on the Origins of the War, 1898–1914, Vol. X, Part II, The Last Years of Peace* (London: His Majesty's Stationery Office, 1938), 426 and 709, and Linda B. Fritzinger, *Diplomat Without Portfolio: Valentine Chirol, His Life and* The Times (London: I. B. Tauris & Co. Ltd., 2006), 81.
46. G.F.R. Henderson, *The Science of War: A Collection of Essays and Lectures, 1991–1903*, ed. Neill Malcolm (London: Longmans, Green, and Co., 1912), 370.
47. Charles Wentworth Dilke and Spenser Wilkinson, *Imperial Defence* (London: Macmillan and Co., 1892), 179.
48. "Lieut.-Colonel G.F.R. Henderson," *Times*, & March 1903, 7.
49. Jay Luvaas, *The Education of an Army: British Military Thought 1815–1940* (Chicago: University of Chicago Press, 1964), 237.
50. Bond, *Victorian Army and the Staff College*, 188.
51. F. N. Maude, "Report of the Royal Commission on the War in South Africa," *United Service Magazine*, v. 28, no. 899 (1903): 26.
52. Lowell J. Satre, "St. John Brodrick and Army Reform, 1901–1903," *Journal of British Studies*, v. 15, no. 2, (1976): 125–6 and James Lees-Milne, *The Enigmatic Edwardian: The Life of Reginald 2nd Viscount Esher* (London: Sidgwick & Jackson, 1986), 125.
53. Serving with Dawkins were Ernest Beckett (Banking), William Mather, M.P. (Engineering), Sir Charles Welby, (Assistant Under Secretary of State for War), Colonel Sir George Clarke (Woolwich Arsenal) and George Gibb (Rail).
54. *Hansard*, House of Commons debate, 4 March 1902, v. 104, cc375–7 and 7 March 1902, v. 104, cc734–831.

55. Wood, *Life and Adventure in Peace and War*, 240–1.
56. "Death of Sir George Farwell," *Times*, 2 October 1915, 2 and [B], "Army Service Corps," *United Service Magazine*, v. 35, no. 946 (1907): 673.
57. *Hansard*, House of Commons debate, 16 May 1901, v. 94, cc281–396.
58. Wessels, ed., *Lord Roberts*, 178, 185 and 237.
59. "Field Force South Africa, List of Officers On, and Attached to, The General Staff," 1 May 1901, Lieutenant General Sir Aylmer Hunter-Weston Papers, National Army Museum, London, 6503-39-8. Hood transferred to the East Kent Regiment in December 1901; see TNA ADM 196/62 (C. Hood).
60. TNA ADM 1/8710/138, Pope-Hennessy, "The Services and a Common Doctrine of War," Senior Officers' War Course, 17 January 1927.

Chapter 7

1. Roberts, *Salisbury*, 42.
2. For services in China, Captains Jellicoe and Warrender were made Commanders of the Bath, while Commanders Beatty, Cradock, and Lieutenant Keyes were meritoriously promoted.
3. On the Boxers and their aims see Jerome Ch'ên, "The Nature and Characteristics of the Boxer Movement—A Morphological Study," *Bulletin of the School of Oriental and African Studies, University of London*, v. 23, no. 2 (1960): 287–308. The name "Boxers" derived from "The Fist of Righteous Harmony" as the society was properly known.
4. A. Henry Savage Landor, *China and the Allies, Vol. I* (New York: Charles Scribner's Sons, 1901), 38.
5. Salisbury to C. MacDonald signal of 11 March 1900 cited in *Correspondence Respecting the Insurrectionary Movement in China* (London: Her Majesty's Stationery Office, 1900), 6.
6. *Ibid*, E. Monson (Paris) to Salisbury signal of 14 March 1900.
7. *Ibid*, Foreign Office to Admiralty letter, 24 March 1900, 11–12 and C. MacDonald to Salisbury signal of 16 April 1900, 23.
8. *Ibid*, C. MacDonald to Salisbury signal of 17 May 1900, 26.
9. *Ibid*, C. MacDonald to Salisbury signal of 21 May 1900 and Salisbury to MacDonald signal of 22 May 1900, 27–8.
10. *Ibid*, C. MacDonald to Salisbury signal of 27 May 1900 and Salisbury to MacDonald signal of 27 May 1900, 29.
11. *London Gazette*, 5 October 1900, no. 27235, 6093.
12. Commander-in-Chief, China to Admiralty signal of 28 May 1900, *Correspondence Respecting the Insurrectionary Movement in China*, 29.
13. *Ibid*, MacDonald to Salisbury signal of 30 May 1900, 30.
14. A. Henry Savage Landor, *China and the Allies, Vol. II* (New York: Charles Scribner's Sons, 1901), 10 and 15.
15. W. Carles to Salisbury signal of 5 June 1900, *Correspondence Respecting the Insurrectionary Movement in China*, 35.

16. *Ibid*, Commander-in-Chief, China to Admiralty signal of 31 May 1900, 31. The ships sent were the battleship *Centurion* (Flag) and the destroyer *Whiting*, joined by the cruiser *Endymion* and the destroyer *Fame*.
17. *Ibid*, Commander-in-Chief, China to Admiralty signal of 4 June 1900, 34.
18. C. MacDonald to Salisbury signal of 4 June 1900, *Correspondence Respecting the Insurrectionary Movement in China*, 34.
19. *Ibid*, C. MacDonald to Salisbury signal of 5 June 1900, 36.
20. *Ibid*, Commander-in-Chief, China to Admiralty signal of 6 June 1900; Admiralty to Commander-in-Chief, China signal of 6 June 1900; Foreign Office to Admiralty letter, 6 June 1900 and Salisbury to C. MacDonald signal of 7 June 1900, 37–9.
21. *Ibid*, Commander-in-Chief, China to Admiralty signal of 7 June 1900, 38.
22. *Ibid*, Commander-in-Chief, China to Admiralty signal of 8 June 1900, 40.
23. *Ibid*, C. MacDonald to Salisbury signals of 8 June 1900, 42–3.
24. *Ibid*, Foreign Office to Admiralty letter, 8 June 1900, 41 and Seymour, *My Naval Career*, 342–3.
25. Foreign Office to War Office letter, 8 June 1900 and Admiralty to Rear Admiral China signal of 15 June 1900, *Correspondence Respecting the Insurrectionary Movement in China*, 41–2 and 56.
26. *Ibid*, St. J. Brodrick to India Office and War Office letter, 15 June 1900, 58.
27. TNA WO 28/302, India Office to Curzon, 18 June 1900.
28. J. Jordan (Peking) to E. Grey letter, 19 December 1911, *Further Correspondence Respecting the Affairs of China: China No. 3 (1912)*, 23; H. B. Vaughan, *St. George and the Chinese Dragon: An Account of the Relief of the Pekin Legation by an Officer of the British Contingent* (London: C. Arthur Pearson, Ltd., 1902), 15–6 and *London Gazette*, 14 May 1901, no. 27313, 3277.
29. TNA WO 28/302, "China Expeditionary Force Order of Battle."
30. "Death of Sir Claude MacDonald," *Times*, 11 September 1915, 5; Lansdowne to C. MacDonald letter, 10 February 1901, *Further Correspondence Respecting Events at Peking: China No. 3* (London: His Majesty's Stationery Office, 1901), 25; Cromer, *Modern Egypt*, *I*, 338 and Savage Landor, *China and the Allies*, *II*, 90.
31. Commander-in-Chief, China to Admiralty signal of 10 June 1900, *Correspondence Respecting the Insurrectionary Movement in China*, 45.
32. Robert Leonhard, "The China Relief Expedition: Joint Coalition Warfare in China Summer 1900," Johns Hopkins University, Applied Physics Laboratory, 11. "The China Relief Expedition Joint Coalition Warfare in China Summer 1900" - DocsLib – accessed 10 March 2024.
33. Seymour, *My Naval Career*, 345 and Savage Landor, *China and the Allies*, *I*, 87.
34. Clive Bigham, *A Year in China, 1899–1900* (London: Macmillan and Co., Limited, 1901), 36.
35. W. Carles to Salisbury signal of 11 June 1900, *Correspondence Respecting the Insurrectionary Movement in China*, 50.
36. "Sir. E. H. Seymour, O.M.," *Times*, 4 March 1929, 11 and Bigham, *Year in China*, 171.
37. *London Gazette*, 5 October 1900, 6095.

Endnotes 241

38. *Ibid.*
39. *Ibid*, 6096 and Seymour, *My Naval Career*, 346–7.
40. *London Gazette*, 5 October 1900, 6097 and 6110.
41. Also rendered as Hildebrand.
42. Rear Admiral China to Admiralty signal of 17 June 1900, *Correspondence Respecting the Insurrectionary Movement in China*, 74.
43. *London Gazette*, 5 October 1900, 6101.
44. *Ibid*, 6112–14.
45. MacDonald to Salisbury signal of 7 August 1900, *Correspondence Respecting the Disturbances in China: China No. 1* (London: His Majesty's Stationery Office, 1901), 62–3.
46. G. Thompson Brown, "Through Fire and Sword: Presbyterians and the Boxer Year in North China," *Journal of Presbyterian History*, v. 78, no. 3 (2000): 197.
47. *Ibid*, J. Bruce to Admiralty signal of 16 June 1900, *Correspondence Respecting the Disturbances in China*, 74.
48. *London Gazette*, 5 October 1900, 6097 and 6110.
49. Leonhard, "China Relief Expedition," 13.
50. TNA ADM 196/86 (E. Seymour).
51. *London Gazette*, 5 October 1900, 6098–6103.
52. Commander-in-Chief, China to Admiralty signal of 3 August 1900, *Correspondence Respecting the Disturbances in China*, 49.
53. *London Gazette*, 5 October 1900, 6106–07.
54. *Ibid*, 6108–09.
55. "Captain James H. T. Burke, R.N.," *Times*, 17 May 1902, 8.
56. Leonhard, "China Relief Expedition," 16.
57. Savage Landor, *China and the Allies*, *I*, 93–94.
58. Rear Admiral China to Admiralty signal of 20 June 1900 and Admiralty to Rear Admiral China signal of 20 June 1900, *Correspondence Respecting the Insurrectionary Movement in China*, 65.
59. Scott, *Fifty Years in the Royal Navy*, 139.
60. "The Fighting at Tien-Tsin," *Times*, 30 August 1900, 6.
61. TNA ADM 196/38 (J. Jellicoe).
62. *London Gazette*, 6 November 1900, no. 27244, 6759–60.
63. Rear Admiral China to Admiralty signal of 21 June 1900, *Correspondence Respecting the Insurrectionary Movement in China*, 67.
64. "Major-General Sir A. R. F. Dorward," *Times*, 26 March 1934, 14.
65. *London Gazette*, 13 July 1900, no. 27210, 4363 and Salisbury to H. Gough (Berlin) signal of 26 June 1900, *Correspondence Respecting the Insurrectionary Movement in China*, 75–6.
66. W. Carles to Salisbury signal, undated, but *ca.* 30 June 1900, *Correspondence Respecting the Insurrectionary Movement in China*, 95.
67. *Ibid*, A. Dorward to Lansdowne signal of 4 July 1900, 98.
68. Savage Landor, *China and the Allies*, *I*, 326.
69. Commander-in-Chief, China to Admiralty signal of 2 July 1900, *Correspondence Respecting the Insurrectionary Movement in China*, 99 and A. S. Daggett, *America*

in the China Relief Expedition (Kansas City: Hudson-Kimberley Publishing Company, 1906), 43.
70. *Correspondence Respecting the Insurrectionary Movement in China*, Salisbury to J. Whitehead (Tokyo) signal of 6 July 1900, 102.
71. *London Gazette*, 6 November 1900, 6762–3.
72. Leonhard, "China Relief Expedition," 29–31.
73. *London Gazette*, 14 May 1901, 3278 and "Death of Sir Alfred Gaselee," *Times*, 1 April 1918, 7.
74. *Correspondence Respecting the Disturbances in China*, Lansdowne to General Office Commanding Hong Kong signal of 18, July 1900, 19 and Hong Kong and Shanghai Bank to Foreign Office letter, 29 July 1900, 39–40.
75. "Report of Events in Peking from June 20th to 14th August, 1900," *Further Correspondence Respecting Events at Peking*, 25.
76. *Correspondence Respecting the Disturbances in China*, E. Seymour to Admiralty letter, 8 August 1900, 176–7.
77. *Ibid*.
78. *London Gazette*, 14 May 1901, 3277.
79. Leonhard, "China Relief Expedition," 38.
80. Vaughan, *St. George and the Chinese Dragon*, 23.
81. *London Gazette*, 6 November 1900, 6763–4 and 14 May 1900, 3277.
82. James Harrison Wilson, *China: Travels and Investigation in the "Middle Kingdom"—A Study of Its Civilization and Possibilities Together with an Account of the Boxer War* (New York: D. Appleton and Company, 1901). 377–9.
83. *London Gazette*, 6 November 1900, 6763–4 and Leonhard, "China Relief Expedition," 48.
84. "Report of Events in Peking from June 20th to 14th August, 1900," *Further Correspondence Respecting Events at Peking*, 31 and Savage Landor, *China and the Allies, II*, 187.
85. C. MacDonald to Salisbury signal of 24 August 1900, *Correspondence Respecting the Disturbances in China*, 105.
86. Hans van de Ven, "Robert Hart and Gustav Detring during the Boxer Rebellion," *Modern Asian Studies*, v. 40, no. 3 (2006): 632.
87. Michael H. Hunt, "The Forgotten Occupation: Peking, 1900–1901," *Pacific Historical Review*, v. 48, no. 4 (1979): 506.
88. Wilson, *China*, 388–90.
89. E, Seymour to Admiralty signal of 13 June 1900, *Correspondence Respecting the Insurrectionary Movement in China*, 53.
90. Admiralty to E. Seymour signal of 8 August 1900, *Correspondence Respecting the Disturbances in China*, 63.
91. *Ibid*, Foreign Office to Admiralty letter, 28 July 1900 and Admiralty to Foreign Office letter, 3 August 1900, 34 and 46.
92. *Ibid*, J. Bruce to Admiral signal of 24 June 1900 and Admiralty to J. Bruce signal of 28 June 1900, 74 and 81.
93. *London Gazette*, 5 October 1900, 6102–13.

Endnotes 243

94. Salisbury to E. Monson (Paris) letter, 7 August 1900, *Correspondence Respecting the Disturbances in China*, 61.
95. *Ibid*, Salisbury to F. Lascelles (Berlin) signal of 9 August 1900, 66.
96. Georg Lynch, *The War of the Civilisations being a Record of a "Foreign Devil's" Experiences with the Allies in China* (London: Longmans, Green, and Co., 1901), 31.
97. *London Gazette*, 5 October 1900, 6108.
98. Leonhard, "China Relief Expedition," 5.
99. Wilson, *China*, xi.
100. Brown, "Through Fire and Sword," *Journal of Presbyterian History*, 198.
101. Bigham, *Year in China*, 166–89.
102. G. P. Gooch and Harold Temperley, eds., *British Documents on the Origins of the War 1898–1914, Vol. III, The Testing of the Entente 1904–6* (London: His Majesty's Stationery Office, 1928), 378–9.
103. *London Gazette*, 14 May 1901, 3277–80; "Admiral G. H. Borrett," *Times*, 11 June 1952, 8 and "Indian Medical Service," *British Medical Journal*, v. 2, no. 2062, July 7 (1900): 68.
104. Savage Landor, *China and the Allies, I,* 374.
105. Lynch, *War of the Civilisations*, 240–4.

Chapter 8

1. *Hansard*, House of Commons debate, 25 February 1904, v. 130, c. 1501.
2. Robert L. Hess, "The 'Mad Mullah' and Northern Somalia," *Journal of African History*, v. 5, no. 3 (1964): 419–20.
3. Douglas Jardine, *The Mad Mullah of Somaliland* (London: Herbert Jenkins Limited, 1923), vii and 15.
4. *Official History of the Operations in Somaliland, Vol. II* (London: Harrison and Sons, 1907), 436 and TNA CAB 37/69/43, J. Grierson, "The Military Situation in Somaliland," 9 March 1904.
5. TNA ADM 116/931, "Journal of the Principal Events connected with Somaliland from 10th to 31st December 1902."
6. *Official History of the Operations in Somaliland, 1901–04, Vol. I* (London: Harrison and Sons, 1907), 81 and 266; *Operations in Somaliland, II*, 417; TNA CAB 37/63/146, Foreign Office memorandum, 24 October 1902; Angus Hamilton, *Somaliland* (London: Hutchinson and Co., 1911), 220 and "Abyssinian Expedition Against the Mad Mullah," *Times*, 19 October 1901, 12.
7. Cobbold assumed the style Cobbold-Sawle by royal warrant in 1932 following the death of his father-in-law, Rear Admiral Sir Charles Graves-Sawle.
8. Hamilton, *Somaliland*, 72 and *London Gazette*, 18 April 1902, no. 27426, 2587–8.
9. TNA CAB 37/63/149, Cranbourne memorandum, 2 November 1902.
10. "Major A. H. C. Hanbury Tracy," *Times*, 5 December 1915, 6 and *Operations in Somaliland, I*, Prefatory Note, 42–60 and 96.
11. TNA ADM 116/931, "Journal of Principal Events connected with Somaliland from 10th to 31st December 1902."

12. *Operations in Somaliland, II*, 335; "Somaliland Expedition," *Times*, 8 November 1902, 7 and Lord Hardinge, *My Indian Years 1910–1916* (London: John Murray, 1948), 101.
13. The presence of a Boer force soon after the termination of hostilities in South Africa speaks to a degree of underappreciated political management.
14. "Somaliland Expedition," *Times*, 4 November 1902, 3.
15. TNA CAB 37/63/165, Lansdowne to R. Rodd signal of 6 December 1902.
16. *Operations in Somaliland, I*, 116–21, 201 and 270.
17. W, C. Coombes and J. B. Wilkie, *The Commission of H.M.S. Naiad 1901 – 1904: Cape, East Indies and Mediterranean Stations* (London: Westminster Press, 1904), 25 and 35 *Operations in Somaliland, II*, 336.
18. *Operations in Somaliland, I*, 149n and 200 and *Operations in Somaliland, II*, 531.
19. *London Gazette*, 2 September 1904, no. 27710, 5638.
20. HMSs *Perseus*, *Naiad*, and *Pomone*.
21. ADM 116/931, "Journal of the Principal Events connected with Somaliland from 1st to 31st January 1903," 13.
22. *Ibid*, 12; TNA ADM 196/42 (E. Pears); ADM 196/137 (G. Bevan); *Operations in Somaliland, I*, 126–32 and 148n; *Operations in Somaliland, II*, 531; Admiral Sir Alexander Bethell Papers, Liddell Hart for Military Archives, King's College, London, 1/3/1–7, General Officer Commanding Somaliland Field Force to Senior Naval Officer Obbia letter, 18 February 1903 and Coombes and Wilkie, *Naiad*, 38–9.
23. Bethell Papers, LHCMA, 1/3/1–7, GOC Somaliland Field Force to Senior Naval Officer letter, 18 February 1903.
24. TNA ADM 196/38 (A. Bethell).
25. TNA ADM 196/141 (A. Silvertop); *Operations in Somaliland, I*, 138 and 147; *Operations in Somaliland, II*, 484 and "Naval and Military Intelligence," *Times*, 25 October 1902, 12.
26. *Operations in Somaliland, I*, 140–6.
27. "Latest Intelligence," *Times*, 24 April 1903, 5 and Hamilton, *Somaliland*, 266–9. Though a reserve battalion, the defense offered by 2/KAR was held most creditable. Plunkett, however, had disobeyed orders in a battle where over 2,000 of the enemy were estimated to have died.
28. Manning remained in theater and assumed command of the First Brigade.
29. C. T. Atkinson, *The Royal Hampshire Regiment, Volume One, To 1914* (Glasgow: Robert Maclehose & Company Limited, 1950), 412.
30. *Operations in Somaliland, I*, 190–5 and 202.
31. TNA ADM 116/931, "Journal of the Principal Events connected with Somaliland from 1st to 30th November 1903," 17.
32. *Operations in Somaliland, I*, 207.
33. *Operations in Somaliland, II*, 338 and 367 and TNA ADM 196/43 (E. Carey).
34. Other sources render the fatality as Stanton.
35. Jardine, *Mad Mullah of Somaliland*, 131–4.
36. TNA ADM 116/930, G. Atkinson-Willes letter to Admiralty, 18 January 1904 and ADM 196/88 (E. Gaunt).

Endnotes 245

37. *Operations in Somaliland, I,* 229–31, 270–5 and 320; *Operations in Somaliland, II,* 378–9 and "Somaliland," *Times,* 9 December 1903, 5.
38. *Operations in Somaliland, I,* 241–2.
39. *Ibid,* 254.
40. *Ibid,* 264–5 and 319. The approval was received on 7 April 1904.
41. TNA ADM 116/930, G. Atkinson-Willes to Admiralty letter, 23 April 1904.
42. *Operations in Somaliland, I,* 281–97.
43. *Ibid;* TNA ADM 196/87 (F. Pekham) and Atkinson, *Royal Hampshire Regiment, I,* 418n.
44. TNA CAB 37/70/62, Lansdowne, "Future Administration of Somaliland," 28 April 1904; ADM 116/930, G. Atkinson-Willes to Admiralty letter, 1 May 1904 and ADM 116/931, "Journal of the Principal Events connected with Somaliland from 1st to 29th February 1904," 23.
45. TNA CAB 37/89/84, W. Churchill, "A Minute on the Somaliland Protectorate," 28 October 1907.
46. *Operations in Somaliland, II,* 370.
47. *Operations in Somaliland, I,* 305.
48. *Ibid,* 308 and *Operations in Somaliland, II,* 583.
49. "Intelligence Duties in Savage Warfare as Exemplified by the Somaliland Campaign," *Report on the Eastern Command Intelligence and Reconnaissance Course, April 1908,* War Office, General Staff, 18 February 1909, Hunter-Weston Papers, NAM 6503-39-16.
50. TNA CAB 37/89/84, W. Churchill, "A Minute on the Somaliland Protectorate," 28 October 1907.
51. TNA CAB 37/119/47, "Proposed Aircraft Expedition to Somaliland," March 1914 and "Flying Officers in Somaliland," *Times,* 13 June 1914, 8.

Chapter 9

1. *Hansard,* House of Commons debate, 3 July 1902, v. 110, cc734–5.
2. See especially C. E. Callwell, *Military Operations and Maritime Preponderance; Their Relations and Interdependence* (Edinburgh: William Blackwood and Sons, 1905).
3. TNA CAB 38/4, CID minutes, 4 January 1904.
4. *Ibid.*
5. *Ibid,* CID minutes, 27 January 1904 and *Official History (Naval and Military) of the Russo-Japanese War, Vol. III* (London: His Majesty's Stationery Office, 1920), 23.
6. B. Vincent, "Artillery in the Manchurian Campaign," *Journal of the Royal United Services Institution,* v. 52, no. 359 (1908): 28.
7. *Russo-Japanese War. Reports from British Officers Attached to the Japanese and Russian Forces in the Field, Vol. I* (London: His Majesty's Stationery Office, 1908), 276.
8. Ardagh, *Sir John Ardagh,* 399n.
9. TNA WO 106/39, M. Gerard to Secretary Army Council letter, 30 March 1905 and "British Naval Attaché in Manchuria," *Times,* 17 March 1905, 3.

10. "General Sir Montagu Gerard," *Times*, 28 July 1905, 6; "Naval and Military Intelligence," *Times*, 4 January 1905, 8 and "Lieut.-Gen. Sir H. C. Holman," *Times*, 28 July 1949, 7.
11. "Admiral Sir William Pakenham," *Times*, 31 July 1933, 7 and TNA ADM 196/88 (W. Pakenham).
12. G. H. Gunns, *Log of H.M.S. "Sutlej," Pacific and China Stations. 1904–1906.* (London: Westminster Press, 1906), 95–8.
13. *Hansard*, House of Lords debate, 8 July 1904, v. 137, c. 1071–9; TNA ADM 196/20 (C. Eyres) and ADM 196/88 (C. Eyres) and *Navy List for July 1904*, 432–3.
14. Duncan Stuart Ferguson, "'Splendid allies' or 'No more deadly enemies in the world?' General Sir Ian Hamilton, the British Military and Japan, 1902–1914," *Journal of the Royal Asiatic Society*, Third Series, v. 20, no. 4 (2010): 526.
15. Vincent cited in *Russo-Japanese War. Reports from Officers Attached to the Japanese Forces in the Field, Vol. 1*, General Staff, War Office, April 1905, 75 and 215–6.
16. *Ibid*, 19. Though identified as an "army," the equivalent unit in contemporary British usage was a corps.
17. *Ibid*, 117.
18. Field Marshal Sir Archibald Armar Montgomery-Massingberd Papers, 2/1, "The Lessons of 1815, 1862, 1866, and 1870 as confirmed by the War in Manchuria," July 1907, Liddell Haft Centre for Military Archives, King's College, London.
19. Philip Towle, "Russo-Japanese War and the Defence of India," *Military Affairs*, v. 44, no. 3 (1980): 113.
20. *Reports from Officers Attached to the Japanese Forces, I*, 6–8 and "Naval & Military Intelligence," *Times*, 8 September 1903, 4.
21. *Reports from Officers Attached to the Japanese Forces, I*, 294–5.
22. *Ibid*, 303 and TNA WO 33/1520, *The Russo-Japanese War: Selection of Reports from Officers Attached to the Japanese Forces, Vol. II*, General Staff, War Office, August 1905, R. T. Toke, "Embarkation of the Japanese 8th Division at Osaka, 3rd to 10th October 1904," 545–6.
23. A contemporary example of a movement going terribly wrong is offered by the *Drayton Grange*. See Michael Tyquin, "SS 'Drayton Grange': The Tragedy of the Last Australian Troopship from the Boer War," *Health and History*, v. 3, no. 2 (2001): 94–103.
24. *Russo-Japanese War. Medical and Sanitary Reports from Officers Attached to the Japanese and Russian Forces in the Field* (London: Eyre and Spottiswoode, 1908), 7 and 47.
25. *Russo-Japanese War. Joint Report by Major G. H. G. Mockler and Captain H. C. Holman, D.S.O.*, War Office, General Staff, 1906, xiii.
26. TNA WO 106/39, M. Gerard to Secretary Army Council letter, 9 September 1904.
27. *Russo-Japanese War. Part I* (London: Harrison and Sons, 1906), 23 and W. D. Bird, *Lectures on the Strategy of the Russo-Japanese War* (London: Hugh Rees, Ltd., 1909), 17–8.

28. "British Assistance to the Japanese Navy during the Russo-Japanese War of 1904–5," *Great Circle*, v. 2, no. 1 (1980): 44.
29. *Official History (Naval and Military) of the Russo-Japanese War, Vol. 1* (London: Harrison and Sons, 1910), 36.
30. *Ibid*, 50 and 59–60 and *Official History of the Russo-Japanese War. Part III. The Siege of Port Arthur* (London: Harrison and Sons, 1909), 25–6.
31. *Russo-Japanese War, I*, 43.
32. *Official History of the Russo-Japanese War, I*, 51–2 ad 64.
33. Telfer-Smollett, "Best Method for Carrying Out the Conjoint Practice of the Navy and Army in Embarkation and Disembarkation," 375.
34. Bird, *Russo-Japanese War*, 24–5.
35. *Ibid*, 65–8.
36. *Official History (Naval and Military) of the Russo-Japanese War, I*, 66–7.
37. *Ibid*, 88–99.
38. *Ibid*, 104–07 and *Official History (Naval and Military) of the Russo-Japanese War, III*, 67.
39. *Official History (Naval and Military) of the Russo-Japanese War, I*, 72–3.
40. *Official History (Naval and Military) of the Russo-Japanese War, Vol. II* (London: Harrison and Sons, 1912), 212–5.
41. *Official History (Naval and Military) of the Russo-Japanese War, I*, 103, 121, 127 and 134–5.
42. *Ibid*, 137–8.
43. *Ibid*, 151 and 215.
44. *Official History of the Russo-Japanese War. Part II. From the Battle of the Ya-Lu to Liao-Yang, Exclusive.* (London: Harrison and Sons, 1908), 65–6.
45. *Official History of the Russo-Japanese War, I*, 167–8.
46. *Ibid*, 487.
47. *Official History of the Russo-Japanese War, II*, 123.
48. *Official History of the Russo-Japanese War, I*, 328–33.
49. *Official History of the Russo-Japanese War, II*, 550.
50. *Ibid*, 537.
51. Alexander R. Bay, "Beriberi, Military Medicine, and Military Authority in Prewar Japan," *Japan Review*, no. 20 (2008): 123–4. During the war, about 250,000 Japanese troops suffered beriberi, with more than 27,000 succumbing. For its part, the Third Army experienced roughly 21,000 cases during its siege of Port Arthur.
52. *Official History of the Russo-Japanese War, III*, 12, 55 and 131–2; *Official History of the Russo-Japanese War, II*, 627–42 and 693–4.
53. *Official History of the Russo-Japanese War, III*, 839–40.
54. *Ibid*, 103–05 and 216.
55. *Ibid*, 835–8.
56. Treaty of Portsmouth, Article IX, https://mjp.univ-perp.fr/traites/1905portsmouth.htm - accessed 25 January 2023.
57. *Official History of the Russo-Japanese War, III*, 216n.

248   The Development of British Amphibious Operations 1882-1914

58. Charles à Court assumed the style Charles à Court Repington in August 1898.
59. "A Plea for History," *Times*, 10 September 1904, 8.
60. Waters, *"Secret and Confidential,"* 294 and "British Assistance to the Japanese Navy," *Great Circle*, 53.
61. TNA WO 33/350, Wellescourt Waters, *Reports on the Campaign in Manchuria in 1904 by Colonel Waters* (London: Eyre and Spottiswoode, 1905).
62. Ernest D. Swinton, *Eyewitness: Being Personal Reminiscences of Certain Phases of the Great War, Including the Genesis of the Tank* (Garden City: Doubleday, Doran & Company, 1933), 28.
63. *Official History of the Russo-Japanese War*, I, 5.
64. Compare the *Russo-Japanese War. Part I* with *Official History (Naval and Military) of the Russo-Japanese War*, I.
65. TNA CAB 24/4, E. Daniel, "Historical Section of the Committee of Imperial Defence," note, 8 June 1917.
66. *Official History of the Russo-Japanese War*, I, 405–08.
67. The Russian Navy performed maritime interdictions beyond the theater of operations while Japanese vessels patrolled the South China Sea.
68. George Morton-Jack, *The Indian Army on the Western Front: India's Expeditionary Force to France and Belgium in the First World War* (New York: Cambridge University Press, 2014), 119.
69. Ian Hamilton, *A Staff Officer's Scrap-Book During the Russo-Japanese War* (London: Edward Arnold, 1906).
70. Liddell Hart Centre for Military Archives, King's College, London, Major-General Sir George Aston Papers, "Diary," entries, 21, 22 January 1910, 8 April 1910, and 20 April 1911.
71. *Reports from Officers Attached to the Japanese Forces*, I, 302–03.

Chapter 10

1. Esher Papers, CAC/ESHR/16/4, "Notes and Supporting Materials Relating to the War Office Reconstitution Committee," interview with P. Girouard, 26 November 1903.
2. Telfer-Smollett, "Best Method for Carrying Out the Conjoint Practice of the Navy and Army in Embarkation and Disembarkation," 373.
3. Esher Papers, CAC/ESHR/16/4, "Notes and Supporting Materials Relating to the War Office Reconstitution Committee."
4. Fitzmaurice, *Granville*, II, 388–95 and 404–05.
5. Tellingly, Salisbury was in Germany when the battle at Omdurman was fought. See Roberts, *Salisbury*, 699.
6. "The Murder of Captain Selby," *Times*, 18 March 1882, 12; "The Late Commander Selby," *Times*, 17 April 1882, 5 and R. Sarell, "The Case of Commander Selby, R.N.," *British Medical Journal*, v. 1, no. 1107 (1882): 376.
7. Gambetta had drafted the note issued in January 1882 and then proposed sending the British and French naval squadrons to Alexandria. See Chamberlain, "Sir Charles Dilke and the British Intervention in Egypt, 1882," 234 and 239–42.

8. Maurice, *Campaign of 1882*, 11.
9. *London Gazette*, 10 April 1885, no. 25460, 1666.
10. Cromer, *Modern Egypt, II*, 52.
11. Preston, ed. *Relief of Gordon*, 15, 47–8, 111, 233, and 236–7.
12. Childers, *Childers, II*, 119.
13. Wolseley, *Soldier's Life*, 55–6. Seymour assumed the style Baron Alcester in November 1882 for services rendered in Egypt.
14. TNA ADM 196/20 (C. Lindsay) and ADM 196/39 (C. Lindsay).
15. Major Spencer Childers, the scion of Hugh Childers, offers one example. Colonel Stanley Clarke, a close friend of the prince of Wales and commanding the Light Camel Regiment represented another, with Major George FitzGeorge, the duke of Cambridge's eldest son, proving a third.
16. "Hamley and Wolseley," *Broad Arrow: Naval and Military Gazette* (15 June 1895): 801 and Luvaas, *Education of an Army*, 155–6.
17. Bond, *Victorian Army and the Staff College*, 132.
18. Wolseley cited in Childers, *Childers, II*, 112 and 132.
19. The many changes adopted are ably recounted in Douglas E. Delaney, *The Imperial Army Project: Britain and the Land Forces of the Dominions and India 1902–1945* (Oxford: Oxford University Press, 2020.)
20. Elmslie, "Lessons to be Derived," 466–70. Beyond the general one of defending the Suez Canal, the exact role a French force would have carried out has not been traced. In their absence, the availability of an Indian contingent assumed greater proportions.
21. Edward E. Bradford, *Life of Admiral of the Fleet Arthur Knyvet Wilson Bart., V.C., G.C.B., O.M., G.C.V.O.* (London: John Murray, 1923), 70–3.
22. "Latest Intelligence," *Times*, 3 July 1882, 5.
23. Goodrich, *Naval and Military Operations*, 165 and Grant, *War in the Soudan*, 50.
24. "Naval and Military Intelligence," *Times*, 22 July 1882, 12.
25. Telfer-Smollett, "Best Method for Carrying Out the Conjoint Practice of the Navy and Army in Embarkation and Disembarkation for War," 368–9.
26. Maurice, *Campaign of 1882*, 65 and Goodrich, *Naval and Military Operations*, 175–7.
27. "Expedition to Egypt," *Times*, 6 October 1882, 7.
28. F. Robert Hunter, "Tourism and Empire: The Thomas Cook & Son Enterprise on the Nile, 1868–1914," *Middle Eastern Studies*, v. 40, no. 5 (2004): 39–40.
29. TNA ADM 196/40 (H. Andoe) and 196/38 (H. Barnard) and Francis Coningsby Hannam Clarke, *Staff Duties: A Series of Lectures Addressed to the Officers of the Staff College* (London: Her Majesty's Stationery Office, 1884), 224–7.
30. TNA ADM 1/6835, War Office, "Personnel of a Naval Brigade necessary to work the Lines of Communication of an Army Corps along 100 miles of River," 27 November 1886.
31. Goodrich, *Naval and Military Operations*, 196 and *London Gazette*, 27 March 1884, no. 25332, 1456.
32. "Naval and Military Intelligence," *Times*, 27 May 1878, 6 and Galloway, *Battle of Tofrek*, 90–1.

33. Tulloch, *Soldier's Sailoring*, 303.
34. *London Gazette*, 2 November 1882, no. 25162, 4879 and Beckett, *Victorians at War*, 10.
35. Esher Papers, CAC/ESHR/2/8, R. Brett to R. Churchill letter, 7 March 1888.
36. Beaver, "Intelligence Division Library," *Journal of Library History*, 207.
37. Montagu-Stuart-Wortley, "My Reminiscences of Egypt and the Sudan (from 1882 to 1889)," *Sudan Notes and Records*, 30.
38. TNA CAB 37/12/22, Wolseley to Hartington memorandum, 8 April 1884; FO 84/1618, W. Miéville to Granville letter, 23 March 1882 and Preston, ed., *Relief of Gordon*, 30.
39. Gleichen, ed., *Anglo-Egyptian Sudan*, I, 204–05.
40. TNA ADM 196/61 (W. Tucker) and ADM 196/86 (A. Wilson).
41. Adye, *Recollections of a Military Life*, 347.
42. *London Gazette*, 6 May 1884, no. 25351, 2079.
43. Goodrich, *Naval and Military Operations*, 69–71 and Sydenham of Combe, "Sea Heresies," *Naval Review*, v. 19, no. 2 (1931): 222.
44. Goodrich, *Naval and Military Operations*, 74 (original emphasis).
45. *Ibid*, 87.
46. P. H. Colomb, *Essays on Naval Defence* (London: W. H. Allen & Co., Limited, 1896), 14n.
47. TNA ADM 116/208, J. Fisher and A. Wilson report, 4 August 1882.
48. Goodrich, *Naval and Military Operations*, 177.
49. Younghusband, *Forty Years a Soldier*, 39–40.
50. TNA CAB 37/13/36, J. S. Rothwell, "England's means of Offence against Russia," 7 July 1884 and J. B. Atlay, *Lord Haliburton: A Memoir of His Public Service* (Toronto: William Briggs, 1909), 200.
51. Gardiner, *Harcourt*, 601–03.

Chapter 11

1. George Aston, *Sea, Land and Air Strategy: A Comparison* (Boston: Little, Brown and Company, 1914), 167.
2. TNA CAB 1/31, General Staff, "The need on a General Staff in the Navy," memorandum, 28 July 1909.
3. A. R. Godwin-Austen, *The Staff and the Staff College* (London: Constable and Company, Ltd., 1927), 85–110.
4. William Robertson, *Private to Field-Marshal* (London: Constable and Company Ltd., 1921), 170.
5. William Marshall, *Memories of Four Fronts* (London: Ernest Benn, Ltd., 1929), xv.
6. TNA FO 800/357, A. Nicolson to Hardinge letter, 18 July 1912 and Harold Nicolson, *Sir Arthur Nicolson, First Lord Carnock: A Study in Old Diplomacy* (London: Constable & Co., 1937), 7–10.

7. Goodrich, *British Naval and Military Operations in Egypt*, 337.
8. Horace Smith-Dorrien, *Memories of Forty-Eight Years' Service* (New York: E. P. Dutton and Company, 1925), 78.
9. Wolseley to A. Alison letter, 9 December 1883, General Sir Archibald Alison Papers, Liddell Hart Centre for Military Archives, King's College, London; and Robertson, *Private to Field-Marshal*, 89–90 and, especially, 107.
10. Charles V. F. Townshend, *My Campaign in Mesopotamia* (London: Thornton Butterworth Limited, 1920), 13.
11. Turner, *Sixty Years*, 294.
12. Esher Papers, CAC/ESHR/4/1, Esher to Knollys letter, 27 May 1906.
13. Cyril Falls, "Edmund Henry Hynman Allenby," in L. G. Wickham Legg, ed., *The Dictionary of National Biography 1931–1940* (London: Oxford University Press, 1949), 7.
14. G. W. Redway, "Staff College Papers, August, 1908," *United Service Magazine*, v. 38, no. 960 (1908): 179.
15. TNA ADM 196/16 (H. Hildyard) and Frederick Maurice, ed., *Sir Frederick Maurice: A Record of His Work and Opinions* (London: Edward Arnold, 1913), 66–8.
16. Wilson Papers, IWM HHW 1/1, Reel 1, "Diary," 24 November 1893, 12 July 1894, and 17 July 1894.
17. Bond, *Victorian Army and the Staff College*, 167; George Aston, *Letters on Amphibious Wars* (London: John Murray. 1920), 110 and Brigadier General Sir James Edmonds Papers, "Foreign Expedition," November 1897, I/2A/14-7, Liddell Hart Centre for Military Archives, King's College, London.
18. Ian F. W. Beckett, *Johnnie Gough, V.C., A Biography of Brigadier-General Sir John Edmond Gough, V.C.* (London: Tom Donovan, 1989), 114.
19. Aston, *Amphibious Wars*, 87–120.
20. *Ibid*, 28 and 56.
21. *Ibid*, 20.
22. *Ibid*, 37–8.
23. *Ibid*, 53–4 and 103–4.
24. *The Tragedy of "The Battle of the Beaches,"* privately printed, Captain Hughes Lockyer Papers, Box 75/56/1, Imperial War Museum, London.
25. Seymour Fortescue, *Looking Back* (London: Longmans, Green and Co., 1920), 91 and Robert Hastings Harris, *From Naval Cadet to Admiral: Half-a-Century of Naval Service and Sport in Many Parts of the World* (London: Cassell and Company, Ltd., 1913), 145.
26. TNA ADM 196/40 (R. Bruce).
27. Chris Madsen, "Rear Admiral Henry John May and the Royal Navy War Course 1900–1904," *Northern Mariner*, v. 31, no. 3 (2022): 310.
28. M. Hankey to Fisher letter, 17 December 1909, Fisher Papers, CAC/FISR/1/9/447.
29. TNA ADM 196/86 (W. Henderson).
30. TNA ADM 196/39 (H. May) and ADM 196/86 (H. May).

31. Bond, *Victorian Army and the Staff College*, 197.
32. George Armand Furse, *Military Expeditions Beyond the Seas, Vol. II* (London: William Clowes & Sons, Limited, 1897), 374 and 384–7.
33. "Major-General Sir Edward May," *Times*, 12 February 1936, 16.
34. Edward S. May, *Principles and Problems of Imperial Defence* (London: Swan Sonnenshein & Co. Limited, 1903), 1 and 58.
35. *Ibid*, 85.
36. *Ibid*, 116–17.
37. "Death of Dr. Lawrence," *Times*, 18 August 1919, 13.
38. TNA CAB 1/31, "Lectures delivered at the R. N. War College, Portsmouth, during the Spring Session, 1911."
39. TNA ADM 196/62 (R. Foster).
40. "Combined Operations, Lecture 1," no date, but *ca*. 1908, Sir Julian Corbett Papers, Box 2, Liddell Hart Centre for Military Archives, King's College, London.
41. *Ibid*.
42. Julian S. Corbett, *Maritime Operations in the Russo-Japanese War, 1904–1905, Volume 2* (Annapolis: Naval Institute Press, 2015), 349.
43. Aston, *Sea, Land and Air Strategy*, vii and 20–4 and Aston, *Letters on Amphibious Wars*, vii.
44. C. Repington to Esher letter, 4 February 1904, Esher Papers, CAC/ESHR/10/24.
45. Callwell, *Military Operations and Maritime Preponderance*, 1–9.
46. W. D. Bird, *A Précis of Strategy* (London: Hugh Rees, Ltd., 1910), 52–3.
47. "Combined Operations, Lecture 4, Command," no date, but *ca*. 1908, LHCMA, Corbett Papers, Box 2.
48. "Combined Strategy for Fleets and Armies," *Times*, 16 July 1907, 15.
49. TNA ADM 196/62 (J. Rose).
50. "Naval and Military Intelligence," *Times*, 20 May 1907, 5.
51. Anon., "Some Notes on the Early Days of the Royal Naval War College," *Naval Review*, v. 19, no. 2 (1931): 245–6.
52. Aston Papers, "Diary," 27 May 1913, LHCMA 1/6.
53. *Ibid*, 11 December 1913 and Aston, *Sea, Land, and Air*, 92–7. It remained, however, that the war orders covering the invasion of the United Kingdom stressed the destruction of the enemy's transports. See TNA ADM 186/621, *C. B. 917J Naval Staff Monograph (Historical), Volume XII, Home Waters— Part III*, Admiralty, Naval Staff, Training and Staff Duties Division, May 1925, 1.
54. Callwell, *Military Operations*, 73–118.
55. C. E, Callwell, *The Life of Sir Stanley Maude* (London: Constable and Company Ltd., 1920), 93–4.
56. H. Wake to R. Plunkett letters, 22 October 1909 and 26 July 1909, Admiral Sir Reginald Aylmer Ranfurly Plunkett-Ernle-Erle-Drax Papers, Churchill Archives Centre, Churchill College, Cambridge, 1/14 and Reginald Plunkett, "The Staff College," *Naval Review*, v. 3, no. 1 (1915): 97–8.
57. Aston, *Sea, Land, and Air Strategy*, 211–3.
58. "Combined Strategy for Fleets and Armies," *Times*, 16 July 1907, 15.

Endnotes 253

59. TNA WO 279/18, "Report on a Conference of General Staff Officers at the Staff College, 7th to 10th January, 1908," 36 and Jim Beach, "The British Army, the Royal Navy, and the 'big work' of Sir George Aston, 1904–1914," *Journal of Strategic Studies*, v. 29, no. 1 (2006): 148.
60. "Combined Strategy for Fleets and Armies," *Times*, 16 July 1907, 15; Keith Jeffrey, *Field Marshal Sir Henry Wilson: A Political Soldier* (Oxford: Oxford University Press, 2006), 68 and C. E. Callwell, *Field-Marshal Sir Henry Wilson Bart., G.C.B., D.S.O. His Life and Diaries, Volume I* (London: Cassell and Company, Ltd., 1927), 69.
61. Beach, "'big work' of Sir George Aston," *Journal of Strategic Studies*, 150.
62. "Lt.-Col. Sir Wilfrid Spender," *Times*, 23 December 1960, 10.
63. "Naval and Military Intelligence," *Times*, 1 October 1906, 11 and "Naval and Military Intelligence," *Times*, 11 May 1907, 8.
64. W. Spender to G. Aston letter, 14 December 1905, LHCMA, Aston Papers, 3/1.
65. TNA ADM 1/6640, "Question of the employment of Royal Marine Officers on the General Staff of the Army," 4 February 1882 and CAB 37/74/14, H. Arnold-Forster, "Summary of the Year's Work at the War Office," 31 January 1905.
66. H. Rawlinson to G. Aston letter, 24 May 1904, LHCMA, Aston Papers, 4/4.
67. "Royal Naval War College," *Times*, 29 May 1908, 16 and TNA WO 25/3917/7 (M. Manifold-Bowman).
68. TNA ADM 1/8272, A. Vyvyan, "Notes for War Staff Committee," no date but *ca.* 1913.
69. TNA ADM 1/7417, "History of the Benin Expedition of 1897," Admiralty, Intelligence Department (No. 561), December 1899.
70. "Imperial Strategy. Scheme No. I. 1907," Staff College, Camberley, 4 February 1907, LHCMA, Montgomery-Massingberd Papers, 2/1.
71. H. Rawlinson to J. Corbett letter, 2 October 1905, LHCMA, Corbett Papers, Box 2.
72. *Ibid.*
73. "Naval and Military Intelligence," *Times*, 11 April 1912, 13.
74. Anon., "Early Days of the Royal Naval War College," *Naval Review*, 241.
75. "Sir Henry Wilson," *Times*, 23 June 1922, 18.
76. "Evidence – Dardanelles Commission (Notes)," 12 October 1916, LHCMA, Aston Papers, 4/7.
77. The quota allocated to the Indian establishment was five officers over the course of 2 years. See George de S. Barrow, *The Fire of Life* (London: Hutchinson & Co., 1942), 41.
78. TNA CAB 6/3, General Staff, "The Possibility of Bringing the Indian Army into Closer Touch with the British Army," 20 March 1905.
79. TNA WO 32/3094, D. Hutchinson to N. Lyttelton memorandum, January 1906.
80. "Lord Kitchener and the Indian Staff College," *Times*, 18 October 1905, 4.
81. H. M. S., "Proposed Indian Staff College," *Times*, 26 December 1900, 5.
82. "Rival Staff Colleges," *Times*, 29 May 1905, 10.
83. "The Indian Staff College," *Times*, 10 April 1905, 10.

84. "Major-General Sir Alfred Bayly," *Times*, 30 June 1928, 16.
85. "Sir Thompson Capper Killed," *Times*, 1 October 1915, 7 and A. Grant Duff to C. Dobell letter, 13 May 1906, Lieutenant Colonel Adrian Grant Duff Papers, Churchill Archives Centre, Cambridge, CAC/AGDF 1/6.
86. TNA ADM 196/61 (H. Drake).
87. *Hansard*, House of Commons debate, 15 July 1897, v. 51, cc161–2.
88. "Lecture Notes," LHCMA, Corbett Papers, Box 1 and H. Rawlinson to J. Corbett letter, 2 October 1905, Box 2.
89. Bird, *Précis of Strategy*, 52–3.
90. See W. D. Bird, *Lectures on the Strategy of the Russo-Japanese War* (London: Hugh Rees, Ltd., 1909); A. I. R. Glasfurd, *Sketches of Manchurian Battle-Fields with a Verbal Description of Southern Manchuria: An Aid to the Study of the Russo-Japanese War* (London: Hugh Rees, Ltd., 1910).
91. G. Warrender to P. Cox letter, 10 December 1907, Sir Percy Cox Papers, GB 165-0341 – 2/14, Box 1, File 2, Middle East Center Archive, St. Antony's College, Oxford, hereafter, MECA.
92. "Gen. Sir George Barrow," *Times*, 20 December 1959, 10.
93. Ian Hamilton had brought Vincent's observations of the Russo-Japanese War to Kitchener's attention in March 1904, though whether the commander-in-chief recalled the instance cannot be claimed. See Liam Caswell, "Born Soldiers Who March Under the Rising Sun: The Russo-Japanese War, Britain's Military Observers, and British Impressions Regarding Japanese Martial Capabilities Prior to the First World War" (master's thesis, Dalhousie University, 2017), 115, http://Caswell-Liam-MA-HIST-December-2017.pdf (dal.ca).
94. Jeffrey, *Field Marshal Sir Henry Wilson*, 82–3.
95. *London Gazette*, 17 June 1910, no. 28385, 4264.
96. TNA CAB 37/55/196, Roberts to Lansdowne signal of 17 August 1900; Alexander Godley, *Life of an Irish Soldier: Reminiscences of General Sir Alexander Godley G.C.B., K.C.M.G.* (London: John Murray, 1939), 105 and Barrow, *Fire of Life*, 46.
97. Every year a few officers successfully negotiating the 2-year course were nonetheless reported as unsuited for employment on the staff. In the close-knit fraternity of *psc* officers, a tendency to be argumentative married with a distinct lack of tack poisoned an officer's future prospects.
98. Commandant Quetta Staff College to Military Secretary letter, 21 September 1909, Major General Thompson Capper Papers, Liddell Hart for Centre for Military Archives, LHCMA, 2/4/17. While attending Camberley Vincent lectured on artillery in the Russo-Japanese War; see B. Vincent, "Artillery in the Manchurian Campaign," *Royal United Services Institution Journal*, v. 52, no. 359 (1908): 28–52.
99. See especially Hamilton, *Scrap-Book*, 52–6.
100. H. Wilson to T. Capper letter, 2 October 1908 - original emphasis - LHCMA, Thompson Capper Papers, 2/4/17.
101. Beckett, *Johnnie Gough*, 139 and 147 and Jeffrey, *Henry Wilson*, 82–3.
102. "Sir Thomas Blamey," *Times*, 28 May 1951, 6.
103. Furse, *Military Expeditions, II*, 393–95.

104. "Diary," 13 May 1912, Grant Duff Papers, CAC/AGDF/2/2 and G. G. Aston, "Combined Strategy for Fleets and Armies; Or '"Amphibious Strategy,'" *Journal of the Royal United Services* Institution, v. 51., no. 354 (1907): 989.
105. TNA ADM 1/7840, Captain T. Jackson, "Landing of the Second Japanese Army, *May 1904*," April 1905.
106. James Willcocks, *With the Indians in France* (London: Constable and Company Ltd., 1920), 96–7 and "Diary," 12 November 1916, Major General Ladislaus Herbert Richard Pope-Hennessy Papers, Imperial War Museum, London, 03/35/1.
107. "Diary," 21 and 22 July 1909, LHCMA, Aston Papers, 1/2.
108. *Ibid*, 19 and 20 August 1909.
109. M. Hankey to Fisher letter, 10 January 1910, Fisher Papers, CAC/FISR/1/9/455 and "War Staff Officer's Qualifying Examination," 13–17 January 1913, Drax Papers, CAC/DRAX/1/22.
110. Michael Howard, "Men Against Fire: Expectations of War in 1914," *International Security*, v. 9, no. 1 (1984): 52–3.
111. LHCMA, Montgomery-Massingberd Papers, 2/1 and Lieutenant Colonel Cecil Allanson personal diary, no date and privately published, 6–7, Sir Robert Rhodes James Papers, Churchill Archives Centre, Churchill College, Cambridge, CAC/RHJS/2/1.
112. TNA ADM 196/143 (C. H. N. James).
113. TNA ADM 203/100.
114. "Naval and Military Intelligence," *Times*, 16 May 1907, 12 and "Naval and Military Intelligence," *Times*, 31 May 1907, 8.
115. TNA ADM 196/143 (R. Bellairs), ADM 196/143 (J. Patterson) and ADM 196/125 (G. Hamilton).
116. TNA ADM 196/62 (J. Rose).
117. TNA ADM 196/62 (St. G. Armstrong).
118. L. Kiggell to G. Aston letter, 11 September 1913, LHCMA, Aston Papers, 4/10.
119. [*Anon.*] "The Staff," *Army Quarterly*, v. 1, no. 1 (1920): 28–30.
120. Arthur, ed. *Wolseley*, 123. His other aides were Walter Adye, Spencer Childers and Arthur Creagh.
121. Snook, "Wolseley, Wilson and the Failure of the Khartoum Campaign," PhD diss., 102.

Chapter 12

1. Telfer-Smollett, "The Best Method for Carrying Out the Conjoint Practice of the Navy and Army in Embarkation and Disembarkation for War, Illustrated By the Experience of the Past," *Royal United Service Institution Journal*, 380.
2. TNA AIR 10/1206, *Manual of Combined Naval, Military and Air Operations, 1925*.
3. TNA WO 33/644, *Manual of Combined Naval and Military Operations*, 2. Following the First World War, the *Manual of Combined Naval and Military Operations* was designated *Confidential Book 967* in naval distribution circles.

4. RUSI held yearly competitions on military topics with those set in 1895 and 1905 specifically addressing amphibious warfare.
5. "Motor-Car Accident," *Times*, 28 August 1912, 7 and "Naval & Military Intelligence," *Times*, 3 August 1904, 6.
6. G. F. MacMunn, "The Best Method for Carrying Out the Conjoint Practice of the Navy and the Army in Embarkation and Disembarkation for War, Illustrated by the experience of the Past," *Journal of the Royal United Services Institution*, v. 49, no. 327 (1905): 508–11 and 520.
7. TNA ADM 1/6888, "Report of the War Office Committee on the result of the Combined Naval and Military Operations at Milford Haven, 1886," January 1887.
8. "Whitsuntide Manoeuvres," *Times*, 26 May 1890, 8 and "The Whitsuntide Manoeuvres," *Times*, 28 May 1890, 6.
9. "The Whitsuntide Manoeuvres," *Times*, 30 May 1890, 5.
10. British exercises of the period usually entailed a "general idea" known to all participants and a "special idea" unique to one side. These set the stage for the lessons to be deduced from the respective serial. See H. H. Wilson, "Staff Tours," *Journal of the Royal United Services Institution*, v. 52, no. 363 (1908): 667–8.
11. "The Naval Manoeuvres," *Times*, 21 July 1900, 15.
12. Jonathan Reed Winkler, "Silencing the Enemy: Cable-cutting in the Spanish-American War," *War on the Rocks*. Accessed 16 March 2023. https://warontherocks.com/2015/11/silencing-the-enemy-cable-cutting-in-the-spanish-american-war/.
13. TNA ADM 1/7417, Admiralty, Intelligence Department, "Report on the Naval Manoeuvres of 1899," December 1899, 38; "The Naval Manoeuvres," *Times*, 5 August 1899, 6 and *Times*, 18 August 1899, 7 and Harris, *From Naval Cadet to Admiral*, 186–7.
14. "Naval and Military Operations at Malta," *Times*, 28 November 1899, 10.
15. Smith-Dorrien, *Forty-Eight Years' Service*, 133–4.
16. "The Organization of Mounted Troops of the Expeditionary Force," unsigned and undated memorandum but most likely by Douglas Haig, *ca.* 1906, Brigadier General Philip Howell Papers, Liddell Hart for Military Archives, King's College, London, 4/2/2.
17. In 1910, a subcommittee of the CID examined the issue of infantry and cavalry synchronization in an overseas expedition. See John Connor, *ANZAC and Empire: George Foster Pearce and the Foundations of Australian Defence* (Cambridge: Cambridge University Press, 2011), 47.
18. Fisher Papers, CAC/FISR/5/7/4190, "French Naval Manoeuvres in the Mediterranean," July 1901.
19. Esher Papers, CAC/ESHR/10/41, J. Fisher to Esher letter, 19 November 1903.
20. J. Fisher to G. Ellison letter, 16 November 1903, Ellison Papers, NAM 8704-35-53 and TNA CAB 38/4, CID minutes, 2 March 1904.
21. "Speech by Sir John French," Ellison Papers, NAM 8704-35-94 – original emphasis and "Naval and Military Co-operation in War," *Times*, 25 November 1903, 7.
22. "Naval & Military Intelligence," *Times*, 8 March 1904, 4 and "Naval & Military Intelligence," *Times*, 11 March 1904, 5.

23. TNA ADM 1/8880, Under Secretary State, War Office (E. Ward) to Admiralty letter, 6 January 1903.
24. TNA CAB 38/4, CID minutes, 4 March 1904.
25. Mortimer Durand, *The Life of Field-Marshal Sir George White, V.C., Vol. II* (Edinburgh: William Blackwood and Sons, 1915), 247.
26. Cost may have been a factor but the more likely reason for the truncated exercise was the present readiness of the fleet.
27. "Combined Naval and Military Manoeuvres," *Times*, 20 April 1904, 10 and TNA WO 33/322, "Extracts from a Report on a Staff Ride Embracing a Disembarkation and the Establishment of a Base as Carried Out by the Staff of the Second Army Corps, April 1904," 4.
28. TNA WO 33/322, "Extracts from a Report on a Staff Ride Embracing a Disembarkation and the Establishment of a Base as Carried Out by the Staff of the Second Army Corps, April 1904," 5–6 and 65–6.
29. Aston, "Combined Strategy for Fleets and Armies," *Journal of the Royal United Services Institution*, 989.
30. P. H. Colomb, *Naval Warfare Its Ruling Principles and Practices Historically Treated* (London: W. H. Allen & Co. Limited, 1895), 209.
31. TNA WO 33/322, "Extracts from a Report on a Staff Ride Embracing a Disembarkation and the Establishment of a Base as Carried Out by the Staff of the Second Army Corps," April 1904, 8.
32. *Ibid*, 66–9.
33. *Ibid*, 69–70.
34. TNA ADM 144/28, W. Henderson, "2nd Army Corps Staff Ride: The Naval Share of Operations," April 1904.
35. George Aston, *Secret Service* (New York: Cosmopolitan Book Corporation, 1930), 90–1.
36. "Naval & Military Intelligence," *Times*, 4 June 1904, 7; "Naval & Military Intelligence," *Times*, 8 June 1904, 12 and "Naval & Military Intelligence," *Times*, 9 June 1904, 13.
37. "Army Corps Training," *Times*, 23 August 1904, 9.
38. "Army Manoeuvres," *Times*, 7 September 1904, 5.
39. "The Military and Manoeuvres," *Times*, 31 August 1904, 4.
40. "Army Manoeuvres," *Times*, 7 September 1904, 5.
41. Wood, *Life and Adventure in Peace and War*, 281–2.
42. Simon Batten, *Futile Exercise: The British Army's Preparations for War 1902–1914* (Warwick: Helion & Company Limited, 2018), 62.
43. *Ibid*, 54.
44. "Some Military Lessons of the Essex Manoeuvres," *Times*, 22 September 1904, 10 and Batten, *Futile Exercise*, 58.
45. "The Army Manoeuvres," *Times*, 9 September 1904, 8.
46. Batten, *Futile Exercise*, 32.
47. Thus, more important than which officers commanded in mock battles, Repington held was the role of the Directing Staff in controlling events. See "Some Military Lessons of the Essex Manoeuvres," *Times*, 22 September 1904, 10.

48. "The Army Manoeuvres," *Times*, 10 September 1904, 10.
49. Repington believed age to be a contributing factor in the loss of these boats as they dated from the 1870s.
50. "The Army Manoeuvres," *Times*, 13 September 1904, 8.
51. "The Army Manoeuvres," *Times*, 14 September 1904, 8.
52. TNA WO 279/8, "Report on Army Manoeuvres, 1904," 16.
53. "The Army Manoeuvres," *Times*, 14 September 1904, 8.
54. "The Army Manoeuvres," *Times*, 8 September 1904, 8; George Aston, *Memories of a Marine* (London: John Murray, 1925), 241 and C.E.W. Bean, *Story of ANZAC from the Outbreak of War to the End of the First Phase of the Gallipoli Campaign, May 4, 1915* (Sydney: Angus & Robertson Ltd., 1941), 194.
55. TNA WO 33/344, "Report of the Naval and Military Conference on Oversea Expeditions," War Office, 1905, 9.
56. TNA WO 279/8, "Report on Army Manoeuvres, 1904," 24.
57. TNA CAB 38/3/53, L. Battenberg, "Remarks on Offensive Over-Sea Expeditions suggested by the War Office as Feasible in the Memorandum on the Military Needs of the Empire in a War with France and Russia (No. 1A, 12th August, 1901)," 1 July 1903. Original emphasis.
58. *Ibid*, 6–7 and 12.
59. "Cavalry Training in Ireland," *Times*, 17 July 1905, 6.
60. "Cavalry Training in Ireland," *Times*, 1 August 1915, 4. In the serial, the *Donegal* represented a cruiser squadron.
61. "Cavalry Training in Ireland," *Times*, 5 August 1905, 8.
62. Fortescue, *Looking Back*, 128. The style marine transport officer operated within the Royal Indian Marine.
63. TNA ADM 196/40 (R. Berkeley); ADM 196/40 (G. Boyes) and ADM 196/40 (J. Hext).
64. TNA ADM 1/7357A, "Benin Expedition" and ADM 196/40 (R. Heriz).
65. TNA ADM 186/610, *C.B. 1585, Naval Staff Monographs, Vol. III*, Admiralty, Naval Staff, Training and Staff Duties Division, July 1921, 6–7 and CAB 38/3/53, Battenberg, "Remarks on Offensive Over-Sea Expeditions suggested by the War Office as Feasible in the Memorandum on the Military Needs of the Empire in a War with France and Russia (No. 1A, 12th August, 1901)," 1 July 1903, 20.
66. TNA ADM 144/28, W. Henderson, "2nd Army Corps Staff Ride: The Naval Share of Operations," April 1904 and TNA ADM 186/610, *C.B. 1585, Naval Staff Monographs, III*, 64.
67. Arthur W. Jose, *The Royal Australian Navy 1914–1918* (Sydney: Angus and Robertson, Ltd., 1941), 407.
68. Douglas Jerrold, *The Royal Naval Division* (London: Hutchinson & Co., 1923), 2.
69. TNA CAB 38/4, Military Department to Secretary of State for India signal, 10 March 1904 and CID minutes, 30 March 1904.
70. TNA CAB 38/10, "Précis of the Minutes of the Committee of Imperial Defence. Meetings 51 to 82. July 17, 1904 to November 24, 1905." On the Secret

Endnotes 259

Intelligence Service, see Keith Jeffrey, *The Secret History of MI6* (New York: The Penguin Press, 2010).
71. P.E.F. Hobbs, "The Best Organisation for the Land Transport of the British Army, having Regard Both to Home Defence and Over-Sea Expeditions," *Journal of the Royal United Services Institution*, v. 47, no. 304 (1903): 645.
72. TNA ADM 1/7859, "*Report of the Naval and Military Conference on Oversea Expedition*," War Office, 1905.
73. TNA CAB 1/31, General Staff, "The need on a General Staff in the Navy," memorandum, 28 July 1909.
74. TNA ADM 196/86 (W. Fawkes) and ADM 196/43 (L. Halsey).
75. AWM 4 1/25/9, Part 4, "J. M. de Robeck memorandum No. C 33," 4 November 1915; TNA WO 33/569, *Manual of Combined Naval and Military Operations*, General Staff, War Office, 1911 and WO 33/644, *Manual of Combined Naval and Military Operations*, General Staff, War Office, 1913.
76. TNA WO 33/644, "*Manual of Combined Naval and Military Operations*," 1913, 7 – original emphasis.
77. MacMunn, "Best Method for Carrying Out the Conjoint Practice of the Navy and the Army," *Journal of the Royal United Services Institution*, 505.
78. TNA WO 33/644, "*Manual of Combined Naval and Military Operations*," 1913, 8, 28–30 and WO 33/569, "*Manual of Combined Naval and Military Operations*," 1911, 7, 24–5.
79. War Office, General Staff, *Field Service Pocket Book* (London: His Majesty's Stationery Office, 1914), 79–83.
80. War Office, General Staff, *Field Service Regulations, Part I, Operations, 1909* (London: His Majesty's Stationery Office, 1914), 67–71 and 231–4. A supplement to the *FSR* was issued by Simla to address items unique to the Indian Army.
81. War Office, General Staff, *Training and Manoeuvre Regulations, 1913*, 78, Hunter-Weston Papers, NAM 6503-39-20.
82. A *Naval War Manual* issued in the post-1918 period would eventually serve a purpose akin to the *FSR* for the navy.
83. *Rifle and Field Exercises for H.M. Fleet* (London: Her Majesty's Stationery Office, 1913); *BR 159 Royal Naval Handbook of Field Training* (London: His Majesty's Stationery Office, 1920) and [W.S.R. King-Hall] "Notes on a Naval Battalion," *Naval Review*, v. 9, read '(1921), 396–7.
84. Lieutenant General Sir T. Kelly-Kenny to General Officer Commanding 1st Army Corps letter 57500/645 of 2 January 1902, Ellison Papers, National Army Museum, London, United Kingdom, 8704–35.
85. TNA ADM 174/377, *Regulations for His Majesty's Transport Service* (London: His Majesty's Stationery Office, 1908) and ADM 186/10, *Regulations for His Majesty's Transport Service* (London: His Majesty's Stationery Office, 1914).
86. TNA ADM 186/610, *Naval Staff Monographs, III*, 67.
87. TNA WO 33/2982, "Naval and Military Staff Tour," Joint Report, November 1907, 6.
88. *Ibid*.

89. "Naval and Military Intelligence," *Times*, 6 June 1907, 5.
90. TNA CAB 38/13, "Notes on Invasion Supplied to Mr Balfour."
91. H. Grant to A. Hunter-Weston letter, 9 December 1909, Hunter-Weston Papers, NAM 6503-39-18 and "The Scottish Army Manoeuvres," *Times*, 27 July 1910, 9.
92. TNA ADM 144/31, "Great Britain Naval Manoeuvres, 1909," 24.
93. "Army Manoeuvres," *Times*, 16 September 1912, 4. The Royal Flying Corps' Naval Wing did provide four aircraft and a portion of the personnel operating an airship, however. See "Aircraft in Manoeuvres," *Times*, 13 September 1912, 5.
94. "Army Manoeuvres 1912," S. Drury-Lowe report, undated, Drax Papers, CAC/DRAX, 1/41 and "Army Manoeuvres," *Times*, 16 September 1912, 4.
95. TNA ADM 196/89 (S. Drury-Lowe); "Capture of Illig," and "Untitled Leader," *Times*, 28 April 1904, 5 and 9.
96. TNA ADM 116/1169 "Criticisms of the 1913 Manoeuvres (Draft)," undated and no author specified.
97. *Ibid*, "Naval Manoeuvres, 1913. Report of Lieutenant-Colonel, RMLI."
98. Rose, "Lessons to Be Derived," *Journal of the Royal United Services Institution*, 709.
99. "The Naval Manoeuvres," *Times*, 18 June 1913, 4 and TNA ADM 116/1214, "Naval Manoeuvres, 1913."
100. TNA ADM 116/1214, "Naval Manoeuvres, 1913," 2.
101. *Ibid*, F. Marshall, "Report," 6 August 1913.
102. *Ibid*, H. Smith-Rewse, "Report," 12 August 1912.
103. Presently, the second sea lord, Jellicoe had detached from the Admiralty to command the Red Fleet in the 1913 summer maneuvers. See TNA ADM 196/38 (J. Jellicoe).
104. TNA ADM 116/1214, "Naval Manoeuvres," 1913, H. Alexander, "Report," 10 August 1913.
105. *Ibid*, E. Seagrave, "Report," 6 August 1913.
106. *Ibid*, H. Street, "Report," 16 August 1913.

Chapter 13

1. Viscount Esher, *To-Day and To-Morrow and Other Essays* (London: John Murray, 1910), 63.
2. TNA FO 800/102, J. S. Ewart, "The Value to a Foreign Power of an Alliance with the British Empire," memorandum, 5 March 1909.
3. Untitled leader, *Times*, 29 September 1900, 9.
4. Sitting with Elgin were Esher, Sir George Taubman-Goldie, Field Marshal Sir Henry Norman, Admiral Sir John Hopkins, Sir John Edge, Sir John Jackson, and Sir John Norman. See *London Gazette*, 16 September 1902, no. 27464, 5951.
5. Untitled leader, *Times*, 26 August 1903, 7.
6. Walter Roch, *Mr. Lloyd George and the War* (London: Chatto & Windus, 1920), 6.
7. TNA FO 800/342, C. Hardinge to A. Nicolson letter, 4 January 1909 and FO 800/353, A. Nicolson to Stamfordham letter, 20 January 1912.

8. *Hansard*, House of Commons, 5 March 1903, v. 118, cc1578–91.
9. TNA CAB 37/40/64, Salisbury minute, October 1895.
10. *Ibid*, Devonshire minute, 3 November 1895 and CAB 37/53/71, Devonshire memoranda, 2 and 21 November 1900.
11. Denis Judd, *Balfour and the British Empire: A Study in Imperial Evolution 1874–1932* (London: Faber and Faber, 2015), 49.
12. *Hansard*, House of Commons, 5 March 1903, v. 118, cc1578–91 and "Diary," 18 July 1912, Duff Papers, CAC/AGDF/2/2.
13. J. O. Baylen, "Politics and the 'New Journalism': Lord Esher's Use of the 'Pall Mall Gazette,'" *Victorian Periodicals Review*, v. 20, no. 4 (1987): 126 and Lees-Milne, *Enigmatic Edwardian*, 141 and 236.
14. Ellison later became Haldane's private secretary when the latter supplanted Arnold-Forster at the War Office.
15. Esher Papers, CAC/ESHR/10/41, J. Fisher to Esher letter, 12 November 1903. Indeed, that risk was more than realized in June 1905 when Fisher joined Esher and Clarke in a joint memorandum. Effectively an addendum to their earlier efforts, this paper set forth the rationale for a general staff including how it should be employed, recruited and manned. That Fisher, now first sea lord, would have been apoplectic if such a paper had been issued by the chief of the general staff to the Admiralty evidently did not worry him. See TNA CAB 37/78/115, "The General Staff," 28 June 1905.
16. Ian F. W. Beckett, *A British Profession of Arms: The Politics of Command in the Late Victorian Army* (Norman: University of Oklahoma Press, 2018), 245.
17. Fraser, *Lord Esher: A Political Biography* (Barnsley: Pen and Sword, 2013), 95 and Alfred Cochrane, "George Sydenham Clarke," in Wickham Legg, ed. *Dictionary of National Biography 1931–1940*, 181.
18. Esher Papers, CAC/ESHR/10/24, L. Amery to Esher letter, 3 November 1903 and "Death of General Kelly-Kenny," *Times*, 28 December 1914, 9.
19. Almeric Fitzroy, *Memoirs, Vol. I* (London: Hutchinson & Co., 1920), 214–5.
20. Bond, *Victorian Army and the Staff College*, 214.
21. Esher Papers, CAC/ESHER/1032, A. Balfour to H. M. King, no date, but February 1904 and Fraser, *Lord Esher*, 161.
22. *War Office (Reconstitution) Committee*, I, 10.
23. Fitzroy, *Memoirs, I*, 190 and Fraser, *Lord Esher*, 104.
24. "Lord Esher," *Times*, 23 January 1930, 17.
25. "Reconstructed Cabinet," *British Medical Journal*, v. 2, no. 2232 (1903): 923.
26. Arnold-Forster's proposed reforms were issued in a series of Command Papers over the course of 1904.
27. Esher Papers, CAC/ESHR/10/44, Arnold-Forster to Esher letters, 21 October 1903 and 13 February 1904.
28. *Ibid*, H. Arnold-Forster to Esher letter, 21 March 1904.
29. Fraser, *Lord Esher*, 20.
30. TNA CAB 37/63/145, Arnold-Forster to Lord Selborne memorandum of 20 October 1902.

31. *Ibid*, H. Arnold-Forster to Selborne memorandum of 20 October 1902, 8–9.
32. Esher Papers, CAC/ESHR/10/44, Arnold-Forster to Esher letter, 29 August 1904.
33. TNA CAB 37/63/166, Selborne memorandum, 12 December 1902.
34. TNA CAB 37/65/35, H. Arnold-Forster, "Notes on the Present System of Army Organization and on Some Suggested Changes," memorandum, May 1903 and Aston, *Memories of a Marine*, 214–5.
35. Telfer-Smollett, "The Best Method for Carrying Out the Conjoint Practice of the Navy and Army in Embarkation and Disembarkation for War, Illustrated By the Experience of the Past," *Royal United Service Institution Journal*, 381.
36. Fitzroy, *Memoirs, I*, 149–56.
37. TNA CAB 38/3, CID minutes, 4 December 1903. Balfour began chairing the CID on 18 November 1903.
38. Esher Papers, CAC/ESHR/10/28, Esher to A. Balfour letter, 30 March 1904 and LHCMA, Aston Papers, J. Fisher to G. Aston letters 18 May 1904.
39. TNA CAB 38/18, CID minutes, 30 May 1911.
40. TNA CAB 38/4, Kitchener, "The Administration of the Army in India," 26 April 1904 and Connor, ANZAC and Empire, 19.
41. Lovat Fraser, *India Under Curzon & After* (New York: Henry Holt and Company, 1911), 35.
42. Lord Hardinge, *My Indian Years 1910–1916*, 31.
43. Nigel Woodyatt, *Under Ten Viceroys: The Reminiscences of a Gurkha* (London: Herbert Jenkins Limited, 1922), 129 and S. D. Pradhan, *Indian Army in East Africa* (New Delhi: National Book Organisation, 1991), 3.
44. TNA CAB 38/8, General Staff, "The Possibility of Bringing the Indian Army into Closer Touch with the British Army," 20 March 1905.
45. Salisbury cited in Keith Jeffrey, "An English Barrack in the Oriental Seas? India in the Aftermath of the First World War," *Modern Asian Studies*, v. 15, no. 3, (1981): 369.
46. TNA CAB 38/7, "Scheme of Re-distribution of the Army in India and Preparation of the Army in India for War," 1904; Fraser, *India Under Curzon*, 406 and Rhodri Williams, *Defending the Empire: The Conservative Party and British Defence Policy 1899–1915* (New Haven: Yale University Press, 1991), 7.
47. Edward M. Spiers, "Haldane's Reform of the Regular Army: Scope for Revision," *British Journal of International Studies*, v. 6, no. 1, (1980), 77.
48. Esher Papers, CAC/ESHR/13/11, "Extracts from the Minutes of the Committee of Imperial Defence Regarding Reinforcements for India," 31 December 1906, 5.
49. TNA WO 95/5235/6, Inspector General of Communications to Deputy Adjutant & Quarter-Master General, General Headquarters, memorandum No. 423/193-L.C., 5 March 1916.
50. Smith-Dorrien, *Forty-Eight Years' Service*, 299.
51. Fraser, *India Under Curzon*, 219–20 and Briton Cooper Busch, *Hardinge of Penshurst: A Study in the Old Diplomacy* (Hamden: Archon Book, 1980), 227.
52. Nicholas d'Ombrain, *War Machinery and High Policy: Defence Administration in Peacetime Britain 1902–1914* (London: Oxford University Press, 1973), 1.

53. "Diary," 20 January and 6 February 1909, LHCMA, Aston Papers, 1/1.
54. TNA CAB 38/9, "The General Staff," 28 June 1905.
55. Nicholas Lambert, "British Naval Policy, 1913–1914: Financial Limitation and Strategic Revolution." *Journal of Modern History*, v. 67, no. 3 (1995): 596–7.
56. Aston, *Memories of a Marine*, 220–1.
57. H. O. Arnold-Forster, "National Defence," *United Service Magazine*, v. 37, no. 954 (1908): 141 and David G. Morgan-Owen, *The Fear of Invasion: Strategy, Policy and British War Planning, 1880–1914* (Oxford: Oxford University Press, 2017), 45–7.
58. TNA CAB 38/9, CID minutes, 20 July 1905.
59. TNA ADM 116/984B, J. Fisher to G. Clarke letter, 12 October 1905.
60. Shawn T. Grimes, "War Planning and Strategic Development in the Royal Navy, 1887–1918 (PHD diss. University of London, 2004)" 78.
61. Neil William Summerton, "The Development of British Military Planning for a War Against Germany, 1904–1914," (PhD diss., University of London, 1970), 31.
62. Gooch and Temperley, eds., *Origins of the War, IV,* 140.
63. Fraser, *Lord Esher*, 173.
64. TNA CAB 17/95, C. Ottley to G. Clarke draft paper "Preparations of Plans for combined Naval and Military Operations in War," no date, but *ca.* 16 July 1905.
65. TNA ADM 1/8997, "Remarks on the Framing of Certain Plans for War with Germany at the Admiralty," no date, but *ca.* May 1909; Esher Papers, CAC/ESHR/10/37, G. Clarke to Esher letter, 15 December 1905, G. P. Gooch and Harold Temperley, eds., *British Documents on the Origins of the War, 1898–1914, Vol. VI, Anglo-German Tension, Armaments and Negotiation, 1907–12* (London: His Majesty's Stationery Office, 1930), 23 and G.P. Gooch and Harold Temperley, eds., *British Documents on the Origins of the War, Vol. VIII, Arbitration, Neutrality and Security* (London: His Majesty's Stationery Office, 1932), 409.
66. John Gooch, *The Plans of War: The General Staff and British Military Strategy c. 1900–1916* (Abingdon: Routledge, 2016), 189–90.
67. Esher Papers, ESHR/16/10, "Notes on a Conference Held at Whitehall Gardens," 19 December 1905.
68. John Gooch, "Sir George Clarke's Career at the Committee of Imperial Defence, 1904–1907," *Historical Journal*, v. 18, no. 3 (1975): 559.
69. George S. Clarke and James R. Thursfield, *Navy and the Nation or Naval Warfare and Imperial Defence* (London: John Murray, 1897), 9–10.
70. TNA ADM 196/20 (C. Ottley), ADM 196/39 (C. Ottley) and ADM 196/87 (C. Ottley).
71. "Rear-Admiral C. L. Ottley," *Times*, 26 September 1932, 17.
72. Grant Duff Papers, CAC/AGDF/1/1, A. Grant Duff to Haldane letter, 21 February 1912.
73. TNA CAB 38/4, War Office, "Strength of the Regular Army and Auxiliary Forces, having regard to Peace and War Requirements," memorandum, 1 May 1904; CAB 2/1, "Committee of Imperial Defence, Subject Index to the Minutes of Meetings 1 to 82" and ADM 196/42 (A. Sykes).

74. TNA ADM 1/7367B, *Cordelia* to Commander-in-Chief letter, 7 February 1898.
75. *Ibid*, H. Drake minute, 12 March 1898.
76. TNA CAB 38/3/53, L. Battenberg, "Remarks on Offensive Over-Sea Expeditions suggested by the War Office as Feasible in the Memorandum on the Military Needs of the Empire in a War with France and Russia" (No. 1A, 12th August, 1901), 1 July 1903.
77. TNA WO 106/40, "Scheme for the Attack of the Canary Islands," 28 February 1906.
78. TNA ADM 116/3111, Director of Military Operations, "Military Policy in the Event of War with France," no date, but *ca*. July 1905.
79. TNA ADM 116/3132 and FO 800/102, War Office memorandum, 8 March 1909.
80. TNA CAB 38/4, War Office, "Strength of the Regular Army and Auxiliary Forces, having regard to Peace and War Requirements," 1 May 1904.
81. TNA CAB 38/12, R. Haldane, "Notes on the Organization and Administration of the Military Forces in the United Kingdom," 18 June 1906.
82. Britain, Prussia, France, Austria and Russia guaranteed the neutrality of Belgium in perpetuity by treaty in 1831. See TNA CAB 38/10, G. Clarke, "Treaty Guarantees and the Obligations of Guaranteeing Powers," 1 August 1905.
83. TNA CAB 38/11, "Notes on a Conference Held at Whitehall Gardens December 19, 1905," 26 January 1906.
84. Bond, *Victorian Army and the Staff College*, 141 and H. de Watteville, "Sir Charles Edward Callwell," in J.R.H. Weaver, ed., *Dictionary of National Biography 1922–1930* (London: Oxford University Press, 1937), 154.
85. Grimes, "War Planning and Strategic Development," 79–81.
86. *Ibid*, 85.
87. Esher Papers, CAC/ESHR/4/1, Esher to J. Fisher letter, 18 February 1906; Esher to G. Clarke letter, 18 February 1906 and Esher to H. M. King letter, 16 February 1906.
88. *Ibid*, Esher to Campbell-Bannerman letter, 1 March 1906.
89. Franklyn Arthur Johnson, *Defence by Committee* (London: Oxford University Press, 1960), 18.
90. Summerton, "Development of British Military Planning," 32. A classified report, *N.I.D. 811*, appearing in July 1906 (not traced) recorded the results to date in the joint planning for overseas expeditions. Its existence is confirmed in TNA ADM 1/8211, "List of Books on Confidential Books, &c., Issued to Flag Officers and Other Officers as Determined by the Admiralty," April 1909.
91. Charles à Court Repington, *Vestigia: Reminiscences of Peace and War* (Boston: Houghton Mifflin Company, 1919), 88 and TNA ADM 196/62 (M. Hankey).
92. Bond, *Victorian Army and the Staff College*, 256–7. It was Campbell-Bannerman who insisted on withholding information about the discussions from the wider cabinet. See Gooch and Temperley, eds., *Origins of the War, III*, 170–9 and *Origins of the War, VI*, 626–9.
93. TNA CAB 1/31, "The need on a General Staff in the Navy," General Staff memorandum, 28 July 1909.

94. Drax Papers, CAC/DRAX, 1/14, H. Wake to R. Plunkett letter, 26 July 1909. Rear Admiral Lewis Bayly commanded the Royal Naval war college and was subsequently appointed to investigate the seizing of an advanced base to support flotilla operations; see TNA ADM 137/452.
95. TNA CAB 38/19, War Office memorandum 130-B, 13 August 1911.
96. TNA WO 106/47, DMO memoranda, 11 and 12 August 1911.
97. Summerton, "Development of British Military Planning," 426.
98. Fraser, *Lord Esher*, 101.
99. TNA CAB 38/19, CID minutes, 23 August 1911.
100. George Riddell, *Lord Riddell's War Diary 1914–1918* (London: Ivor Nicholson and Watson, 1933), 13.
101. Roch, *Lloyd George and the War*, 31–3 and Fitzroy, *Memoirs, I*, 377.
102. Wilson did not shine scholastically at Eton and then finished second from the bottom in his entry examination. He did, however, secure three firsts in his examinations leading to lieutenant and then gained a first in gunnery when specializing. See Bradford, *Sir Arthur Knyvet Wilson*, 4 and 20 and TNA ADM 196/14 (A. Wilson).
103. Fisher Papers, CAC/FISR/1/9/474, Fisher to C. Ottley letter, 25 February 1910.
104. See TNA CAB 1/31 for James Thursfield's articles in *The Times* from 13 October 1909 through 3 March 1910 calling for the creation of an Admiralty war staff and a naval staff college. Concurrently, Beresford continued his crusade for the establishment of a war staff at the Admiralty; see Lord Charles Beresford, *The Betrayal: Being a Record of Facts Concerning Naval Policy and Administration from the Year 1902 to the Present Time* (London: P. S. King & Son, 1911).
105. Paul Guinn, *British Strategy and Politics 1914–1918* (Oxford: Oxford University Press, 1965), 21.
106. Grimes, "War Planning and Strategic Development," 206.
107. TNA CAB 37/108/136, A. Wilson, "Naval War Staff," 30 October 1911.
108. TNA CAB 37/112/106, W. Churchill, "Memorandum on the General Naval Situation," 30 September 1912.
109. TNA ADM 137/452, W. Churchill to L. Bayly letter, 21 January 1913.
110. A. W. A. Pollock, "Naval War Staff," *United Service Magazine*, v. 44, no. 999 (1912): 482–3.
111. Reginald McKenna Papers, Churchill Archives Centre, Churchill College, Cambridge, 4/7, hereafter, CAC/MCKN, W. Churchill minute, no date, but *ca.* 1 January 1912.
112. TNA ADM 1/7170, A. Haliburton to Admiralty letter, 12 August 1893; ADM 1/7220, R. Thompson to Admiralty letter, 17 February 1894, and ADM 1/7859, C. Ottley minute, 7 February 1905 and Esher Papers, CAC/ESHR/16/6, *War Office (Reconstitution) Committee, I*, 5 and 100. A joint body to coordinate air matters between the services was established in 1912. Chaired by John Seely, the secretary of state for war, it fell into hiatus following his resignation in 1914.
113. TNA ADM 196/42 (S. Colville) and ADM 196/42 (W. Grant). David Beatty, another closely connected to the army courtesy of service in Sudan and China filled the position at the time of its formal disestablishment in 1908.

114. TNA CAB 37/69/38, Salisbury memorandum, 4 March 1904.
115. d'Ombrain, *War Machinery*, 71–3. In 1913, Captain Arthur Vyvyan noted overseas attack planning was being done at the behest of the CID. See TNA ADM 1/8272, A. Vyvyan, "Notes for War Staff Committee," no date but *ca.* 1913.
116. John P. MacKintosh, "Role of the Committee of Imperial Defence before 1914," *English Historical Review*, v. 77, no. 304 (1962): 494–6.
117. TNA CAB 19/26, Cmd. 8610, "Report of the Commission Appointed by Act of Parliament to Enquire into the Operations of War in Mesopotamia Together with a Separate Report By Commander J. Wedgwood, D.S.O., M.P., and Appendices, 1917," and, hereafter, "Mesopotamia Report," 96; ADM 186/608, *C.B. 917B, Naval Staff Monograph (Historical), Volume IV, Monograph 15, Naval Operations in Mesopotamia and the Persian Gulf*, Admiralty, Naval Staff, Training and Staff Duties Division, July 1921, 18 and Christopher Brice, *The Thinking Man's Soldier: The Life and Career of General Sir Henry Brackenbury 1837–1914* (Solihull: Helion and Company, Ltd., 2015), 222.
118. TNA CAB 38/18, "The Desirability of such a General Uniformity of Organisation throughout the Military Forces of the Empire as may Facilitate Their Rendering Mutual Support and Assistance," General Staff memorandum, 12 May 1911.
119. *Ibid.*
120. *Ibid.*
121. TNA CAB 38/15, J. Chancellor, "Colonial Defence – Précis of Important Events connected with the Question of Colonial Naval Contributions," memorandum, 30 April 1909.
122. TNA CAB 38/18, CID minutes, 26 May 1911.
123. TNA CAB 38/16, "Questions Requiring Inter-Departmental Consideration," War Office to CID memorandum, 22 February 1910.
124. TNA CAB 53/14, "Some General Principles of Imperial Defence," Oversea Sub-Committee memorandum, 12 March 1928.
125. Jeffrey Grey, "White, Sir Cyril Brudenell (1876–1940)," *Australian Dictionary of Biography* via http://adb.anu.edu.au/biography/white-sir-cyril-brudenell-1032 – accessed 26 July 2023 and Jose, *Royal Australian Navy 1914–1918*, 375.
126. TNA CAB 38/17, J. R. Chancellor, "Position in the Event of War with a European Power," 24 January 1911 and David Killingray, "The Idea of a British Imperial Army," *Journal of African History*, v. 20, no. 3 (1979): 422.
127. James Willcocks, *From Kabul to Kumassi: Twenty-Four Years of Soldiering and Sport* (London: John Murray, 1904), 295.
128. Wolseley to J. Maurice letter, 12 January 1895, Major General Sir Frederick Barton Maurice Papers, Liddell Hart Centre for Military Archives, King's College, London, 2/2/23.
129. TNA CO 534/17, Colonial Office to Somaliland Protectorate letter, 20 November 1913.
130. TNA CO 534/4, DMO to Colonial Office letter, 11 December 1906.
131. S. C. Ukpabi, "The Origins of the West African Frontier Force," *Journal of the Historical Society of Nigeria*, v. 3, no. 3 (1966): 491.

132. TNA CO 534/3, Uganda Protectorate to Colonial Office letter, 16 August 1905.
133. TNA CAB 37/45/49, Roberts to Lansdowne letter, 25 November 1897.
134. TNA CAB 37/50/56, Wolseley to Lansdowne letter, 24 August 1899.
135. D. S. Macdiarmid, *The Life of Lieut. General Sir James Moncrieff Grierson, K.C.B., C.V.O., C.M.G., A.D.C.* (London: Constable & Company, Ltd., 1923), 271–2.
136. TNA CO 445/31, W. Egerton to L. Harcourt letter, 7 September 1911.
137. TNA CO 534/3, Uganda Protectorate to Elgin letter, 6 March 1906.
138. TNA CAB 38/18, "South Africa – Scale of Attack," CID memorandum, 3 May 1911 and WO 106/46, Gleichen memorandum, no date, but 1905.
139. TNA WO 106/47, Methuen to Haldane letter, 8 March 1909.
140. TNA CO 534/12, "Inspection Report on the 3rd, Battalion King's African Rifles," 18 December 1910.
141. TNA ADM 196/63 (C. Crawley).
142. George S. Clarke, *Imperial Defence* (London: The Imperial Press Limited, 1897), 149.
143. TNA CAB 38/3, "Defence of India," War Office report, 23 June 1903.
144. Morton-Jack, *Indian Army on the Western Front*, 2.
145. Gordon Corrigan, *Sepoys in the Trenches: The Indian Corps on the Western Front 1914–15* (Stroud: Spellmount, 2006,), 3 and Douglas M. Peers, "The Indian Rebellion, 1857–1858," in Stephen M. Miller, ed., *Queen Victoria's Wars: British Military Campaigns, 1857–1902* (Cambridge: Cambridge University Press, 2021), 37.
146. TNA FO 800/107, J. Grierson, "The Feasibility of a Turkish Force Invading Egypt, by way of the Sinai Peninsula," 23 February 1906.
147. TNA FO 800/106, G. Clarke, "The Egyptian Frontier Question," 8 May 1906 and ADM 1/8884, C. Ottley minute, 13 August 1906.
148. G. P. Gooch and Harold Temperley, eds., *British Documents on the Origins of the War 1898–1914, Vol. V, The Near East: The Macedonian Problem and the Annexation of Bosnia, 1903–9* (London: His Majesty's Stationery Office, 1928), 82–83 and 191.
149. TNA CAB 38/11, CID minutes, 11 May 1906.
150. *Ibid*, G. Clarke, "The Egyptian Frontier Question," 9 May 1906.
151. TNA CAB 38/12, "Turco-German Invasion of Egypt," French note, 16 July 1906 and Esher Papers, CAC/ESHR/10/46, French to Esher letter, 9 May 1906.
152. *Ibid*, "Turco-German Invasion of Egypt," remarks by Lord Cromer on Sir John French's memorandum, 23 July 1906.
153. TNA CAB 38/12, "A Turco-German Invasion of Egypt," Esher memorandum, 24 July 1906.
154. Esher Papers, CAC/ESHR/10/36, G. Clarke to Esher letter, 3 August 1906.
155. After suffering 14,000 casualties at Port Arthur, General Kiten Nogi adopted siege tactics to reduce the Russian position. Ultimately successful, total Japanese losses amounted to over 60,000. See *Russo-Japanese War. Reports from British Officers Attached to the Japanese and Russian Forces in the Field, Vol. II* (London: His Majesty's Stationery Office, 1908), 376, 415 and 425.
156. TNA CAB 38/12, CID minutes, 26 July 1906.

157. C. E. Callwell, *Experiences of a Dug-Out 1914–1918* (London: Constable & Company, 1920), 88.
158. *Ibid*, 87.
159. TNA CAB 38/12, General Staff, "Possibility of a Joint Naval and Military Attack upon the Dardanelles," memorandum, 19 December 1906.
160. TNA ADM 137/899, M. Hankey to W, Churchill memorandum, 24 November 1914.
161. TNA CAB 38/12, "Remarks by the Director of Naval Intelligence on the Attached Memorandum," 20 December 1906.
162. TNA CAB 38/13 minutes, 28 February 1907.
163. Callwell, *Experiences of a Dug-Out*, 97.
164. TNA FO 800/48, E. Grey to Kitchener letter, 8 May 1912.
165. *Ibid*, Kitchener to E. Grey letter, 2 June 1912.
166. *Ibid*, Kitchener to E. Grey letter, 19 May 1912.
167. Morton-Jack, *Indian Army on the Western Front*, 112 and Hardinge, *My Indian Years*, 33.
168. The conclusion is drawn from TNA WO 95/5117/5, No. 1 Indian Mountain Artillery Brigade. "War Diary," 29 September and 1, 5 and 7 October 1914.
169. TNA CAB 37/105/27, "Mediterranean Fleet," Churchill memorandum, 15 March 1911.
170. TNA CAB 38/18, Commander-in-Chief, East Indies to Government of India letter, 22 April 1911.
171. TNA CAB 38/19, CID minutes, 14 December 1911.
172. *Ibid*, "Persian Gulf" CID report, 14 July 1911; CAB 37/115/39, "Bagdad Railway and Persian Gulf," Foreign Office and Indian Office joint memorandum, 3 May 1913 and CAB 37/87/36, "Report," [Baghdad Railway] no date, but *ca*. 26 March 1907.
173. TNA CAB 38/12, "Colonial Garrisons," CDC memorandum, 31 May 1906.
174. TNA CAB 38/18, CID minutes, 26 May 1911.
175. TNA FO 800/345, A. Nicholson minute, 22 July 1911.
176. Fisher Papers, CAC/FISR/1/4/139, Battenberg to J. Fisher letter, 7 November 1904.
177. TNA CAB 38/14, "Reinforcements and Draft required to be Despatched to India during the First Year of a War with Russia," 24 June 1908.
178. TNA CAB 38/11, General Staff, "Infantry Garrisons of Gibraltar and Malta," memorandum, 29 May 1906.
179. TNA CAB 38/18, CID minutes, 29 May 1911 and Dilke and Wilkinson, *Imperial Defence*, 50–1.
180. TNA ADM 116/984B, J. Fisher to G. Clarke letter, 12 October 1905.
181. TNA CAB 38/9, appendix to CID minutes, 26 July 1905.
182. "Naval and Military Intelligence," *Times*, 13 January 1906, 7.
183. TNA CAB 38/29, "List of Papers of the Committee of Imperial Defence," no date, but *ca*. 1914.
184. *Ibid*, "Questions Requiring Inter-Departmental Consideration," War Office to CID memorandum, 22 February 1910 and FO 800/359, M. Hankey to A. Nicolson letter, 7 November 1912.

185. TNA CAB 38/19, "Submarine Cable Communications in Time of War," report to CID, 11 December 1911.
186. TNA WO 106/48, H. Drake to General Staff memorandum, no date *ca.* 1905.
187. TNA ADM 116/900B, "Standing Orders for the Guidance of the Commander-in-Chief, or Commodore, on the Pacific Station," Admiralty, 27 July 1903.
188. "Combined Strategy for Fleets and Armies," *Times*, 16 July 1907, 15.

Chapter 14

1. J. Fisher to Selborne letter, 19 December 1899 cited in Arthur J. Marder, ed., *Fear God and Dread Nought: The Correspondence of Admiral of the Fleet Lord Fisher of Kilverstone, Vol. I, The Making of an Admiral, 1854–1904* (London: Jonathan Cape, 1952), 172.
2. TNA ADM 196/87 (H. Jackson).
3. TNA ADM 1/8386/213, F. Sturdee, "Plans for Combined Offensive Action on the Outbreak of War," 21 July 1914
4. M. L. Dockrill, "Lloyd George and Foreign Policy Before 1914," in *Lloyd George; Twelve Essays* ed., A.J.P. Taylor, (London: Hamish Hamilton, 1971), 19.
5. Ross Anderson, "Battle of Tanga, 2–5 November 1914," *War in History*, v. 8, No. 3 (2001): 295 and Fisher Papers, CAC/FISR/1/24/1346, M. Hankey to Fisher letter, 23 April 1917.
6. TNA CAB 21/3, M. Hankey to H. Asquith memorandum, 5 August 1914.
7. "Diary," 30 January and 17 February 1914, LHCMA, Aston Papers.
8. TNA ADM 137/452, W. Churchill to H. Asquith letter, 31 July 1914
9. "Admiral of the Fleet Sir H. B. Jackson," *Times*, 16 December 1929, 19. For convenience, the body will be referred to as the "Combined Operations Committee," though contemporaries often referred to it as the "Offensive Sub-Committee."
10. TNA ADM 196/87 (H. Jackson) and R. MacGregor Dawson, "The Cabinet Minister and Administration: A. J. Balfour and Sir Edward Carson at the Admiralty, 1915–17," *Canadian Journal of Economic and Political Science*, v. 9, no.1 (1943): 11.
11. TNA ADM 196/61 (G. Aston).
12. TNA CAB 38/28, "Committee on Combined Operations in Foreign Territory."
13. "Diary," 23 January 1912 and M. Hankey to G. Aston letter, 29 February 1912, LHCMA, Aston Papers.
14. "Diary," 18 April, 3 and 24 November 1913, LHCMA, Aston Papers, 1/6, and "Admiral Sir Lewis Bayly," *Times*, 17 May 1938, 18.
15. Admiralty to Adjutant General Royal Marines letter M.0916/14, 24 July 1914, LHCMA, Aston Papers, 4/5.
16. *Ibid*, "Diary," 2 August 1914, 1/7.
17. C. E. Callwell, *Small Wars: Their Principles and Practice* (London: Harrison and Sons, 1906).
18. Charles Callwell, *The Effect of Maritime Command on Land Campaign Since Waterloo* (Edinburgh: William Blackwood and Sons, 1897) and *Military Operations*

and Maritime Preponderance: Their Relations and Interdependence (Edinburgh: William Blackwood and Sons, 1905).

19. Callwell, *Experiences of a Dug-Out*, 8; "Sir C. E. Callwell," *Times*, 17 May 1928, 18 and *London Gazette*, 18 August 1914, no. 28873, 6499.
20. "General Sir Ian Hamilton," *Times*, 13 October 1947, 8 and John Lee, *A Soldier's Life: General Sir Ian Hamilton, 1853–1947* (London: Macmillan, 2000), 89.
21. "General Sir Edmund Barrow," *Times*, 5 January 1934, 7 and Younghusband, *Memories in Peace and War*, 242.
22. "Sir Rowland Sperling," *Times*, 9 January 1965, 12 and TNA FO 800/91, Emmott to E. Grey letter, 6 August 1914.
23. John M. Carland, "Enterprise and Empire: Officials, Entrepreneurs, and the Search for Petroleum in Southern Nigeria, 1906–1914." *International History Review*, v. 4, No. 2, May 1982, 194.
24. *Ibid*, 202 and "Sir G. V. Fiddes," *Times*, 24 December 1936, 14.
25. TNA ADM 186/608, *Naval Staff Monograph, II,* 134.
26. *Hansard*, House of Commons debate, 3 August 1914, v. 65, cc1809–32; TNA FO 800/166, F. Bertie to W. Tyrrell letter, 4 August 1914 and E. Grey to F. Bertie (Paris) signal of 2 August 1914, *Correspondence Respecting the European Crisis: Miscellaneous No. 6* (London: His Majesty's Stationery Office, 1914), 74. The commitment did not extend to protecting French shipping in the Mediterranean—a point the Admiralty sought to correct. See TNA ADM 186/618, *C.B. 917F, Naval Staff Monographs (Historical), Vol. VIII, The Mediterranean 1914–1915*, Admiralty, Naval Staff, Training and Staff Duties Division, March 1923, 263.
27. TNA FO 800/166, F. Bertie to E. Grey letter, 4 August 1914 and F. Bertie to W. Tyrrell letter, 4 August 1914.
28. TNA ADM 186/610, *Naval Staff Monographs, III,* 27.
29. K. M. Wilson, "The British Cabinet's Decision for War, 2 August 1914," *British Journal for International Studies*, v. 1, no. 2 (1975): 154 and Roch, *Lloyd George and the War*, 86–90. Those eventually resigning were Viscount Morley (lord president of the council) and John Burns (president of the Board of Trade).
30. TNA ADM 186/608, *Naval Staff Monographs, East Africa,* 136. As a consequence of reducing the Mediterranean Fleet in 1912–1913, India assumed a greater role in the reinforcement of Egypt in wartime. See Gooch and Temperley, eds., *Origins of the War, X, Part II,* 592.
31. Nauru's transmitter was disabled by its German operators on 9 September 1914 when an Australian raiding party appeared; see Jose, *Royal Australian Navy 1914–1918,* 70.
32. TNA ADM 186/605, *C.B. 917, Naval Staff Monographs, Vol. I,* Admiralty, Training and Staff Duties Division, November 1920, 72–3; ADM 186/592, *O.U. 6039, Naval Operations in the Cameroons 1914*, Admiralty, Training and Staff Duties Division, August 1919; and AWM 4 1/1/1, Part 1, Admiralty to Rear Admiral Australian Fleet signal of 19 August 1914.
33. "*S.380, Lieutenant Harold Bedwell Remark Book,*" entry of 11 August 1914 (privately held) and AWM 4 1/1/3, Part 1, Secretary of State for the Colonies to Department of External Affairs Australia signal of 13 October 1914.

34. Jose, *Royal Australian Navy 1914–1918*, 49–50.
35. TNA ADM 186/610, *Naval Staff Monographs, III*, 9–10.
36. *Hansard*, House of Lords debates, 25 August 1914, v. 17, cc501–04. Tellingly, this decision was taken without recourse to consideration by the war council, which had last met on August 5.
37. TNA CAB 37/51/105, Wolseley memorandum, 29 December 1899. It was also the conclusion of Major H. G. Thomson in 1915 as he handled the requests of gunners serving in Mesopotamia who sought to return home with the idea of enlisting in one of the new armies to gain early promotion. See WO 95/5117/2, 1/5 Hampshire Battery, Royal Field Artillery, "War Diary," 30 June 1915.
38. *Hansard*, House of Lords debate, 28 August 1914, v. 17, cc549–51; TNA FO 800/375, Hardinge to A. Nicolson letter, 2 October 1914 and CAB 37/162/32, Hardinge, "Mesopotamian Campaign," December 1916; Willcocks, *With the Indians in France*, 15 and 322 and J. E. Edmonds, *Military Operations France and Belgium, 1914: Antwerp, La Bassée, Armentières, Messines, and Ypres October–November 1914* (London: Macmillan and Co., Limited, 1925), 92; hereafter, *Military Operations France and Belgium, 1914, II*.
39. Esher Papers, CAC/ESHR/13/10, "Report of the Standing Sub-Committee of the Committee of Imperial Defence appointed to enquire into the question of Oversea Transport of Reinforcements in Time of War," 16 June 1910, 4; E. C. H. [Ernest Charles Holtom], *Two Years' Captivity in German East Africa being the Personal Experiences of Surgeon E. C. H., Royal Navy* (London: Hutchinson & Co., 1918), 4 and TNA ADM 186/605, *Naval Staff Monographs, I*, 10.
40. Nearly 77,000 British regulars were serving in India in August 1914. See *Statistics of the Military Effort of the British Empire during the Great War 1914–1920* (London: His Majesty's Stationery Office, 1922), 777.
41. Fisher Papers, CAC/FISR/1/23/1284, "The Dardanelles Commission. Thursday, 28th September, 1916. Fifth Day," 70–1.
42. H. H. Asquith, *The Genesis of the War* (London: Cassell and Company, Limited, 1923), 223–4.
43. TNA CAB 38/28, Combined Operations Committee minutes, 6 August 1914. "Report on the Opening of the War," Historical Section, CID, 1 November 1914.
44. Julian A. Corbett, *History of the Great War, Naval Operations, Vol. I* (London: Longmans, Green and Co., 1920), 128.
45. TNA WO 106/46, "Military Policy in a War with Germany," 1908.
46. TNA CAB 42/1, War Council minutes, 5 August 1914 and Viscount French, *1914* (London: Constable and Company, Ltd., 1919), 5.
47. TNA CAB 38/28, "Report on the Opening of the War," Historical Section, CID, 1 November 1914 and Avner Offer, "The Working Classes, British Naval Plans and the Coming of the Great War," *Past and Present*, no. 107 (1985): 221.
48. TNA CAB 38/28, "Report on the Opening of the War," Historical Section, CID, 1 November 1914.
49. TNA CAB 41/35, H. Asquith to George V letters, 11 August and 22 September 1914. This included British officers serving in Indian regiments and British officers serving in British battalions then stationed in India. In turn, the Admiralty

also retained officers of the Royal Indian Marine home on leave. Their absence was keenly felt in Mesopotamia in late 1915 when IEF D's flotilla expanded. See BL IOR/L/MIL/17/5/3243, Army Headquarters India, "War Diary," 29 December 1915; and IOR/L/MIL/17/16/22, Crewe to Hardinge signal of 16 September 1914.
50. TNA ADM 186/608, *Naval Staff Monographs, IV, Cameroons*, 160–3.
51. *Ibid*, 166 and 211–2 and CAB 24/3, Sub-Committee on Territorial Changes' Second Interim Report, 22 March 1917.
52. TNA ADM 186/608, *Naval Staff Monographs, IV, Cameroons*, 162–3 and CAB 38/28, Combined Operations Committee minutes, 17 August 1914.
53. *London Gazette*, 30 May 1916, no. 29604, 5428.
54. "Brig.-Gen. C. H. P. Carter," *Times*, 26 October 1943, 6 and TNA ADM 186/608, *Naval Staff Monographs, IV, Cameroons*, 184.
55. TNA CAB 21/3, "Recommendations of the Sub-Committee of Imperial Defence which considered the question of offensive operations against German Colonies," 6 August 1914.
56. *British Amphibious Operations of the First World War* to be published by Pen and Sword.
57. TNA ADM 186/608, *Naval Staff Monographs, IV, Cameroons*, E. Grey to F. Bertie signal of 10 August 1914, 207; FO 800/91, F. Butler to W. Tyrrell letter, 15 October 1914 and "Colonel F. C. Bryant," *Times*, 29 March 1956.
58. TNA CAB 38/28, Combined Operations Committee minutes, 29 August 1914.
59. "Admiral Sir Cyril Fuller," *Times*, 3 February 1942, 7.
60. TNA CAB 24/3, Sub-Committee on Territorial Changes' Second Interim Report, 22 March 1917.
61. *Ibid* and "Admiral Sir Cyril Fuller," *Times*, 3 February 1942, 7.
62. *Anon.*, "Notes on the Cameroons: By a Member of the West African Expeditionary Force," *Geographical Journal*, v. 48, no. 5 (1916): 404.
63. TNA CAB 38/28, Combined Operations Committee minutes, 29 September 1914.
64. Lovett Elango, "The Anglo-French 'Condominium' in Cameroon, 1914–1916: The Myth and the Reality," *International Journal of African Historical Studies*, v. 18, no. 4 (1985): 658.
65. TNA ADM 196/125 (L. Braithwaite).
66. TNA CAB 38/28, Combined Operations Committee minutes, 16 September 1914.
67. Edmund Dane, *British Campaign in Africa and the Pacific 1914–1918* (London: Hodder and Stoughton, 1919), 30 and TNA ADM 186/612, *C.B. 917C, Eastern Squadrons*, 164 and CO 417/430, F. Trench to Secretary War Office letter, 24 February 1906.
68. TNA CO 417/430, "Military Situation in German South-West Africa," General Staff memorandum, 28 June 1905.
69. "Obituary. Major-General Sir H. T. Lukin," *Times*, 17 December 1925, 18 and TNA CAB 24/3, Sub-Committee on Territorial Changes, Second Interim Report, 22 March 1917 and Willcocks, *With the Indians in France*, 20.

70. Gooch and Temperley, eds., *Origins of the War, X, Part II*, 480.
71. W. Whittall, *With Botha and Smuts in Africa* (London: Cassell and Company, Ltd., 1917), 3–6 and 158.
72. Willcocks, *With the Indians in France*, 20.
73. TNA CAB 38/28, E. Barrow, "Expedition against German East Africa," 18 September 1914.
74. TNA CAB 24/3, Appendix K, Sub-Committee on Territorial Changes, Third Interim Report, 28 March 1917.
75. TNA CAB 42/6, "Views of the General Staff on the Present Situation at Salonica and in the Balkans, with Deductions as to Our Wisest Course of Action There—November 23, 1915."
76. TNA CAB 24/3, "Sub-Committee on Territorial Changes," Fourth Interim Report, 17 July 1917.
77. Jonathan E. Helmreich, "The End of Congo Neutrality," *The Historian* (1966): v. 28, no 4, 615.
78. E. Goschen (Berlin) to E. Grey signal of 29 July 1914 and E. Grey to E. Goschen signal of 30 July 1914, *Correspondence Respecting the European Crisis*, 46 and 55.
79. TNA CAB 24/3, "Sub-Committee on Territorial Changes," Fourth Interim Report, 17 July 1917.
80. Keith Moore, "The Royal Society's War Committee on Engineering 1914–19," *Notes and Records of the Royal Society of London*, v. 62, no. 3 (2008): 316.
81. Drax Papers, CAC/DRAX/4/8, "Dardanelles Commission, First Report, 1917, Cd. 8490," 10.
82. Corbett, *Naval Operations, I*, 124.
83. Imperial War Museum, London, Norman Macleod Papers, 05/63A, "Diary," 10–14 September 1914.
84. TNA ADM 196/61 (G. Aston); LHCMA, Aston Papers, "Diary," 25 and 27 August 1914; Imperial War Museum, London, Vice Admiral Wilfred Henderson Papers, "The Antwerp Expedition," 22 April 1915, Misc. 207, Item 3003 and Lieutenant Colonel Kenneth Henderson Papers, IWM/10942/DS/MISC/2, "Unpublished Memoir," 112–3.
85. TNA ADM 196/62 (J. Rose).
86. TNA ADM 137/6, J. Rose to H. Jackson note, no date but *ca.* 4 October 1914.
87. McKenna Papers, CAC/MCKN/3/22/85 J. Jellicoe to R. McKenna letter, 23 May 1915; Grimes, "War Planning and Strategic Development," 234–6 and Summerton, "Development of British Military Planning," 225–6.
88. "The War Day By Day," *Times*, 3 August 1914, 4.
89. Bond, *Victorian Army and the Staff College*, 299; Callwell, *Experiences of a Dug-Out*, 12–48 and Ian Hamilton, *The Soul and Body of an Army* (London: Edward Arnold & Co., 1921), 40–1.
90. TNA ADM 186/605, *Naval Staff Monographs, I*, 107–08.
91. TNA CAB 24/2, M. Hankey, "The General View of the War," memorandum, 31 October 1916.
92. *Ibid*, H. Jackson, "Summary of Naval Situation," memorandum, 8 February 1916.

93. TNA ADM 186/612, *Naval Staff Monographs, V*, 9–14 and FO 800/91, L. Harcourt to E. Grey letter, 23 September 1914.
94. TNA CAB 42/1, War Council minutes, 1 December 1914, 7 January and 8 January 1915.
95. Kitchener retained sizable land holdings in East Africa, though no evidence has been found to suggest this interest influenced his view of the unfolding campaign.
96. TNA FO 800/102, C. Callwell to E. Crowl letter, 22 August 1914 and C. Callwell and E. Grey to H. Kitchener letter, 22 August 1914; George Morton-Jack, *The Indian Empire at War: From Jihad to Victory, The Untold Story of the Indian Army in First World War* (London: Little, Brown, 2018), 138 and Callwell, *Experiences of a Dug-Out*, 47, 63 and 110.
97. Jose, *Royal Australian Navy 1914–1918*, 152.
98. TNA CAB 24/1, J. French, memorandum, 3 January 1915.
99. *Ibid*, D. Lloyd George, "Suggestions as to a Military Position," 1 January 1915; CAB 41/35, H. Asquith to George V, letter, 9 October 1914 and CAB 37/128/30, Kitchener, "The War," 31 May 1915.
100. TNA ADM 186/622, *C.B. 917K, Naval Staff Monographs (Historical), Vol. XIII, Home Waters—Part IV, From February to July 1915*, Admiralty, Training and Staff Duties Division, October 1925, 6.
101. Spenser Wilkinson, *Britain at Bay* (New York: G. P. Putnam's Sons, 1909), 66–9.
102. TNA CAB 24/1, Esher, "After Six Months of War," 27 January 1915.
103. TNA CAB 42/1, War Council minutes, 11:30 a.m., 4 p.m. and 6:30 p.m., 28 January 1915.
104. TNA CAB 24/1, Esher, "After Six Months of War," 27 January 1915.
105. *Ibid*, M. Hankey, "Attack on the Dardanelles," 2 February 1915.
106. TNA CAB 42/1, War Council minutes, 6:30 p.m., 28 January 1915.
107. TNA CAB 24/1, War Staff, "Alexandretta and Mesopotamia," 17 March 1915.
108. On seizing Alexandretta to isolate Mesopotamia, see AWM4 1/8/4, "Egyptian Expeditionary Force (EEF) Intelligence Diary," 15 August 1916.
109. Callwell, *Experiences of a Dug-Out*, 171.
110. TNA ADM 137/6, E. Barrow to H. Jackson letter, 12 October 1914.

Index

'Abdallāhi b. Muhammad at-Ta'īshī, see Khalīfa
Adye, Lieutenant General Sir John, 8, 43
Alexandra, HMS, 5, 223n, 224n
Alexandria, 2-4, 8, 51, 57, 61, 96, 104, 107, 113, 232n, 248n
  bombardment, 5-6, 50, 97-8, 100, 105, 134
  rioting, 10, 15-7, 63
Algerine, HMS, 57, 63
Alison, Major General Sir Archibald, 7, 97, 100, 224n
Arnold-Forster, Hugh, 91, 120, 158, 162, 261n
Asquith, Henry, 163, 169-71, 186-88, 191, 194, 201
Aston, Colonel George, 93, 108, 111-12, 116-21, 125, 129, 131, 141, 145, 153, 186, 189, 192, 200
Atkinson-Willes, Rear Admiral George, 77-9
Altham, Colonel Edward, 73, 136

Baker, Sir Samuel, 15-6, 23
Baker, Valentine, 3, 11-3, 15-6, 18-9, 51, 97, 227n
Balfour, Arthur, 83, 146, 155-59, 162, 166, 171, 184, 262n
Ballard, Captain George, 38, 137, 142, 166-67
Baring, Sir Evelyn, 12, 14, 16-8, 20, 23, 44-5, 100
  see also Lord Cromer

Barrow, General Sir Edmund, 189-90, 200
Battenberg, Admiral Prince Louis, 142, 164, 187
Bayly, Captain Edward, 57, 62, 69
Bayly, Admiral Sir Lewis, 119, 189, 265n
Beatty, Admiral of the Fleet Earl Beatty, 44, 55, 239n, 265n
Beresford, Admiral Lord Charles, 24, 27-8, 44, 98-9, 104, 163, 168, 265n
Bird, Lieutenant Colonel, 116, 124-25
Boyes, Vice Admiral, 142-43
Brett, Reginald, 2, 33, 103, 156, 222n
  see also Esher

Bright, John, 4, 6
Brisk, HMS, 56, 67
Brodrick, William St. John, 53, 58
Bruce, Rear Admiral James, 61, 63, 68
Buller, General Sir Redvers, 13, 24-5, 28, 47-8, 229n

Callwell, Colonel Charles, 116, 118, 125, 166, 179, 189, 193-94, 202, 204
Campbell-Bannerman, Sir Henry, 156, 166-67, 171, 264n
Cambridge, George, Duke of, 23, 30, 249n
Capper, Colonel Thompson, 124-26
Centurion, HMS, 62, 69, 240n
Chamberlain, Joseph, 4, 46, 190
Chemulpo, 87-88, 96
Childers, Hugh, 8, 249n

Churchill, Winston, 81, 169-70, 181, 187-88, 191, 200
Clarke, Major General Sir Andrew, 15, 22, 134
Clarke, Sir George, later Lord Sydenham, 105, 138, 145, 156-57, 159, 162-63, 166, 171, 178, 224n, 261n
Cobbe, Colonel Alexander, 73, 75
Colville, Admiral Sir Stanley Cecil, 43, 171
Committee of Imperial Defence, 91-3, 113, 119, 130, 137, 144, 155, 157, 159-88, 191, 194-95, 198-99, 256n
Committee on Combined Operations, 187-88, 193, 199-200
Compton, Spencer, *see* Marquess of Hartington and Duke of Devonshire
Corbett, Sir Julian, 115-22, 124-25, 167, 193
Cradock, Captain Christopher, 55, 61
Creagh, Major General Sir O'Moore, 65, 125
Cromer, Earl, 30, 44
Curzon, George, 160, 190

Dardanelles, 82, 130, 178-81, 184, 203-204
Dawkins, Clinton, 53, 154, 238n
Devonshire, Duke of, 156, 159, 222n
Digna, Osman, 17-9, 30, 32-4, 44
Dilke, Sir Charles, 15, 228n
Dobell, Brigadier General Charles, 191, 194-96
Doris, HMS, 49-50
Dorward, Brigadier General Arthur, 58, 62-3
Drury-Lowe, Captain Sydney, 79, 151

Egerton, Major General Sir Charles, 43, 76-9

Elgin, Earl of, 154, 156, 260n
Ellison, Lieutenant Colonel Gerald, 156-57, 261n
El Teb, 16, 19, 26
Esher, Viscount, 110, 145, 154, 156-59, 162, 165-67, 170, 178, 188, 203, 222n, 260n, 261n
Euryalus, HMS, 8, 16
Eyres, Captain, 83-4

Fairfax, Captain Henry, 9-10
Fashoda, 15, 44
Fawkes, Rear Admiral Sir Wilmot, 140, 145
Field Service Regulations, 77, 84, 125, 139, 148, 157, 259n
Fisher, Admiral Sir John, 6, 49, 99, 104, 130, 135-37, 145-46, 156-57, 162-64, 166-67, 178-79, 184, 187-88, 261n
Fox, HMS, 78-9
French, Field Marshal Sir John, 49, 137, 140-41, 145, 150-51, 173, 178

Gaselee, Lieutenant General Sir Alfred, 63-6, 68-9
Gerard, General Sir Montagu, 83, 86
Girouard, Lieutenant Colonel Sir Percy, 42, 96
Gladstone, William, 1, 4, 7, 12, 15, 20, 22-3, 28-31, 34, 42, 81, 96-8, 233n
Goodrich, Lieutenant Commander Caspar, 5, 101, 105-106
Gordon, Major General Charles, 12, 15, 17-23, 25-31, 44, 61, 96-7, 100, 102, 228n
Gough, Major John, 75, 111
Graham, Major General Gerald, 9, 18-9, 30, 32-4, 51, 73, 75, 98, 102, 105, 112

Grenfell, General Sir Francis, 42, 135-36, 157
Grey, Sir Edward, 178, 187, 191, 193, 198
Grierson, Major General James, 162, 167, 175, 179

Haig, Lieutenant General Sir Douglas, 111, 125, 127, 150
Haldane, Richard, 129, 167, 170, 187-88, 191, 200, 261n
Halsey, Commander Lionel, 49, 142, 145
Hamilton, General Sir Ian, 84-5, 93, 95, 126, 189-91, 194, 254n
Hammill, Commander Tynte, 22, 24, 102
Hankey, Captain Maurice, 130, 163-64, 167, 187-89, 191
Hardinge, Lord, 109, 160, 181
Harris, Rear Admiral Robert, 49-50
Harrison, Colonel Richard, 2, 102
Hassan, Muhammad Abdullah *aka* "Mad Mullah", 71, 75, 79, 104, 175
Hartington, Marquess of, 1, 2, 14, 15, 20-3, 31, 33, 98, 154
Hermione, HMS, 56, 67
Hewett, Rear Admiral Sir William, 8-10, 15-20, 22, 79, 97-8
Hext, Captain John, 11, 39, 143
Hicks, Lieutenant Colonel William, 13-4, 16, 21, 97, 227n
Higgins, Pearce, 114-15
Hood, Captain Horace, 44, 78-9, 239n
Hoskins, Rear Admiral Anthony, 9, 104
Hoskins, Colonel Reginald, 191, 194
Hyacinth, HMS, 78-9

Inflexible, HMS, 5-6, 223n, 224n
Iris, HMS, 9-10

Jackson, Admiral Sir Henry, 152-53, 187-89, 191-92, 194-95, 197-99, 201-202
Jellicoe, Admiral of the Fleet Earl, 55, 63, 152, 200, 239n, 260n

Kenna, Colonel Paul, 74, 78
Keppel, Commander Colin, 44-5, 78
Keyes, Admiral of the Fleet Lord, 55, 239n
Khalīfa, 34, 44
Khartoum, 11-2, 14-8, 20-3, 25, 27-8, 30-2, 34, 42, 44, 98
King's African Rifles, 72-6, 175-76, 191, 194, 244n
King's Royal Rifle Corps, 74, 118
Kitchener, Field Marshal Lord, 22, 42-5, 53, 76, 95, 111, 123-25, 160, 177, 180-81, 190-91, 200-202, 204, 254n, 274n
Kuroptakin, General, 83, 86

Ladysmith, 49-50, 52
Lake, Brigadier General Percy, 138-39
Lawrence, Rev. Thomas, 114-15
Lloyd George, David, 187, 203
Lyttelton, General Sir Neville, 43, 162, 180, 184

McKenna, Reginald, 129, 168-70, 191
MacDonald, Sir Claude, 56-8, 61, 66-7
Macpherson, Major General Sir Herbert, 10, 38, 99
Mahdī (Muhammad Ahmad ibn al-Saiyid "Abd Allāh), 13-4, 17-8, 20, 22, 28, 30-2, 34, 44, 71, 105, 228n
Malet, Sir Edward, 7, 224n, 227n
Manning, Brigadier General William, 73-7, 175, 224n

Manual of Combined Naval and Military Operations, 122, 133-53
Marchand, Major Jean-Baptiste, 45, 236n
May, Lieutenant Colonel Edward, 114, 126, 141
May, Rear Admiral Henry, 113, 224n
Methuen, Lieutenant General Lord, 50-1, 175
Milner, Sir Alfred, later Viscount, 12, 49, 190
Mohawk, 77-9
Moncrieff, Lynedoch, 14, 97
Monarch, HMS, 5, 9, 223n
Mowatt, Sir Francis, 137, 154
Mukden, 83, 90-1

Naiad, 73, 77, 244n
Noel, Admiral Sir Gerald, 84, 136
Northbrook, Earl of, 14-5, 23, 34, 98

Omdurman, 27, 34, 44, 74, 248n
Ottley, Captain Charles, 130, 163, 171, 179-80, 189
Orion, HMS, 9-10
Orlando, HMS, 57, 62-3

Pakenham, Captain William, 83-4
Paris, Colonel Archibald, 51, 200
Perseus, HMS, 74, 77-8, 244n
Phillimore, Admiral Sir Richard, 55, 79
Pomone, HMS, 73-4, 78, 244n
Port Arthur, 84-5, 87-90, 94, 128, 169, 179, 247n, 267n
Powerful, HMS, 49-50

Rawlinson, Brigadier General Sir, 119, 121, 131, 186
Rawson, Lieutenant Wyatt, 10, 98

Repington, Charles à Court, 91, 123, 140-41, 167, 201, 248n, 257n, 258n
Rimington, Major General Michael, 143, 150
Rolfe, Commander Ernest, 8-9, 18-9
Rose, Colonel John, 131, 200
Royal Marine Artillery, 7, 43, 124, 144, 225n
Royal Marine Light Infantry, 7, 131, 225n

Scott, Admiral Sir Percy, 5, 49-50, 63
Salisbury, Marquess of, 17, 31-2, 34, 38, 42, 44, 47, 52, 55-6, 156, 160, 171, 248n
Seymour, Admiral Sir Beauchamp, 3-5, 7, 17, 98, 103-104, 134, 148, 224n, 225n, 249n
Seymour, Vice Admiral Sir Edward, 10, 56-60, 62-5, 67-8, 79, 95-6, 104
Sherwood Foresters, 135, 139
Silsili, Fort, 4-5
Slade, Captain Edmond, 120, 150, 167, 181, 184
Smith-Dorrien, Major General Horace, 4, 54, 109
Sperling, Rowland, 189-91, 195
Stephenson, Lieutenant General Sir Frederick, 20, 22-4, 43
Stewart, Lieutenant Colonel Donald, 11, 15, 17, 20, 25
Stewart, Brigadier General Sir Herbert, 23, 25-8, 232n
Suakin, 11-4, 16-9, 21-3, 30-3, 36, 43, 102, 104, 106, 113, 143
Swayne, Lieutenant Colonel Eric, 72-3, 76, 79

Tamai, 19, 58
Tel-el-Kebir, 2, 10, 104

Temeraire, HMS, 5, 223n
Terrible, HMS, 49-50, 58, 63
Togo, Vice Admiral, 83-4, 87-8, 91, 128
Tokar, 6, 14, 16, 18-9
Tulloch, Major Alexander, 2-4, 9

Urabi, Colonel Ahmed, 1-3, 6, 8, 10, 12, 14, 40, 98, 232n

Vincent, Major Berkeley, 84-85, 125-27, 254n

Wake, Major Hereward, 118-19, 168
Wardrop, Major Frederick, 27, 132
West African Frontier Force, 173, 175, 191, 196
White, Lieutenant General Sir George, 38, 48
Wilson, Admiral of the Fleet Sir Arthur, 19, 104, 162, 168-70, 199-200, 265n
Wilson, Colonel Sir Charles, 11, 26-9, 44, 100, 232n
Wilson, Field Marshal Sir Henry, 42, 111, 120, 125-27, 149-50, 168, 189
Wolseley, General Sir Garnet, 7-11, 14-5, 17, 20-5, 28-31, 34, 40, 42, 48, 74, 95-6, 98-101, 103-04, 110-11, 132, 148, 162, 174-75, 232n, 236n
Wood, Field Marshal Sir Evelyn, 12, 16, 24, 48, 137-39, 145-46, 227n